Classical Subjects Creatively Taught™

LATIN Alive!
BOOK 3

Karen Moore
Gaylan DuBose

Latin Alive! Book 3
© Classical Academic Press, 2013
Version 1.2

ISBN: 978-1-60051-084-7

All rights reserved. This publication may not be reproduced, stored in a retrieval system, or transmitted, in any form or by any means, without the prior written permission of Classical Academic Press.

Classical Academic Press
515 S. 32nd Street
Camp Hill, PA 17011

www.ClassicalAcademicPress.com

Scripture labeled "Vulgate" is taken from the Latin Vulgate.

Subject Editor: Edward J. Kotynski

Project Editor: Lauraine E. Gustafson

Cover, illustrations, and design: Lenora Riley

PGP.08.18

Latin Alive! Book 3

Table of Contents

Suggested Schedule vii

Preface ix

Unit 1

Chapter 1 1
- **Section 1.** Declension Review (p. 2)
- **Section 2.** Irregular Noun: *Vīs* (p. 4)
- **Section 3.** Noun Case Review (p. 5)
- **Section 4.** The Gerund (p. 5)
- **Section 5.** The Gerundive (p. 7)

Chapter 2 11
- **Section 6.** Verb Review (p. 12)
- **Section 7.** Ablative of Agent and Means (p. 15)
- **Section 8.** Participle Review (p. 15)
- **Section 9.** Impersonal Verbs (p. 17)
- Reading: "*Arborēs ad Rogōs Faciendōs Caeduntur*," Liber VI (fragment), Ennius

Chapter 3 21
- **Section 10.** Verb Review: Perfect System (p. 22)
- **Section 11.** Perfect Passive Participle (p. 25)
- **Section 12.** Deponent Verbs (p. 26)
- **Section 13.** PUFFV Verbs and the Ablative Case (p. 28)
- Reading 1: "*Dē Bellō Hannibalicō*," Liber VIII (fragment), Ennius
- Reading 2: "*Fabiī Cunctātōris ēlogium*," Liber IX (fragment), Ennius

Chapter 4 33
- **Section 14.** Subjunctive Mood (p. 34)
- **Section 15.** Present Subjunctive (p. 34)
- **Section 16.** Subjunctive of Irregular Verbs (p. 36)
- **Section 17.** Translating the Subjunctive (p. 37)
- Reading: *M. Catonis Dē Agrī Cultūrā, Praefatio*, Cato

Chapter 5 42
- **Section 18.** Imperfect Subjunctive (p. 43)
- **Section 19.** Imperfect Subjunctive for Deponent Verbs (p. 44)
- **Section 20.** Conditions With the Indicative (p. 45)
- **Section 21.** Subjunctive Conditions: Future Less Vivid (p. 46)
- Reading 1: *Dē Agrī Cultūrā*, iii, *Prima Pars*, Cato
- Reading 2: *Dē Agrī Cultūrā*, iii, *Secunda Pars*, Cato

Chapter 6 51
- **Section 22.** Perfect Subjunctive (p. 52)
- **Section 23.** Pluperfect Subjunctive (p. 53)
- **Section 24.** Sequence of Tenses (p. 55)
- **Section 25.** Indirect Command (p. 55)

Reading 1: *Dē Agricultūrā*, xiii, Varro
Reading 2: *Dē Agricultūrā*, xiii, Varro

Unit 1 Reading 61
Historical Reading: "An Overview of Early Latin Literature," by Alden Smith of Baylor University
Latin Reading: *Dē Linguā Latīnā*, V.iv, Varro

Unit 2

Chapter 7 70
- **Section 26.** Purpose Review (p. 71)
- **Section 27.** Purpose Clauses (p. 72)
- **Section 28.** Future Imperative (p. 73)

Reading: *Epistula Cornēliae, Matris Gracchōrum*, Nepos

Chapter 8 77
- **Section 29.** Indirect Question (p. 78)
- **Section 30.** Indirect Statement (p. 79)
- **Section 31.** Time Relative (p. 80)
- **Section 32.** Exclamatory Accusative (p. 81)

Reading: *Ōrātiō in Catilīnam Prīma*, Cicero

Chapter 9 86
- **Section 33.** Irregular Verb: *Fīō* (p. 87)
- **Section 34.** Ablatives in Comparative Phrases (p. 89)
- **Section 35.** Ablative of Respect (Specification) (p. 91)

Reading: *Dē Bellō Gallicō*, I:i–ii, Caesar

Chapter 10 100
- **Section 36.** Result Clause (p. 101)
- **Section 37.** Purpose Clause vs. Result Clause (p. 102)
- **Section 38.** *Cum* Clauses (p. 103)

Reading: *Ab Urbe Conditā*, XXX.xxx, Livy

Chapter 11 109
- **Section 39.** Conditional Review (p. 110)
- **Section 40.** Contrary-to-Fact Conditionals (p. 111)
- **Section 41.** Doubting Clauses (p. 113)

Reading: *Hannibal*, Nepos

Chapter 12 118
- **Section 42.** Clauses of Fearing (p. 119)
- **Section 43.** Genitive and Ablative of Quality (or Description) (p. 120)

Reading: *Naturalis Historia*, *Liber* XXXVI, *Caput* XIV, Pliny the Elder

Unit 2 Reading 127
Historical Reading: "Pons Mulvius," by Christopher R. Schlect of New St. Andrew's College
Latin Reading: *Bellum Catilīnae IX et X*, Sallust

Unit 3

Chapter 13 135
- **Section 44.** Latin Poetry: Meter and Scansion (p. 136)
- **Section 45.** Elision (p. 138)
- **Section 46.** Lyric Poetry (p. 139)

Reading 1: *Catullus I. ad Cornelium*
Reading 2: *Catullus LI. ad Lesbiam*

Chapter 14 145
- **Section 47.** Relative Clause of Characteristic (p. 146)
- **Section 48.** Dative of Direction (p. 147)
- **Section 49.** Dactylic Hexameter (p. 148)

Readings 1–6: *Aeneid*, I.i–xxxiii, Vergil

Chapter 15 158
- **Section 50.** Compound Verbs and the Dative Case (p. 159)
- **Section 51.** Objective Genitive (p. 160)
- **Section 52.** More on Meter (p. 160)

Reading 1: "A Poet's Thoughts on Cleopatra After the Battle of Actium," *Ode* I.xxxvii, Horace
Reading 2: "The Poet Believes He Will Achieve Immortality," *Ode* III.xxx, Horace

Chapter 16 168
- **Section 53.** Proviso Clause (p. 169)
- **Section 54.** *Dum* Clauses (p. 169)
- **Section 55.** Poetry Review (p. 170)

Readings 1–3: *Metamorphoses*, *Liber V*, Ovid

Unit 3 Reading 182
Historical Reading: "The Latin Poetry of John Milton," by Grant Horner of The Master's College
Latin Reading: *Elegia secunda, Anno ætatis 17. In obitum Præconis Academici Cantabrigiensis*, Milton

Glossaries

Vocabulary by Chapter... 189

Alphabetical Glossary... 201

Contributors 249

Selected Bibliography 251

Appendices

Appendix A: Pronunciation Guide 253

Appendix B: Reference Charts 257

Appendix C: Abbreviations 279

Appendix D: Noun Cases and Their Common Uses 281

Appendix E: Parsing, Declining & Conjugation Worksheets.................................. 283

Suggested Schedule

This suggested schedule assumes a class period that meets 4–5 times per week, for approximately 50–55 minutes per day.

STEP 1: VOCABULARY (1/2–1 DAY)
- Discuss chapter university motto.
- Orally review new vocabulary list and discuss derivatives.

STEP 2: GRAMMAR (2–3 DAYS)
- Read 1–2 sections per day and complete the exercises for those sections.
    - The number of sections completed each day will depend on the length and level of difficulty. Students will move through some chapters and sections more quickly than others.
    - This step may sometimes require 2 days in order to complete the grammar lessons for the chapter.

STEP 3: SENTENCE TRANSLATION (2 DAYS)
- Just before the chapter reading there is at least one exercise devoted to sentence translation. These sentences review the grammar lessons introduced in the chapter, and often prepare students for the chapter reading.
- After students have completed the translations, review each sentence. This is a critical juncture in the chapter as it will provide an opportunity to make sure that the students understand how to apply the lessons.

STEP 4: CHAPTER READING (3–4 DAYS)
The following are two suggestions for utilizing this exercise. Varying the approach from time to time with different chapters will increase the students' reading proficiency.

1. Oral Translation
a. Have students write a rough draft of their translation.
b. When finished, put English translation aside.
c. Read through passage first in Latin, then in English.
d. Use reading comprehension questions to discuss passage.
e. Allow students to rewrite a final copy of translation.

2. Sight Translation

This approach may seem slow and awkward at first, but will improve with practice.

    a. Read through passage aloud in Latin twice.

    b. Use reading comprehension questions to discuss passage.

    c. Read through passage again in English.

    d. Students write a translation in English.

STEP 5: QUIZ (1/2 DAY)

- You may want to administer an oral or written quiz to students (see p. x in the teacher's edition for guidelines).
- Quizzes should primarily assess the students' knowledge of the vocabulary and grammar taught in each chapter.

REPEAT!

- Following the quiz, students may either begin the next chapter with Step 1, or enjoy some supplemental activities (see the Supplemental Lessons section below).
- Teachers can combine Step 5 with Step 1 to make a shorter and more time efficient "week."

SUPPLEMENTAL LESSONS

Latin Alive! Book 3 provides a great wealth of supplemental activities to enrich the students' understanding of and appreciation for the Latin language. There are a variety of ways to implement these supplemental activities.

- *Colloquāmur:* These segments provide a wide variety of ways to practice Latin aloud in a conversational manner.
- **Challenge Boxes:** The questions/challenges in these boxes often compliment the chapter reading and would greatly add to a time of discussion after reading the passage.
- **Derivative Detective & Latin in Math/Science:** Any of the activities that accompany these segments may be useful as extra credit assignments.

These supplemental lessons and activities may also fill valuable time after completing an exercise or a quiz. In a classroom setting, some students will often finish faster than others. These exercises may be used to fill what we like to call "wise time."

UNIT REVIEW (3–4 DAYS)

- Read English introduction either as a class or independently.
- Follow chapter reading guidelines (see Steps 1–4).
- You may want to assign the multiple-choice reading comprehension questions as an independent exercise or complete them together as a class.
  - If completed individually, be sure to discuss together afterward.
- After the students have finished their final translation of the passage, they may take the unit test. These are included in appendix F of the teacher's edition.

Preface

Attention Students:

We have written this text just for you, the young teen in the dialectic stage of learning (the School of Logic or Rhetoric). As the third book in the Latin Alive! series, this book will build upon the foundation provided in the first two books. This book will teach you to read, understand, and even construe original Latin texts, which represent some of the greatest literature ever written.

You will find the following in this book:

- **Pronunciation:** A pronunciation guide is included as an appendix to the text. This guide will help you recall all the rules for syllabication and accent you learned in *Latin Alive! Book 1* and *Book 2* (*LA1* and *LA2*). These rules will become very important in the poetry section found in unit 3.
- **Glossaries:** Each chapter begins with vocabulary and English derivatives. At the back of this book we have provided both a Latin-to-English and an English-to-Latin glossary for each of these vocabulary lists.
- **Grammar Lessons:** These sections in each chapter provide clear, concise, and complete grammatical instruction that is written just as we teach in our classrooms. Grammatical exercises follow each lesson to help you practice what you have just learned.
- **Sentence Translation Exercises:** These exercises appear toward the end of each chapter. They will help you apply what you have practiced in the grammatical exercises and prepare you for the chapter reading.
- **Chapter Readings:** The readings in this book will provide you with a survey of Latin literature from the earliest writings of Ennius to the writings of Vergil and Ovid under the reign of Augustus. Each reading is authentic, unadapted Latin.
- **Reading Chapters:** Each unit concludes with a reading chapter designed to review the preceding lessons. The reading chapters resemble the format of the reading comprehension portion of the National Latin Exam and both the multiple choice and essay sections of the Advanced Placement Latin Exam. These unit reviews have been intentionally designed to increase reading comprehension skills and to familiarize you with the rhetorical devices commonly found in Latin literature.
- **Reading Helps:** Each reading, whether in a regular chapter or a reading chapter, contains the following helps:
    - <u>Character lists</u> that describe the characters appearing in each story.
    - An <u>extra glossary</u>, which contains words italicized in the text. This glossary will allow you to see on which words you can expect help.
    - At the end of the passage, we have provided <u>translations for some phrases</u>, which appear in bold type in the passage. This feature allows us to introduce you to classical idioms and expressions that frequently appear in Latin literature or especially difficult words and phrases in the text.
    - <u>Reading comprehension questions</u>, in both Latin and English, which follow each reading.

- **Historical Vignettes:** We are honored to have some outstanding classicists and historians as contributing writers for each of our unit review chapters. In these pieces, they share their expertise and love for literature.
  - Alden Smith, Associate Dean of the Honors College of Baylor University
  - Christopher R. Schlect, historian and Academic Dean of New St. Andrew's College
  - Grant Horner, Professor of Renaissance Literature at The Master's College
- **Poetry Unit:** Most of the readings in the Latin Alive! series have consisted of prose. Now we are excited to offer you an opportunity to experience the beauty of poetry. Unit 3 concludes the grammar studies via a study of the masters of Latin poetry: Catullus, Vergil, Horace, and Ovid. You will learn about the more common styles of Latin poetry, their Greek origins, and the poets they inspired through the ages.
- **Bonus Material:** In addition to all of the aforementioned, we have provided some of the following segments in each chapter to supplement your lessons.
  - **Colloquāmur:** Improve your command of Latin by increasing your oral proficiency. These activities appear regularly throughout the text and offer practical and sometimes entertaining ways to apply your Latin skills in and out of the classroom.
  - **Scrībāmus:** This new section will challenge you to imitate the grammatical concepts and literary styles you are studying throughout the text.
  - **Derivative Detective:** Build your English vocabulary through activities that demonstrate how we can trace modern words back to an ancient vocabulary.
  - **Culture Corner:** Through these windows to the past, you will learn more about the Romans, their lives, their history, and their traditions.
  - **Latin in Science/Math:** Learn why Latin is called the language of the sciences. These segments connect the vocabulary you are learning to the many different branches of science and math.
  - **About the Author:** In this text you will have the opportunity to read a variety of Latin literature from the time of Ennius to the era of Vergil and Ovid. These segments will introduce you to the authors who penned these great works.
  - *Est Vērum!* These short segments will provide interesting tidbits of information about the author or subjects of the chapter readings.
  - **Legacy:** The poetry unit (unit 3) will feature segments that demonstrate how the legacy of these ancient poets lives on in later writers of this genre of literature.
- The completion of this book will conclude your Latin grammatical study, which means that you will be amply prepared to read and comprehend Latin texts. While you will encounter some readings as you go through this book, Classical Academic Press also offers a dedicated reader, *Latin Alive! Latin Reader*, which will provide you with the opportunity to read Latin without spending so much time learning grammar.

NOTE TO TEACHERS & PARENTS:

As with the previous books in the Latin Alive! series, this text includes clear, concise, and complete grammatical instruction, making it user-friendly for the novice Latin teacher. As seen in the list of features above, it also incorporates a great number of exercises and additional activities, making a supplemental text quite unnecessary. We have, however, created a teacher's guide for this text in order to aid you in the classroom. This guide includes not only answers and translations, but also teacher tips, tests, additional classroom projects, and a resource guide accumulated from our combined teaching experience of more than sixty-five years.

It is our hope that you will enjoy learning Latin with this textbook as much as we have enjoyed creating it for you.

S.D.G.,

Karen Moore & Gaylan DuBose

Vita sine litteris mors est.
Adelphi University, NY

This motto is adapted from letter 82 in Seneca the Younger's *Epistulae morales ad Lucilium*, which says, "*Otium sine litteris mors est, et hominis vivi sepultura.*"

Chapter 1

- Section 1. Declension Review
- Section 2. Irregular Noun: *Vīs*
- Section 3. Noun Case Review
- Section 4. The Gerund
- Section 5. The Gerundive

VOCABULARY

LATIN	ENGLISH	DERIVATIVES
Nouns		
colōnus, colōnī, m.	farmer, (sometimes) a tenant farmer	(colonize)
cornū, -ūs, n.	horn; wing (of an army)	(cornet)
frūctus, -ūs, m.	fruit; profit, benefit	(fructose)
fūr, fūris, m./f.	thief (used as a term of reproach to slaves)	(furtive)
iniūria, -ae, f.	wrong, injury; insult, offense	(injury)
lacus, -ūs, m.	lake, pond, large body of water	(loch)
lēx, lēgis, f.	law	(legislate)
māiōrēs, māiōrium, m./f. pl. (cf. the comparative form of magnus)	ancestors	
mercātor, mercātōris, m.	merchant	(commercialize)
opus, operis, n.	work	(operative)
praedium, praediī, n.	farm, landed estate	(praedial)
sapientia, -ae, f. (cf. sapiens)	wisdom	(sapient)
silva, -ae, f.	woods, forest	(Pennsylvania)
vīs, vīs, f.	force, power; (pl.) strength, troops, forces	(vis)
Verbs		
invītō, -āre, -āvī, -ātum (cf. vitare, "to avoid")	to invite, entertain, summon	(invite)
nesciō, -īre, -īvī, -ītum	to not know, to be ignorant of	(nescience)

Adjectives, Adverbs, Conjunctions, etc.

| vetus, veteris, adj. | old, ancient | (veteran) |

Section 1. Declension Review

A noun is the name of a person, a place, a thing, or an idea. In Latin there are five groups of nouns called declensions. Each declension shares a group of case endings. We usually find the base of a noun by removing the genitive singular ending. Review the following charts, paying special attention to the genitive singular, since that form, besides providing the base, tells us to which declension the noun belongs.

A. First Declension

Masculine and Feminine (e.g., *familia, -ae,* f.)

Case	Singular	Plural
Nom.	familia	familiae
Gen.	familiae	familiārum
Dat.	familiae	familiīs
Acc.	familiam	familiās
Abl.	familiā	familiīs

Nota Bene: When a declension has more than one gender declined with the same endings, a noun of only one gender will appear in the charts. Assume that if more than one gender is mentioned under the name of the declension, it is declined the same way as the example. This statement applies to all five declensions.

As you know from *LA1* and *LA2*, there is another case, called the vocative, which is used for direct address. The vocative is exactly like the nominative except that nouns ending in *-us* in the nominative have that ending changed to *-e* to form the vocative and nouns ending in *-ius* have that ending changed to *-ī* to form the vocative (e.g., *colōnus* would become *colōne* in the vocative and *fīlius* would become *fīlī* in the vocative). Because the focus of this book is not on conversational Latin, the authors have opted to not include the vocative in the chapters. (However, the vocative is included for reference in the noun charts found in appendix B.)

B. Second Declension

Masculine (e.g., *colōnus, -ī,* m.)

Case	Singular	Plural
Nom.	colōnus	colōnī
Gen.	colōnī	colōnōrum
Dat.	colōnō	colōnīs
Acc.	colōnum	colōnōs
Abl.	colōnō	colōnīs

Nota Bene: The second declension masculine is the only declension in which the vocative differs from the nominative.

Neuter (e.g., *praedium, -ī,* n.)

Case	Singular	Plural
Nom.	praedium	praedia
Gen.	praediī	praediōrum
Dat.	praediō	praediīs
Acc.	praedium	praedia
Abl.	praediō	praediīs

C. Third Declension

Masculine and Feminine (e.g., *lēx, lēgis*, f.)

Case	Singular	Plural
Nom.	lēx	lēgēs
Gen.	lēgis	lēgum
Dat.	lēgī	lēgibus
Acc.	lēgem	lēgēs
Abl.	lēge	lēgibus

Caveat Discipulus: For the third declension, the nominative form is not determined by the genitive form. Both nominative and genitive forms must be memorized.

Neuter (e.g., *opus, operis*, n.)

Case	Singular	Plural
Nom.	opus	opera
Gen.	operis	operum
Dat.	operī	operibus
Acc.	opus	opera
Abl.	opere	operibus

D. Fourth Declension

Masculine and Feminine (e.g., *frūctus, frūctūs*, m.)

Case	Singular	Plural
Nom.	frūctus	frūctūs
Gen.	frūctūs	frūctuum
Dat.	frūctuī	frūctibus
Acc.	frūctum	frūctūs
Abl.	frūctū	frūctibus

Neuter (e.g., *cornū, cornūs*, n.)

Case	Singular	Plural
Nom.	cornū	cornua
Gen.	cornūs	cornuum
Dat.	cornū	cornibus
Acc.	cornū	cornua
Abl.	cornū	cornibus

E. Fifth Declension

Feminine or Masculine (e.g. *rēs, reī*, f. and *diēs, diēī*, m.)

Case	Singular	Plural
Nom.	rēs/diēs	rēs/diēs
Gen.	reī/diēī	rērum/diērum
Dat.	reī/diēī	rēbus/diēbus
Acc.	rem/diem	rēs/diēs
Abl.	rē/diē	rēbus/diēbus

Caveat Discipulus: The *e* in fifth declension nouns is short in the genitive and dative singular if preceded by a consonant and long if preceded by a vowel.

Exercise 1. Identify the stem of the following nouns and tell to which declension each noun belongs.

1. manus, manūs — man, 4th
2. familia, familiae — famili, 1st
3. genū, genūs — gen, 4th
4. servus, servī — serv, 2nd
5. pater, patris — patr, 3rd
6. arbor, arboris — arbor, 3rd
7. cīvis, cīvis — civ, 3rd
8. oppidum, oppidī — oppid, 2nd
9. fidēs, fideī — fid, 5th
10. cornū, cornū — corn, 4th
11. mercātor, mercātōris — mercator, 3rd
12. silva, silvae — silv, 1st
13. genus, generis — gener, 3rd
14. cultus, cultūs — cult, 4th
15. vir, virī — vir, 2nd
16. fūr, fūris — fur, 3rd
17. lacus, lacūs — lac, 4th
18. lēx, lēgis — leg, 3rd
19. māiōrēs, māiōrium — maior, 3rd
20. sapientia, sapientiae — sapienti, 1st

Showing an alliance concluded between two Germanic tribes, this woodcut is modeled after a bas-relief from the Column of Marcus Aurelius in Rome.

SECTION 2. Irregular Noun: *Vīs*

In addition to these five noun declensions, there is one irregular noun listed in this chapter's vocabulary list. The noun *vīs, vīs*, meaning "force" or "strength," is very unusual. The singular forms decline in an irregular manner. The plural forms decline like the third declension i-stem. Take care to memorize these forms well.

CASE	SINGULAR	PLURAL
NOM.	vīs	vīrēs
GEN.	vīs	vīrium
DAT.	vī	vīribus
ACC.	vim	vīrēs/vīrīs
ABL.	vī	vīribus

Caveat Discipulus: It is sometimes easy to mistake this irregular noun for the second declension *vir, virī*, or with the second-person present tense of *volō* and *nōlō*.

Exercise 2. Identify the case and number of each of the following nouns. Write down all possibilities.

1. frūctūs — Gen, Singular | Nom, Plural | Acc, Plural | Voc, Plural
2. fūribus — Dat, Plural | Abl, Plural
3. rēs — Nom, Singular | Nom, Plural | Acc, Plural | Voc, Singular | Voc, Plural
4. colōnōrum — Gen, Plural
5. agricola — Nom, Singular | Abl, Singular | Voc, Singular
6. lacū — Abl, Singular
7. vim — Acc, Singular

8. mercātōris ~~Gen, singular~~ ~~Nom, singular~~ ~~Voc, singular~~
9. cīvis ~~Gen, singular~~
10. cīvium ~~Gen, plural~~ ~~Acc plural~~ ~~Voc plural~~
11. praedia ~~Nom, plural~~ ~~Acc Plural~~ ~~Voc, Plural~~
12. lēgis ~~Gen, singular~~
13. lēgēs ~~Nom, Plural~~ ~~Acc, Plural~~ ~~Voc, Plural~~
14. operum ~~Gen, Plural~~ ~~Dat Plural~~ ~~Abl, Plural~~
15. virīs ~~Acc, singular~~ ~~Voc, singular~~
16. opus ~~Nom, singular~~ ~~Acc, singular~~

SECTION 3. Noun Case Review

The case of a noun will help you determine that noun's job, or how that noun functions in a sentence. You have now learned most of the uses for all seven noun cases. Look at the following list and then take a moment to see how many uses you can recall for each case. Check your list against the one provided in appendix D.

- Nominative — Subject, Predicate Nom.
- Genitive — Possession, Material, Origin, partitive
- Dative — Indirect object, reference, Special verbs/Adjectives, possession, Purpose, Agent
- Accusative — Direct object, prepositional phrases — time, space, Place to which
- Ablative — Place where/from, separation, manner, accompaniment, agent, means, respect, cause
- Vocative — Direct address
- Locative — Place where

Exercise 3. Provide the case of each underlined word in the following sentences. Using the context clues, discern the function or job of each underlined word. (Do not be concerned if you cannot yet translate or comprehend the full meaning of the sentences. You will work on those skills in chapter 3.)

1. <u>Maiōrēs</u> nostrī <u>fūrem</u> damnāvērunt. — S. Nom / Acc. D.O. / Acc
2. Existimāvērunt <u>cīvem</u> malum esse <u>peiōrem</u> quam fūrem. — Acc S / Pr Acc
3. <u>Virum</u> bonum <u>virtūte</u> laudābant. — Acc DO / Abl, because
4. <u>Colōnus</u> bonus laudātur ā nostrīs <u>maiōribus</u>. — Nom. S / Abl, Agent
5. Ita ad <u>oppidum</u> frūmentum ferēbant bonī <u>agricolae</u>. — Acc OP / Nom. S
6. Laudem dedērunt <u>maiōrēs</u> bonīs <u>mercātōribus</u>. — Nom S / Dat, Indirect object / Reference
7. Ex <u>agricolīs</u> multī <u>virī</u> bonī vēnērunt. — Abl PhP / Nom. S
8. Laudat <u>virēs</u> <u>militum</u>. — Acc DO / Gen
9. Sunt <u>virī</u> quī in <u>familiā</u> suā nōn laetī sint. — Nom S / Abl PW
10. Urbem magnā <u>vī</u> hostēs <u>vincent</u>. — Abl, means
11. Fēmina <u>fructūs</u> <u>virīs</u> dedit. — Acc, DO / Dat Indirect object / Reference
12. Parāte <u>praedia</u> <u>militibus</u>! — Acc DO / Dat Reference

SECTION 4. The Gerund

The gerund is a verbal noun. The English gerund is a verb with the suffix *-ing* that functions as a noun (e.g., *walking*). Because it is a noun, the gerund has case, number, and gender. The gerund is always neuter and always singular. It can appear in any of the oblique cases (genitive, dative, accusative, ablative). The gerund never appears in the nominative case.

As a verb, the gerund also has tense and voice. The translation of the gerund is always present and active. It does not have a subject, but can take a direct object. Latin, however, will usually employ the gerundive rather than the gerund if a direct object is being expressed (see section 5).

A. FORMATION: present stem + *-nd* + second declension neuter singular endings

	1ST CONJ.	2ND CONJ.	3RD CONJ.	3RD *-io* CONJ.	4TH CONJ.
GEN.	amandī	videndī	agendī	capiendī	audiendī
DAT.	amandō	videndō	agendō	capiendō	audiendō
ACC.	amandum	videndum	agendum	capiendum	audiendum
ABL.	amandō	videndō	agendō	capiendō	audiendō

Nota Bene:
- The gerund is always neuter singular.
- Note that the third *-io* and fourth conjugation verbs have an *-ie-* before the gerund ending. This is the same present stem as seen in the imperfect and future active tenses.
- The gerund never appears in the nominative case. Latin will use an infinitive instead (i.e., *errāre hūmanum est* "to err is human" or "erring is human").

Exercise 4. Provide the gerund for each verb in the case requested.
1. Accusative: expiāre — *expiandum*
2. Dative: accēdere — *accedendo*
3. Genitive: vidēre — *videndi*
4. Ablative: frangere — *frangendo*
5. Dative: venīre — *veniendo*
6. Genitive: āmittere — *amittendi*
7. Accusative: metuere — *metuendum*
8. Dative: pultāre — *pultando*
9. Ablative: invītāre — *invitando*
10. Genitive: dīcere — *dicendi*
11. Dative: ferre — *ferendo*
12. Accusative: peccāre — *peccandum*
13. Genitive: nescīre — *nesciendi*
14. Ablative: habēre — *habendo*
15. Accusative: facere — *faciendum*
Bonus: Nominative: agere — *agere*

B. TRANSLATION

Remember, the gerund never acts as a subject or as a direct object. It does, however, have several other uses depending on the case in which it appears. Let's break down the five cases to see how the gerund may be used in each one.

Nominative: *Currere* (inf.) *facile est.* *Running* is easy.

The Latin gerund does not appear in the nominative case. Instead, Latin uses the subjective infinitive. In other words, the Latin infinitive is the subject of the sentence. In English, however, we often translate the infinitive as an English gerund, ending in *-ing*.

Genitive: Amōrem *currendī* habet. He has a love *of running*. (without a DO)
Amōrem bellum *gerendī* habet. He has a love *of waging war*. (with a DO)

The genitive form of the gerund exemplifies a new use of the genitive called the objective genitive, which will be studied in greater detail in a later chapter. For now, note how the English translation uses a prepositional phrase beginning with "of." This preposition is usually the best way to translate most Latin phrases using the genitive case.

Virī ad oppidum *bellum gerendī causā* adveniunt.
The men arrive at the town *for the sake of waging war*.

The genitive gerund can also accompany *causā* to show purpose.

Dative: Aptus *regendō* est. — He is fit *for ruling*.
Aptus gentēs *regendō* est. — He is fit *for ruling* the nations.
īnstrūmentum *pugnandō* — an instrument for *fighting*

The gerund in the dative case often accompanies a special verb or adjective that typically appears with a dative noun, as seen in the first two examples. It may also show purpose.

Accusative: Domum *ad dormiendum* vēnit. — He came home *to sleep*.
Sumus parātī ad *pugnandum*. — We are prepared *for fighting*.

The gerund in the accusative case has only one purpose: to show purpose. Latin uses *ad* + the accusative gerund for purpose statements where English would use an infinitive.

Ablative: Vincit Rōmam, modo *vīvendō*. — He conquers Rome just *by living*.
Hic fortis *pugnandō* perit. — This brave man dies *from fighting*.

The ablative gerund has several uses typical of the ablative case: means, manner, cause, and comparison. The ablative gerund also appears as the object of the prepositions *ab*, *dē*, *ex*, *in*, and sometimes *prō*.

Exercise 5. Translate the following gerund phrases.
1. īnstrūmentum edendō — *Instrument for eating*
2. regendī causā — *for the sake of ruling*
3. ad vincendum — *To conquer*
4. aptus audiendō [vēritātem] — *Fit for hearing*
5. in vīvendō — *In living*
6. ars dīcendī — *The art of speaking*
7. modus operandī — *The way of working*
8. locum [artem] discendō — *place for learning*
9. ad vīvendum — *To live*
10. onus probandī — *burden of showing to be real*

SECTION 5. The Gerundive

A. FORM

The gerundive is a verbal adjective. It differs from the gerund in that it is used to modify a noun or pronoun the same way in which an adjective would. Thus, while the gerundive appears similar to the gerund (hence the similar names), it differs in that the gerundive may decline in any case, number, or gender.

CASE	MASCULINE	FEMININE	NEUTER
Nom.	agendus	agenda	agendum
Gen.	agendī	agendae	agendī
Dat.	agendō	agendae	agendō
Acc.	agendum	agendam	agendum
Abl.	agendō	agendā	agendō
Nom.	agendī	agendae	agenda
Gen.	agendōrum	agendārum	agendōrum
Dat.	agendīs	agendīs	agendīs
Acc.	agendōs	agendās	agenda
Abl.	agendīs	agendīs	agendīs

Nota Bene: The gerundive declines like first and second declension adjectives.

Exercise 6. Using what you have learned about the gerund and the gerundive, decline the plural forms of the gerundive for the following verbs.

1. docēre – masculine   *docendī, docendōrum, docendīs, docendōs, docendīs*
2. invītāre – feminine   *invitandae, invitandarum, invitandis, invitandas, invitandis*
3. nescīre – neuter   *nescienda, nesciendarum, nesciendis, nescienda, nesciendis*

B. Translation

You may recall from *LA2* that the gerundive is also known in Latin as the future passive participle. Thus it is often translated "to be _____ed/en."

fēmina *amanda*	a woman *to be loved*
crūstula *edenda*	cookies *to be eaten*

If you think about an action that is on your "to do" list (agenda), it is often something that must be done. In the same manner, the gerundive often carries a sense of obligation or necessity.

Fēmina amanda est.	The woman must be loved.
	(lit., The woman is to be loved.)
Crūstula edenda sunt nōbīs.	The cookies must be eaten by us.
	(lit., The cookies are to be eaten.)

English, however, prefers an active sentence to a passive for expressions with an agent. So an alternate way to express the second sentence would be the following:

We have to eat the cookies.

Notice that in the preceding examples the gerundive is joined by a form of the verb *esse*. Latin grammarians give this construction the fancy title of passive periphrastic. The dative of agent is used instead of *ā/ab* with the ablative with this construction.

There are some ideas that can be expressed with either the gerund or the gerundive.

Exempli gratia:

Rēx aptus gentēs *regendō* est.	The king is fit *for ruling* the nations.
Rēx aptus *gentibus regendīs* est.	The king is fit *for ruling the nations*.
	(lit., The king is fit *for the nations being ruled*).*

Which of the preceding examples use the gerund? Which use the gerundive?

You can see clearly that these are two different ways of expressing the same idea.

*Nota Bene: Translations should never resemble the "literal" translations given above. They are only given for illustrative purposes.

Exercise 7. Underline the gerundive in each of the following sentences and circle the word it modifies. Then translate.

1. Nesciō virum laudandum magis quam hunc. *I do not know a man that needs to be praised more than this one.*
2. Colōnī mercātōrēsque ad praedium vetus sunt invitandī. *The farmers and merchants must be invited to the ancient estate.*
3. Māter in mēnsā līberīs frūctūs edendōs pōnit. *The Mother places fruit on the table for the children to eat.*
4. Lēgēs parendae scrībī cum sapientiā debent. *The laws to be obeyed must be written with wisdom.*
   Hint: *scrībī* – passive form *scrībere*
5. Mī fīlī, fūrēs et virī malī sunt vītandī. *My son, thieves and bad men must be avoided.*
6. Parāvimusne nāvēs lacuī nāvigandō? *Have we prepared the ships for sailing on the lake?*
7. Vītābis iniūriam vītandō pugnō. *You will avoid injury by avoiding fight.*
8. Prō prīmā lūce diēī opus agendum erat. *Before the 1st light of day, the work had to be done.*
9. Edendīs multīs crūstulīs crēscēs maximē corpore. *Eating many cookies, you will increase in body.*
10. Animal parvum bēstiās saevās in silvā arbore ascendendā effugit. *The small animal escaped from the savage beasts in the forest by climbing up a tree.*

Exercise 8. Read and discuss the following quotations.
1. ad astra per aspera (Motto of Kansas) To the stars through difficulties
2. mens sana in corpore sano (Juvenal) A sound mind in a sound body
3. Dux [erat] femina facti. (Vergil) A woman was the leader of the deed
4. Docendo discimus. (Seneca) We learn by teaching
5. Ipse dixit. (used by Cicero and many others) He himself said.
6. Crescit eundo. (Motto of New Mexico) Increases as it goes / It grows as it goes
    Hint: *Eundo* is the gerund form of the irregular verb *ire*.
7. Labor omnia vincit. (Vergil) Work conquers all
8. Timendi causa est nescire. (Seneca) The cause of fearing is ignorance
9. iustitia omnibus (Motto of the District of Columbia) Justice for all
10. Labora summa vi, pauca desidera. (Marcus Aurelius) Work with highest power, desire few things
11. Carthago delenda est! (Cato the Elder) Carthage must be expunged!
12. ad eundum audacter quo nullus homo ante ivit (Dux Kirkus) to boldly go where no man has gone before.
13. Veterem iniuriam ferendo invitamus novam [iniuriam]. (Publilius Syrus) Carrying an old injury invites a new one
14. Deus his quoque finem dabit. (Vergil) God will give an end to these things also.
15. ad captandum vulgus (unknown) To capture the multitude
16. vir bonus, dicendi peritus (definition of an orator, Cato the Elder) A good man, an expert in speaking
    Hint: *peritus* – skilled

Derivative Detective

We have formed English words from Latin words for centuries. Some Latin elements, such as the noun *rēs*, have English derivatives in a different part of speech. The suffix *-fy* added to the root *rē-* makes an English verb from a Latin noun. (The suffix *-fy* is from the Latin *faciō*, meaning "make" or "do.") So the English word *reify* means "make into a thing." The suffix *-ate* makes the noun *lēx* into a verb (*legislate*) in a manner similar to the process for *reify*. The suffix *-ize* in *civilize* functions in the same way. The suffix *-ile* (from the Latin suffix *-ilis*, an adjective-forming suffix in Latin) makes the Latin noun *vir* into an English adjective—*virile*—based *in toto* on *virīlis*, meaning "like a man" or "manly."

Make each of the following Latin words into an English derivative of the different, specified part of speech. Use an English dictionary if necessary.
- fūr (adjective) furtive
- lēx (adjective) legal
- frūctus (verb) fructifying
- deus (verb) deify
- mors (verb) mortified

For each of the following Latin words, provide an English derivative that is the same part of speech as the Latin word given but which has a different meaning.
- pater paternity
- opus opera
- colōnus colony
- frūctus fruition
- cīvis civilian
- cornū corn
- lēx legislator

Colloquāmur!

Use the following questions and responses to review the adjectives in the sentences translated throughout this chapter. Use some "eye" Latin to figure out what the responses mean.

Interrogātiō: Cūius est numerī?　　What number is it?
Respōnsum: Singulāriter est.　　*It is singular*
　　　　　　　Plūrāliter est.　　*It is plural*

Interrogātiō: Quō est cāsū?　　In what case is it?
Respōnsum: Cāsū nōminātīvō est.　　*It is the nominative case*
　　　　　　　Cāsū genitīvō est.　　*It is the genitive case*
　　　　　　　Cāsū datīvō est.　　*It is the dative case*
　　　　　　　Cāsū accūsātīvō est.　　*It is the accusative case*
　　　　　　　Cāsū ablātīvō est.　　*It is the ablative case*
　　　　　　　Cāsū vocātīvō est.　　*It is the vocative case*
　　　　　　　Cāsū locātīvō est.　　*It is the locative case*

Interrogātiō: Cūius est generis?　　What gender is it?
Respōnsum: Est virīlis.　　*It is masculine*
　　　　　　　Est muliebris.　　*It is feminine*
　　　　　　　Est neutrālis.　　*It is neuter*

Interrogātiō: Quid significat?　　What does it mean?

Scrībāmus! (Let's Write!)

In this book, we are introducing a new segment that will encourage you to compose your own original pieces of Latin. This first writing assignment will be a short one. You have seen many mottoes for people, groups, states, and countries. Compose your own personal Latin motto. You may wish to take into account your own talents, goals, and interests, or those of your family.

Da optimum opus, et dande ludere.

129/134　　96%

Oportet eum regnare.
King's College, Pennsylvania

This is adapted from 1 Corinthians 15:25 of the Vulgate: "Oportet autem illum rēgnāre dōnec pōnat omnēs inimīcōs sub pedibus ēius."

Chapter 2

- Section 6. Verb Review
  - Present System, Active and Passive
- Section 7. Ablative of Agent and Means
- Section 8. Participle Review
- Section 9. Impersonal Verbs

VOCABULARY

LATIN	ENGLISH	DERIVATIVES
Nouns		
fremitus, -ūs, m.	a roaring, murmuring	(fremitus)
secūris, secūris, f.	axe, hatchet	
Verbs		
caedō, caedere, cecīdī, caesum (cf. caedes)	to cut down, to kill	(caesarian)
cavō, -āre, -āvī, -ātum	to make hollow, to hollow out	(excavate)
cōgitō, -āre, -āvī, -ātum	to think, to consider	(cogitate)
existimō, -āre, -āvī, -ātum	to judge a thing according to its value	(estimate)
licet, licēre, licuit *or* licitum est	it is allowed for *x* (dat.) to *y* (inf.); *x* (dat.) may *y* (inf.)	
oportet, oportēre, oportuit	it is proper/right for *x* (acc.) to *y* (inf.); *x* (acc.) should *y* (inf.)	
praestō, praestāre, praestitī, praestitum	to place before, to present; to be outstanding, to be distinguished; to prevail; to overcome; to stand before	
prōmittō, prōmittere, prōmīsī, prōmissum	to let go forward, to send forth; to promise	(promise)
sonō, sonāre, sonuī, sonitum	to sound, to resound, to make a noise	(sonic)
vīsō, vīsere, vīsī, vīsum	to look at carefully, to contemplate	(visage)
Adjectives, Adverbs, Conjunctions, etc.		
frondōsus, -a, -um, adj.	full of leaves, leafy	(frond)

Section 6. Verb Review

You likely recall that Latin has four verb conjugations, or groups of verbs. The conjugation for each verb may be identified by the verb's stem, which is found like this:

stem = second principal part – *re*

This stem is called the present stem and may be used to form verbs in the present system (*id est* present, imperfect, and future) in both the active and passive voices.

The charts in this section show the three tenses in the present system for a first conjugation verb. You may need to review verbs of the other conjugations by looking at the reference charts in appendix B. Remember that first and second conjugations tend to follow the same patterns. Third and fourth conjugation verbs sometimes follow a different pattern.

A. Present Tense

1. Active Voice

All conjugations: present stem + active personal endings

First Conjugation: I praise, I am praising, I do praise

Person	Singular	Plural
1	laudō (I praise)	laudāmus (we praise)
2	laudās (you praise)	laudātis (you praise)
3	laudat (he/she/it praises)	laudant (they praise)

2. Passive Voice

All conjugations: present stem + passive personal endings

First Conjugation: I am praised, I am being praised

Person	Singular	Plural
1	laudor (I am praised)	laudāmur (we are praised)
2	laudāris/laudāre* (you are praised)	laudāminī (you are praised)
3	laudātur (he/she/it is praised)	laudantur (they are praised)

__Caveat Discipulus__: Notice that the second-person singular now shows an alternate form. At first glance, it may seem like an infinitive, but the context of the sentence will reveal differently.

Nota Bene:
- Note that the stem is the same for both the active and passive voices.
- Note carefully that the second-person singular has an alternative form, which looks like the infinitive.
- Note the stem vowel in the passive third-person singular is long (it is short in the active voice).
- Refer to the reference charts in appendix B to see examples of conjugations 2–4.

Queen Dido of Carthage on the funeral pile, a scene from Virgil's *Aeneid*

Exercise 1. Considering the patterns shown for *laudāre*, conjugate the verbs *habēre* and *aperīre* in the present active and present passive. Include the alternative ending for the second-person singular present passive. Also be sure to include English translations. (Hint: You can see models for the second and fourth conjugations in the reference charts in appendix B.)

B. Imperfect Tense

1. Active Voice

First and second conjugation: present stem + -*ba*- + active personal endings

Third and fourth conjugation: present stem + -*ēba*- + active personal endings

First Conjugation: I was praising, I used to praise, I kept on praising, I praised

Person	Singular	Plural
1	laudābam (I was praising)	laudābāmus (we were praising)
2	laudābās (you were praising)	laudābātis (you were praising)
3	laudābat (he/she/it was praising)	laudābant (they were praising)

2. Passive Voice

First and second conjugation: present stem + -*ba*- + passive personal endings

Third and fourth conjugation: present stem + -*ēba*- + passive personal endings

First Conjugation: I was praised, I was being praised, I used to be praised

Person	Singular	Plural
1	laudābar (I was praised)	laudābāmur (we were praised)
2	laudābāris/laudābāre (you were praised)	laudābāminī (you were praised)
3	laudābātur (he/she/it was praised)	laudantur (they were praised)

Nota Bene:

- Note that the tense marker is the same for both the active and passive voices.
- Remember that the first and second conjugations use the tense marker -*ba*-. The third and fourth conjugations use the tense marker -*ēba*-.
- Refer to the reference charts in appendix B to see examples of the imperfect tense for conjugations 2–4.

Exercise 2. Considering the patterns shown for *laudāre*, conjugate the verbs *rapere* and *invenīre* in the imperfect active and passive. Be sure to include English translations. (Hint: Remember that *rapere* is a third conjugation *-io* verb. You can see models for the third *-io* and fourth conjugations in appendix B.)

C. Future Tense

1. Active Voice

First and second conjugation: present stem + -*b* (*i, o, u*)- + active personal endings

First Conjugation: I shall praise, I shall be praising

Person	Singular	Plural
1	laudābō (I shall praise)	laudābimus (we shall praise)
2	laudābis (you will praise)	laudābitis (you will praise)
3	laudābit (he/she/it will praise)	laudābunt (they will praise)

2. Passive Voice

First and second conjugation: present stem + -b (i, o, u)- + passive personal endings

First Conjugation: I shall be praised

Person	Singular	Plural
1	laudābor (I shall be praised)	laudābimur (we shall be praised)
2	laudāberis/laudābere (you will be praised)	laudābiminī (you will be praised)
3	laudābitur (he/she/it will be praised)	laudābuntur (they will be praised)

Nota Bene:

- Note that the tense marker is the same for most endings in the active and passive voices.
- Note carefully that the second-person singular has a vowel change. The active tense ending is -*bis*. The passive endings are -*beris* or -*bere*.
- Remember that the first and second conjugations use the tense marker -*b (i, o, u)*-. The third and fourth conjugations use the tense marker or -*e*- (with the exception of -*a*- in the first-person singular).
- Refer to appendix B to see examples of the future tense for conjugations 2–4.

Exercise 3. Considering the patterns shown for *laudāre*, conjugate the verbs *ferre* and *placēre* in the future active and passive. Include English translations. (Hint: Remember that although *ferre* is classified as an irregular verb, it follows the conjugation pattern for the third conjugation in the imperfect and future tenses.)

In order to review verbs in the present system in the other conjugations, you will need to refer to either the paradigms in appendix B or your notes from *LA1* and *LA2*.

Exercise 4. For each verb below, give the person, number, tense, and voice.

1. laudāmur — 1st, Plural, Present, Passive
2. occupābunt — 3rd, Plural, Future, Active
3. cōgitābis — 2nd, Singular, Future, Active
4. parābās — 2nd, Singular, Imperfect, Active
5. laudantur — 3rd, Plural, Present, Passive
6. cōgitō — 1st, Singular, Present, Active
7. occupābāmur — 1st, Plural, Imperfect, Passive
8. vīsent — 3rd, Plural, Future, Active
9. sonābantur — 3rd, Plural, Imperfect, Passive
10. cavābit — 3rd, Singular, Future, Active
11. prōmittēminī — 2nd, Plural, Future, Passive
12. caeduntur — 3rd, Plural, Present, Passive

Exercise 5. Change each verb in exercise 4 from active to passive or from passive to active, keeping the same person, number, and tense.

1. laudāmus
2. occupābuntur
3. cōgitāberis
4. parābāris
5. laudant
6. cōgitor
7. occupābāmus
8. vīsentur
9. sonābant
10. cavābitur
11. prōmittētis
12. caedunt

Exercise 6. Translate the following sentences.
1. Hic vir praestat. — This man is outstanding.
2. Ille puer quaerit, "Cūr?" — That boy asks, "Why?"
3. Nostrae fēminae bonae semper laudantur. — Our good women are always praised.
4. Ā nōbīs bonae fēminae semper laudābuntur. — By us good women will always be praised.
5. Agricolae fortissimī prōmittēbant bonum labōrem. — The strongest farmers promised good work.
6. Discipulī sē in eō studiō occupant. — The students occupy themselves in this study.
7. Quid in animō habēs? — What do you have in mind?
8. Quās rēs parābit illa puella? — What things will that girl prepare?

9. Quae rēs parābuntur ab illā puellā? *What things will be prepared by that girl?*
10. Lēx laudābitur ā virō illō. *The law will be praised by that famous man.*
    Hint: When a form of *ille* follows the noun it modifies, it can mean "that famous."

Section 7. Ablative of Agent and Means

The passive voice indicates that someone or something (the subject) is acted upon by an agent. The agent is sometimes left to be inferred from the context, but when it is expressed, in Latin we show the agent by using *ā* or *ab* with the ablative case.

Exempli Gratia:
Frūmentum portātur.   The grain is carried.
Frūmentum ā servō portātur.   The grain is carried <u>by a servant</u>.

When a thing is used to perform the action, Latin uses the ablative case without a preposition. This is called the ablative of means.

Exempli Gratia:
Frūmentum carrō portātur.   The grain is carried <u>by a cart</u>.

Both ablatives can be in the same sentence.

Exempli Gratia:
Frūmentum carrō ā servō portātur.   The grain is carried by the servant by cart.
                                      (i.e., The servant carries the grain by cart.)

Exercise 7. Translate the following sentences, which contain the ablative of agent or means constructions.
1. Ager ab agricolā parābātur. *The field was being prepared by the farmer.*
2. Silva sonābat fremitū bellī. *The forest was sounding with the roaring of the war.*
3. Illa rēs ab omnibus bonīs virīs condemnābitur. *That thing will be condemned by all good men.*
4. Frūctūs emēbantur ā mercātōre. *The fruits were being bought by the merchant.*
5. Arborēs frondōsae in silvā secūribus hominum caeduntur. *The leafy trees in the forest are chopped by the axes of the men.*
6. Omne opus nostrum ā patre nostrō laudātur. *All of our good work is praised by our father.*
7. Ā cīve malō bona lēx nōn laudābitur. *The good law will not be praised by the bad citizen.*

Section 8. Participle Review

In chapter 1, we reviewed the gerund, a verbal noun. The basic idea behind the gerund is that a verb, showing action, is grammatically transformed into a noun. It thus expresses the idea of the action. A participle is a verbal adjective. It is a verb that is grammatically transformed into an adjective. It is thus part adjective and part verb. As an adjective, it will have case, number, gender, and the ability to modify nouns. As a verb, the participle will have tense, voice, and the ability to take a direct object. We will review the most commonly used participles over the next few chapters. Let's begin with the present participle.

Present Participle

a. Formation: present stem + *-ns, -ntis*   age-ns

The present participle consists of the present stem plus the ending *-ns* (in the nominative singular only) and *-ntis*. These participles decline as third declension i-stem nouns or adjectives.

SINGULAR		
Case	Masculine/Feminine	Neuter
Nom.	agēns	agēns
Gen.	agentis	agentis
Dat.	agentī	agentī
Acc.	agentem	agēns
Abl.	agentī/agente	agentī/agente
Voc.	agēns	agēns

PLURAL		
Case	Masculine/Feminine	Neuter
Nom.	agentēs	agentia
Gen.	agentium	agentium
Dat.	agentibus	agentibus
Acc.	agentēs/agentīs	agentia
Abl.	agentibus	agentibus
Voc.	agentēs	agentia

Nota Bene:

- The stem vowel -*e*- is long only in the nominative singular. This is true for all conjugations: (first) *amāns, amantis*; (second) *vidēns, videntis*; (third) *agēns, agentis*; (third -*iō*) *capiēns, capientis*; (fourth) *audiēns, audientis*.
- Third -*iō* and fourth conjugation both have an -*ie*- before the participial ending (see examples in preceding note).
- The ablative singular has two endings: one resembles third declension nouns, the other third declension adjectives. Section 8b will discuss when to use these forms.
- The accusative plural commonly appears as -*īs* in the writings of certain authors, such as Vergil.

Exercise 8. Transform the following verbs into the present participle with the requested case, number, and gender.

1. caedere (nominative, singular, neuter) *caedens*
2. cavāre (dative, plural, feminine) *cavantibus*
3. cōgitāre (accusative, singular, masculine) *cogitantem*
4. existimāre (genitive, plural, neuter) *existimantium*
5. frangere (ablative, plural, masculine) *frangentibus*
6. occupāre (dative, singular, feminine) *occupanti*
7. praestāre (nominative, plural, masculine) *praestantes*
8. prōmittere (accusative, plural, neuter) *promittentia*
9. sonāre (genitive, singular, feminine) *sonantis*
10. vīsere (ablative, singular, masculine) *visente, visenti*

b. Translation

The present active participle demonstrates action that occurs *at the same time* as that of the main verb. The English present participle typically uses the ending -*ing*, particularly when functioning as an adjective. In Latin, the adjectival participle will use the third declension adjective ending for the ablative singular: -*ī*.

| Uxor **amāns** virum cūrat. | The **loving** wife cares for her husband. |
| Vir **ab uxōre amantī** cūrātur. | The husband is cared for **by his loving wife**. |

Both of the above examples demonstrate the adjectival use of the present active participle. Latin also uses participles as nouns or, more accurately, uses participles that modify an unexpressed or understood noun.

| **Currēns** est fessus. | **The one running** is tired. |
| | **He who is running** is tired. |

In the preceding example, it is understood that the participle modifies a noun that is unexpressed. That unseen noun must refer to a singular person. Notice how English needs to add an expressed subject ("one") and often employs a relative pronoun to translate this participle. Latin uses participles much more often than English. When the participle acts as a noun, or has an object, it is sometimes better to translate the participle as a dependent clause. When functioning as a noun, the present participle uses the third declension noun form of the ablative singular: short -*e*.

> Currentēs sunt fessī.   **Those who are running** are tired.
>
> Flōrēs ab **currente** calcābātur.   The flowers were being trampled by **the one running**.
> *or*
> The flowers were being trampled by **the one who was running**.

Caveat Discipulus: Gerund vs. Present Participle

Students sometimes confuse the gerund (verbal noun) with the participle (verbal adjective). To help discern the difference, remember the following clues:

Gerund	Present Participle
• The gerund will have the letters *-nd-* just before the ending.	• The present participle will have the letters *-ns* or *-nt-*.
• The gerund will decline as a second declension neuter noun.	• The present participle will decline as a third declension adjective or noun.
• The gerund always acts as a noun representing an action.	• The present participle will always act as an adjective describing another noun, even if that noun is not seen in the sentence.

Exercise 9. Identify and parse the present participle or gerund in each of the following sentences. Then translate.

1. Virī caedentēs arborēs frondōsās decem hōrās labōrābant.
2. Expellite hostēs terram nostram occupantēs!
3. Vīsentibus ille pugnāre ferōcius quam omnēs vidētur.
4. Duo virī mūrum altissimum vīsendī causā ascendent.
5. Magnus fremitus quercū in silvā cadente creātur.
6. Imperātor amantēs patriam salūtāvit magnā ōrātiōne.
   Hint: What single English word could represent *amantēs patriam*?
7. Ferte secūrēs et īnstrūmenta vōbīscum alia aedificandō.
8. We created a small boat by hollowing out a tree.
9. The falling trees resound with a great roar through the whole forest.
10. The children drive off the wolf by throwing stones.
11. Thinking often about his family, the father wrote many letters.

Section 9. Impersonal Verbs

Impersonal verbs are actually a misnomer grammatically. The fact is that a specific or actual person is not the subject of an impersonal verb; but as we know, the third-*person* ending can take a neuter subject. So, while there is no person involved in the colloquial sense, there is in grammatical usage. In English we use the placeholder "it" for our impersonal verbs, which Latin usually does not do so. For instance, notice the following expressions:

> It is right to do this.
> It is not permissible for us to run in the building.

In the first sentence, if we asked the question "What is right?" the answer would be "to do this." In a sense, this phrase is the subject and we could rephrase the statement as "To do this is right." The word "it" can either be seen as a placeholder or as a marker to let the listener/reader understand that a phrase is coming that will explain the pronoun. Very frequently we use this impersonal construction when we want to be general and inclusive. In the first example, if one asked the question "For whom is it right to do this?" the answer would be "everyone" or "anyone." On the other hand, the second example seems odd in English because we generally use personal constructions when we are being specific and exclusive. The second example might better be written as "We are not allowed to run in the building." Even if the second sentence were truncated and no subject expressed, as in "It is not permissible to run in the building," we might prefer to make it personal and make the subject generic, as in "One is not permitted to run in the building."

There are all sorts of ways to make these phrases more pleasing to the English speaker's ear. As a result, we generally shy away from a literal way of translating these constructions.

Unlike English speakers, the Romans had no qualms about keeping the impersonal verb even when the subject was expressed. Readers will always see these verbs in the third-person singular. For this reason, these verbs are listed in the dictionary (and in this chapter's vocabulary list) differently than most verbs. Look through the list and see if you can identify the two impersonal verbs.

Now look at these two impersonal verbs within a Latin sentence. What is the subject for each of these verbs?

> Oportet nōs hoc facere.
>
> Nōn licet nōbīs currere in aedificō.

To discern the subject, ask yourself:

> Quid oportet? (nōs)
>
> Quid nōn licet? (nōbīs)

In Latin, the subject of an impersonal verb is usually an infinitive along with its subject and object (if they are expressed). You may recall from *Latin Alive! Book 2* that an infinitive can act as the subject of a sentence or phrase (see *LA2*, section 65). When the infinitive phrase acts as a subject it is considered neuter and singular, thus fitting the third-person singular nature of an impersonal verb. Also note that for *oportet* the person for whom something is fitting is in the accusative case (subject of the infinitive), while for *licet* the person for whom something is permitted is in the dative case (dative of reference).

Regular verbs may also act in an impersonal manner and often do so in the passive voice.

> Vidētur esse bonum pullō.   It seems good to the chicken.

Exercise 10. Translate the following famous quotations from Latin literature. Watch for impersonal verbs.

1. Cui peccare licet, peccat minus. (Ovid)
2. Gutta cavat lapidem, non vi, sed saepe cadendo. (Ovid)
   Hint: *gutta* – a drop/dripping
3. Non licet omnibus adire Corinthum. (Horace)
   Hint: *Corinthus* – Corinth, Greek city, luxurious travel destination
4. Salus populi suprema lex [est]. (Cicero, motto of Missouri)
5. Caritate te benevolentia oportet esse, non armis. (Cicero)
   Hint: *cāritāte* – affection; *benevolentiā* – kindness
6. Non omne quod licet honestum est. (*Corpus Iuris Civilis*)
7. Ab ovo usque ad mala. (Horace)
8. Divina natura dedit agros, ars humana aedificavit urbes. (Tibullus)
9. Aegroto, dum anima est, spes esse dicitur. (proverb)
   Hint: *aegrōtō* – sick man
10. Quod licet Iovi non licet bovi. (proverb)

Chapter Reading

"ARBORĒS AD *ROGŌS* FACIENDŌS CAEDUNTUR"

Fragment from Ennius, *Liber VI*, unadapted

Incendunt arbusta per alta, secūribus caedunt,

Percellunt magnās quercūs, exciditur īlex,

Fraxinus frangitur atque *abiēs* consternitur alta.
Pīnūs procerās pervortunt: omne sonābat
Arbustum fremitū silvae frondōsae.

Glossary

rogus, -ī, m.	funeral pyre
incendō, incendere, incendī, incēnsum	to burn, to set fire (cf. *incendium*)
arbustum, -ī, n.	plantation, a vineyard planted with trees, grove of trees
percellō, percellere, perculī, perculsum	to beat down, to strike down
excīdō, excīdere, excīdī, excīsum	*ex + caedō*
īlex, īlicis, f.	holly, holm-oak
fraxinus, -ī, m.	ash tree
abiēs, abietis, f.	silver fir
consternō, consternere, constrāvī, constrātum	to strew, to scatter; to knock over
pīnus, -ūs, f.	pine tree (this word also commonly appears as a second declension noun: *pīnus, pīnī*)
prōcērus, -a, -um, adj.	*altus, longus*
pervortō, pervortere, pervortī, pervorsum	to turn upside down (cf. *per + vertere*)

Caveat Discipulus: There are several trees named in this chapter reading. Notice that each tree is feminine in gender even if it is in a declension that does not have many feminine nouns (second and fourth declensions). The names of trees are often feminine "PAIN" words. That is, they are feminine in gender despite their declension.

Respondē Latīnē!

1. Quōmodo virī arborēs caedunt?
2. Quālēs arborēs in silvā sunt?
3. Cūr caedunt arborēs?

About the Author

ENNIUS

Ennius was known to the Romans as "the father of Roman poetry." He was born Quintus Ennius in Calabria, Italy, and lived c. 239–170 BC. To put his lifetime into a historical context, Ennius was born just after the end of the First Punic War (241 BC) and lived through the tumultuous events of the Second Punic War. We know that he served as a centurion in Sardinia during this war. This means he was an eyewitness to some very exciting and very dangerous times for Rome. Some of the events of these times are recorded in his writings. Unfortunately, very little of his work has survived to the present day. Most of what remains are fragments—portions of poems and stories—many contained within the writings of other Roman authors. What we do know of Ennius is that he was highly regarded by later Roman authors. We see his influence in the writings of men such as Cicero, Vergil, and Livy, writers hailed as the greatest of their day. Truly, Ennius does deserve the title "the father of Roman poetry" or even of Roman literature.

Derivative Detective

For each of the following verbs, form an English noun or adjective. Define each English word you write down.

1. laudō — laudable: deserving praise
2. parō — preparatory: to prepare, something to prepare
3. occupō — occupation: possession
4. cōgitō — cogitation: focused thought
5. existimō — estimable: worthy of great respect
6. quaerō — requirement: need

Colloquāmur!

CLASSROOM REQUESTS

Impersonal verbs work very well for classroom conversation. Think how many times you need to ask your teacher's permission to go somewhere or do something. In Latin, the polite way to ask permission would be with the impersonal verb *licet* with a pronoun in the dative case.

Licet mihi – is it permitted for me? May I?

Licet nōbīs – is it permitted for us? May we?

Brainstorm some common requests that you can use each day in your classroom. Here are a few to get you started. Translate them before moving on to Game Time.

- Licet mihi īre ad lātrīnam? — May I go to the bathroom?
- Licet mihi īre ad fontem aquae? — May I go to the water fountain?
- Licet nōbīs labōrāre/studēre cum amīcīs? — May we study with friends?

Game Time!

Play *Magister, licetne mihi?*, also known as "Teacher, May I?"

1. Use your cardinal numbers to complete the phrase. A list of these numbers is provided in appendix B.

    Licetne mihi ambulāre (number) passūs?

2. Add some adjectives to describe your paces, such as *magnōs passūs, parvōs passūs, celerēs passūs, tardōs passūs*.
3. As a class, brainstorm other requests that you can make of your teacher.

Et facta est lux.
Morehouse College, Georgia

This motto is adapted from Genesis 1:3 of the Vulgate: "Dixitque Deus fiat lux et facta est lux."

Chapter 3

- Section 10. Verb Review: Perfect System
  - Perfect Tense
  - Pluperfect Tense
  - Future Perfect Tense
- Section 11. Perfect Passive Participle
- Section 12. Deponent Verbs
  - Indicative Mood
  - Participles
  - Imperative Mood
- Section 13. PUFFV Verbs and the Ablative Case

VOCABULARY

LATIN	ENGLISH	DERIVATIVES
Nouns		
ōrātor, ōrātōris, m. (cf. ōrō, ōrāre)	orator, speaker	(orator)
Verbs		
circumeō, circumīre, circumīvī/circumiī, circuitum	to go around; to enclose	(circuit)
cōnsequor, cōnsequī, cōnsecūtus sum (cf. sequor)	to follow, to go after; to obtain	(consequence)
cunctor, cunctārī, cunctātus sum (cf. cunctātiō)	to delay; to hesitate (+ inf.)	
faeneror, faenerārī, faenerātus sum	to lend [money] at interest; to drain by extortion	
gignō, gignere, genuī, genitum	to beget, to bear, to bring forth	(genitive)
gradior, gradī, grēssus sum	to walk, to step	(grade)
habeō, habēre, habuī, habitum	to have, to hold; to consider	(habit)
hortor, hortārī, hortātus sum	to encourage, to exhort	(exhortation)
misceō, miscēre, miscuī, mixtum	to mix, to mingle	(miscellaneous)

morior, morī/morīrī, mortuus sum (cf. mortuus)	to die	(mortuary)
nītor, nītī, nīsum sum/nīxum sum (cf. nīsus)	to strive, to exert oneself, to make an effort	
pōnō, pōnere, posuī/posīvī, positum	to put, to place	(deposit)
redeō, redīre, rediī/redīvī, reditum	to go back, to come back, to return	
Adjectives, Adverbs, Conjunctions, etc.		
perīculōsus, -a, -um, adj. (cf. perīculum)	dangerous	(perilous)
hinc, adv.	from this, from here	
quom (archaic form of cum, conj.), adv.	when	

Nota Bene: Some of the verbs in this vocabulary list are deponent. Memorize the principal parts carefully. Can you guess which verbs in this list are deponent? They should look unusual. (You will learn more about deponent verbs later in this chapter.)

Section 10. Verb Review: Perfect System

All verbs in all conjugations follow the same pattern when conjugating in the tenses of the perfect system: perfect, pluperfect, and future perfect. There are no exceptions for this rule, not even among irregular verbs. If you can conjugate one verb in the perfect system, you can conjugate and recognize them all. As Vergil said in *Aeneīs II*, "... ab uno disce omnes."

A. Perfect Tense

1. Active Voice

All conjugations: perfect stem (third principal part) + perfect active endings

Person	Singular	Plural
1	habuī (I held, have held, did hold)	habuimus (we held, have held, did hold)
2	habuistī (you held, have held, did hold)	habuistis (you held, have held, did hold)
3	habuit (he/she/it held, has held, did hold)	habuērunt/habuēre* (they held, have held, did hold)

*****Caveat Discipulus***: Notice that the third-person plural now shows an alternate form. At first glance, the alternate form may seem like an infinitive, but if you look closely you will notice that the perfect stem remains. It occurs quite often in Latin literature, especially in poetry.

Considering the example of *habuēre*, what are the alternate forms of the following third-person plural verbs?

posuērunt

genuērunt

circumīvērunt

existimāvērunt

2. Passive Voice

Participial stem (fourth principal part) + present active form *esse*

The perfect tense, passive voice, is the fourth principal part plus the present tense of *sum*. Since the fourth principal part is a participle, or verbal adjective, its form will change both number and gender to agree with its subject. Many verbs, such as *esse*, do not have passive forms. If you are wondering why, try to use these same words in the passive voice in English. Their meanings just will not transfer into the passive voice.

Person	Singular	Plural
1	habitus, -a, -um sum (I was held)	habitī, -ae, -a sumus (we were held)
2	habitus, -a, -um es (you were held)	habitī, -ae, -a estis (you were held)
3	habitus, -a, -um est (he was held)	habitī, -ae, -a sunt (they were held)

Exercise 1. Conjugate the verbs *laudāre* and *esse* in the perfect active tense. Conjugate *laudāre* in the perfect passive tense as well. Include the English translation for each form. For the passive voice of *laudāre*, assume the masculine gender.

B. PLUPERFECT TENSE

1. Active Voice

All conjugations: perfect stem + -era- + active personal endings

The pluperfect tense, active voice, is formed on the perfect stem. Notice that the tense indicator is -era-; in effect, this tense is the perfect stem plus the imperfect tense of *sum*. The pluperfect tense shows the earlier of two actions which both occur in the past or an action by or at a certain time in the past. Consider the following examples:

Before you arrived, I had left.

By three o'clock Friday, I had left.

Person	Singular	Plural
1	habueram (I had held)	habuerāmus (we had held)
2	habuerās (you had held)	habuerātis (you had held)
3	habuerat (he/she/it had held)	habuerant (they had held)

2. Passive Voice

Participial stem (fourth principal part) + imperfect active form *esse*

The pluperfect tense, passive voice, is the fourth principal part plus the imperfect tense of *sum*. Notice that the tense indicator -era- found in the active voice also appears in the passive voice.

Person	Singular	Plural
1	habitus, -a, -um eram (I had been held)	habitī, -ae, -a erāmus (we had been held)
2	habitus, -a, -um erās (you had been held)	habitī, -ae, -a erātis (you had been held)
3	habitus, -a, -um erat (he had been held)	habitī, -ae, -a erant (they had been held)

Exercise 2. Conjugate the verbs *pōnere* and *īre* in the pluperfect active tense. Conjugate the verb *pōnere* in the pluperfect passive tense; assume the feminine gender. Include the English translation for each form.

C. FUTURE PERFECT TENSE

1. Active Voice

All conjugations: perfect stem + -eri- + active personal endings

The future perfect tense, active voice, is formed on the perfect stem. Basically, the tense indicator is -eri-; in effect, this tense is the perfect stem plus the future tense of *sum*. Be mindful of the *o* in the first-person singular and be careful not to put a *u* into the ending of the third-person plural. The future perfect tense shows the earlier of two actions which both occur in the future or an action by a certain time in the future.

Notice the examples below.
> By the time you (will) arrive, I shall have left.
> By three o'clock Friday, I shall have left.

The future perfect tense appears more frequently in Latin than it does in modern English.

Person	Singular	Plural
1	habuerō (I shall have held)	habuerimus (we shall have held)
2	habueris (you will have held)	habueritis (you will have held)
3	habuerit (he/she/it will have held)	habuerint (they will have held)

2. Passive Voice

Participial stem (fourth principal part) + future active form *esse*

Person	Singular	Plural
1	habitus, -a, -um erō (I shall have been held)	habitī, -ae, -a erimus (we shall have been held)
2	habitus, -a, -um eris (you will have been held)	habitī, -ae, -a eritis (you will have been held)
3	habitus, -a, -um erit (he/she/it will have been held)	habitī, -ae, -a erunt (they will have been held)

Exercise 3. Conjugate the verbs *audīre* and *ferre* in the future perfect tense, both active and passive. Include the English translation for each form. For the passive voice, assume the neuter gender for each verb.

Exercise 4. Translate the following verb phrases into Latin. Consider carefully the tense and voice of each.

1. I have gone around
2. I will have gone around
3. you (s.) are praised
4. you (s.) were praised
5. he had considered
6. it had been considered
7. she was considering
8. we were hearing
9. we were heard
10. you (pl.) have been brought forth
11. you (pl.) had been brought forth
12. they were being placed
13. they have been placed
14. they had placed
15. I had placed
16. I had been placed
17. I was being placed
18. he seized
19. she has been seized
20. it will have been seized

Exercise 5. Translate the following sentences.

1. Quem quaeritis?
2. Virō parcite!
3. Placuitne?
4. Laudāvērunt illam lēgem.
5. Cēpistīne fūrem?
6. Colōnus frūctum laudāverit ante eam emēs.
7. Agricola praedium ēmerat.
8. Existimāverō rem ante eam emam.
9. Redīverat mercātor.
10. Ā nōbīs frūctūs crās emptae erunt.
   Hint: *crās* = tomorrow
11. The citizens had not praised those laws.
12. The merchant was praised by that man.
13. The pretty girl had been praised by the boy.
14. The boy was praised by that girl.
15. We had bought the fruit.

24

SECTION 11. Perfect Passive Participle

Latin participles appear in only three tenses: present, future, and perfect. You reviewed the present active participle in the previous chapter. The present participle occurs only in the active voice. The perfect participle occurs only in the passive voice.

A. FORMATION: participial stem + *-us, -a, -um*   āctus, -a, -um

The perfect passive participle uses the participial stem, formed from the fourth principal part. In fact, the fourth principal part truly is the perfect passive participle. So if you have diligently memorized all principal parts for all verbs, then you already have this one memorized. The perfect passive participle declines like first and second declension adjectives.

SINGULAR			
NOM.	āctus	ācta	āctum
GEN.	āctī	āctae	āctī
DAT.	āctō	āctae	āctō
ACC.	āctum	āctam	āctum
ABL.	āctō	āctā	āctō

PLURAL			
NOM.	āctī	āctae	ācta
GEN.	āctōrum	āctārum	āctōrum
DAT.	āctīs	āctīs	āctīs
ACC.	āctōs	āctās	ācta
ABL.	āctīs	āctīs	āctīs

B. TRANSLATION

The perfect passive participle demonstrates action that has already happened *before* that of the main verb. This participle is best translated as "____ed" or "having been ____ed." (Sometimes rather than ending with *-ed* the translated verb will end in *-n* or even *-t*." Consider, for example, "having been shown" or "having been thought.")

| Uxor **amāta** virum cūrat. | The **loved** wife cares for her husband. |
| Currus **āctus** celerrimē cursum vīcit. | The chariot, **having been driven** very fast, won the race. |

As in the case with other adjectives, a participle may sometimes be substantive. That means that the noun it modifies is not specifically expressed, but understood.

| **Amāta** virum cūrat. | The loved (woman) cares for her husband. |
| Cursum **āctus** celerrimē vīcit. | The (one) driven very fast won the race. |

Caveat Discipulus: It is sometimes easy to confuse a perfect passive participle with the perfect passive indicative. In order to distinguish between the two, always look around for a form of *esse*. If you see a linking verb nearby it may not be a participle.

| Currus celerrimē āctus est. | The chariot was driven very fast. |
| Currus celerrimē āctus vīcit. | The chariot, driven very fast, won. |

Exercise 6. Form the nominative singular of the perfect passive participle for each of the following verbs, then translate.

Example: amāre: amātus, amāta, amātum = loved, having been loved
1. habēre — habitus, habita, habitum (held, having been held)
2. vīsere — vīsus, vīsa, vīsum (considered, having been considered)
3. cōgitāre — cōgitātus, cōgitāta, cōgitātum (thought, having been thought)
4. miscēre — mixtus, mixta, mixtum (mixed, having been mixed)
5. nescīre — nescītus, nescīta, nescītum (unaware, having been unaware)
6. pōnere — postus, posta, postum (put, having been put)
7. occupāre — occupātus, occupāta, occupātum (seized, having been seized)
8. dīcere — dictus, dicta, dictum (said, having been said)
9. capere — captus, capta, captum (captured, having been captured)
10. cavēre — cavātus, cavāta, cavātum (hollowed, having been hollowed)
11. redīre — reditus, redita, reditum (returned, having been returned)
12. petere — petītus, petīta, petītum (attacked, having been attacked)
13. promittere — promissus, promissa, promissum (promised, having been promised)
14. gerere — gestus, gesta, gestum (borne, having been borne)
15. docēre — doctus, docta, doctum (taught, having been taught)

Exercise 7. Translate the following sentences. Be careful to watch how the perfect passive participle may be used. (Hint: Look first for the main verb, which will have a personal ending. If you see a form of *esse*, look to see if a participle is near. If so, it may be part of the main verb.)
1. Nōnne negābis cōnsilium habitum perīculōsum ā multīs? — Will you not refuse the plan considered dangerous by many?
2. Hoc cōnsilium habitum est ā multīs esse perīculōsum. — This plan was considered by many to be dangerous.
3. Verba dicta ab ōrātōre bonō vulgus mōvērunt. — The words spoken by the good speaker moved the multitude.
4. Flōrēs caeruleī rubrīque flāvīque ā puellīs in silvā vīsī sunt. — The blue, red and yellow flowers were seen by the girls in the wood.
5. Colōnī arborēs frondōsās caesās ā secūribus ad praedium ferēbant. — The farmers were carrying the leafy trees cut down by axes to the estate.
6. Vīs mixta cum sapientiā ducī bene serviet. — Strength mixed with wisdom will serve the leader well.
7. Multī līberī mātrī beātae genitī erant. — Many children had been born to the happy mother.
8. Multa posita bona in forō ā mercātōribus vidēbāmus. — We will see many things put in the market by the merchants.
9. Familiae propter mīlitēs redditōs tūtōs maximē gaudent. — The families rejoice greatly on account of the soldiers returned safely.
10. Hinc diēbus tribus fūr captus prō iūdiciō missus erit. — Three days hence the thief having been captured will be sent before court.

SECTION 12. Deponent Verbs

A. INDICATIVE MOOD

Deponent (from *dē*, "down, aside" + *pōnō*, "put") verbs are passive in form but active in meaning. They have put aside their active *forms*; they have put aside their passive *meanings*. In the indicative mood, deponent verbs conjugate like the passive voice for that tense and that verb conjugation.

The second principal part is the present passive infinitive. Deponent verbs of the first conjugation will have a second principal part ending in *-ārī*, the second conjugation in *-ērī*, the third conjugation in *-ī*, and the fourth conjugation in *-īrī*. Compare the principal parts of deponent verbs to those of regular verbs and you will see that each principal part represents the same grammatical form.

First-Person Singular, Present Indicative	Present Infinitive	First-Person Singular, Perfect Indicative
amō (I love)	amāre (to love)	amāvī (I loved)
cōnor (I try)	cōnārī (to try)	cōnātus sum (I tried)

Deponent verbs do not list a fourth principal part in any dictionary. Why is that?

Exercise 8. The following chart contains some common and important deponent verbs. Identify the conjugation of each verb.

cōnor, cōnārī, conātus sum	1st	to try
vereor, verērī, veritus sum	2nd	to fear
loquor, loquī, locūtus sum	3rd	to speak
gradior, gradī, grēssus sum	3rd	to step, to walk
orior, orīrī, ortus sum	4th	to rise
arbitror, arbitrārī, arbitrātus sum	1st	to think
hortor, hortārī, hortātus sum	1st	to urge, to encourage
polliceor, pollicērī, pollicitus sum	2nd	to promise
morior, morīrī, mortuus sum	4th	to die

Exercise 9. Conjugate the following deponent verbs in the tense requested. Include both the Latin and English for each conjugation.
- Present: cōnor
- Imperfect: vereor
- Future: loquor
- Perfect: gradior (use masculine)
- Pluperfect: morior (use neuter)
- Future Perfect: hortor (use feminine)

B. Participles

The participles for deponent verbs will look identical to those for regular verbs. The difference is that a perfect passive participle for a deponent verb will always be translated with an active meaning.

    hortāns = encouraging   hortātum = encouraged, having encouraged

    moriēns = dying   mortuus = dead, having died

The only form of the deponent that is translated *passively* is the future passive participle (the gerundive). The future passive periphrastic is also translated passively.

    hortandus = to be encouraged   hortandus est = he is to be encouraged

    conandum = to be tried   conandum est = it must be tried

C. Imperative Mood

It is important to note the present imperative forms of deponent verbs. The imperative singular employs the alternate second-person singular passive ending *-re*; the present imperative plural employs the regular second-person passive ending of *-minī*. The negative imperative will use the imperative form of the verb *nōlō, nōlle* and the true deponent infinitive. Here are the imperatives of the common deponent verb *cōnor* (to try).

Singular	Plural
cōnāre (try!)	cōnāminī (try!)
nōlī cōnārī (don't try!)	nōlīte cōnārī (don't try!)

Notice that the singular form looks like the second principal part of a non-deponent verb, but is really the ending *-re* for the second-person singular.

Exercise 10. Form the positive and negative imperatives, both singular and plural, for the following verbs. Take care to determine whether the verb is regular or deponent.

1. habēre
2. hortārī
3. cunctārī
4. redīre
5. morīrī
6. pōnere
7. gradī
8. nītī
9. miscēre
10. consequī

Exercise 11. Translate the following sentences.

1. Colōnum sequere ad praedium!
2. Consequiminī fūrēs et pecūniam captam!
3. Līberī, pārēte parentibus!
4. Nōlī pecūniam illī agricolae faenerārī!
   Hint: *pecūniam* – money
5. Parāte sē bellō!
6. Nōlī oppugnāre frātrem tuum!
7. Gradere ā virō malō; eum verēre!
8. Loquiminī nōbīscum dē lēgibus, sī tibi placet!
9. Encourage (pl.) the soldiers prepared for battle!
10. Do not talk (pl.) while the teacher is talking!
11. Do not hesitate (s.) to tell Father this!
12. Strive (s.) to be honest always!

SECTION 13. PUFFV Verbs and the Ablative Case

You may recall that there is a group of special intransitive verbs which govern the dative case, meaning they take a direct object in the dative case instead of the accusative. Can you remember a few?

In a similar manner, there is a group of five deponent verbs, which, along with their compounds, govern the ablative. This means they take an ablative object instead of the accusative. We can remember them easily as the "PUFFV" (puffy) verbs.

Potior – to gain possession of*

Ūtor – to use

Fruor – to enjoy

Fungor – to perform

Vescor – to feed upon

*__Nota Bene__: *Potior* can also govern the genitive.

Chapter 3

Exercise 12. Read and discuss the following famous quotations.

1. Dulce et decorum est pro patria mori. (Quintus Horatius Flaccus—Horace)
2. Acta est fabula. (words signifying the end of a play, also reputed to be Augustus Caesar's dying words)
3. Et dignitate tua frui tibi et fortunis licebit. (Cicero)
   Hint: *dignitate* – dignified position
4. Vitiis nemo sine nascitur. (Horace)
5. Aut vincere aut mori. (Roman motto)
6. Amicus certus in re incerta cernitur. (Ennius quoted by Cicero, *Laelius* 17.64)
7. Multi famam, conscientiam pauci verentur. (Pliny)

Exercise 13. Translate the following sentences.

1. Ea rēs est tam perīculōsa.
   Hint: *tam* – so
2. Maiōrēs nostrī hoc in lēgēs creātās ā senātū posīvērunt.
3. Maiōrēs nostrī illum fūrem prō iūdiciō prōmissum condemnāverant.
4. Exisitmāvērunt cīvem, quī faenerātus est, pēiōrem quam fūrem.
5. Hinc licet exisitimare.
6. Et quom virum bonum laudābant, ita laudābant bonum agricolam et bonum colōnum.
7. Ex agricolis milites fortibus fortes gignuntur.
8. Nolite cunctari consequi sapientiam doctam ā patre!
9. Eō in studiō occupati sunt.
10. Praedium quom parare cogitabis, habe in animo multa bona.

Chapter Reading: Reading 1

"DĒ BELLŌ HANNIBALICŌ"

Fragment from Ennius, *Liber VIII*, unadapted

Postquam *Discordia taetra*
Bellī ferrātōs postēs portāsque *refrēgit*.
Pellitur ē mediō sapientia, vī geritur rēs,
Spernitur orator bonus, *horridus* miles amātur.
Haut doctis dictis *certantes* sed *maledictis*
Miscent inter sese *inimicitiam* *agitantes*.
Non *ex iūre manu consertum* sed magis *ferrō*
Rem repetunt, regnumque petunt, *vādunt* solidā vī.

PHRASES: Reading 1

ex iūre – *idiomatically*: in a lawsuit, in a court of law

manū cōnsertum – to spar (lit., to join together with the hand) **cōnsertum = cōnsertum est**. The original text omits the helping verb. Such an omission is called ellipsis. Poets would often omit words that their readers would naturally expect or understand as being implied in order to fit the meter of the poem. *Cōnsertum est* is an impersonal passive. Where we would have "they sparred" in English, Latin has "it was sparred."

ferrō – *gladiō*

GLOSSARY: Reading 1

Use your "eye" Latin to discern the meaning of the underlined words in the reading.

Discordia, -ae, f.	Discord, goddess of strife
taeter, taetra, taetrum, adj.	foul, hideous, offensive
ferrātus, -a, -um, adj.	of iron (cf. *ferrum*)
postis, postis, m.	a doorpost
refrēgit	re + *frēgit* (from *frangō, frangere*)
spernō, spernere, sprēvī, sprētum	to spurn, to despise, to scorn
haut (also spelled *haud*), adv., emphatic negative	Not at all! By no means!
certō, -āre, -āvī, -ātum	to contend, to struggle (cf. *certamen*)
maledīcō, maledīcere, maledīxī, maledictum	to abuse, to speak ill, to curse (*male* + *dīcere*)
sēsē	*sē* (refl. pro.)
inimīcitia, -ae, f.	enmity (antonym for *amīcitia*)
aitantēs	*dīcentēs*
cōnserō, cōnserere, cōnseruī, cōnsertum	to join together (in a hostile manner, as in a militant context)
repetō, repetere	re + *petere*
vādō, vādere	to rush, to hasten

RESPONDĒ LATĪNĒ! READING

1. Quis est dea in fābulā?
2. Quis spernitur? Quis amātur?
3. Quid aiunt?
4. Quid hostis petit?

Chapter Reading: Reading 2

"FABIĪ CUNCTĀTŌRIS *ĒLOGIUM*"

Fragment from Ennius, *Liber IX*, unadapted

Ūnus homō nōbīs *cunctandō* restituit rem.
Nōn enim *rumōrēs* pōnēbat ante salūtem.
Ergō postque *magisque* virī nunc glōria *clāret*.

GLOSSARY: Reading 2

Use your "eye" Latin to discern the meaning of the underlined words in the reading.

ēlogium, -ī, n.	tombstone inscription, eulogy
cunctandō	the gerund form of the deponent *cunctor*
magisque (*magis* + *que*, irr. CpAdj)	more (in this instance, it is "and more")
clāreō, clārēre	to shine bright

RESPONDĒ LATĪNĒ! READING 2

1. Cūr homō ūnus laudātur?
2. Quandō virī glōria clāret?

Culture Corner

THE WAR WITH HANNIBAL

The Second Punic War, also known as the War with Hannibal, was a source of great inspiration for many Roman writers. Indeed, this war was a pivotal event in the history of Rome. At the end of the First Punic War, Rome was poised to become a world power. The Romans had, for the first time, expanded their landholdings past the natural borders of Italy, gaining the islands of Sicily, Corsica, and Sardinia.

At this moment in history rose Rome's greatest nemesis, Hannibal Barca. Hannibal had been trained from childhood by his father, the great general Hamilcar, to hate Rome, to seek its destruction, and to avenge Carthage. Historians would later anoint Hannibal as the greatest military genius of antiquity.

Hannibal and his forces brought Rome to its knees and very nearly destroyed her. Few Roman generals had any success against Hannibal. His cunning and gift for strategy allowed him to outmaneuver many on their home turf. One general who did have some measure of success was Fabius Cunctator. Fabius had learned from watching his compatriots that a head-on battle against Hannibal was always disastrous. He also knew that Hannibal's army was limited in size and resources. Hannibal depended upon supplies coming a great distance from Carthage and upon the local Gallic and Italian tribes, who he was sure would betray Rome and join his army. Fabius therefore did not engage Hannibal in open battle but instead followed him all across Italy. He harassed Hannibal's army with small raids and frustrated the supply lines. At first the Romans were greatly frustrated by Fabian's tactics of hit, run, and delay. Later, however, as Hannibal's army weakened, they began to appreciate the wisdom of his strategy. Fabius was hailed as a great general and even a savior of Rome.

Ennius's records of the Second Punic War served as a resource for later authors, including Livy and Vergil. Vergil, in his magnum opus, the *Aeneid*, adapts the lines of Ennius you just read as he offers praise to the virtue of Fabius: "*unus qui nobis cunctando restituis rem*" (*Aeneid* VI, ln. 846). Livy wrote an extensive account of the Second Punic War in Books 21–30 of *Ab Urbe Condita*, an exhaustive account of the history of Rome since the founding of the city. It was this book which inspired many of the stories you read in *Latin Alive! Book 1*. The complete story of the War with Hannibal as recorded by Livy is still available today, now in both Latin and English. Check to see if a copy is in your local library.

Logical Latin

1. Some of you may have the opportunity to study logic. As part of your studies, you will find that many of the terms you must learn and use regularly are Latin. Translate the following logic terms into English, then research what each term means.

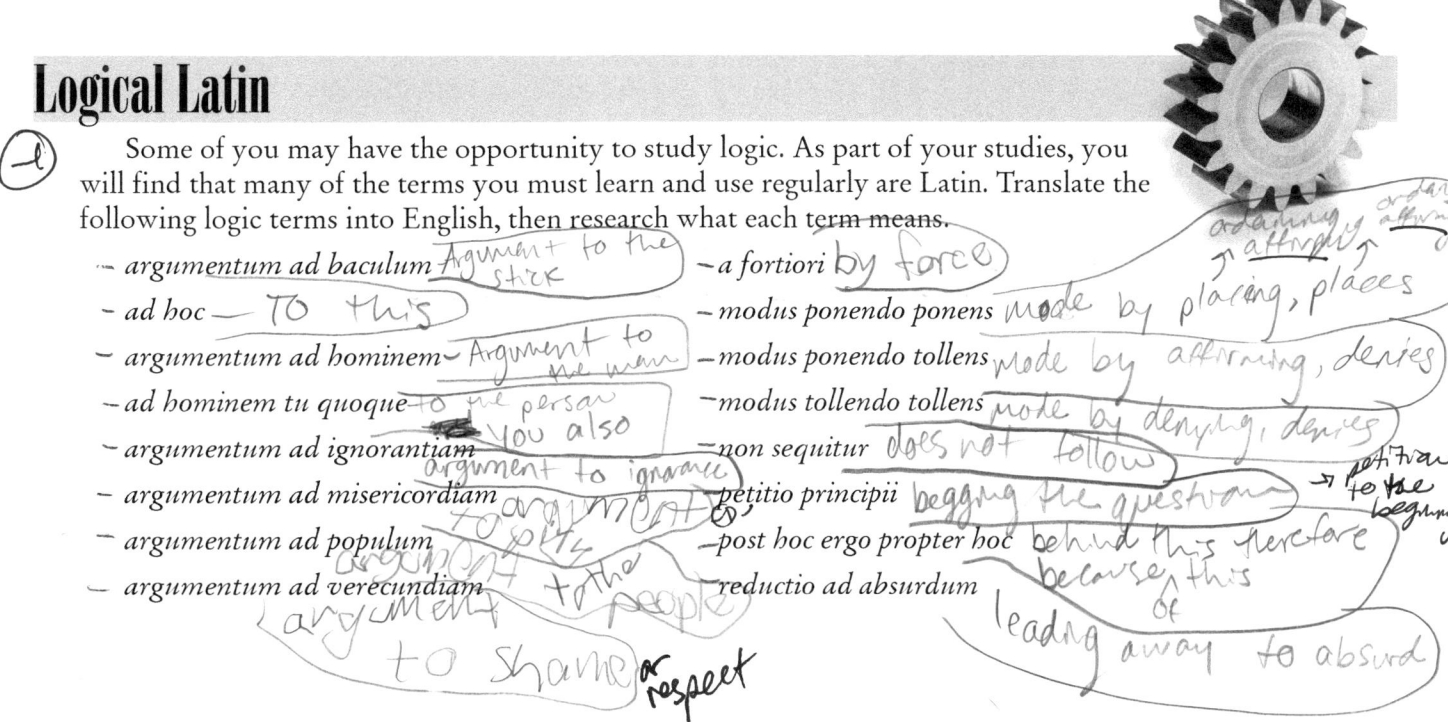

- argumentum ad baculum
- ad hoc
- argumentum ad hominem
- ad hominem tu quoque
- argumentum ad ignorantiam
- argumentum ad misericordiam
- argumentum ad populum
- argumentum ad verecundiam
- a fortiori
- modus ponendo ponens
- modus ponendo tollens
- modus tollendo tollens
- non sequitur
- petitio principii
- post hoc ergo propter hoc
- reductio ad absurdum

Colloquāmur!

Use the following questions and responses to review the nouns in the sentences translated throughout this chapter. Use some "eye" Latin to figure out what the responses mean.

Interrogātiō: Quid/Ubi est verbum? What/where is the word?

Interrogātiō:	Cūius est persōnae?	What person is it?
Respōnsum:	Prīmae persōnae est.	*It is first person*
	Secundae persōnae est.	*It is second person*
	Tertiae persōnae est.	*It is third person*

Interrogātiō:	Cūius est numerī?	What number is it?
Respōnsum:	Singulāriter est.	*It is singular*
	Plūrāliter est.	*It is plural*

Interrogātiō:	Cūius est temporis?	What tense/time is it?
Respōnsum:	Praesentis est.	*It is present*
	Imperfectī est.	*It is imperfect*
	Futūrī est.	*It is future*
	Perfectī est.	*It is perfect*
	Plūs quam perfectī est.	*It is pluperfect*
	Futūrī exactī est.	*It is future perfect*

Interrogātiō:	Cūius est vōcis?	What voice is it?
Respōnsum:	Est actīvī.	*It is active*
	Est passīvī.	*It is passive*

Interrogātiō:	Cūius est coniugātiōnis?	What conjugation is it?
Respōnsum:	Est prīmae coniugātiōnis.	*It is first conjugation*
	Est secundae coniugātiōnis.	*It is second conjugation*
	Est tertiae coniugātiōnis.	*It is third conjugation*
	Est quartae coniugātiōnis.	*It is fourth conjugation*

Interrogātiō:	Quid significat?	What does it mean?
	Quid est subiectīvum?	*What is the subject?*

Scrībāmus! (Let's Write!)

In chapters 2 and 3, you read fragments from the poetry of Ennius. Exercise your Latin composition skills by writing a short Latin poem in the form of a haiku. The haiku, a form of Japanese poetry, is among the shortest of this literary genre. It is known for its compact yet powerful means of expression. The haiku should consist of three lines, seventeen syllables *in toto*. The first line should consist of only five syllables, the second line has seven syllables, and the third line another five syllables. This is a wonderful way to begin exploring Latin poetry, as the Romans wrote their poetry with regard to the number and rhythm of syllables as opposed to rhyme. (This book will provide a study of Latin poetry in unit 3.) The haiku typically contains themes related to nature or emotion, but you may write a bit of poetry to commemorate a person, as Ennius does in the chapter reading.

Example:
Arborēs altae
Ilex, fraxinus, quercus
Caesae nunc absunt

Imparat erant
Malo draco apparuit
Et pluit ignem

vox clamantis in deserto
Dartmouth College, New Hampshire
This motto is taken from John 1:23 of the Vulgate.

Chapter 4

- Section 14. Subjunctive Mood
- Section 15. Present Subjunctive
  - Active and Passive Voices
- Section 16. Subjunctive of Irregular Verbs
- Section 17. Translating the Subjunctive
  - Potential
  - Deliberative
  - Optative
  - Jussive
  - Hortatory

VOCABULARY

	LATIN	ENGLISH	DERIVATIVES
Nouns			
	duplum, -ī, n.	a double amount	(duplex)
	mercātūra, -ae, f.	trade, buying and selling (used disparagingly)	(mercantile)
	quadruplum, -ī, n.	a quadruple amount	(quadruplets)
Verbs			
	existimō, -āre, -āvī, -ātum	to estimate, count	
	fruor, fruī, frūctus/fruitus sum (+ abl.)	to have the benefit of, to enjoy	(fruit)
	īnstituō, īnstituere, īnstituī, īnstitūtum	to undertake, to begin, to decide to do; to put in place	(institute)
	sustineō, sustinēre, sustinuī, sustentum	to hold up, to support, to sustain	(sustenance)
Adjectives, Adverbs, Conjunctions, etc.			
	amplus, -a, -um, adj.	large, wide, spacious, ample, grand; distinguished	(amplify)
	invidiōsus, -a, -um, adj.	envious; hateful, spiteful, seething	(invidious)
	stabilis, -e, adj.	stable, firm, steady	(stable, stability)

(handwritten annotation: "The voice of one crying in the desert")

strēnuus, -a, -um, adj.	brisk, prompt, active, vigorous	(strenuous)
studiōsus, -a, -um, adj.	eager to (+ inf.); eager for (+ gen.)	(studious)
interdum, adv.	sometimes, occasionally, now and then	
item, adv. (cf. īdem)	likewise, in the same way	
suprā, adv.	above	(superior)
tam, adv.	so	
vērum, adv.	truthfully	(verily)
nisi, conj.	if not, unless; except	

SECTION 14. Subjunctive Mood

There are three moods, or modes, for Latin (and English) verbs: the indicative, the imperative, and the subjunctive. The indicative mood makes a statement or asks a question (i.e., it *indicates* something). The imperative makes a command (cf. *imperō, imperāre*). The subjunctive (*subiungō*, "to join under") has many subordinating uses (i.e., used in subordinate or dependent clauses), but in this chapter we will focus on its independent uses, among which are the optative and the potential subjunctive. The subjunctive mood is used to represent a wide variety of ideas which will be explained one at a time in subsequent chapters. In English these two are expressed often by the helping verbs "would" or "may/might." For example:

Potential: I would do that.
I might see you tomorrow.

Optative: Would that you loved me.
May you be blessed.

A knowledge of the subjunctive mood is vital to reading and comprehending classical Latin, both prose and poetry. Be warned that the subjunctive in Latin has many uses and may be translated in several different ways. The following charts show the subjunctive expressing *potential*, something that may or may not happen, be happening, or have happened. These are independent uses of the subjunctive (i.e., the subjunctive used alone in a sentence). We will discuss this use of the subjunctive in more detail later in section 17.

SECTION 15. Present Subjunctive

The present subjunctive looks very similar to the present indicative. The difference is in the characteristic vowel that appears just before the personal ending. To form the present subjunctive, we continue to use the present stem and the personal endings you have already learned. Latin adds a new set of vowels as a subjunctive marker to designate the new mood.

present stem + subjunctive marker + personal endings

The first and third conjugations switch their characteristic letters. Second and fourth conjugations will add an *-a-* to the stem vowel. One way to remember these vowel changes is with the phrase: W<u>e</u> <u>e</u>at c<u>a</u>v<u>ia</u>r.

The translation in the following chart is only one of several possibilities. You will learn to translate the subjunctive more exactly when you see it in sentences—the context will help guide your reading. For now, use this translation model to practice conjugating and translating the subjunctive.

PRESENT ACTIVE SUBJUNCTIVE

Singular

1st Conj.	2nd Conj.	3rd Conj.	3rd -io Conj.	4th Conj.
laudem (I may praise)	habeam (I may hold)	mittam (I may send)	capiam (I may seize)	audiam (I may hear)
laudēs (you may praise)	habeās (you may hold)	mittās (you may send)	capiās (you may seize)	audiās (you may hear)
laudet (he may praise)	habeat (she may hold)	mittat (it may send)	capiat (he may seize)	audiat (she may hear)

Plural

laudēmus (we may praise)	habeāmus (we may hold)	mittāmus (we may send)	capiāmus (we may seize)	audiāmus (we may hear)
laudētis (you may praise)	habeātis (you may hold)	mittātis (you may send)	capiātis (you may seize)	audiātis (you may hear)
laudent (they may praise)	habeant (they may hold)	mittant (they may send)	capiant (they may seize)	audiant (they may hear)

Nota Bene:
- Notice that the macra patterns for the endings are consistent throughout all conjugations. The vowels are short in the first-person singular and in the entire third person; elsewhere, the subjunctive markers have a macron.
- The third *-io* mimics the pattern for fourth conjugation.
- All translations use the potential subjunctive (see section 17A).

To form the passive voice of the present subjunctive, simply replace the active personal endings with those for the passive voice: *-r, -ris, -tur, -mur, -minī, -ntur*.

PRESENT PASSIVE SUBJUNCTIVE

Singular

1st Conj.	2nd Conj.	3rd Conj.	3rd -io Conj.	4th Conj.
lauder (I may be praised)	habear (I may be held)	mittar (I may be sent)	capiar (I may be seized)	audiar (I may be heard)
laudēris (you may be praised)	habeāris (you may be held)	mittāris (you may be sent)	capiāris (you may be seized)	audiāris (you may be heard)
laudētur (he may be praised)	habeātur (she may be held)	mittātur (it may be sent)	capiātur (he may be seized)	audiātur (she may be heard)

Plural

laudēmur (we may be praised)	habeāmur (we may be held)	mittāmur (we may be sent)	capiāmur (we may be seized)	audiāmur (we may be heard)
laudēminī (you may be praised)	habeāminī (you may be held)	mittāminī (you may be sent)	capiāminī (you may be seized)	audiāminī (you may be heard)
laudentur (they may be praised)	habeantur (they may be held)	mittantur (they may be sent)	capiantur (they may be seized)	audiantur (they may be heard)

Nota Bene:

- Notice that the macra pattern on the endings is consistent with passive indicative verbs. The first-person singular and third-person plural are both short. The rest of the verbs have a long vowel in the ending.
- Note in particular that the third-person singular is now long, though it is short in the active subjunctive.
- The third -*io* mimics the pattern for fourth conjugation.
- All forms use the potential subjunctive (see section 17A). Students may also use the helping verb "would" (e.g., I would praise).

Exercise 1. Conjugate and translate the verbs listed below in the present subjunctive in both the active and passive voices. You will need to be sure you know to which conjugation each verb belongs. Use the translation for the *potential subjunctive* that was modeled for you in the previous examples.

1. pōnō
2. moneō
3. existimō
4. serviō

Exercise 2. Change the verbs below from active to passive, keeping the same person and number. Look carefully at each verb to first determine the mood: indicative or subjunctive. (Hint: All verbs are in the present tense.)

1. mittis
2. audīs
3. laudētis
4. habet
5. portāmus
6. portētis
7. instituunt
8. sustineam
9. existimētis
10. fruitur

Section 16. Subjunctive of Irregular Verbs

Just as they are in the indicative, some verbs are irregular in the subjunctive. Memorize the present subjunctive of the irregular verbs in this section. If you were to translate these verbs, you would translate them with the English auxiliary verb "would."

Person	Verb	Singular	Plural
1	sum (to be)	sim (I may be)	sīmus
2		sīs	sītis
3		sit	sint
1	volō (to wish)	velim (I may wish)	velīmus
2		velīs	velītis
3		velit	velint
1	nōlō (not to want)	nōlim (I may not want)	nōlīmus
2		nōlīs	nōlītis
3		nōlit	nōlint
1	mālō (to prefer)	mālim (I may prefer)	mālīmus
2		mālīs	mālītis
3		mālit	mālint
1	ferō (to carry)	feram (I may bear)	ferāmus
2		ferās	ferātis
3		ferat	ferant
1	eō (to go)	eam (I may go)	eāmus
2		eās	eātis
3		eat	eant

Nota Bene:

- The subjunctive forms of *esse* and *volo* share a common pattern, with the vowel *-i-* appearing between the stem and ending.
- The subjunctive forms of *volō* and its compounds (*nōlō* and *mālō*) consist of the infinitive + *i* + a personal ending.
- The subjunctive forms of *ferre* and *īre* follow the subjunctive pattern for third conjugation verbs.
- The compounds of *sum* are formed like *sum* (e.g., *possim, possīs,* etc.). Likewise, the compounds of *eō* and *ferō* are formed like their respective roots.

Exercise 3. Change the following verbs from indicative to subjunctive, keeping the same person, number, and voice.

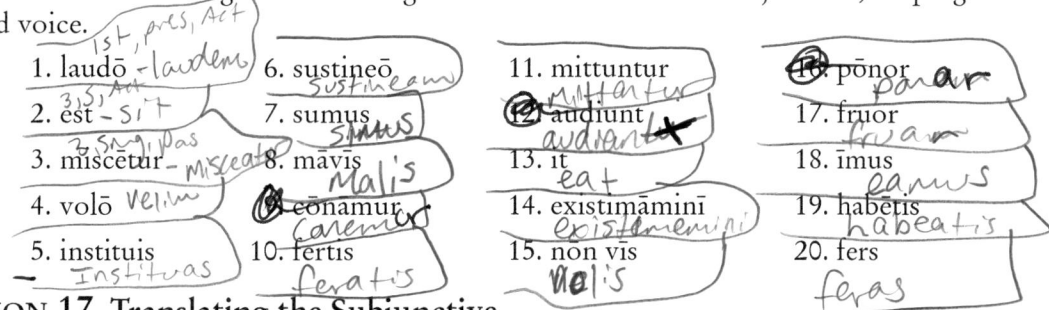

1. laudō
2. est
3. miscētur
4. volō
5. instituis
6. sustineō
7. sumus
8. māvīs
9. cōnāmur
10. fertis
11. mittuntur
12. audiunt
13. it
14. existimāminī
15. nōn vīs
16. pōnor
17. fruor
18. īmus
19. habētis
20. fers

SECTION 17. Translating the Subjunctive

The subjunctive has a variety of different independent uses. An independent use of the subjunctive means that the subjunctive verb is part of the main sentence; it is not included in a dependent clause. You have been introduced to one independent use—the potential subjunctive. Other common independent uses are the optative, deliberative, and the jussive.

A. POTENTIAL (FROM *POTĒNS*, "ABLE")

The potential subjunctive expresses something that is possible; it is *able* to happen. You can translate the potential subjunctive using the auxiliaries "would," "may," and "might." When expressing the negative—something that is not able to happen—use *nōn*.

    In bellō pugnētis.   You would/may fight in the battle.
    Trāns flūmen nōn eās.   You would/may not go across the river.

B. DELIBERATIVE (FROM *DĒLĪBERĀRE*, "TO CONSIDER")

The deliberative subjunctive asks a question. It considers a) what one ought to do, or b) what one might do. In this manner it is often used for rhetorical questions. As such, it is considered either a subcategory of the potential subjunctive or the hortatory subjunctive. The deliberative subjunctive is frequently in the first-person singular.

    Quid faciam?   What shall I do?

C. OPTATIVE (FROM *OPTĀRE*, "TO WISH")

The optative expresses a wish or a desire that something would/would not happen. A positive wish is expressed by *utinam*, a negative wish by *nē* or *nē utinam*. This adverb is a compound formed from *ut + nam* (oh, that!). It is best rendered as "I wish that," "would that," "oh, that," "if only," and so forth.

    Utinam nōbīscum sīs.   I wish that you would be with us.
                              Would that you would be with us.

    Utinam nē adveniās.   I wish that you would not come.
                              If only you would not come.

It can also refer to events in the past or the present using the pluperfect or imperfect subjunctives, respectively.

    Utinam nōbīscum fuissēs. I wish that you had been with us (then).
    Utinam nōbīscum essēs.   I wish that you were with us (now).

D. Jussive (from *iubēre*, "to order")

The jussive subjunctive is a polite command given in the third person. It is not as strong as the imperative mood (most often given in the second person), but it is a command nonetheless. You can translate these using the auxiliary "let." A good example of the jussive subjunctive is *Caveat discipulus* (Let the student beware).

Mīlitēs imperātōrī pāreant.   Let the soldiers obey the general.
Nē senātus malōs audiat.   Let the Senate not listen to bad men.

E. Hortatory (from the Latin *hortārī*, "to encourage")

When the jussive subjunctive appears in the first person it is often called hortatory. The hortatory subjunctive is an exhortation. It is very similar to the optative subjunctive in that it, too, communicates a desire. The hortatory, however, is usually in the first-person plural and issues a mild command or exhortation. When negative, the hortatory is preceded by *nē*.

Pugnāmus prō patriā!   Let us fight for our country!
Trāns flūmen nē eāmus.   Let us not go across the river.

Exercise 4. Translate these famous quotations. Identify the use of the subjunctive in each one.

1. Caveat emptor.
2. Cēdant arma togae. (Motto of Wyoming)
3. Crēdās nōn dē puerō scrīptum, sed ā puerō. (Pliny the Younger)
4. Quod utinam īnspectāre possīs timōrem dē illō meum. (Cicero)
5. Deus misereātur. (Psalm 66:2, Vulgate; Psalm 67:1, KJV)
6. Quid autem est, quod tū nōn audeās? (Cicero)
7. Gaudeāmus igitur iuvenēs dum sumus. (opening line of an old German student song)
8. Mē miseram! Quid iam crēdās? Aut cūr crēdās? (Terence)
9. Utinam id sit, quod spērō. (Terence)

Exercise 5. Enjoy translating these familiar English quotations into Latin. **Hint:** Use the present subjunctive for each one.

1. May the force be with you. (Obi Wan Kenobi)
2. He would make a lovely corpse. (Charles Dickens)
3. Let us go forth to lead the land we love. (John F. Kennedy)
   Hint: The infinitive cannot show purpose (see sections 4–5).
4. What God has joined together, let no man separate. (Jesus)
5. Where shall I go? What shall I do? (Scarlett O'Hara)
6. If I only had a brain. (The Scarecrow)
   Hint: brain – *cerebrum, -ī*, n.

Exercise 6. Parse and label the following sentences.

- For nouns and adjectives give the case, number, and gender.
- For verbs give the person, number, tense, voice, and mood.
- Use the following abbreviations to label the sentences:

S	subject	pro.	pronoun
V	verb	PrAdj	predicate adjective
LV	linking verb	adj.	attributive adjective
DO	direct object	adv.	adverb
IO	indirect object	OP	object of a preposition.
PrN	predicate nominative/noun		

1. Rēs perīculōsa sit.
2. Maiōrēs nostrī haec in lēgibus posuērunt.
3. Habuērunt fūrem condemnārī duplī.
4. Habēbant maiōrēs nostrī faenerātōrem peiōrem quam fūrem.
5. Faenerātōrem exīstimāvērunt condemnārī quadruplī.

Before You Read!

SUPERLATIVE REVIEW

A superlative adjective describes the highest degree possible. Latin often signals the superlative degree with the ending *-issimus, -issima, -issimum*. In other cases, when the stem of the adjective ends in an *-r*, the *-r* is doubled: *pulcherrimus*. A select group of adjectives will signify the superlative with a double *-l*: *similis, dissimilis, facilis, difficilis, gracilis, utilis*. Practice forming the superlative degree for the following adjectives (the first two have been done for you). Then translate both the positive and superlative forms. Watch for the *-issi-* in the chapter reading that follows.

Positive	Superlative
dulcis – sweet	dulcissimus – sweetest, most sweet, very sweet
benignus – kind	benignissimus – kindest, most kind, very kind
amplus – large	amplissimus – largest, most large, very large
stabilis – stable	stabilissimus – stablest, most stable, very stable
similis – similar	similissimus – most similar, very similar
honestus – honest	honestissimus – honestest, most honest, very honest
miser – miserable	miserissimus – miserablest, most miserable, very miserable
facilis – easy	facilissimus – easiest, most easy, very easy

Chapter Reading

FROM *M. CATONIS DĒ AGRĪ CULTŪRĀ*, THE *PRAEFĀTIŌ*

Est interdum **praestāre** mercātūrīs rem quaerere, **nisi tam** perīculōsum **sit**, et item foenerārī, **sī tam** honestum. Māiōrēs nostrī sīc habuērunt et ita in lēgibus posīvērunt: fūrem duplī condemnārī, foenerātōrem quadruplī. **Quantō pēiōrem** cīvem *existimārint* foenerātōrem quam fūrem, hinc licet existimāre. Et virum bonum *quom* laudābant, ita laudābant: bonum agricolam bonumque colōnum; amplissimē laudārī existimābātur quī ita laudābātur. Mercātōrem autem strēnuum studiōsumque **reī quaerendae** existimō, vērum, ut suprā dīxī, perīculōsum et calamitōsum. At ex agricolīs et virī fortissimī et mīlitēs strēnuissimī gignuntur, maximēque pius *quaestus* stabilissimusque consequitur minimēque invidiōsus, minimēque male **cōgitantēs** sunt quī in eō studiō occupātī sunt. Nunc, **ut ad rem redeam, quod promīsī, īnstitūtum** principium hoc erit.

Phrases

Est . . . praestāre – it is distinguished

nisi tam . . . sit – if it were . . . not so

sī tam – if it [were] . . . so

quantō pēiōrem – how much worse

reī quaerendae – of seeking property (This is a gerundive phrase.)

cōgitantēs – thinking (This is a present active participle.)

ut ad rem redeam – to return to the point, in order that I may return to the point

quod promīsī – as/which I promised. *Quod* is a relative pronoun referring to the *ut* clause, and is therefore neuter.

īnstitūtum – (having been) put into place (This is a perfect passive participle as a part of a perfect passive indicative with *erit*.)

GLOSSARY

Use your "eye" Latin to discern the meaning of the underlined words in the reading.

existimārint .... they considered (This is a syncopated form from *existima[ve]rint*; this is a perfect subjunctive in an indirect question, a construction to be learned later in this book.)

quom .... *cum* (This conjunction belongs logically before the word *virum*.)

quaestus, -ūs, m. .... way of making money, occupation

RESPONDĒ LATĪNĒ!

1. Quae rēs perīculōsa sit?
2. Quae rēs nōn sit honesta?
3. Quem condemnāvērunt duplī nostrī patrēs?
4. Quis est pēior, foenerātor aut fūr, secundum (according to) maiōrēs nostrōs?
5. Unde vēnērunt mīlitēs strēnuissimī?

ANSWER IN ENGLISH!

1. What occupation does Cato describe as hazardous?
2. How many times did the Romans even more ancient than Cato condemn a thief?
3. How can we judge how the ancient Romans felt about trade and thievery?
4. From which class do the bravest and strongest soldiers come?
5. What is the subject to which Cato promises to return?

About the Author

MARCUS PORCIUS CATO

Marcus Porcius Cato, known also as Cato the Elder, Cato the Orator, and Cato the Censor, was born in 234 BC. He lived an especially long life for that time period, dying in 149 at the age of eighty-five. His old Plebeian family lived in his birthplace, Tusculum, which was an ancient town of Latium within ten miles of Rome. He was born in Tusculum, an ancient town of Latium located within ten miles of Rome. His ancient Plebian family had lived in Tusculum for generations. Growing up on his father's farm in the Sabine country, Cato acquired qualities of simplicity, frugality, honesty, austerity, and patriotism. He never abandoned these qualities. For generations, Cato was the embodiment of the great Roman virtues, both to Romans and non-Romans alike. The love of the soil he acquired in his youth remained with him always. He became the owner of large estates and plantations peopled partially and worked to a large degree by slaves. (His writing includes passages on how to treat slaves.) The ancient Romans knew Cato also as a great general, philosopher, orator, historian, and legal mind.

Derivative Detective

WORDS FROM DEPONENT AND SEMI-DEPONENT VERBS

There are two important semi-deponent verbs in Latin. They are called *semi-deponent* because they are regular verbs in the present system and deponent verbs in the perfect system. They are *audeō, audēre, ausus sum* (to dare) and *gaudeō, gaudēre, gāvīsus sum* (to rejoice).

Considering the Latin meanings you have learned for deponent and semi-deponent verbs so far in this textbook, give the meaning of each word below. It is all right to use an English or Latin dictionary to complete this exercise.

- inconsequential *of no importance*
- sequential *in a sequence*
- function (noun and verb) *natural activity for something (work in a certain way)*
- utility *useful thing*
- fructify *make something productive*
- audacity *willingness for risks*
- fruition *fulfilled*
- sequel *a followup*
- gaudy *extravagantly showy*
- possessive *demanding total attention and love of source*
- audacious *bold*
- perfunctory *action/gesture carried out w/ minimum effort/reflection*

Culture Corner

EARLY LATIN LITERATURE: LIVIUS ANDRONICUS

Livius Andronicus was a Greek from Tarentum. We know him by that name because, having been captured in the war with Pyrrhus, he became the property of the Livius clan. His master freed him as a reward for teaching the children of the clan. As a *libertus* he continued to teach and even wrote a textbook. Since Greek children learned to read with the works of Homer, and since there was no Latin "Homer," Andronicus produced for Latin-speaking children a Latin translation or adaptation of the *Odyssey*. This poem is in a complicated ancient Latin verse form called Saturnians. The textbook created by Andronicus was still in use during the time of Augustus, though the language was by then archaic and considered uncouth. Andronicus also wrote hymns for special occasions and set up a guild for writers in the temple of Minerva.

Est Vērum! (It's True!)

Many scholars consider all Latin before 75 BC to be Old Latin.

Statue of Tiber outside the Capitoline museum in Rome

Non ministrari, sed ministrare.
Belhaven University, Mississippi

Not to be ministered but to minister

Chapter 5

- Section 18. Imperfect Subjunctive
- Section 19. Imperfect Subjunctive for Deponent Verbs
- Section 20. Conditions with the Indicative
  - Simple Present
  - Simple Past
  - Simple Future
- Section 21. Subjunctive Conditions: Future Less Vivid

VOCABULARY

LATIN	ENGLISH	DERIVATIVES
Nouns		
adulēscentia, -ae, f.	youth	(adolescent, adolescence)
aetās, aetātis, f.	age, lifetime (*Aetās* is the contracted form of *aevitās*, which in turn is from *aevum*, meaning "eternity," "time," or "lifetime.")	(coeval, medieval)
aqua, -ae, f.	water	(aquatic)
dōlium, -ī, n.	a large jar for storing wine	
fundus, -ī, m.	farm, estate (cf. praedium) (This word originally meant "soil" or "ground." The meaning "farm," then, is a type of synecdoche.)	(fundamental)
olea, -ae, f.	olive, olive tree	
tempestās, tempestātis, f.	storm	(tempest, temper)
torcular, torculāris, n. (i-stem)	a wine press, an oil press	(torque, torture)
Verbs		
accēdō, accēdere, accēssī, accēssum	to approach, to come near	(accede)
cōnserō, cōnserere, cōnsēvī, cōnsitum	to sow, to plant	
dēiciō, dēicere, dēiēcī, dēiectum	to throw down, to hurl down (cf. dē + iaciō)	(dejected)

expediō, expedīre, expedīvī/ expediī, expedītum	to set free; to be useful	(expedite)
soleō, solēre, solitus sum (semi-deponent)	to be accustomed	
ADJECTIVES, ADVERBS, CONJUNCTIONS, etc.		
oleārius, -a, -um, adj.	of oil, for oil	
vīnārius, -a, -um, adj.	of wine, for wine	
continuō, adv.	immediately	
diū, adv.	for a long time	
nē, adv.	not (used to introduce a negative purpose; often translates as "so that not" or "lest")	
quotannīs, adv.	every year	
nēve, conj.	and not, or not (an alternate form is neu)	
ut or utī, conj.	(with the indicative) as; when; (with the subjunctive) in order that, to	

SECTION 18. Imperfect Subjunctive

Forming the imperfect subjunctive is the easiest task there is in learning Latin. The imperfect subjunctive for most verbs is the second principal part plus the regular personal endings. This method of formation is for all verbs in Latin, even irregular ones. (There is an added step, which you will learn later in this chapter, for forming the imperfect subjunctive for deponent verbs.)

As you learned in chapter 4, there are many ways to translate the subjunctive. For the imperfect subjunctive in this chapter, translate the subjunctive verbs as indicating potential, using the English auxiliary "might be" and the ending *-ing*. (The helping verb "would" may also be used, depending upon the context of the sentence.)

A. ACTIVE VOICE

PERSON	SINGULAR	PLURAL
1	habērem (I might be holding)	habērēmus (we might be holding)
2	habērēs (you might be holding)	habērētis (you might be holding)
3	habēret (he/she/it might be holding)	habērent (they might be holding)

B. PASSIVE VOICE

PERSON	SINGULAR	PLURAL
1	habērer (I might be being held)	habērēmur (we might be being held)
2	habērēris (you might be being held)	habērēminī (you might be being held)
3	habērētur (he/she/it might be being held)	habērentur (they might be being held)

Nota Bene:
- The stem for the imperfect subjunctive retains the long vowel of the infinitive. This is true for all infinitives that have a long vowel. The third conjugation, however, will retain the short vowel for its infinitives.
  Exempli Gratia: amārem, habērem, mitterem, audīrem
- The final vowel is long in the first-person plural and throughout the second person in the active voice. In the passive voice the third-person singular also has a long final vowel.

Irregular verbs form the imperfect subjunctive in the same manner as regular verbs: infinitive + personal endings.

Exempli Gratia: essem, īrem, ferrem, vellem

Exercise 1. Following the examples of the verb *habēre*, conjugate the verbs *expedīre* and *esse* in the imperfect active subjunctive. Conjugate *parāre* and *accēdere* in the imperfect passive subjunctive. Include the English translations.

Exercise 2. Translate these subjunctive verbs from Latin into English.

1. praestārēmus
2. laudārēminī
3. īrētis
4. occupāret
5. cogitārem
6. possēmus
7. vellent
8. parārentur
9. poneret
10. ferrēmur
11. laudārēs
12. occupārentur

Section 19. Imperfect Subjunctive for Deponent Verbs

To form the imperfect subjunctive for deponent verbs, follow these steps.

1. Change the form of the second principal part from passive to active. Look at the following examples.

   faenerārī becomes *faenerāre*
   pollicērī becomes *pollicēre*
   sequī becomes *sequere*
   orīrī becomes *orīre*

2. Add the endings to the theoretical infinitive you have formed.

Imperfect Subjunctive for a Deponent Verb

Person	Singular	Plural
1	sequerer (I might follow)	sequerēmur (we might follow)
2	sequerēris (you might follow)	sequerēminī (you might follow)
3	sequerētur (he/she/it might follow)	sequerentur (they might follow)

Nota Bene: Semi-deponent verbs form their imperfect subjunctives for the present stem as though they were regular verbs instead of deponent.

Exercise 3. Following the example of *sequī*, conjugate the verbs *faenerārī* and *nītī* in the imperfect subjunctive. Include the English translations.

Exercise 4. In the person and number indicated, form the imperfect subjunctive for each of the following verbs. Translate each form with the potential translation.

1. faeneror – 1st/plural
2. nītor – 3rd/plural
3. cōnor – 2nd/singular
4. morior – 2nd/plural
5. arbitror – 3rd/singular
6. vereor – 3rd/plural
7. consequor – 1st/singular
8. gradior – 1st/plural

SECTION 20. Conditions With the Indicative

You may recall from chapter 15 of *LA2* that one use of the adverbial clause is to show a condition. A conditional statement is an adverbial clause that sets forth a condition, a requirement or prerequisite, for an action. Consider how English expresses a condition.

> If you are well, then I am well.

English expresses a condition with an "if . . . then" statement. Sometimes the word "then" is expressed, sometimes it is merely implied.

> If you are well, I am well.

The simple condition in Latin uses the same structure.

> Sī bene tibi est, bene mihi est.

In both English and Latin the conditional statement consists of two parts: the protasis and the apodosis. The protasis (the adverbial clause) contains the actual condition—it is the *if* statement. The apodosis contains the conclusion—it is the *then* statement. In the following examples, circle the apodosis and underline the protasis.

> If you work now, then you can play later.
>
> You were allowed to eat ice cream, if you ate all of your dinner.
>
> If you stand on that table, it will break.

Simple conditions always use the indicative mood. This is because a simple condition implies nothing about what may or may not happen; it simply indicates the condition. Unreal conditions (see section 21) indicate conditions that are either unlikely to happen or are contrary to fact. Latin uses the adverb *sī* to introduce a positive condition. The adverbs *nisi* (unless) or *sī nōn* (if not) introduce a negative condition.

A. SIMPLE PRESENT: protasis and apodosis – present indicative

Sī studēs, tū bene agis.	If you study, you are doing well.
Nisi studēs, tū bene nōn agis.	If you do not study, you are not doing well.

B. SIMPLE PAST: protasis and apodosis – imperfect or perfect indicative

Sī studuistī, tū bene ēgistī.	If you studied, you did well.
Sī nōn studistī, tū bene nōn ēgistī.	If you did not study, you did not do well.

C. *SIMPLE FUTURE (FUTURE MORE VIVID): protasis and apodosis – future indicative

Sī studēbis, tū bene agēs.	If you will study, you will do well.
	If you study, you will do well.

Nota Bene:

- The simple future is often called the *future more vivid*. This is because it is presented as a vivid possibility. We will contrast this use with the *future less vivid* in the next section, which presents a less likely and thus less vivid possibility.

- English sometimes uses a present tense verb to imply a future tense action—this is virtually the rule in subordinate clauses.

- Authors occasionally replace the apodosis with an imperative verb.

Exercise 5. Underline the protasis and circle the apodosis in each of the following conditional statements. Then translate.

1. Sī arborēs nunc cōnserēmus, tum frūctūs quotannīs habēbimus. — *If we plant trees now, then we will have fruit every year*
2. Semper laetus eram, sī tū mēcum aderās. — *I was always happy, if you were near with me*
3. Sī id aedficābis, venient. — *If you build it, they will come*
4. Tibi dōlium ferre possum, sī ūlla dōlia vīnāria nōn habēs. — *I am able to bring a jar for you, if you do not have any wine jars*
5. Mitte cōpiās continuō, sī bellum ab hoste dēclarātur. — *Send forces immediately, if war is declared by the enemy*
6. Vērum, sī fūr captus est tum ad iūdicium missus est. — *Truly, if the thief is captured, then he has been sent to court*
7. Sī līberī sunt strēnuī, tum dīc eōs currere in agrīs. — *If the children are active, then say that they are to run in the fields*
8. Sī hīc cunctāris, tum domum ante noctem nōn adveniēs. — *If you are delayed here, then you will not arrive home before night*
9. Mēnsa dōlium nōn sustinēbit, nisi stabilis erit. — *The table will not support the jar, unless it will be made stable*
10. Sī satis oleārum habēs, fer eās ad torcular. — *If you have enough olives, bring them to the press*

SECTION 21. Subjunctive Conditions: Future Less Vivid

Simple conditions contain verbs in the indicative mood: some present tense, some past tense, and some future tense (with the occasional imperative thrown in). This is because each statement in a simple condition implies nothing about whether the condition may or may not be met; it simply states the condition.

In contrast to simple conditions using the indicative, the subjunctive is used in conditions that are either contrary to fact or unlikely to occur (unreal conditions). There are several types of subjunctive conditions. In this chapter we will learn the future less vivid.

In section 20, you learned that future more vivid presents a condition that is likely to happen. As a result, the indicative mood is used. In contrast, future less vivid means that the fulfillment of the condition is unlikely or less probable. To express this unlikelihood, Latin uses the subjunctive mood.

FUTURE LESS VIVID: protasis and apodosis – present subjunctive

Translate: If ____ should/were to ____, then ____ would ____.
If ____ happens to ____, then ____ would ____.
If ____ were to ____, then ____, would ____.

Exempli Gratia:

Sī studeās, tū bene agās.   If you should/were to study, you would do well.

(Notice how, in this sentence, the condition is presented not only as hypothetical but also as unlikely to occur.)

Here's an example of future more vivid (future indicative):

Sī studēbis, tū bene agēs.   If you (will) study, you will do well.

Exercise 6. Identify whether each conditional is future more vivid or future less vivid. Then translate.

1. [FMV] Fessī erimus, sī celerrimē currēmus. — *we will be tired, if we will run very fast*
2. [FLV] Fessī nōn sīmus, nisi celeriter currāmus. — *we may not be tired, unless we would run quickly*
3. [FMV] Nisi id quaerēs, id nōn inveniēs. — *Unless you will seek, you will not find*
4. [FLV] Sī quaerās, inveniās. — *If you seek, you might find*
5. [FMV] Sī saxum erit gravissimum, tum tū id tollere nōn poteris. — *If the rock will be very heavy, then you will not be able to lift it*
6. [FLV] Sī saxum sit gravissimum, tum tū id nōn tollās. — *If the rock were very heavy, then you might not be able to lift it*
7. [FLV] Sī mē ad fundum cōnsequāminī, vōbīs oleās dēmōnstrem. — *If you were to follow me to the farm, I might show you the olives*
8. [FMV] Sī mē ad fundum cōnsequēminī, vōbīs oleās dēmōnstrābō. — *If you follow me to the farm, I will show you the olives*
9. Unless you (will) give the animals water immediately, Father will be angry. — *Nisi aquam animālibus continuō dabis, tum pater īrātus erit.*
10. If you should give water to the animals, then Father would be happy. — *Sī aquam animālibus dēs, tum pater laetus sit.*
11. If you (will) have a good press, then the work will be done well. — *Sī bonum torcular habēbis, tum opus agētur bene.*
12. If you should/were to have a good press, then the work would be done well. — *Sī bonum torcular habeās, tum opus agātur bene.*
13. A great storm would blow down the olives, if it should come. — *Tempestās magna dēiciat oleās, sī veniat.*
14. The storm will blow down the olives, if it comes (if it will come). — *Tempestās dēiciet oleās, sī veniet.*

Chapter Reading: Reading 1

M. PORCI CATONIS *DĒ AGRĪ CULTŪRĀ*, III

Prima Pars

Prīmā adulēscentiā patrem fāmiliae agrum cōnserere studēre oportet. Aedificāre diū cōgitāre oportet, cōnserere cōgitāre nōn oportet, sed facere oportet. Ubi aetās accēssit ad annōs XXXVI, tum aedificāre oportet, sī agrum cōnsitum habeāt. **Ita** *aedificēs*, **nē** villa fundum *quaerat* nec fundus villam. Patrem familiae villam rūsticam bene aedificātam habēre expedit, cellam oleāriam, vīnāriam, dōlia multa, **utī lubeat** cāritātem exspectāre: et **reī et virtūtī et glōriae** erit. Torculāria bona habēre oportet, ut opus bene efficī possit. Olea ubi lecta *siet*, oleum *fiat* continuō, nē *corrumpātur*. *Cōgitātō* quotannīs tempestātēs magnās venīre et oleam dēicere solēre.

PHRASES: Reading 1

Ita . . . nē – thus . . . not

utī lubeat – so that it may be pleasing

reī et virtūtī et glōriae – for the business/property, respect, and glory

GLOSSARY: Reading 1

Use your "eye" Latin to discern the meaning of the underlined words in the reading.

aedificēs	The subjunctive, here, is used as a kind of mild imperative: "you should build" instead of "build."
quaerat	seek, lack (i.e., the buildings and farmland should correspond)
cāritās, cāritātis, f.	honor, esteem; high price
siet	an archaic form of *sit* (present subjunctive)
fiat	This is the present passive subjunctive for *faciō*, which you will learn in a later chapter. Translate it as "let it become."
corrumpō, corrumpere, corrūpī, corrumptum	to spoil
cōgitātō	future active imperative of *cōgitō* (The future imperative is used instead of the present imperative, especially in verbs of knowing, remembering, or considering. Translate it as "consider" or "remember.")

RESPONDĒ LATĪNĒ! READING 1

1. Cuī necesse est cōnserere studēre?
2. Quā aetāte pater familiae aedificāre oportet?
3. Sī agricola torculāria bona habeat, quae rēs bene efficī possit?
4. Quandō veniunt tempestātēs?
5. Quis glōriam et bonum pretium et virtūtem habeat?

Chapter Reading: Reading 2

M. PORCĪ CATONIS *DĒ AGRĪ CULTŪRĀ*, III

Secunda Pars

Sī *cito* sustūleris et *vāsa* parāta erunt, *damnī* nihil erit ex tempestāte et oleum *viridius* et melius *fiet*. Sī in terrā et *tabulātō* olea nimium diū erit, *pūtēscet*, oleum foetidum *fiet*. Ex *quāvis* oleā oleum viridius et bonum *fierī* potest, sī *temperī* faciēs. In *iūgera olētī* CXX vāsa *bīna* esse oportet, sī *olētum* bonum beneque *frequēns cultum*que erit. *Trapētōs* bonōs *prīvōs inparēs* esse oportet; sī orbēs *contrītī* sient, ut *conmutāre* possīs. . . .

PHRASES: Reading 2

iūgera olētī CXX – olive grove of 120 *iūgera* (An *iūgerum* is a measure of land about 2,800 square feet or about two-thirds of an acre.)

GLOSSARY: Reading 2

Use your "eye" Latin to discern the meaning of the underlined words in the reading.

cito	quickly
vāsa, -ōrum, n. pl.	(agricultural) implements
damnum, -ī, n.	loss (*damnī* is a partitive genitive meaning "nothing of loss" = "no loss")
viridis, -e, adj.	green (here it is comparative)
fiet	the future passive of *faciō* ("will become")
tabulātō	[on] the floor
pūtēscet	will spoil, will become putrid
quāvis	whatever *x* (noun) you please (notice the ablative case when translating)
fierī	to become
temperī	early, on time
olētum, -ī, n.	olive yard
bīnī, -ae, -a	two apiece
frequēns	close together (cf. frequent and frequently)
cultus, -a, -um, adj.	cultivated, tilled
trapētus, -ī, m.	olive mill, oil mill
prīvōs	individual(ly), each its own
inparēs	of unequal size
contrītī sient	*contrītī sint* they should be worn down
ut	might be better understood before *si*
conmutō, -āre	to change entirely

RESPONDĒ LATĪNĒ! READING 2

1. Quandō patrem familiae aliter agricolam vāsa parāre oportet?
2. Sī damnī nihil ex tempestāte vēnerit, quāle oleum erit?
3. Ubi oleās nimium diū manēre nōn oportet?
4. Sī oleae nimium diū in terrā aut tabulātō mānserint, quāle erit oleum?
5. Ubi necesse est agricolās oleum facere?

Culture Corner

ROMAN VILLA

During the earliest days of Rome, when *Roma* designated only "the city," there were many small farms. The farmers lived on and were the sole operators of the farms. These farms were the first villas. As time went by, dwellers of the city of Rome began to branch out commercially, with many of them becoming owners of farms or villas. They did not, of course, do the actual farm work: rather, they employed a *vilicus* to oversee the work of the *familia rustica*. According to Harold Whetstone Johnson, in his book *The Private Lives of the Romans*, the *familia rustica* was the "slaves that were employed upon the vast estates that long before the end of the Republic had supplanted the small farms of the earlier day."[1] Eventually there developed two types of villa, the *villa rustica* and the *villa urbana*.

While the *villa rustica* was a true working farm, the *villa urbana* was an often elaborate country home near a city such as Rome. The master and his family would be able to travel to the *villa urbana* for a visit of a night or two. During the Empire there were many *villae* around the Bay of Naples. Remains of these estate houses can be seen around Pompeii and Herculaneum. The Isle of Capri was an especially popular place for wealthy families to build villas. Many of these elaborate villas had mosaic floors. Some even had central heating by means of the hypocaust, a hot-water heating system under the floor. These villas featured many of the characteristics of the *domus*, such as the atrium and the peristyle.

Some of these elaborate villas were eventually known as palaces, such as the "palace" at Fishbourne in the south of England. These palaces eventually had walls and were the architectural and defensives forerunners of the castles of medieval Europe. Originally, people began to build villas because they could be more spacious than a *domus*, the size of which was constricted by the walls of the cities. In the end, however, the villas themselves were surrounded by walls.

VILLA ROMANA DEL CASALE

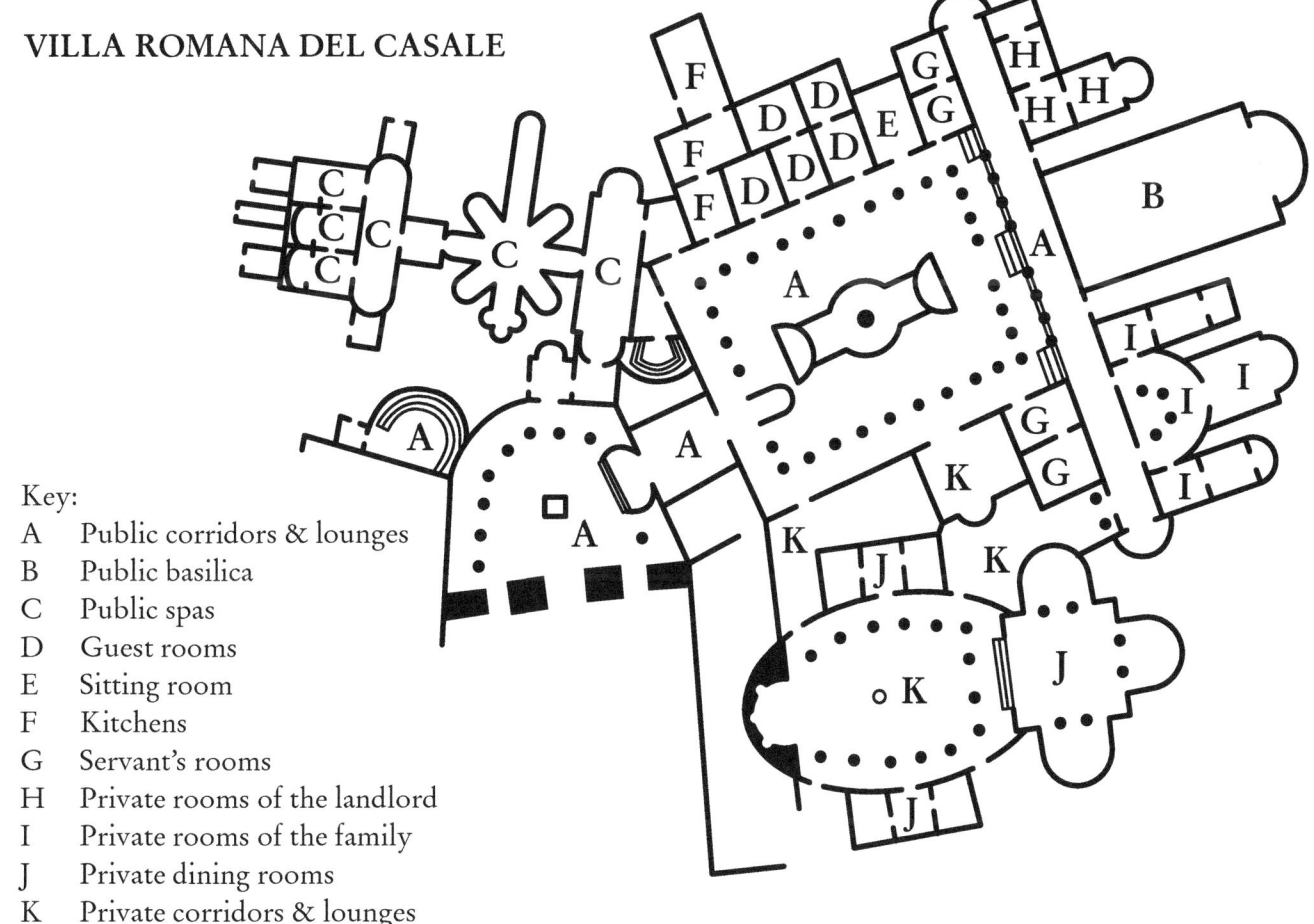

Key:
A Public corridors & lounges
B Public basilica
C Public spas
D Guest rooms
E Sitting room
F Kitchens
G Servant's rooms
H Private rooms of the landlord
I Private rooms of the family
J Private dining rooms
K Private corridors & lounges

---

1. Harold Whetstone Johnson, *The Private Lives of the Romans* (Honolulu, HI: University Press of the Pacific, 2002), 95.

Colloquāmur!

Use the following questions and responses to review the nouns in the sentences translated throughout this chapter. Use some "eye" Latin to figure out what the responses mean.

Interrogātiō: Quid/Ubi est verbum? — What/where is the verb?

Interrogātiō: Cūius est persōnae? — What person is it?
Respōnsum: Prīmae persōnae est. — *It is first person*
— Secundae persōnae est. — *It is second person*
— Tertiae persōnae est. — *It is third person*

Interrogātiō: Cūius est numerī? — What number is it?
Respōnsum: Singulāriter est. — *It is singular*
— Plūrāliter est. — *It is plural*

Interrogātiō: Cūius est temporis? — What tense/time is it?
Respōnsum: Praesentis est. — *It is present*
— Imperfectī est. — *It is Imperfect*
— Futūrī est. — *It is future*
— Perfectī est. — *It is Perfect*
— Plūs quam perfectī est. — *It is Pluperfect*
— Futūrī exactī est. — *It is future perfect*

(93%)

Interrogātiō: Cūius est vōcis? — What voice is it?
Respōnsum: Est actīvī. — *It is Active*
— Est passīvī. — *It is Passive*

137 / 147

Interrogātiō: Cūius est modī? — What mood is it?
Respōnsum: Indicātīvī est. — *It is Indicative*
— Imperātīvī est. — *It is Imperative*
— Subiectīvī est. — *It is Subjunctive*

Interrogātiō: Cūius est coniugātiōnis? — What conjugation is it?
Respōnsum: Est prīmae coniugātiōnis. — *It is first conjugation*
— Est secundae coniugātiōnis. — *It is second conjugation*
— Est tertiae coniugātiōnis. — *It is third conjugation*
— Est quartae coniugātiōnis. — *It is fourth conjugation*

Interrogātiō: Quid significat? — What does it mean?
— Quid/Ubi est subiectīvum? — *Where is the subject*

Est Vērum!

On some old portraits, you will see the person's name written along with the year the portrait was painted and, for example, *aet.su. xxiii*. The last three items tell how old the subject was at the time the portrait was painted: "in his/her own age twenty-three."

Translation: A True Likeness of John Babington in the Year of His Own Age, 31.

Palmam qui meruit ferat.
University of Southern California

Chapter 6

- Section 22. Perfect Subjunctive
  - Perfect Active Subjunctive
  - Perfect Passive Subjunctive
- Section 23. Pluperfect Subjunctive
  - Pluperfect Active Subjunctive
  - Pluperfect Passive Subjunctive
- Section 24. Sequence of Tenses
- Section 25. Indirect Command

VOCABULARY

	LATIN	ENGLISH	DERIVATIVES
Nouns			
	ānser, ānseris, m.	goose	
	arvum, -ī, n.	plowed land, field (cf. arāre, "to plow")	
	dīum, -ī, n.	open air, open sky	
	faenum, -ī, n.	hay	
	frīgus, frīgoris, n.	cold, coolness	(frigid)
	hiems, hiemis, f.	winter	(hiemal)
	pābulum, -ī, n.	food, fodder for animals	(pabulum)
	plaustrum, -ī n.	wagon, cart	
	stabulum, -ī, n.	standing room, quarters, a stable	(stable)
	sūs, suis, c.	pig, sow, hog	
	tēctum, -ī, n.	roof, house (by synecdoche)	
	vīlicus, -ī, m.	overseer of a villa	
Verbs			
	cōnficiō, cōnficere, cōnfēcī, cōnfectum	to put together, to finish	
	mācerō, -āre, -āvī, -ātum	to soften	(macerate)

perfundō, perfundere, perfūdī, perfūsum	to pour over	
saliō, salīre, saluī, saltum	to spring, to leap, to jump	
vetō, vetāre, vetuī, vetitum	to forbid, to prohibit	(veto)
ADJECTIVES, ADVERBS, CONJUNCTIONS, etc.		
aliquot, indec. adj.	some, several	
plānus, -a, -um, adj.	flat, level, even	(plane)
pluvius, -a, -um, adj.	rainy, of rain	(pluviometer)
praesertim, adv.	especially, chiefly	

SECTION 22. Perfect Subjunctive

In the last few chapters you learned the subjunctive mood for the present system. Did you notice that there was a tense missing? The present system normally includes the present, imperfect, and future tenses, and it would seem that we have skipped over the future. You should be happy to know that there are only four tenses in the subjunctive mood: present, imperfect, perfect, and pluperfect. The future and future perfect do not exist with this new mood. That leaves only two tenses left for you to learn in the subjunctive mood.

A. PERFECT ACTIVE SUBJUNCTIVE

perfect stem + tense indicator -eri + active personal endings

Perfect Subjunctive: Active Voice

PERSON	SINGULAR	PLURAL
1	habuerim	habuerīmus
2	habuerīs	habuerītis
3	habuerit	habuerint

Nota Bene:

- Latin forms the perfect subjunctive for irregular verbs in the same manner as for regular verbs: third principal part + *-eri* + personal endings

Exempli Gratia: fuerim, īverim, tulerim, voluerim

Caveat Discipulus: The perfect active subjunctive can look very similar to the future perfect active indicative. Look up the chart for the future perfect active indicative in appendix B and compare the two. How are they alike? How are they different?

Exercise 1. Conjugate the verbs *salīre* and *posse* in the perfect active subjunctive and in the future perfect active indicative.

B. PERFECT PASSIVE SUBJUNCTIVE

fourth principal part + present subjunctive of *esse*

Recall how you were instructed to form the perfect passive indicative (see section 10). This tense uses the fourth principal part and the present indicative of the verb *esse*. The perfect subjunctive is formed in a similar manner with a slight twist. The perfect passive subjunctive is the fourth principal part plus the *present subjunctive* of *esse*. All verbs, even irregular ones, in all conjugations form the perfect passive subjunctive the same way.

Perfect Subjunctive: Passive Voice

PERSON	SINGULAR	PLURAL
1	habitus sim	habitī sīmus
2	habitus sīs	habitī sītis
3	habitus sit	habitī sint

Nota Bene:

- Just as with the perfect passive indicative, the fourth principal part may use the masculine, the feminine, or the neuter endings. The gender will depend on the subject.
    - Vir habitus sit.
    - Fēmina habita sit.
    - Saxum habitum sit.
- Latin forms the perfect subjunctive for irregular verbs in the same manner as for regular verbs: fourth principal part + *sim*.

Exercise 2. Conjugate the verb *cōnficere* and *ferre* in the present passive subjunctive and the perfect passive subjunctive, using the feminine forms.

Exercise 3. Parse the following verbs, identifying the person, number, tense, voice, and mood. Also indicate if a verb is deponent. Do *not* translate.

Caveat Discipulus: Multiple possibilities may exist for some of the following verbs, so include *all* possibilities.

1. cōnficeret — 3, S, Impf, A, Sub
2. mācerent — 3, Pl, Pr, A, Sub
3. dēiectum es — 2, S, Perf, P, Ind
4. expedient — 3, Pl, F, A, Ind
5. solēbam — 1, S, Impf, A, Ind
6. existimārēris — 2, S, ~~F~~ I, P, Sub
7. institūtum sit — 3, S, Perf, P, Sub
8. perfūderim — 1, S, Perf, A, Sub
9. salīrēs — 2, S, Impf, A, Sub
10. frūctūs erātis — 2, Pl, Plu, P, Ind — Deponent
11. sustentī sīmus — 1, Pl, Perf, P, Sub
12. habuerō — 1, S, Fut Perf, A, ~~I~~
13. morīrētur — 3, S, Impf, (P), Sub — Deponent
14. miscēbis — 2, S, Fut, A, Ind
15. cavāverint — 3, Pl, Perf, A, Sub / 3, Pl, Fut Perf, A, Ind
16. hortātus sim — 1, S, Perf, A, Sub
17. cōgitēs — 2, S, Pr~~~~, A, Sub
18. occupāverimus — 1, S, Perf, A, Sub / 1, Pl, Fut Perf, A, Ind
19. praestēminī — 2, Pl, ~~Pr~~ (P), Sub — Deponent
20. possint — 3, Pl, Pr, A, Sub

SECTION 23. Pluperfect Subjunctive

A. Pluperfect Active Subjunctive

perfect stem + -*isse* + active endings

The pluperfect active subjunctive is the perfect stem plus -*isse* plus the usual endings. Another way to look at this formation is that the pluperfect subjunctive in the active voice is the perfect active infinitive plus the usual endings. Can you compare this method of formation to any other you have learned in Latin?

Pluperfect Subjunctive: Active Voice

Person	Singular	Plural
1	habuissem	habuissēmus
2	habuissēs	habuissētis
3	habuisset	habuissent

Nota Bene:

- Latin forms the perfect subjunctive for irregular verbs in the same manner as for regular verbs: third principal part + *-isse* + personal endings.

Exempli Gratia: fuissem, tulissem, īvissem, voluisssem

Exercise 4. Conjugate the verbs *mācerāre* and *velle* in the pluperfect active subjunctive and the imperfect active subjunctive.

B. Pluperfect Passive Subjunctive

fourth principal part + imperfect subjunctive of *esse*

The pluperfect passive subjunctive continues the traditional pattern of the perfect passive tenses. This tense is the fourth principal part plus the imperfect subjunctive of *esse*.

Person	Singular	Plural
1	habitus essem	habitī essēmus
2	habitus essēs	habitī essētis
3	habitus esset	habitī essent

Nota Bene:

- Just as with the perfect passive indicative, the fourth principal part may use the masculine, the feminine, or the neuter endings. The gender will depend on the subject:
  - Vir habitus esset.
  - Fēmina habita esset.
  - Saxum habitum esset.
- Latin forms the pluperfect subjunctive for irregular verbs in the same manner as for regular verbs: fourth principal part + *esse* + personal endings.
- Just as the pluperfect active subjunctive is the perfect active infinitive with the endings added, the pluperfect passive subjunctive is the perfect passive infinitive with the endings added.

Exercise 5. Conjugate the verb *perfundere* in the pluperfect passive subjunctive; use the neuter form.

Exercise 6. Change the mood of the following verbs from indicative to subjunctive, keeping the same person, number, tense, and voice. Do *not* translate.

Exempli Gratia: habeō → habeam

1. mācerābātur
2. vidēs
3. bibunt
4. saluerās
5. cēpī
6. habitus erat
7. erātis
8. hortābar
9. scīvistī
10. perfūsa erunt
11. possunt
12. versāris
13. exit
14. metuēbās
15. fers
16. cōnfēcerātis
17. solēbāmus
18. mixtī erāmus
19. moritī sunt
20. cōgitāvit

Section 24. Sequence of Tenses

You have already learned the independent uses for the subjunctive mood—uses such as potential, jussive, and optative. There are also a number of dependent uses for the subjunctive, many of which are introduced by the adverb *ut* (that). Roman writers used certain tenses of the subjunctive in these dependent clauses. Grammarians call this pattern of usage the sequence of tenses. The sequence of tenses often mirrors our own manner of speaking in English. Therefore, one of the key indicators of a good tense translation is that it sounds natural. You will need to understand this sequence in order to read and translate dependent clauses using the subjunctive. (Section 25 will introduce the first of these clauses, which is indirect command.)

There are two sequences of tense: primary and secondary.

- If the main verb is in the present (either indicative or subjunctive), future, or future perfect tense, the sequence is primary.
- If the main verb is in any tense indicating action in the past, the sequence is secondary.
- In primary sequence, we use the present subjunctive to show an action that is incomplete at the time of the main verb. This means that at the time of the main verb, the action in the subordinate clause is either currently happening or about to happen.
- In secondary sequence, we use the imperfect subjunctive to show incomplete action.
- In primary sequence, we use the perfect subjunctive to show action completed at the time of the main verb. This means that at the time of the main verb, the action in the subordinate clause has already occurred.
- In secondary sequence, we use the pluperfect subjunctive to show completed action.

Chart for Sequence of Tenses

Sequence	Main Verb	Subjunctive Verb
Primary	Non-past	Present for Incomplete Action Perfect for Completed Action
Secondary	Any time in the past	Imperfect for Incomplete Action Pluperfect for Completed Action

Section 25. Indirect Command

positive: *ut* + subjunctive   negative: *nē* + subjunctive

Recall that in chapter 4 you learned that Latin commands can be expressed in independent clauses with the subjunctive mood (see section 17). We call these hortatory subjunctives when they are in the first person and jussive subjunctives when in the third person. The imperative mood is used for a direct second-person command.

Pugnēmus prō patriā!	Let us fight for our country! (hortatory)
Pugnent prō patriā!	Let them fight for their country! (jussive)
Pugnāte prō patriā!	(You) Fight for your country! (imperative)

When reporting a command indirectly, Latin uses the subjunctive regardless of the person(s) receiving the command. The direct command becomes a dependent clause within the main sentence. The main verb is a verb of commanding, telling, encouraging, asking, or begging (among others); the command itself is introduced in the positive by *ut* and in the negative by *nē*. (Examples of such verbs include *imperō*, *dīcō*, *hortor*, *rogō*, and *petō*.)

1. Prō patriā pugnēmus!
   Let us fight for our country!
   Rēx imperat nōs *ut prō patriā pugnēmus*.
   The king orders us *to fight for our country*.
   (lit., "in order that we may fight for our country")

2. Pugnāte prō patriā!
   Fight for your country!
   Rēx imperāvit vōs *ut prō patriā pugnārētis*.
   The king ordered you *to fight for your country*.
   (lit., "in order that you might fight for your country")

3. Nōlī pugnāre cum frātre! Do not fight with your brother!	Māter monet tē *nē pugnēs cum frātre.* Mother warns you *not to fight with your brother.* (lit., "lest you fight with your brother")
4. Pugnet nōn cum frātre! Let him not fight with his brother!	Māter monuit eum *nē pugnāret cum frātre.* Mother warned him *not to fight with his brother.* (lit., "lest he fight with his brother")

Nota Bene:

- Note that *ut* introduces positive commands—commands "to do" something.
- Note that *nē* introduces negative commands—commands "not to do" something.
- Note that the rules for the sequences of tenses still apply.
- Note that the *incomplete* tenses (present and imperfect) are used since commands always refer to the future.

Caveat Discipulus: There are two verbs that *do not* use this construction to communicate a command: *iubeō* and *vetō*. These two verbs will use an infinitive. In addition, verbs of wishing (such as *volō* and *nōlō*) can take either an infinitive or a subjunctive.

Māter vetuit eum pugnāre cum frātre.	Mother forbade him to fight with his brother.
Volō tē advenīre hodiē. Volō ut adveniās hodiē.	I want you to arrive today.
Nōlō eum pugnāre. Nōlō ut is pugnet.	I do not want him to fight.

Indirect commands do not necessarily have to appear with a verb that blatantly expresses command. Sometimes a command can be a strong suggestion of obligation or necessity. Thus the passive periphrastic may also introduce such a clause. You will recall from *LA2* that the passive periphrastic is the future passive participle (i.e., gerundive) plus a form of *esse* (see *LA2*, section 63). When the passive periphrastic introduces an indirect command it will take on an impersonal form.

faciendum est   it must be done/made

Faciendum est ut fenestrae perspicī ad orientem possint.
> It must be done that the windows are able to be looked through to the east.
> (I order you to) make the windows face east.

Remember, when an agent is shown, the passive periphrastic will use the dative case instead of the ablative with *ā* or *ab*.

Faciendum *tibi* est ut fenestrae perspicī ad orientem possint.
> It must be made *by you* that the windows are able to be looked through to the east.
> You must make it that the windows face east.

Videndum est ut līberī vestēs calidiōrēs gerant.
> It must be seen to that the children wear warmer clothes.

Exercise 7. Underline the indirect command in each sentence. Translate the full sentence. Remember to carefully consider the sequence of tenses in each sentence, especially as you translate from English to Latin.

1. Cōnsul nōs hortātur ut patientiam habeāmus.
2. Vīlicus imperāvit servōs ut et faenum et aquam in stabulum ferrent.
3. In villā faciendum bovibus est ut stabula caldiōra hieme sint.
4. Vīlicus iussit frūmentum ferrī in stabulum antequam frīgus hiemis accederet.
5. Persuādēbitne tandem senātōribus ut illum virum malum damnent?
6. Providendum erat vīlicō ut opus omne ante hiemem cōnficerētur et familia in frīgore cūrārētur.
7. Agricola rogāverat puerōs ut frūmentum in agrīs cōnsererent.
8. Do the laws forbid (*vetō*) me to throw rocks at the farmer's pigs?
9. Vetantne lēgēs mē iactāre saxa ad suēs agricolae?
10. The geese will soon persuade (*persuādeō*) you not to throw rocks at them!
11. The consul ordered (*imperō*) the watchmen to go into the forum of the city.
12. It must be made that the stable has big roofs and the carts are able to be in it.
13. I beg (*precor*) my children to choose to follow wisdom.

Chapter Reading: Reading 1

MARCUS TERENTIUS VARRO, *DE AGRICULTURA*, XIII

In villā **facienda** stabula ita [sunt], ut *būbīlia* sint ibi, hieme quae possint esse caldiōra. *Frūctus*, **ut est** vīnum et oleum, locō plānō in *cellīs* [sit], item ubi *vāsa* vīnāria et oleāria esse possint faciendum [est]; *āridus*, **ut est** *faba* et faenum, in *tabulātīs*. Familia *ubi versētur* providendum [est], sī fessī opere aut frīgore aut calōre [sunt], ubi *commodissimē* possint sē *quiēte recipērāre*. Vīlicī proximum ianuam *cellam* esse oportet eumque scīre, quī introeat aut exeat noctū quidve ferat, praesertim sī ōstiārius est nēmō. In prīmīs **culīna videnda [est] ut sit admōta**, quod ibi hieme *antelūcānīs* temporibus aliquot rēs cōnficiuntur: cibus parātur ac capitur. Faciundum [est] etiam plaustrīs ac cēterō instrūmentō omnī in *cohorte*, ut satis magna sint tēcta, *quibus* caelum pluvium [est] inimīcum.

PHRASES: Reading 1

facienda – *facienda sunt* (ellipsis)

ut est – such as

culīna **videnda [est] ut sit** *admōta* – Latin often uses personal constructions where English would use the impersonal. Latin: "The kitchen must be seen in order that it is placed nearby." English: "It must be seen (to) that the kitchen be placed nearby."

GLOSSARY: Reading 1

Use your "eye" Latin to discern the meanings of the underlined words in the reading.

būbīle, būbīlis, n.	an ox stall
frūctus	*here,* produce that is wet
cella, -ae, f.	storeroom; small room
vās, vāsis, n. (plural forms *vāsa, vāsōrum*)	a vessel
āridus	*here,* produce that is dry
faba, -ae, f.	bean
tabulātum, -ī, n.	floor, a floored area (as opposed to dirt)

ubi..	(to be translated before *familia*)
versor, versārī...................................	to dwell
commodissimē..................................	most suitably, comfortably, or advantageously
quiēs, quiētis, f.	rest
reciperō, -āre, -āvī, -ātum (= *recuperō*)	to recuperate, to recover
ōstiārius, -ī, m.	doorkeeper, porter (cf. *os*, "mouth, opening, port")
culīna, -ae, f.	kitchen
admoveō, admovēre, admōvī, admōtum........	to place, to move near
antelūcātus, -a, -um, adj.....................	happening before daybreak (cf. *ante* + *lux*)
cohors, cohortis, f.	an enclosure, a yard (especially for cattle)
quibus	(the antecedent is *plaustrīs* and *īnstrūmentō*)

RESPONDĒ LATĪNĒ! READING 1

1. Quid necesse est aedificāre in villā? *būbīle et stabula*
2. Quandō būbīlia erunt calidiōra? *in hieme*
3. Quae rēs sunt āridae? *faba et faenum*
4. Cūr cellam vīlicī proximam iānuam esse oportet? *ut sciret qui intro eat aut exeat in nocte*
5. Quae rēs est inimīca plaustrīs et aliīs īnstrūmentīs? *magna pluvia*

Chapter Reading: Reading 2

MARCUS TERENTIUS VARRO, *DĒ AGRICULTŪRĀ*, XIII

Haec enim, sī intrā clausum in cōnsaeptō et sub dīō, fūrem modo nōn metuunt, adversus tempestātem nocentem nōn resistunt. Cohortēs in fundō magnō duae aptiōrēs: **ūna ut interius conpluvium habeat lacum, ubi aqua saliat, quī intrā stȳlobatās, cum velit, sit sēmipiscīna**. Bovēs enim ex arvō aestāte reductī hīc bibunt, hīc perfunduntur, nec minus ē pābulō cum redierunt ānserēs, suēs, porcī. In cohorte exteriōre lacum esse oportet, ubi mācerētur lupīnum, item alia quae dēmissa in aquam ad ūsum aptiōra fīunt.

PHRASES: Reading 2

ūna . . . sēmipiscīna – such that the one more to the inside may have a pool within the stylobates where water flows [and] which, when desirable, may become a fishpond (read the word order as: *ut ūna interius conpluvium habeat lacum intrā stȳlobatās, ubi aqua saliat, quī, cum velit, sit sēmipiscīna*.)

GLOSSARY: Reading 2

Use your "eye" Latin to discern the meanings of the underlined words in the reading.

haec..	the antecedent is *plaustrīs* and *īnstrūmentō* from the end of the previous reading
clausum, -ī, n.	enclosure (cf. *claudere*, "to close off")
consaeptum, -ī, n............................	a fenced in enclosure
adversus + acc.	against
cohors, cohortis, f.	an enclosure, a yard (especially for cattle)
ut	translate before *ūna*
interius	toward the center
conpluvium, -ī, n. (also *compluvium*)	the roofless space (often a square or rectangle) in the center of a Roman house through which the rain falls into the impluvium (or rain pool) below; here possibly used as an adjective describing *lacum*.

saliat	could mean "may flow" or "may gush" here
stȳlobata, -ae, m.	the pedestal of a row of columns
sēmipiscīna, -ae, f.	a small fish pond; a half fish pond made by dividing a tank
cum	translate first in the clause
porcī	probably boars (male pigs) as opposed to *suēs*, "sows" (female pigs)
lupīnum, -ī, n.	the lupine, a plant that looks like a bluebonnet with seeds edible when soaked (usually in salt water). The Romans spread cultivation of the plant throughout the empire.
fīunt	they become, they are made

RESPONDĒ LATĪNĒ! READING 2

1. Quem tēcta metuunt?
2. Quantae cohortēs aptiōrēs in fundō magnō?
3. Quandō bovēs redūcentur ex arvīs et bibent aquam ē lacū?
4. Quid agent ānserēs et suēs et porcī aestāte ubi rediērunt ad lacum?
5. Quid fit aptius ad ūsusm ubī mācerētur?

About the Author

MARCUS TERENTIUS VARRO

Varro was born around the area of what is now Rieti, Italy. He was a supporter of Pompey and held the office of *praetor* as well as the offices of tribune and aedile. He worked with Gaius Julius Caesar in the matter of land reforms around 59 BC. Caesar forgave him his support of Pompey at the time of the Battle of Pharsalus, and in 47 BC appointed Varro to oversee the public library at Rome. After Caesar's death, though, Marc Antony proscribed him. When Augustus came into power, Varro was again in favor. Varro was one of the most prolific of Roman writers, composing at least seventy-four works. (Some say he produced as many as 500 works.)

Latin in Science

In chapter 8 of *LA2*, you were introduced to the scientific or taxonomic nomenclature for a variety of animals in the wild. Such names are a help not only to scientists who research these wild creatures, but also to veterinarians and farmers who raise animals. These taxonomic names often have two parts: genus (from Latin *genus*, "family") and species (from Latin *species*, "form, shape, kind"). Often the genus name is the same as the Latin word for that general type of animal. The species name is often a Latin word that describes a characteristic unique to that animal, such as its appearance. Using your language detective skills and a Latin dictionary, draw lines to match the farm animals with their proper taxonomic name.

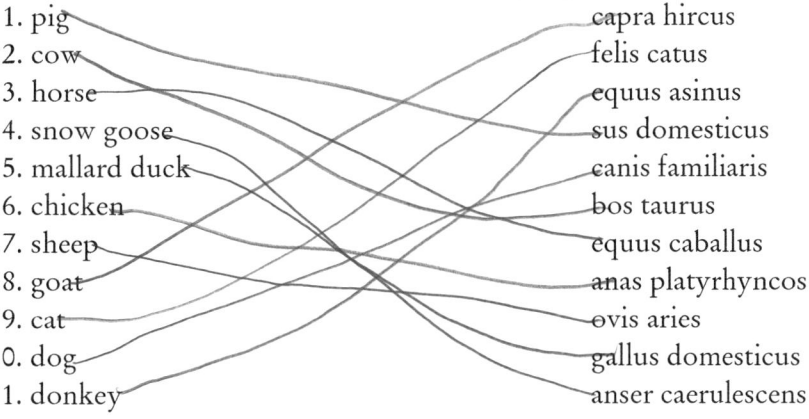

1. pig
2. cow
3. horse
4. snow goose
5. mallard duck
6. chicken
7. sheep
8. goat
9. cat
10. dog
11. donkey

capra hircus
felis catus
equus asinus
sus domesticus
canis familiaris
bos taurus
equus caballus
anas platyrhyncos
ovis aries
gallus domesticus
anser caerulescens

Game Time!

Old MacDonald could have learned a thing or two from Varro about farming! Use what you have learned about the Latin names of farm animals to compose your own rendition of the popular children's song "Old MacDonald Had a Farm." When it comes time to make the animal sounds, you will need to draw upon what you have learned about Latin phonics. Use what you know about Latin pronunciation to write out the sounds each animal makes. You can refer to the pronunciation guide (appendix A) in the back of your text to help you.

Senex Varrō fundum habet, ī-ae-ī-ae-ō.
Et in fundō habet __felis__, ī-ae-ī-ae-ō.
Cum __me-au__, __me-au__ hīc
Et __me-au__, __me-au__ ibi
hīc __me-au__, ibi __meau__, ubīque __me-au__, __me-au__.
Senex Varrō fundum habet, ī-ae-ī-ae-ō.

Old Varro has a farm, ee-i-ee-i-o.
And on his farm he has a __cat__, ee-i-ee-i-o.
with a __meow__, __meow__ here
and a __meow__, __meow__ there
here a __meow__, there a __meow__, everywhere a __meow__, __meow__.
Old Varro has a farm, ee-i-ee-i-o.

113/128   88%

Roman mosaic of a farmer

Unit 1 Reading

READING AND REVIEW FOR CHAPTERS 1–6

An Overview of Early Latin Literature

Alden Smith, Baylor University

While ancient cultures were, generally speaking, far from static, the kind of dramatic paradigm shifts that occurred among the Romans from the beginning of the republic to the end of the empire were relatively rare in antiquity. (The implications of the change from the Roman republic to empire will remind some fans of the situation and plot of the *Star Wars* movies.) Yet, well before that unofficial titular transformation, big changes were afoot in Italy. In the *urbs* proper there was, in 509 BC, the expulsion of the kings, which marked the beginning of a far more democratic form of government than had existed during the monarchy (753–509 BC). This new government was that of the *res publica*, or "public thing." In the fourth through second centuries BC, there was the conflict (and occasionally concord) of the "orders," or "ranks," of citizenry, today sometimes harshly called "class warfare." Worse than mere disagreements and grumpiness, there were even the Social Wars—physical battles, in this case—near the beginning of the first century BC. Most of the problems in the republican period seemed to stem from the fact that Rome was being thrust, for better or for worse, into the position of world leadership. To adjust to that role, Rome had to redefine herself.

The aforementioned shift from republic to empire began in earnest in 133 BC, when King Attalus of Pergamum bequeathed his inherited share of Alexander the Great's empire to Rome. The Senate was in a bit of a quandary as to what to do with this new territory, which was home to one of the finest libraries in antiquity. How should the gift of this territory be handled? Tiberius Gracchus had a radical idea—it was not accepted and in part lead to his assassination—having to do with the distribution of Pergamum's land. The way the Senate chose to address the problem soon after Gracchus's death is recorded in a decree.[1] A good bit of debate in the Senate followed. After Eumenes III, who claimed to be Attalus's true successor, fell to the Roman general Marcus Perperna, the Senate formally accepted the bequest, making Pergamum the Roman province of Asia (129 BC). Meanwhile, Rome became an economic hub, taking in much but offering few tangibles in return. The port at Puteoli, which until the first century AD was the primary dock of Rome, eventually was replaced by a more modern facility at Ostia, built by the emperor Claudius closely following plans that Julius Caesar had drawn up. Rome thus got a new and closer "mouth" for its import business, one reflected in the numerous floor mosaics that are still extant in Ostia's mercantile hall (*Piazza delle Corporazioni*).

---

1. Wilhelm Dittenberger, *Orientis Graeci Inscriptiones Selectae* (Leipzig, Germany: S. Hirzel, 1905), 2.435.

In Roman literature, meanwhile, there were similar signs of growth not unrelated to Rome's growing global sway. Such development did not happen all at once, and was not a "new" thing, since before Rome ruled the world, Alexander the Great had shown how broad even Macedonian dominion, both militarily and culturally, could be. Although Alexander the Great's empire slowly dissipated politically, it did not disintegrate in terms of scholarly influence. Much of the reason for that had to do with a single building (and the institutions that grew up around that building), namely, the famous library at Alexandria, which was even finer than the library at Pergamum. This edifice made the city of Alexandria, located on the northern coast of Egypt, the principal seat of higher learning. Scholar-poets such as Callimachus and Apollonius of Rhodes spent many years in that library carefully researching the poems they would write. They passed on that legacy of careful literary craftsmanship to the Romans, who, though there was no public library in Rome until the time of Augustus, eagerly adopted their model.

Throughout this time of rapid political expansion, rampant economic excitement, and ravenous importing and exporting—especially of government, which was the city's chief export—Rome's own literary brand was being developed. It was, at first, highly indebted to literature coming from the east, particularly Greek literature, but also was derived from Rome's and Italy's own unique cultural traditions and history. The earliest known Roman poet was Livius Andronicus (ca. 284–204 BC), who hailed from Tarentum and whose *cognomen* likely indicates Greek ancestry. Livius exemplifies the indebtedness to both traditions, for he renders the Homeric epics into Latin in the Saturnian meter, a poetic rhythmical pattern unique to the Italic peninsula.[2] Though most of his work is lost, some fragments of his *Odyssey* do remain and, fortunately, the opening line is preserved: "*Virum mihi, Camena, insece versutum*" (Tell me, Camena [Italian Muse], about a clever man). Livius was himself just such a clever man, for he blazed the way in Roman literature, also composing the first Latin comedies and tragedies, staged in 240 BC to celebrate the Roman victory over the Carthaginians in the First Punic War.[3]

The next great Roman poet was Gnaeus Naevius, born in ca. 270 BC in Campania.[4] He fought in the First Punic War and only near the middle of his life turned his hand to writing plays, which he did from about 235 BC on, producing mostly comedies but writing several tragedies as well. His comedies were a mixture of those with Roman themes (known as *fabulae togatae*) and those based on Greek originals (*palliatae*). In the prologue to his *Andria*, Terence tells us of Naevius's penchant for *contaminatio*, the practice of blending Greek and Roman sources. He also wrote an epic entitled *Punica*, which was the story of the first war against the Carthaginians. Like the plays that were "*togatae*," this poem made Romanness a major poetic theme, one that would be borne out again in Virgil's *Aeneid* and, well before that, in the *Annales* of Ennius.[5]

The greatest of the early Roman poets was this last poet—Quintus Ennius. Various ancient sources tell us that Ennius was born in 239 BC at Rudiae (modern Rugge) in southeastern Italy (viz. the heel of the boot). Aulus Gellius reports that he claimed to have had "three hearts" (*tria corda habere sese dicebat*)[6] because he spoke Oscan, as well as Greek and Latin. When serving in Sardinia as a soldier, he made the acquaintance of the quaestor Marcus Porcius Cato, whose tutor in Greek literature he became. He followed Cato back to Rome[7] and there lived out his life as the city's unofficial poet laureate.[8] His most famous work remains his *Annales*, a poetic history of Rome offering a year-by-year, rather than thematically arranged, presentation of Roman history in poetic form. He knew and interacted with other poets of that time, including Marcus Pacuvius, his nephew, and Caecilius Statius. Among the most famous quotations attributed to Ennius is a funerary epigram on poetic immortality: *Nemo me lacrimis decoret nec funera fletu / faxit. Cur? uolito uiuus per ora uirum*, "Let no one decorate me with tears nor perform funeral rites with weeping. Why? I will fly, alive, on the lips of men."[9]

Like Ennius, his uncle, there was yet another southerner, Marcus Pacuvius, who would become an important figure in the Roman literary scene. Born in the last quarter of the third century in Brindisium,

---

2. E.H. Warmington, *Remains of Old Latin*, vol. 2 (Cambridge, MA: Harvard University Press, 1936; rpt. 1967), vii-xiv.
3. Warmington, vol. 2, x.
4. Aulus Gellius, *Noctes Atticae*, 1.24; cf. Warmington, vol. 2, xiv.
5. Warmington, vol. 2, xiv-xvii.
6. Aulus Gellius, *Atticae Noctes*, 17.17.1.
7. Cornelius Nepos, *Cato*, 1.4.
8. cf. Warmington, vol. 2, xvii-xviii.
9. Warmington, vol. 1, "Epigrams 9-10," 402.

Pacuvius followed his uncle to Rome, where he not only composed tragedies but also made a reputation for himself as a great artist. Though his paintings do not survive—among which the most famous seems to have been that of Hercules in the Forum Boarium—various sources tout his artistry (e.g., Pliny, *Historia Naturalis*, 35.19) Like the other poets mentioned here, Pacuvius's poetry survives only in fragmentary form.[10]

Many other poets who shaped the early stages of Latin literature should be mentioned at least briefly. Among these are Accius, the splendid Roman tragedian of the second century BC, who lived to a very great age and who was an acquaintance of Cicero.[11] A close contemporary of Accius was the great early Roman satirist Gaius Lucilius, whose influence on Horace, Persius, and Juvenal cannot be underestimated. He was a member of the literary circle around P. Cornelius Scipio Aemelianus (known as the Scipionic Circle). We have some 1,400 lines of Lucilius that have survived in fragmentary form. These show that he had little compunction about naming and reproaching his "enemies."[12]

As we near the beginning of the first century BC, we come across two further names important in the development of early Latin literature; these are Aelius Stilo and Lucius Afranius. Afranius was born near the end of the second century BC. His comedies, mostly *togatae*, were vignettes of daily life in ancient Rome and were recognized by many as thoroughly well crafted (such as Cicero, who mentions Afranius's linguistic dexterity on more than one occasion). Though Quintilian's judgment of Afranius is less favorable, the lasting impact of Afranius can be seen in the number of other authors' references to him.[13]

Aelius Stilo is perhaps best known for being Varro's teacher. Stilo wrote prose works (now lost) that treated the subject of philology, the study of words, their meanings, and their origins.[14] He was known both for his wide learning and range and for his fluidity, each of which facets of his style influenced Varro.

Finally, we should consider Gaius Lucilius, a writer who developed the one genre that Quintilian would call "all ours," viz. satire. Though admittedly the roots of satire lie in Greek literature, in terms of literary genre Quintilian's vaunt is essentially correct, as Lucilius blazed the way with stinging barbs that would not only influence subsequent writers in this genre, most notably Horace and Juvenal, but would even have an impact on poets such as Catullus, whose invective hendecasyllables find inspiration in Lucilius's work.

While many others could be mentioned, each of these writers noted here laid the groundwork for a robust literary future for the Romans, a future that is for us a distant past, yet one made forever vivid through the great works of literature of their literary heirs that we still enjoy reading today.

Before You Read

In this reading, Varro puts forth etymologies for several Latin words. While his conclusions are interesting and fun to read, we must not consider the etymologies accurate, as Roland G. Kent, who edited *Varro on the Latin Language* (Loeb Classical Library, 2006), points out in his introduction to this work. Linguists and classicists have learned much about the origin of words since the time Varro wrote.

VARRO: *DĒ LINGUĀ LATĪNĀ*, V.IV

CHARACTERS

Quintus Ennius: an early Roman poet

Gaius Lucilius: the earliest Roman satirist

Marcus Pacuvius: a Roman dramatist, nephew to Ennius

Aelius Stilo: Varro's teacher

Afranius: Roman comic poet

---

10. Warmington, vol. 2, xvii-xix.
11. Warmington, vol. 2, xxi.
12. cf. Michael Coffey, *Oxford Classical Dictionary*, 3rd ed. (New York: Oxford University Press, 1996), 887.
13. cf. Jarrett T. Welsh, "Quintilian's Judgment of Afranius," *The Classical Quarterly*, 60 (Cambridge, MA: Cambridge University Press, 2010), 121-22.
14. G.B. Conte, *Latin Literature: A History* (Baltimore, MD: The Johns Hopkins University Press, 1994), 124, 572-73.

The square brackets are put around words that are not actually in the original text but that may be inferred and supplied; in other words, the square brackets in this article indicate ellipses.

1 "Via" quidem iter, quod ea *vehendō teritur*, iter item "*āctus*," quod
2 *agendō teritur*; etiam "*ambitus*" iter, quod circumeundō teritur: nam
3 *ambitus* [est] circuitus; ab eōque Duodecim Tabulārum interpretēs "*ambitus*
4 "*pariētis*" circuitum esse dēscrībunt. Igitur "tera" [facta erat] terra et ab eō
5 poētae *appellārunt summa* terrae quae sōla *terī* possunt, "*sola* terrae." Terra,
6 ut putant, eadem et "humus;" *ideō* **Ennium in terram cadentīs dīcere**:
7 "*Cubitīs pīnsībant* humum;" et **quod terra sit humus,** *ideō* is "humātus"
8 mortuus, quī terrā *obrutus*; ab eō quī Rōmānus *combustus* est, sī in sepulcrum
9 ēius abiecta *glēba* nōn est aut sī os exceptum est mortuī ad familiam
10 pūrgandam, dōnec in pūrgandō humō est *opertum* (ut *pontificēs* dīcunt) **quod**
11 **inhumātus sit,** familia *fūnesta* manet. Et dīcitur "humilior," quī ad humum
12 *dēmissior, īnfimus* "humillimus," quod in mundō *īnfima* humus. *Hūmor*
13 hinc. Itaque ideō Lūcīlius: "Terra abiit in *nimbōs* hūmōremque." Pācuvius:
14 "Terra exhālat auram atque aurōram hūmidam;" "hūmidam" hūmectam;
15 hinc ager ūlīginōsus "hūmidissimus;" hinc "*ūdus*" "ūvidus;" hinc "*sūdor*" et
16 "*ūdor*." **Īs sī quamvīs** *deorsum* in terrā, **unde sūmī pote,** "*puteus*;" nisi *potius*
17 quod *Aeolīs* dīcēbant **ut *pytamon* sic *pyteon*** ā *potū*, nōn ut nunc
18 *phrear*. Ā *putīis* oppidum **ut Puteolī,** quod *incircum* eum locum aquae
19 frīgidae et caldae multae, nisi ā *pūtōre* potius, quod *pūtidus* odōribus saepe ex
20 sulphure et *alūmine*. Extrā oppida **ā puteīs** "*puticulī*," quod ibi in puteīs
21 *obruēbantur* hominēs, nisi potius, ut Aelius scrībit, "*puticulī*" quod
22 *pūtēscēbant* ibi cadāvera prōiecta, quī locus pūblicus *ultrā Ēsquiliās*. Itaque
23 eum Afrānius "**putilucōs**" in *Togātā* appellat, quod inde *suspiciunt* per
24 puteōs lūmen.

Phrases

Ennium in terram cadentīs dīcere – [They think] that Ennius speaks of [men] falling to the ground (This continues the indirect statement begun with *putant* in the previous sentence. *Cadentīs* is accusative plural.)

quod terra sit humus – inasmuch as ground (terra) is earth (humus)

quod inhumātus sit – inasmuch as he is unburied/not under the earth

Īs sī quamvīs – if you go however much *or*, if *īs* is read as *is*: if anyone (lit., "if he as you wish")

unde sūmī pote – read as *unde sūmī ūdōrem pote est* ("whence it is possible for moisture to be taken up")

ut *pytamon* sic *pyteon* – *ut . . . sic* means "as well as . . . no less"; Varro seems to be using a fancy version of *nōn modo . . . sed etiam*, meaning "not only . . . but also"

ut Puteolī – read as *nōtum ut Puteolī*

ā puteīs – read as *sic nōminātī ā puteīs*

putilucōs – "wells of light" (a made-up word not to be mixed up with *puticulōs*; this is a pun on *puteus*, "well," and *lūx*, "light")

Glossary

Use your "eye" Latin to discern the meaning of the underlined words in the reading.

vehō, vehere, vexī, vectum	to carry, to convey, to ride
terō, terere, trīvī, trītum	to rub, to wear down, to wear away
āctus, m.	a driving passage, therefore a road in this context (from *agō*, "drive")
ambitus, -ūs, m.	a going around, circumference, winding
interpres, interpretis, c.	a mediator, a negotiator, a messenger
pariēs, pariētis, m.	wall (usually the wall of a house)
appellārunt	*appellavērunt* (syncopated perfect)
summa	the highest parts
solum, solī, n.	soil, topmost layer of the ground
ideō, adv.	on that account, therefore, for that reason, for that purpose
cubitum, cubitī, n.	elbow
pīnsō, pīnsere, pīnsī, pīnsum	to crush, to stamp (*pīnsībant* = *pīnsēbant*)
humus, -ī (f.)	ground (*Humus* is one of the few feminine words in the second declension; also, it has the locative *humī*.)
obruō, obruere, obruī, obrutum	to cover up, to bury
combūrō, combūrere, combussī, combustum	to burn; to cremate
sepulcrum, -ī, n.	grave, tomb (for a body or ashes)
glēba, -ae, f.	a clod (of earth)
operiō, operīre, operuī, opertum	to cover, to cover over
pontifex, pontificis, m.	Roman high priest/priest
fūnestus, -a, -um, adj.	mournful
dēmissior, dēmissius, CpAdj.	lower, more downcast
infimus, -a, -um, adj.	lowest
hūmor, hūmōris, m.	moisture, fluid
nimbus, -ī, m.	cloud
aura, -ae, f.	air; breeze; daylight
aurōra, -ae, f.	dawn, daybreak
hūmectus, -a, -um, adj.	wet
ūlīginōsus, -a, -um, adj.	moist, wet, marshy
ūdus/ūvidus, -a, -um, adj.	wet, damp, moist
sūdor, sūdōris, m.	sweat
ūdor, ūdōris, m.	moisture
deorsum, adv.	down, down low, way down, far down
potis, pote	[it is] possible
puteus, puteī, m.	well
potius	rather (CpAdv of *potis, pote*; possibly a deliberate play on the words *puteus, pytamon, pyteon,* and *potus*)
Aeolīs (Greek nominative plural)	The Aeolians
pytamon	(a supposedly Aeolian word for "well")
pyteon	(a supposedly Aeolian word for "well")
potus, -ūs, m.	drink
phrear	(a Greek word for "well")
incircum	around
pūtor, pūtōris, m.	a bad smell
pūtidus, -a, -um, adj.	rotten, stinking
alūmen, alūminis, n.	alum (or one of a group of various other chemical compounds formed near volcanic activity)
puticulī, puticulōrum, m.	a pauper's graveyard where the corpses were buried in pits; especially referring to the one outside the Esquiline in Rome
pūtēscō, pūtēscere, pūtuī	to become rotten

ultrā, prep. + acc. .... on the other side of, on the far side of
Ēsquiliae, Ēsquiliārum, f. .... the Esquiline hill in Rome
Togāta, -ae, f. .... Togata, a type of Roman comedy with its setting in Rome instead of in Greece
suspiciō, suspicere, suspexī, suspectum .... to look up at

Rhetorical Devices

REPETITION: ALLITERATION AND ANAPHORA

Alliteration is the repetition of consonant sounds. Traditionally, the sounds are the initial sounds of words; however, alliteration can also refer to the repetition of consonants at the beginnings of syllables as well as at the beginnings of words. Alliteration is what makes tongue twisters such as "Sally sells seashells down by the seashore" and the tongue twisters at the end of this chapter. The alliteration in the first sentence in the reading in this unit review is a perfect example of alliteration based on initial sounds of both words and syllables.. Study the sentence carefully to see how the alliteration works. Read the sentence aloud to appreciate its full beauty. Can you find other examples of alliteration in the reading from Varro?

Anaphora is another form of repetition: it is the repetition of words at the beginning of clauses, sentences, or lines of poetry. Orators such as Cicero were especially fond of the use of anaphora to drive home points.

Both alliteration and anaphora have been used in rhetoric and poetry down through the ages. Anglo-Saxon poetry, especially the folk epic *Beowulf*, makes extensive use of alliteration. For example:

Then was it great wonder that the wine-hall

Withstood the fierce fighters[15]

When poetry does not rhyme—and rhyme is a relatively modern technique—other poetic devices are what make poetry poetry. Statesmen familiar with Latin and with the poetry of the Romans from Cicero to Churchill have used anaphora effectively. Consider these lines from Winston Churchill's famous address to the people of Britain in World War II.

We shall not flag or fail. We shall go on to the end. We shall fight in France, we shall fight on the seas and oceans, we shall fight with growing confidence and growing strength in the air, we shall defend our island, whatever the cost may be, we shall fight on the beaches, we shall fight on the landing grounds, we shall fight in the fields and in the streets, we shall fight in the hills. We shall never surrender.[16]

As you continue in this textbook, you will learn to recognize and appreciate examples of alliteration and anaphora as well as of many other rhetorical devices.

---

15. James M. Garnett, trans., *Beowulf*, ln. 771-772, accessed August 1, 2012, <http://www.perseus.tufts.edu/hopper/text?doc=Perseus%3Atext%3A2003.01.0003%3Acard%3D710>.
16. This is an excerpt from an address delivered by Winston Churchill to the House of Commons on June 4, 1940. You can find the full speech at the following: <http://www.winstonchurchill.org/learn/speeches/speeches-of-winston-churchill/128-we-shall-fight-on-the-beaches>.

Question & Answer

For each of the following exercises, circle the letter of the correct answer.

1. According to lines 1 and 2 of the reading, a "road" receives that name because _____.
   a. people walk there
   b. cattle used to wander there
   c. transportation, possibly of goods in wagons, wears down the surface
   d. it is paved

2. How did the interpreters of the Twelve Tables describe the circumference of a wall?
   a. as something sharp
   b. as a circuit
   c. as the part of the wall that protrudes
   d. as the narrowest part of a wall

3. What rhetorical figure appears in the first two lines of the reading?
   a. alliteration
   b. synchysis
   c. chiasmus
   d. hyperbole

4. Why is the ground called *terra*?
   a. because poets wanted to call it that
   b. because the earth is trod/ground down
   c. because *terra* has a more pleasing sound than *sola*
   d. because people might confuse *sola* and *sōla*

5. What is the best interpretation of *cadentīs* in line 6?
   a. slaughters
   b. persons yielding the road
   c. persons falling
   d. murderers

6. If a family keeps unburied a bone of a dead family member, what is the effect of that action upon the family?
   a. They will not be able to perform a certain cleansing rite.
   b. They will be mournful as long as the bone is unburied.
   c. They must burn the bone as soon as possible.
   d. There is not any adverse effect.

7. From lines 11 and 12 of the passage, what can you determine about the English verb "humiliate"?
   a. It comes from a Latin word meaning "moisture," because humiliation makes a person cry.
   b. Humiliation makes a person feel as low as the ground.
   c. Humiliation can make people blush.
   d. It originally referred to an unburied corpse.

8. According to Varro, who wrote that the earth disappears into the clouds?
   a. Afranius
   b. Pacuvius
   c. Lucilius
   d. Ennius

9. Quoting Pacuvius, Varro states that _____.
   a. the dawn can be damp
   b. the dawn is a quiet time with no breeze or wind
   c. the dawn is golden
   d. the dawn comes from a cloud

10. What is the nature of the land mentioned in line 15?
    a. extremely dry
    b. extremely low
    c. marshy
    d. moderately damp

11. Varro states that the Latin word for sweat is connected to _____.
    a. a Greek word
    b. an Aeolian term
    c. moisture
    d. exercise

12. What quality explains the origin of the Aeolian word for river?
    a. its color
    b. its water
    c. its potability
    d. its current

13. What surrounded the town of Puteoli?
    a. hot springs
    b. cold springs
    c. both A and B
    d. none of the above

14. What did Aelius write about little pits/burial wells?
    a. Bodies used to be put into them to rot.
    b. They were called pits because they had been dug.
    c. They were always filled to the top with cadavers.
    d. They were never used for anything except collecting water.

15. Where were the public cemeteries in Rome, according to this reading?
    a. in the Forum
    b. on the Capitoline Hill
    c. both A and B
    d. none of the above

16. Quōmodo viae terēbantur?
    a. itinere
    b. vehendō
    c. agenda
    d. equiīs

17. Quī nōmen "sola terrae" summīs terrae dedērunt?
    a. Aeoliī
    b. Pacuvius
    c. interpretēs lēgum
    d. poētae

18. Quae rēs prōicī super sepulchrum Rōmānī inhumātī debet?
    a. ossa
    b. vestēs virī
    c. glēba
    d. vehiculum

19. Quid est pars verbī "putilucus" in Afraniī Togatā?
    a. putidus
    b. pudor
    c. phrear
    d. lumen

Unit 1 Reading
68

20. Quis aut quid purgārī debet?
   a. familia mortuī
   b. ossa
   c. sepulchrum
   d. mortuus

Game Time!

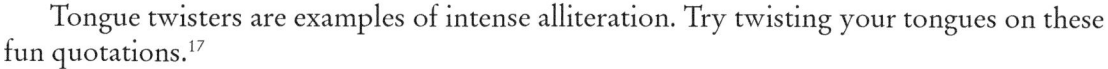

Tongue twisters are examples of intense alliteration. Try twisting your tongues on these fun quotations.[17]

Te te, ro ro, ma ma, nu nu, da da, te te, la la, te te!

(properly: Te tero, Roma, manu nuda, date tela, late te!)

Translation: "I will destroy you, Rome, with my bare hands, give arms and hide yourself!" This sentence is said to have been pronounced by Hannibal (or even by Alaric the Visigoth) as he neared the gates of Rome.

O Tite tute Tati, tibi tanta, tyranne tulisti! (Ennius)

Translation: "O thou tyrant, Titus Tatius, such great troubles you brought upon yourself!"

In mari meri miri mori muri necesse est.

Translation: "In a sea of delightful wine a mouse may only die."

Summergimurne?

Translation: Are we sinking?

Quantum materiæ materietur marmota monax si marmota monax materiam possit materiari?

Translation: "How much wood would a woodchuck chuck if a woodchuck could chuck wood?"

A garden and courtyard in the middle of a ruined villa in Herculaneum, Italy.

---

17. All of the tongue twisters in this section are taken from *Archimedes' Laboratory*, "Antique Puzzles," accessed August 1, 2012, <http://www.archimedes-lab.org/latin.html>.

Salus populi suprema lex esto.
University of Missouri
This motto is taken from Cicero's Oration, *Dē Lēgibus*, Book III, Part III.

Chapter 7

- Section 26. Purpose Review
  - Dative of Purpose
  - Gerund or Gerundive
  - Supine
- Section 27. Purpose Clauses
- Section 28. Future Imperative

VOCABULARY

LATIN	ENGLISH	DERIVATIVES
Nouns		
molestia, -ae, f.	trouble, annoyance	(molest)
pausa, -ae, f.	pause, end	(pause)
prex, precis, f.	prayer	(imprecation)
quisquam, quaequam, quicquam/ quidquam, indef. pro. (cf. quis, quid)	anyone, anything	
senecta, -ae, f. (cf. senex)	old age	(senectitude)
sententia, -ae, f.	opinion, feeling	(sentiment, sentence)
vīta, -ae, f.	life	(vital)
Verbs		
adversor, adversārī, adversātus sum	to oppose, to resist (+ dat.)	(adversary)
lubet/libet, lubēre, lubuit	(impersonal) it is pleasing	
opitulor, opitulārī, opitulātus sum (cf. ops)	to bring aid, to help, to assist	
pudeō, pudēre, puduī (cf. pudendus)	to make ashamed, to shame	(pudency)
tolerō, -āre, -āvī, -ātum	to bear, to endure, to tolerate, to sustain	(tolerate)
Adjectives, Adverbs, Conjunctions, etc.		
dēnique, adv.	and then, finally	
ecquandō, inter. adv. (cf. ec- [in the word ecce] + quandō)	ever, at any time (often carries an attitude of indignation)	
praeterquam, adv. (cf. praeter)	except for, other than	
adversum/adversus, prep. (+ acc.)	against	(adverse)

SECTION 26. Purpose Review

Have you ever noticed how English can express the same idea, the same concept, through a variety of patterns? Consider, *exempli gratia*, the following three sentences, which all express the same purpose.

1. Julia came as a help to her mother.
2. Julia came to help her mother.
3. Julia came so that she might help her mother.

All three of these sentences express the same idea. A young lady named Julia has arrived at some place. Why did she arrive there? For what purpose? To help her mother. Each of these sentences, however, uses a different means to express the same idea.

Latin also uses a variety of constructions to express purpose. In this chapter you will learn a new construction for purpose, but first let us review a few with which you are already familiar. You have already learned three such purpose constructions in *LA2*: 1) dative case (dative of purpose or double dative), 2) the gerund or gerundive with *ad* and the accusative or with *causā* or *grātiā* and the genitive case, and 3) the accusative supine with a verb of motion.

A. Dative of Purpose

The dative of purpose appears when the purpose may be expressed as a noun. This construction often appears along with the dative of reference. When both the dative of purpose and the dative of reference work together (as in the second of the following examples), we call the construction a **double dative**.

Iulia **auxiliō** vēnit.	Julia came **as a help**.
Iulia **auxiliō** mātrī vēnit.	Julia came **as a help** for her mother.

B. Gerund or Gerundive

Both the gerund and the gerundive may appear in the accusative case with the preposition *ad* or with *causā/grātiā* in order to express purpose.

Iulia **ad iuvandum** vēnit.*	Julia came **to help**.
Iulia **ad iuvandam** mātrem vēnit.	Julia came **to help** her mother.
	(lit., Julia came to/for the mother to be helped.)

*__Nota Bene__: The accusative of the gerund with *ad* cannot take a direct object. In other words, the following would not be possible: *Iulia ad iuvandum mātrem vēnit.*

Iulia iuvandī causā/grātiā vēnit.	Julia came for the sake of helping.
Iulia mātrem iuvandī causā/grātiā vēnit.	Julia came for the sake of helping her mother.
Iulia iuvandae mātrae causā/grātiā vēnit.	Julia came to help her mother.
	(lit., Julia came for the sake of her mother to be helped.)

The gerundive, which is a verbal adjective, may agree with another noun. This noun, since it is the subject of a passive verb, may be translated into English as the object of an active idea.

C. Supine

The supine is the fourth principal part of a verb. The supine may appear in the accusative case with a verb of motion to express purpose. Notice that, since the supine is still a verb, it may take a direct object. (The ablative supine, however, cannot take a direct object.)

Iulia **iūtum** vēnit.	Julia came **to help**.
Iulia **iūtum** mātrem vēnit.	Julia came **to help** her mother.

Caveat Discipulus: You may notice that English often renders a purpose phrase in a manner that resembles an infinitive. Classical Latin prose *never* uses the infinitive to express purpose. To write *Iulia adiuvāre mātrem vēnit* would be incorrect.

Exercise 1. Underline the purpose phrase in each sentence. Then translate the sentence.

1. Pater flōrēs dōnō mātrī mīsit.   *The father sent flowers as a gift to the mother.*
2. Dēnique vīlicus ānseribus suibusque stabulō tēctum aedificāvit.
3. Fīlius oblātum precem ad templum īvit.
4. Servus vēnit ad pābulum dandum animālibus.
5. Magistrātus dīcendī causā ad forum īvit.
6. Praeterquam iste, nēmō ad rem pūblicam pudendam tantō cum studiō labōrāvit.
7. Amīcī agricolae vīsum fundum advēnērunt.
8. Ecquandō domum quisquam opitulāndī causā parentibus veniet?
9. Virī ad tēcta facienda arborēs caedunt.
10. Puerī bovibus faenum pābulō ab agrīs ferunt.

SECTION 27. Purpose Clauses

Another way to show purpose in Latin is with a subjunctive *ut* clause, much like the clause you learned for indirect command. In fact, these two clauses are related not only in their grammatical construction, but also in their syntactical purpose. Consider for a moment that a command does carry with it a sense of purpose.

> Mater me imperat ut cubiculum pūrgārem.   My mother commands me to clean the room.
> My mother commands me so that I may clean my room.

What is the purpose of the command? The purpose is to get me to clean my room.

The key word that signals an indirect command in this sentence is "commands." Such words always signal an *ut* clause expressing indirect command. For a purpose clause, however, a verb of command will not appear. The translation of *ut*, however, will communicate a sense of purpose in the action, just as the English phrase "so that."

> Mater me ad cubiculum mittit ut id purgam.   My mother sends me to my room so that I may clean it.

Aside from a commanding verb, the *ut* clause appears the same for purpose as it does for indirect command. When positive, the Latin conjunction *ut* (or *utī*) introduces positive purpose clauses. When negative, the purpose clauses are introduced by *nē*. The clause will follow the sequence of tenses introduced in chapter 6.

Since a purpose is something unfulfilled and therefore incomplete, the subjunctive verb in a purpose clause will always be in the present tense in primary sequence and in the imperfect tense in secondary sequence.

Study the following examples in order to learn how purpose clauses may be translated.

1. Caesar in castra venit ut cum Labiēnō dīcat.
   Caesar is coming into the camp in order that he may speak with Labienus.
   Caesar is coming into the camp so that he may speak with Labienus.
   Caesar is coming into the camp to speak with Labienus.

2. Caesar in castra vēnit ut cum Labiēnō dīceret.
   Caesar came into the camp in order that he might speak with Labienus.
   Caesar came into the camp so that he might speak with Labienus.
   Caesar came into the camp to speak with Labienus.

3. Pugnāmus nē vincāmur.
   We are fighting lest we be conquered.
   We are fighting so that we may not be conquered.

4. Pugnāvimus nē vincerēmur.
   We fought lest we be conquered.
   We fought so that we might not be conquered.

Nota Bene: Note the use of "may" in primary sequence in English and "might" in secondary sequence. In these types of translations the English and Latin are very similar. "May" (present subjunctive) in English follows only non-past verbs while "might" (imperfect subjunctive) follows only past tense verbs.

Exercise 2. Underline the purpose phrase in each of the following sentences and identify which type of purpose clause is being employed. Then translate the sentences.

1. Stabula aedificāmus ut animālia calida sint.
2. Stabula aedificēmus ad animālia calenda.
3. Nōbīs dēnique fābulās vītae tuae saepe memorā, utī eās in senectā nostrā in memoriā cārē teneāmus.
4. Oportet nōbīs stabula bona aedificāre nē animālia frīgore moriantur.
5. Licet tibi aedificāre tēctum stabulō animālibus.
6. Bovēs ad bibendum dūxerant.
7. Bovēs ad aquam dūxerant ut biberent.
8. Locum plānum piscīnae līberīs petimus.
9. Locum plānum petit utī piscīnam habeat.
10. Lubet opitulārī quōquam quī caret ut omnēs molestiā līberēmur.
11. Lubet opitulārī molestiā ad aliōs līberandōs.
12. In castra īmus quaesītum ducem.
13. Eāmus in castra nē fūrēs nōs inveniant.
14. Pausa facienda ōrātiōnis est, nē ōrātor sententiam turbae contrā rem pūblicam advertat.

Section 28. Future Imperative

Until now you have only seen the present tense of the imperative mood, used for direct commands.

venī	venīte
dic	dicite
hortāre	hortāminī

While the present is by far the most common tense for the imperative mood, it is not the only tense. Imperative verbs may appear in the future tense as well. The future tense is useful for a command that is not meant to be obeyed only in the present—now—but also far into the future as a general principle or law. Thus verbs such as *scīre* (to know), *habēre* (to consider), and *meminī* (to remember) often appear as future infinitives. When in the future tense, the suffix *-tō* appears in the second-person singular (you) or third-person singular (he, she, it). The connecting vowel for each verb will be the same as the connecting vowel for the present active indicative (*ā, ē, i, ī* for the first through fourth conjugations, respectively).

Exempli Gratia:

scītō

habētō

mementō

hortator

Another common future imperative is the verb *estō*. This imperative, however, is third person: "let it be." This imperative is often seen instead of the jussive subjunctive *sit* in many mottoes and ancient proverbs. This is because the future imperative is often used of timeless commands, such as in law.

In the same manner as the present imperative, the future imperative has plural forms used to give commands to more than one person (*-tōte*). The plurals for the verbs in the preceding examples are *scītōte*, *habētōte*, and *mementōte*. The plural of *estō* is *estōte*.

Exercise 3. Form the future imperative for the following verbs.

1. petere
2. tolerāre
3. placēre
4. sentīre
5. agere
6. facere
7. hortārī
8. venīre
9. miscēre
10. nescīre

Exercise 4. Read and discuss the meaning or significance of the following quotations.

1. Lux esto! (Kalamazoo College motto)
2. Scito te ipsum. (Socrates, Oracle at Delphi)
3. Esto perpetua! (Motto for both the State of Idaho and University of Idaho)
4. Do ut des. (ancient maxim)
5. Primum, vir esto! (Baker University, Kansas)
6. Legum servi sumus ut liberi esse possimus. (Cicero)
7. Memento Alamonem! (Texenses)
8. Cura nihil aliud nisi ut valeas. (Cicero)
9. Borea flante, ne arato. (Pliny the Elder)
   Hint: *borea* – north wind

Cornelia Gracchus and her sons

Chapter Reading

The following is an excerpt from a letter written by Cornelia to her son, Gaius Gracchus. It was recorded for posterity by the biographer Cornelius Nepos. Cornelia was the matriarch of the Gracchi family. You can read more about her and her famous sons, Tiberius and Gaius, in the Culture Corner segment of this chapter.

VERBA EX EPISTULĀ CORNĒLIAE GRACCHŌRUM MĀTRIS EX EŌDEM LIBRŌ CORNĒLIĪ NEPŌTIS EXCERPTA.

Verbīs conceptīs *dēierāre* **ausim**, praeterquam quī Tiberium Gracchum *necārunt*, nēminem inimīcum tantum molestiae tantumque labōris, quantum tē ob hās rēs, mihi tradidisse: quem oportēbat omnium eōrum, quōs *antehāc* habuī līberōs, *partīs* tolerāre atque cūrāre ut quam minimum *sollicitūdinis* in senectā habērem, utīque, *quaecumque* agerēs, ea vellēs maximē mihi placēre, atque utī nefās habērēs rērum māiōrum adversum meam sententiam quicquam facere, praesertim mihi, cuī parva pars vītae *superest*. Nē id quidem tam breve spatium potest opitulārī, *quin* et **mihi adversēre** et rem pūblicam *prōflīgēs*? Dēnique quae pausa erit? Ecquandō *dēsinet* familia nostra īnsānīre? Ecquandō modus eī reī habērī poterit? Ecquandō *dēsinēmus* et habentēs et *praebentēs* molestiīs īnsistere? Ecquandō *perpudēscet* miscendā atque perturbandā rē pūblicā? Sed sī *omnīnō* id *fierī* nōn potest, ubi ego mortua erō, petitō *tribūnātum*: **per mē** facitō quod lubēbit, cum ego nōn sentiam. Ubi mortua erō, *parentābis* mihi et invocābis deum parentem. In eō tempore nōn pudēbit tē **eōrum deum** precēs *expetere*, quōs vīvōs atque praesentēs relictōs atque desertōs habuerīs? Nē ille *sīrit* Iuppiter tē ea perseverāre nec tibi tantam dēmentiam venīre in animum! Et sī perseverās, **vereor nē** in omnem vītam tantum labōris culpā tuā recipiās, utī in nūllō tempore *tūte* tibi placēre possīs.

Phrases

ausim – I would dare (cf. *audere*)

mihi adversēre = *mihi adversēris* (This is an alternative form for the second-person singular.)

per mē – as far as concerns me

eōrum deum – of those gods (i.e., his ancestors whom he ignored while they were alive, but seeks the council of now that they are dead)

vereor nē ... recipiās – I am afraid that/I fear that ... you will receive (this is a fear clause, which you will be learning in chapter 12)

utī ... possīs – that ... you are able (This is a result clause, which you will be learning in chapter 10.)

Glossary

Use your "eye" Latin to discern the meanings of the underlined words in the reading.

dēierō, -āre, -āvī, -ātum	to take an oath
necārunt	*necāvērunt*
antehāc, adv.	before this time (cf. *ante* + *hāc*)
partīs	*partēs* (remember that i-stem nouns can have an alternative acc. pl. ending in *-ēs*)
sollicitūdō, sollicitūdinis, f.	anxiety, uneasiness of mind
quīcumque, quaecumque, quodcumque, pro.	whoever, whatever
supersum, superesse, superfuī	to be left, to remain (cf. *super* + *esse*)
quin	from; but that (after a negative main clause of hindering; e.g., to keep someone from doing something; here the word acting as a verb of hindering is *opulārī*)
prōflīgō, -āre, -āvī, -ātum	to overthrow, to dash to ground, to cast down utterly
dēsinō, dēsinere, dēsivī	to cease to (+ inf.)
īnsistō, īnsistere, īnsistitī	(+ dat.) to stand upon
praebeō, praebēre, praebuī, praebitum	to hold forth, to offer
perpudēscō, perpudēscere	to be thoroughly ashamed
omnīnō	adverbial form of *omnis*, at all, wholly
fīō, fierī, factus sum	to become, to happen
tribūnātus, -ī, m.	tribuneship
parentō, -āre, -āvī, -ātum	to offer solemn sacrifice in honor of a parent or close relative
deum	*deōrum* (sycopation)
expetere	*ex* + *petere*
sirit	*siverit* the perfect subjunctive form of *sinere*
tūtē ≈ tū ipse	an emphatic form of the pronoun *tū* (or, possibly, an adverb of *tūtus*)

RESPONDĒ LATĪNĒ!

1. Quī sunt fīliī clārī Cornēliae?
2. Quī Cornēliae maximum molestiae dedērunt?
3. Cūr Gāius rērum māiōrum adversum sententiam mātris quicquam nōn facere dēbet?
4. Quō tempore Cornelia Gāium petere tribūnātum vult? Cūr?
5. Amāsne mātrem tuam, et vīs maximē eī placēre?

About the Author

CORNELIA, MATER GRACCHORUM

Few of Rome's families possess the renown of the Gracchi. The matriarch of this famous clan was Cornelia, the daughter of Scipio Africanus, famed general of the Second Punic War. She married Tiberius Sempronius Gracchus, a tribune for the plebeians who also served twice as a consul and later as a censor. Together they had twelve children, but only one daughter and two sons—Tiberius and Gaius Gracchus—reached adulthood. The elder Tiberius died while his children were still young, so Cornelia saw to their education. She hired the best Greek tutors for training in rhetoric, political science, and even martial arts. The promising youths seemed to excel in everything. Valerius Maximus relates to us that once a noble woman was showing off her fine jewelry to Cornelia. She then asked Cornelia to show her finest jewels. Without hesitation, Cornelia left the room and returned with her two sons, and responded, *"Haec ornamenta sunt mea."*[1] Cornelia gained such a reputation for the manner in which she raised her children that, according to the historian Plutarch, King Ptolemy VI of Egypt even proposed marriage, offering to make her his queen. She, however, preferred to remain loyal to her husband's memory and to their children.

The Gracchi brothers grew in distinction and prominence, which many credited directly to the education their mother provided. Tiberius, nine years older than his brother, was the first to make a name for himself. He served under Scipio the Younger, his brother-in-law,[2] in the Third Punic War. Upon his return to Rome, Tiberius was made a tribune of the plebeians as was his father before him. After the war the plebeians brought complaints to Tiberius that the land promised them for their war service was being taken away by the rich patricians. Tiberius spent the remainder of his career pursing land reform, which was greatly opposed by the wealthy landowners. At first Tiberius used proper and lawful means to accomplish reform, but as each attempt was frustrated he began to use tactics that some found less than honorable. Nevertheless, Tiberius had won great popularity with the people, and the patricians found him increasingly difficult. Eventually, they assassinated Tiberius and those with him and threw their bodies in the Tiber.

Gaius was not yet thirty when his brother was murdered. For a time he kept himself out of public affairs, but eventually he, too, joined public service. He first served as a quaestor in Sardinia. Upon his return home, he pursued the tribuneship. The nobility opposed this ambition, but people from all over Italy demanded the office for him. Once elected, Gaius never ceased to remind the people of his brother's murder, which he called an execution by the Senate without trial. He, too, pushed for land reform and other measures on behalf of the plebians, and he, too, incurred the hatred of the Senate. Eventually, he was chased down and murdered.

Upon the death of her sons, Cornelia moved to the town of Misenum. There, she continued to live as a woman of great distinction. She entertained many guests with great hospitality; among them were the learned men of Greece and foreign princes. Cornelia, a very learned woman herself, entertained her guests with stories of her famous father and with the deeds and misfortunes of her sons. Cornelia came to be viewed as the ideal woman of Rome, and so Rome honored her with a statue of brass bearing this inscription, *"Cornelia, Mater Gracchorum."*[3]

Scrībāmus!

That was quite a guilt trip that Cornelia laid on Gaius, wasn't it? It seemed as though it was pretty effective, too. Using a few purpose clauses and perhaps a few of Cornelia's tactics, compose your own guilt trip in Latin. Try to persuade a friend to do something he or she may not want to do (e.g., help you with your homework, try a new food, attempt a new hobby, etc.).

Est Vērum!

Legend has it that the elder of the Gracchi brothers, Tiberius, was the first Roman at the end of the Third Punic War to scale the walls of Carthage.

---

1. Valerius Maximus, *Facta et Dicta Memorabilia*, 4.4, edited by Karl Friedrich Kempf. Available at: <http://www.perseus.tufts.edu/hopper/text?doc=urn:cts:latinLit:phi1038.phi001.perseus-lat1:4.4>.
2. Scipio the Younger, the adopted son of Scipio Africanus, married Cornelia's only surviving daughter.
3. Plutarch, *Lives of the Noble Grecians and Romans*, trans. by John Dryden, ed. by A.H. Clough. Available at: <http://ebooks.adelaide.edu.au/p/plutarch/lives/>.

Vincit qui se vincit.
Ricker College, ME

Chapter 8

- Section 29. Indirect Question
- Section 30. Indirect Statement
- Section 31. Time Relative
- Section 32. Exclamatory Accusative

VOCABULARY

LATIN	ENGLISH	DERIVATIVES
Nouns		
audācia, -ae, f.	boldness, audacity (cf. audax)	(audacious)
coniūrātiō, coniūrātiōnis, f.	conspiracy	
cūra, -ae, f.	care, concern	(curator)
iūssus, iūssūs, m.	an order (cf. iubeō)	(jussive)
patientia, -ae, f.	patience, experience	(patient)
vigilia, vigiliae, f.	a watching for the security of a place; sentinels, soldiers keeping watch (cf. vigilō)	(vigilant)
Verbs		
abūtor, abūtī, abūsus sum	to use fully, to abuse (cf. ūtor)	(abuse)
arbitror, arbitrārī, arbitrātus sum	to think, to judge (cf. arbiter, arbitrium)	(arbitration)
dēsum, dēesse, dēfuī, dēfutūrum	to lack, to fail	
ēlūdō, ēlūdere, ēlūsī, ēlūsum	to ward off, to evade, to elude; to mock	(elusive)
iactō, -āre, -āvī, -ātum	to throw repeatedly or energetically, to throw about; (with the reflexive) to gesticulate	
precor, precārī, precātus sum	to pray, to entreat	
properō, -āre, -āvī, -ātum	to hurry, to hasten	
vītō, -āre, -āvī, -ātum	to avoid	

Adjectives, Adverbs, Conjunctions, etc.		
ācer, ācris, ācre, adj.	sharp, eager; severe, fierce	(acrid)
perniciōsus, -a, -um, adj.	destructive, ruinous	(pernicious)
praeclārus, -a, -um, adj.	very famous, excellent	
nimis, adv.	too much	
tandem, adv.	finally, at last, in the end; I ask, I pray (in urgent questioning)	
ac or atque, conj.	and	

SECTION 29. Indirect Question

Indirect question is just one subcategory of indirect discourse. **Indirect discourse**, or, in Latin, *ōrātiō oblīqua* (an indirect speech), is essentially reporting what someone else said. What they said, however, could be a statement, a command, or even a question. In the previous chapter, we looked at how to report someone else's command in Latin. In this chapter, we're going to take a look at the other two forms of indirect discourse: indirect question and indirect statement (see section 30).

Indirect question, like indirect command, will use a dependent clause that includes a subjunctive verb. Here's how indirect question is formed:

interrogative pronoun, adjective, or adverb + subjunctive verb

You have already learned how to ask a direct question in Latin: simply use an interrogative and an indicative verb.

"Ubi es?"   Where are you?

"Quid facit?"   What is he doing?

An indirect question takes a direct question and, rather than quoting what is asked, describes or reports what is asked. It is a subordinate clause introduced (as in indirect statements) by a "verb of the head." Remember, "verbs of the head" describe actions that your head (i.e., brain, eyes, ears, and mouth) does. When reporting a question, Latin will use the subjunctive instead of the indicative. In the examples below, notice the difference between the indirect question and the direct question from which it comes (positioned underneath).

Marcus rogābit <u>ubi sīs</u>.   Marcus will ask <u>where you are</u>.
Marcus rogābit, "Ubi es?"   Marcus will ask, "Where are you?"

Māter voluit scīre <u>quid faceret</u>.   Mother wanted to know <u>what he was doing</u>.
Māter voluit scīre, "Quid facit."   Mother wanted to know, "What is he doing?"

The preceding examples cover the present and imperfect tense in such questions, but what about the future? Remember, Latin does not have a future subjunctive. Instead, Latin uses the future active periphrastic (also called the first periphrastic). The active periphrastic consists of a future active participle accompanied by a form of *esse*.

> factūrus es — You are about to do
> Marcus rogat quid factūrus sīs. — Marcus asks what you are about to do.
> Marcus asks what you will do.

Nota Bene:

- The active periphrastic uses the subjunctive mood when it appears in an indirect question.
- Notice how the direct question becomes a dependent clause in the indirect statement. This dependent clause is always introduced by a question word—an interrogative pronoun, adjective, or adverb.
- Verbs of asking, knowing, telling, *et cetera*, will introduce an indirect question.
- Note the sequence of tenses between the main verb (in the indicative) and the verb in indirect question (in the subjunctive).

Exercise 1. Underline the indirect question or command in each sentence. Translate the sentences. Remember to carefully consider the sequence of tenses in each sentence.

1. Cōnsul senātōrēsque ubi Catilīna fuisset nōn rogāvēre.
2. Rēs pūblica postulat hominēs omnēs nē lēgēs ēlūdant.
3. Cicerō intellegit quid Catilīna actūrus sit.
4. Scīent senātōrēs quid vir mālus et amīcī proximā nocte ēgerint?
5. Cicerō senātum ōrat ut Catilīnam sapienter arbitrārentur.
6. Volimus scīre quī senātor reī pūblicae satis factūrus sit.
7. Cicerō audīverat quantī hominēs cum Catilīnā fuissent.
8. Puella frātrem petit nē eam ēlūdat.
9. Cicerō nōs quaesīvit ut habērēmus arbitrium in tē, vehemēns et grave arbitrium.
10. Do you think we do not perceive what you did last night?
11. We know whom you will bring together.
12. Cicero asks why Catiline lives.
13. We wanted to know who had killed Titus Gracchus.
14. We want to know who will kill Titus Gracchus.
15. Mother ordered (*iubeō*) us to hasten to speak to our father.

SECTION 30. Indirect Statement

You may recall from *LA2* (chapter 23) that **indirect statement** is simply a statement that the speaker is reporting; therefore, the construction usually follows verbs of saying, knowing, thinking, observing, hearing, seeing, etc. This construction is also known as indirect discourse.

English often uses a conjunction introducing a dependent clause to report an indirect statement. We have seen repeatedly how Latin uses participles and infinitives where English uses dependent clauses. The same holds true for indirect statement. Compare how English and Latin express indirect statement in the following examples.

> Audiō tē agere bene. — I hear that you are doing well.
> Audīvī tē agere bene. — I heard that you were doing well.
> Scīsne mē hunc audīre? — Do you know that I am hearing this?
> Scīsne hunc audītum īrī? — Do you know that this will be heard?
> Putō Lūciam esse pulcherrimam — I think that Lucy is very beautiful!

Instead of using a conjunction to introduce a dependent clause, Latin uses an accusative subject with an infinitive. The literal translation of *Audiō tē agere bene*—"I hear you to do well"— is certainly not how we would speak in English. It is important, therefore, not to translate the Latin "literally," but in the way a person would normally speak in English.

SECTION 31. Time Relative

You may remember that in indirect statement, the tense of the infinitive in indirect statement cannot be taken by itself or absolutely, but must be translated *relative* to or dependent upon the tense of the main verb. This is what we call **time relative**. Briefly review the tenses of the Latin infinitive in the following chart. Observe how the time of the infinitive relates to the time of the main verb in the explanations that appear below the chart.

	PRESENT	PERFECT	FUTURE
infinitive	amāre	amāvisse	amātūrum esse
	amārī	amātum esse	amātūrum īrī
time relative	same time as main verb	prior to main verb	after main verb

This differs from the sequence of tenses for the subjunctive you learned in chapter 6 (section 24). How does the sequence of tenses differ from time relative?

- **Time Relative:** the relationship of time between a main verb and a participle or infinitive.
  - Present tense: indicates action at the *same time* as the main verb
  - Future tense: indicates action at a time *after* the main verb
  - Past tense: indicates action at a time *before* the main verb
- **Sequence of Tenses:** indicates which tenses of the subjunctive may be employed in subordinate clause in sequence with a given tense of an indicative verb in the main clause of a sentence. The rules for the sequence of tenses divide all verbs into two groups based on the tense of the main verb: primary and secondary.
  - Primary: all main verb tenses that express *present* or *future* time
    - same time expressed by the *present* subjunctive
    - time prior expressed by the *perfect* subjunctive
  - Secondary: all main verb tenses that express *past* time
    - same time expressed by *imperfect* subjunctive
    - time prior expressed by *pluperfect* subjunctive

Hint: Remember, the Latin sequence of tense functions almost identically to the English sequence of tense. Make your translation sound natural (cf. section 24).

EXAMPLES OF TIME RELATIVE

1. If the Latin infinitive is in the present tense, it should be translated <u>at the same time</u> as the action of the main verb.

   Canis fēlem <u>esse</u> fortem scīvit.

   The dog knew that the cat <u>was</u> brave.

   Canis fēlem fortem <u>esse</u> scit.

   The dog knows that the cat <u>is</u> brave.

   Scietne fēlem <u>esse</u> fortem canis?

   Will the dog know that the cat <u>is</u> brave?

2. If the Latin infinitive is in the perfect tense, it should be translated as <u>time prior</u> to the action of the main verb.

Canis fēlem cēnam suam iam <u>ēdisse</u> scīvit.	The dog knew that the cat already <u>had eaten</u> his dinner.
Canis fēlem cēnam suam iam <u>ēdisse</u> scit.	The dog knows that the cat already <u>has eaten</u> his dinner.
Scietne fēlem cēnam suam iam <u>ēdisse</u> canis?	Will the dog know that the cat already <u>has eaten</u> his dinner?

3. If the Latin employs a future infinitive, it should be translated as <u>time after</u> the action of the main verb.

Canis fēlem cēnam suam iam <u>ēsūrum esse</u> scīvit.	The dog knew the cat <u>would eat</u> his dinner.
Canis fēlem cēnam suam <u>ēsūrum esse</u> scit.	The dog knows the cat <u>will eat</u> his dinner.
Scietne canis fēlem cēnam suam <u>ēsūrum esse</u>?	Will the dog know that the cat <u>will eat</u> his dinner?

Exercise 2. Underline the indirect statement in each sentence. Translate each sentence.

1. Cicerō saepe dīcēbat Catilīnam senātuum patientiā Rōmānōrum abūtī.
2. Cicerō clāmat Catilīnam esse audāciōrem.
3. Catilīna, nōnne sentīs patēre tua cōnsilia?
4. Senātus virum mālum, ipsum senātōrem, nocte contrā rem pūblicam cōnsilia cēpisse intellēxit.
5. Omnēs Catilīnam in senātum ventūrum esse scīvērunt.
6. In senātū cōnsul clāmāvit P. Scīpiōnem Ti. Gracchum interfēcisse.
7. Senātōrēs audīvērunt Cicerōnem clēmentem vidērī nōlle.
8. Cōnsul putat senātum dēesse.
9. Dīcēsne senātum dēfutūrum esse?
10. Dīximus senātum dēfuisse.

Section 32. Exclamatory Accusative

Latin uses the accusative case when expressing an exclamation. These exclamations are often not in complete sentences. Instead, they are fragments, often just a couple of words.

| O poor me! | Ō mē miserum! |
| O fortunate republic! | Ō fortūnātam rem pūblicam! |

Since the exclamatory accusative is usually a fragment or set apart by commas, it is fairly easy to recognize. Readers need only remember that the accusative is often used for such exclamations and need not be attached to or depend on another sentence or clause.

Exercise 3. Read and discuss the meaning or significance of the following quotations. Watch for indirect discourse and the exclamatory accusative.

1. Aegroto, dum anima est, spes esse dicitur (Cicero)
   Hint: *dicitur* – it is said

2. GETA: o scelera, o genera sacrilega, o hominem inpium!
   SOSTRATA: me miseram! quidnam est quod sic uideo timidum et properantem Getam? (Terence, *Adelphoe*)
   Hint: *quidnam – nam quid* (now/for why?); *Geta* – Geta, a man's name; *Sostrata* – Sostrata, a woman's name

3. Āit omnia pecunia effici posse; dare, profundere oportere, si velis vincere. (Cicero, *In Verrem*)

4. Nullum est iam dictum quod non dictum sit prius (Terence)

5. O curas hominum! O quantum est in rebus inane! (Lucilius)
   Hint: *ināne* – emptiness, futility

6. Praeclarum custodem ovium, lupum! (Cicero)
   Hint: *custōs, custōdis*, c. – watchman, protector; *ovis, ovis*, f. – sheep.; *lupus, lupī*, m. – wolf

7. O me miserum! O me infelicem! Revocare tu me in patriam, Milo, potuisti per hos: ego te in patria per eosdem retinere non potero? (Cicero, *Pro Milone*)
   Hint: Milo is the name of a person whom Cicero is defending in this speech; *īnfēlix* – antonym of *fēlix*; *retineō* – to retain, to keep back, to keep

8. Ingratus est qui beneficium se accepisse negat quod accepit. (Seneca, *De Beneficiis*)
   Hint: *ingrātus* – antonym of *grātus*; *beneficium, -ī*, n. – kindness

9. Ridentem dicere verum quid vetat? (Horace)
   Hint: *Quid* should be translated first.

Before You Read!

Alternative Verb Form

Remember that the second person singular passive form has an alternative ending: *-re*. This sometimes looks like an infinitive!

Indicative Passive
   amāre = amāris
   amābāre = amābāris
   amābere = amāberis

Subjunctive Passive
   amēre = amēris
   amārēre = amārēris

This applies to deponent verbs, too, because they use the passive forms.
   hortāre = hortāris

Cicero uses this alternative form often, so watch for it carefully in the chapter reading. Before you begin, practice writing the alternative forms for these verbs:

arbitrāris	sentiēbāre
arbitrāre	teneāris
vidēreris	teneāre
vidērere	notēris
vastāberis	notēre
vastābere	capiēris
sentiēbāris	capiēre

Chapter Reading

M. TULLĪ CICERŌNIS *ŌRĀTIŌ IN CATILĪNAM PRĪMA* (HABITA IN SENĀTŪ)

Characters

Marcus Tullius Cicero: consul of Rome in 63 BC, speaking to the Senate

Lucius Sergius Catilina: an impoverished aristocrat plotting to overthrow the Roman Republic

Roman Senators: the audience

I. *Quō* ūsque tandem abūtēre, Catilīna, patientiā nostrā? Quam diū etiam furor iste tuus nōs ēlūdet? Quem ad fīnem sēsē *effrēnāta* iactābit audācia? *Nihil*ne tē nocturnum praesidium Palātī, nihil urbis vigiliae, nihil timor populī, nihil *concursus* bonōrum omnium, nihil hic *mūnītissimus* habendī senātūs locus, nihil hōrum ōra voltūsque movērunt? Patēre tua cōnsilia nōn sentīs, *cōnstrictam* iam hōrum omnium *scientiā* tenērī coniūrātiōnem tuam nōn vidēs? Quid proximā, quid *superiōre* nocte ēgerīs, ubī fuerīs, quōs convocāverīs, quid cōnsiliī cēperīs, **quem nostrum ignōrāre arbitrāris**? Ō tempora, ō mōrēs! Senātus haec intellegit. Cōnsul videt; hic tamen vīvit. Vīvit? *immo* vērō etiam in senātum venit, *fit* pūblicī cōnsiliī *particeps*, notat et designat oculīs ad caedem ūnum *quemque* nostrum. Nōs autem fortēs virī **satis** facere **reī pūblicae** vidēmur, sī istīus furōrem ac tēla vītēmus. Ad mortem tē, Catilīna, dūcī iussū cōnsulis iam prīdem oportēbat, in tē cōnferrī pestem, quam tū in nōs omnīs iam diū **māchināris**.

II. *An* vērō vir amplissimus, P. Scīpiō *pontifex maximus*, Ti. Gracchum mediocriter *labefactantem* statum reī pūblicae *prīvātus* interfēcit; Catilīnam **orbem terrae** caede atque incendiīs vastāre cupientem nōs cōnsulēs perferēmus? Nam illa nimis antīqua *praetereō*, **quod** C. Servīlius Ahala Sp. Maelium *novīs rēbus* studentem manū suā occīdit. Fuit, fuit *ista quondam* in hāc rē pūblicā virtūs, ut virī fortēs acriōribus *suppliciīs* cīvem perniciōsum quam acerbissimum hostem coercerent. Habēmus senātūs consultum in tē, Catilīna, vehemēns et grave, nōn deest reī pūblicae cōnsilium neque auctōritās hūius ōrdinis; nōs, nōs, dīcō *apertē*, cōnsulēs dēsumus.

Phrases

quem nostrum ignōrāre arbitrāris – This sentence is somewhat difficult due to the fact that the indirect questions precede the main clause. The interrogatives *quid . . . quid . . . ubi . . . quōs . . . quid* are all introduced by the verb *ignōrāre* in the main clause *quem nostrum ignōrāre arbitrāris*.

satis – the direct object of *facere*; *reī pūblicae* is a dative of advantage; *vidēmur* ≈ *cōgitāmus* (i.e., we seem to ourselves, ≈ we think)

māchināris – you contrive. Astute readers will notice that the Latin uses the present tense here instead of the perfect tense, which would be expected. When expressing a duration of time, Latin authors will use *iam* with the present tense to express an action that began in the past, but continues into the present.

orbem terrae – circle of land = world

quod – can be translated as "that" and the whole phrase interpreted much like an indirect statement

ut . . . coercerent – that . . . they forced (this is a result clause—see chapter 10 for more information about these—so it must be translated indicatively)

Glossary

Use your "eye" Latin to discern the meanings of the underlined words in the reading.

quō	to what end? why? (directional adverb)
effrēnō, effrēnāre, effrēnāvī, effrēnātum	to unbridle
nihil	(for all instances in this sentence) not at all (accusative of respect *or* adverbial accusative: "with respect to nothing" or "nothingwise")
praesidium, -ī, n.	protection, escort, garrison
Palātium, Palātī, n.	Palatine, one of the seven hills of Rome
concursus, concursūs, m.	union, meeting
mūnītissimus	highly fortified (superlative adjective)
cōnstrictam	bound, enclosed (perfect passive participle)
scientia, -ae, f.	knowledge
superior, superius, adj.	previous, earlier (comparative of *superus, -a, -um*)
immo, adv.	nay rather, on the contrary
fit	he is made, he becomes
particeps, participis, m.	participant
quisque, quidque	each
pestis, pestis, f.	plague; destruction, ruin

an	can it be that (introducing direct questions with a note of surprise or indignation)
pontifex maximus	chief Roman priest
labefactō, labefactāre, labefactāvī, labefactāctum	to cause to shake or to totter
prīvātus, -a, -um, adj.	private; (as a noun) private citizen
praetereō, -īre, -iī, -itum	to pass over, to omit
novae rēs	revolution
iste, ista, istud	(here) such
quondam, adv.	once, formerly
supplicium, -ī, n.	punishment
apertē, adv.	openly

RESPONDĒ LATĪNĒ!

1. Quā rē abūtētur Catilīna?
2. Quae rēs ēlūdit senātōrēs Rōmānōs?
3. Quālis est audācia Catilīnae?
4. Quis timet?
5. Quis videt omnia cōnsilia Catilīnae?
6. Quis fit particeps cōnsiliōrum omnium senātūs?
7. Secundum Cicerōnem hāc in ōrātiōne quid vastārī cupit Catilīna?
8. Temporibus antīquīs quis erat pēior Rōmānīs, cīvis perniciōsus vel hostis?
9. Quī dēsunt?
10. Quōmodo dīcit cōnsul?

Bust of Marcus Tullius Cicero

About the Author

MARCUS TULLIUS CICERO

Marcus Tullius Cicero was born on January 3, 106 BC, in the Italian town of Arpinum. Though his family was wealthy and of the equestrian order, none of its members had ever served in high political office; for this reason, Cicero was known as *novus homo*, a new man, when he sought the office of consul. Besides being a politician, he was a philosopher and lawyer. He has long been known as Rome's greatest orator. After being proscribed by the Second Triumvirate, he died in exile on December 7, 43 BC.

During the time when Gaius Julius Caesar was dictator, Cicero championed a return to and preservation of the traditional republican government for Rome. After Caesar's death, Cicero made an enemy of Marcus Antonius, against whom he made a series of speeches known as the "Philippics." It was this enmity with Antonius that brought about Cicero's murder.

Interesting Facts: Cicero married a wealthy woman named Terentia when he was twenty-seven years old. They were married for about thirty years. According to Plutarch, Terentia was a strong-willed woman who "took more interest in her husband's political career than she allowed him to take in household affairs."[1] Cicero and Terentia divorced c. 51 BC. Cicero and Terentia had a daughter, Tullia, and a son, Marcus. After the divorce, Cicero married a young girl named Publilia, perhaps for her money. Terentia lived to be 103 years old.

---

1. Elizabeth Rawson, *Cicero: A Portrait*, London: Bristol Classical Press, 2009, 25.

Culture Corner

CICERO AND CATILINE

According to Cicero, who was consul in 63 BC, Lucius Sergius Catiline wanted not only to murder the consul but also to overthrow the government. Catiline advocated *tabulae novae*, a cancelation of debts. Naturally, this idea gained great favor with Rome's impoverished, but did not find favor with conservatives such as Cicero. Gaius Julius Caesar did not speak out against Catiline, and some of Catiline's ideas were put in place by Caesar nearly twenty years after Catiline's death. Cicero, like Sallust writing after him and drawing upon his letters and speeches, dredges up many past crimes he says Catiline committed. He even accused Catiline of murdering his own son. In his second oration against Catiline, Cicero identifies the six groups who, he says, made up Catiline's supporters: wealthy men highly in debt, men in debt who see revolution as a path to power, veterans of Sulla's army who have lived beyond their means, financially strapped men who thought they could solve their problems by joining Catiline, criminals, and the dissolute young men of the city. We have only the words of Cicero and Sallust to go on. Winners, of course, write history; perhaps we shall never know the whole truth about the Catilinarian conspiracy.

This fresco, "Cicero Denounces Catiline," by Cesare Maccari (1840–1919), shows a handsome and young-looking Catiline sitting alone with his head bowed (in the foreground of the painting) being denounced by an old-looking Cicero (the one standing with his hands spread in an oratorical gesture). This picture, along with comments made by many authors, has led many to believe that Catiline was a hot-headed rebellious youth while Cicero was a wiser, cooler-headed, more stable personality. In actually, Cicero was only a little older than Catiline.

Colloquāmur et Scrībāmus!

Be a Roman reporter! Use what you have learned about indirect discourse to write a short report in Latin on an event that has happened recently. This event may have taken place at school or at home. You can interview your friends and family and report what the eyewitnesses observed.

Est Vērum!

Cicero and Catiline were about the same age. They first became acquainted during the social wars when they were serving with Strabo. Taylor Caldwell wrote a novel called *A Pillar of Iron* in 1965 in which she says that Catiline and Cicero were schoolmates. Though it is a wonderfully entertaining novel which shows much research and good knowledge of the period, that particular detail is inaccurate.

Lux fiat.

University of California Berkley, CA

This motto is taken from Genesis 1:3 of the Vulgate: "*Dixitque Deus fiat lux et facta est lux.*"

Chapter 9

- Section 33. Irregular Verb: *Fīō*
  - Present System, Indicative and Imperative
  - Perfect System, Indicative
  - *Fīō*, Subjunctive Mood
- Section 34. Ablatives in Comparative Phrases
  - Ablative of Comparison
  - Ablative of Degree of Difference
- Section 35. Ablative of Respect (Specification)

VOCABULARY

LATIN	ENGLISH	DERIVATIVES
Nouns		
occāsus, -ūs, m.	the setting of the heavenly bodies; the west; fall, destruction (cf. occidō)	
prōvincia, -ae, f.	province	(provincial)
septentriōnēs, septentriōnum, m. pl. (also spelled septemtriōnēs)	the seven ploughing oxen (a constellation); the north	(septentrional)
Verbs		
attingō, attingere, attigī, attāctum	to touch	
commeō, -āre, -āvī, -ātum	to go up and down, to come and go, to visit frequently	
contineō, continēre, continuī, contentum	to hold together, to keep together; to keep in, to surround, to contain	(content)
fīō, fierī, factus sum	to occur, to happen; to be made, to be done	
incolō, incolere, incoluī	to inhabit, to dwell (in) (cf. īncola)	
occidō, occidere, occidī, occāsum	to fall, to fall down	(occasion)
orior, orīrī, ortus sum	to rise	(Orient)

pertineō, pertinēre, pertinuī	to reach, to extend (to)	(pertinent)
praecēdō, praecēdere, praecēssī, praecēssum	to go before, to precede, to surpass	(precedent)
ADJECTIVES, ADVERBS, CONJUNCTIONS, etc.		
fīnitimus, -a, -um, adj.	neighboring, adjacent	(finite)
longus, -a, -um, adj.	long	(long)
longē, adv.	by far	
minus, CpAdv.	less; not very (comparative form of parvus)	
proptereā, adv.	on that account, therefore	
saepe, adv.	often	
undique, adv.	from/on all sides, from everywhere, everywhere	

SECTION 33. Irregular Verb: *Fīō*

Latin has one more irregular verb that you must learn. It is a very common verb you have already seen a number of times in the readings for this book. Latin uses the verb *fīō, fierī* as the passive form of *faciō, facere* in the present system.

Rōmānī Cicerōnem cōnsulem **faciunt**.　　The Romans **make** Cicero consul.
Cicerō ā Rōmānīs cōnsul **fit**.　　Cicero **is made** consul by the Romans.

As the passive form of *facere, fierī* will appear in many of the same uses and idioms in which you have seen *facere*. The indirect command (sometimes called a jussive noun clause) is one such common use.

A. PRESENT SYSTEM, INDICATIVE AND IMPERATIVE

Notice that even though the verb *fierī* may have a passive meaning, it uses the active voice endings in the present system. The endings for the present system are the same as for all regular verbs. What makes this verb irregular is the abnormal infinitive *fierī*. This word ends in an *-ī* instead of the expected *-e* (it is the only passive form in the present system). This irregular verb, however, will form its stem in a normal manner.

second principal part – *rī* = stem
fie/rī = fie

Like the third conjugation, the final *-e-* of the stem is a short, weak vowel. When an ending is added, it drops after the previous *ī* (except in the case of the third-person plural, where it changes to *u*). It forms just like normal third *-iō* and fourth conjugations.

Present Indicative

PERSON	SINGULAR	PLURAL
1	fīō	fīmus
2	fīs	fītis
3	fit	fīunt

Nota Bene:
- Note that the stem *fī-* adds the normal personal endings for the present active even though the meaning is passive.
- The *ī* is long in every person except the third-person singular.
- The patterns for the imperfect and future tenses are similar to those for the third *-iō* and fourth conjugation.
- The first- and second-person plural forms are exceedingly rare and may in fact never be seen in Latin literature.

Present Imperative

Singular	Plural
fī (become!)	fīte (become!)
nōlī fierī (do not become!)	nōlīte fierī (do not become!)

Nota Bene: The imperative of *fīō* is never used except in early poetry.

Exercise 1. Using what you have learned about indicative verb tenses, conjugate the irregular verb *fierī* in the imperfect and future active indicative. (Hint: Check your answers with the grammatical charts provided in appendix B.)

B. Perfect System, Indicative

The verb *fierī* shares the same forms in the perfect system as its counterpart *facere*. Look again at the vocabulary list for this chapter. There you will notice that the entry for *fīō* has only three principal parts and the last of these is *factus sum*. This word is, in fact, the perfect passive of *facere*.

Exercise 2. Give the passive equivalent for the following forms of *facere*. Translate both forms. (Hint: Use *fīō* for the present system.)

Active	Translation	Passive	Translation
faciō	I make	fīō	I am made, I become
facitis			
facit			
faciēs			
faciēmus			
faciam			
faciēbat			
faciēbant			
facere			
fēcit			
fēcistī			
fēceram			
fēcerātis			
fēcerimus			
fēcerint			

C. *Fīō*, Subjunctive Mood

In the subjunctive mood, *fierī* continues to use patterns very similar to that of regular verbs. Once again the irregularity comes in the unusual verb stem found in the second principal part. Look at the forms for the present and imperfect subjunctive. How do these paradigms compare to regular verbs?

Present Subjunctive

Person	Plural	Singular
1	fīāmus	fīam
2	fīātis	fīās
3	fīant	fīat

Imperfect Subjunctive

Person	Plural	Singular
1	fierēmus	fierem
2	fierētis	fierēs
3	fierent	fieret

Nota Bene:

- Note that the present subjunctive vowel pattern is *iā*. This is similar to the *-ia-* found in the present subjunctive of third *-io* and fourth conjugation verbs.
- The pattern for the imperfect subjunctive follows the same as that for all other verbs. The notable difference is that the infinitive *fierī* will change the final vowel to *fiere* to more closely resemble the regular infinitives.
- Just as with the indicative mood, the subjunctive uses the passive forms of *facere* for the perfect passive system.
  - perfect passive subjunctive = *factus sim*
  - pluperfect passive subjunctive = *factus essem*

Exercise 3. Using what you have learned about *fierī* and *facere*, conjugate the perfect passive indicative and the perfect passive subjunctive for these verbs in the masculine gender. Remember, these two verbs will share the exact same chart in the perfect tense. (Hint: Check your answers with the grammatical charts provided in appendix B.)

Exercise 4. Transform the following subjunctive active forms of *facere* into the passive voice, keeping the same person, tense, number, and mood. Do not translate. (Hint: You will use *fiō* in the present system.)

1. faciās
2. faciant
3. faciāmus
4. faceret
5. facerētis
6. facerem
7. fēcerīs
8. fēcerīmus
9. fēcerim
10. fēcissent
11. fēcissēt
12. fēcissētis

Section 34. Ablatives in Comparative Phrases

In *LA2*, you studied how to compare nouns and manner of action in Latin. *Exempli gratia*, what is being compared in these two sentences?

Marcus is taller than Rufus.   Marcus est altior quam Rufus.

Marcus runs faster than Rufus.   Marcus celerius currit quam Rufus.

You learned that every adjective and every adverb has a comparative and superlative degree for this very purpose. Take a moment to review these forms. (A more extensive chart is provided in the reference section in appendix B).

Part of Speech	Positive	Comparative	Superlative
Adjective	laetus, -a, -um	laetior, laetius	laetissimus, -a, -um
	fortis, forte	fortior, fortius	fortissimus, -a, -um
Adverb	laetē	laetius	laetissimē
	fortiter	fortius	fortissimē

Nota Bene:
- *Laetus* shows the forms for first and second declension adjectives. *Fortis* shows the forms for the third declension adjectives.
- Notice that the comparative form for all adjectives declines like a third declension adjective. The superlative form for all adjectives declines like a first and second declension adjective.
- Be aware that the comparative adverb looks just like the neuter singular accusative form of the comparative adjective. (This phenomenon could be considered a development of the adverbial accusative *or* accusative of respect.)

Caveat Discipulus:

There is a set of irregular comparatives that does not follow these rules. Refer to the reference section (appendix B) to review a list of common irregular comparatives.

When reading comparative phrases in Latin, you will soon notice that a number of different ablative constructions often accompany these phrases. The following are some of the most common constructions.

A. Ablative of Comparison

Latin authors sometimes use the adverb *quam* (than) to show comparison between two words appearing in the same case. On other occasions, however, they prefer to use the ablative case instead of the adverb *quam* to show comparison. Compare the following two sentences.

Pater meus est fortior **quam pater tuus**.   My father is braver **than your father**.

Pater meus est fortior **patre tuō**.   My father is braver **than your father**.

Notice that in the second sentence the object that would have followed "than" is now in the ablative case.

B. Ablative of Degree of Difference

Another ablative that you will often see alongside comparisons is the ablative of degree of difference. This ablative shows how much (or to what degree) something differs in the comparison. Common words that appear as degree of difference are *multō* (by much, much), *tantō* (by so much, so much), *paucīs* (by little, few), and *paulō* (by a little more).

Puer celerius quam amīcī **multō** cucurrit.   The boy ran faster than his friends **by much**.
   The boy ran **much** faster than his friends.

The degree of difference may also refer to space or time.

Mīlitēs **parī spatiō** sēparātī sunt.   The soldiers were separated **by an equal space**.

Post eum **duābus diēbus** dōmum advēnistī.   You had arrived home after him **by two days**.

Exercise 5. Identify the underlined ablative constructions. Then, translate the complete sentences.

Caveat Discipulus: More than one construction may appear in a single sentence.

1. Orgetorix <u>multō</u> dīvitior quam aliī Helvētiī erat.
2. Orgetorix erat dīvitior <u>reliquīs Helvētiīs</u>.
3. Helvētiī fortius pugnāvērunt <u>aliīs</u> ē Rōmānīs.
4. Illās prōvinciās duās, proptereā, magnum flūmen <u>minimō</u> sēparāvit.
5. We have sown more grain on the farm (in) <u>this year</u> than [use *quam*] (in) <u>the first year</u>.
6. Do conspiracies occur <u>much</u> more often?
7. Geese are certainly able to jump <u>much</u> higher <u>than pigs</u>.
8. I believe that youth is more eager to wage war <u>than wise old age</u>.

SECTION 35. Ablative of Respect (Specification)

The ablative of respect, or specification, often appears without a preposition to show in what specific respect something exists or something is done. This use of the ablative answers the question "In what respect?" or "In what way?"

Ille fit dux **nōmine** sōlō.	That man became a leader **in name** only.
Puer hic **linguā** celerior quam **mente** est.	This boy is quicker **in tongue** than **in mind**.
Praecēdis omnēs **virtūte**.	You surpass all **in courage**.

Nota Bene: The adjectives *dignus* and *indignus* often appear with the ablative of respect. English best interprets this phrasing with the preposition "of."

Dominus est dignus **omnī honōre et laude**.	The Lord is worthy **of all honor and praise**.

The supine may also show respect when it appears in the ablative case. Remember that the supine is a fourth declension noun formed from the fourth principal part of the verb. It can appear only in the accusative (showing purpose) or the ablative (showing respect). The ablative supine is used to show respect when it appears with adjectives or the nouns *fās*, *nefās*, and *opus est* (the latter meaning "there is need"). There are five such supines that appear commonly in Latin literature: *audītū*, *cognitū*, *dictū*, *factū*, and *vīsū*.

Here are some examples of their use:

Quid nōbīs dictū opus est?	What need is there for us to speak?
horribile vīsū!	horrible to see!*

Nota Bene: With adjectives, the ablative supine often forms a kind of interjection, such as the English "a horrible sight" or "it was awful to look at."

Caveat Discipulus: The ablative supine does *not* take an object.

Exercise 6. Underline and identify the ablative construction in each sentence. Then translate. *Caveat*: You have learned many uses of the ablative case, and a variety of these uses will appear in this passage and in the chapter reading.

Caveat Discipulus: More than one construction may appear in a single sentence.

1. Illī virī reliquōs mīlitēs virtūte praecēdunt.
2. Sōl aureus ab extrēmīs terrae fīnibus oritur.
3. Vīlicus ā villā tribus diēbus aberit ad equum petendum.
4. Sī suēs in arvum illum ēgeris, undique locī nātūrā animālia continēbuntur.
5. Audāciā et vitiō nēmō erat praeclārior istō fūre!
6. Lacus prōvinciam nostram ab illā dīvidit.
7. In ōrātiōne, saepe iactō mē plus frātre.
8. Omnēs populī linguā, īnstitūtīs, et lēgibus inter sē differunt.
9. Vīsum bēstiās in lūdō magnō eāmus! Mīrābile vīsū!
10. Prōvincia fīnitima fīnibus est minora, quod lacus magnōs nōn pertinet.

Exercise 7. Read and discuss the meaning or importance of the following quotations.

1. Brevis ipsa vita est sed malis fit longior. (Publilius Syrus)
2. Dīxitque Deus, "Fiat lux!" Et facta est lux. (Genesis 1:3, Vulgate)
3. Veniat regnum tuum fiat voluntas tua sicut in caelo et in terra. (Pater Noster, Matthew 6:10, Vulgate)
4. Ex nihilo nihil fit. (ancient proverb)
5. Facilius est multa facere quam [unum] diu. (Quintilian)
6. Leve fit, quod bene fertur, onus. (Ovid)
7. Omnia iam fient quae posse negabam. (Ovid)

8. Orator fit, sed poeta nascitur. (ancient proverb)

9. Qui maiora cupit saepe minora capit. (medieval maxim)

10. Quidvis recte factum [est] quamvis humile, praeclarum [est]. (ancient proverb)

11. Nil homine terra peius ingrato creat. (Ausonius)

12. Mirabile dictu! (Vergil)

Before You Read!

ELLIPSIS

Ellipsis is the omission of one or even more words that must be supplied to make a sentence grammatically complete. We could say that the elements of this omission are understood; for example, when we say in English, "Open the door," the subject "you" is understood. In Latin poetry we often see the expression *haec sēcum*, which literally means "these things to himself." We must supply some form of *dīcō* to make the meaning complete. We see this tag as often as we do in Latin because, since Latin has no quotation marks, the writer must in some way indicate to the reader that the speaker has finished talking. The most common word left out is a form of the word *sum, esse, fuī, futūrum*—even if they are part of a periphrasis (a combination of words involving *sum*). For example, *ego peritus* = *ego peritus sum* (I am dead/have died).

How does Caesar use ellipsis in the second line of the reading?

Notice what is understood in the following examples:

    beātī pauperēs spīritū   Happy **are** the poor in spirit.

The verb *sunt* is understood.

    ubi tū Gāius, ego Gāia   Where you **are** Gaius, I **am** Gaia.

Es and *sum* are understood.

Chapter Reading: Reading 1

DĒ BELLŌ GALLICŌ I:I–II

CHARACTERS: Reading 1

Gāius Iūlius Caesar, Gāiī Iūliī Caesaris, m.: author and narrator, the conqueror of Gaul

Belgae, -ārum, m.: the Belgians

Aquitānī, -ōrum, m.: the Aquitanians, a tribe living in modern-day southwest France

Celtae, -ārum, m.: the Celts, several tribes living in and around the northern Pyrenees Mountains

Galliī, -ōrum, m.: Gauls; the Roman name for the Celts (not all of the inhabitants of Gallia)

Germānī, -ōrum, m.: Germans

Helvētiī, -ōrum, m.: the Helvetians, a tribe living in what is today Switzerland

Sēquanī, -ōrum, m.: the Sequani, a tribe of eastern Gaul

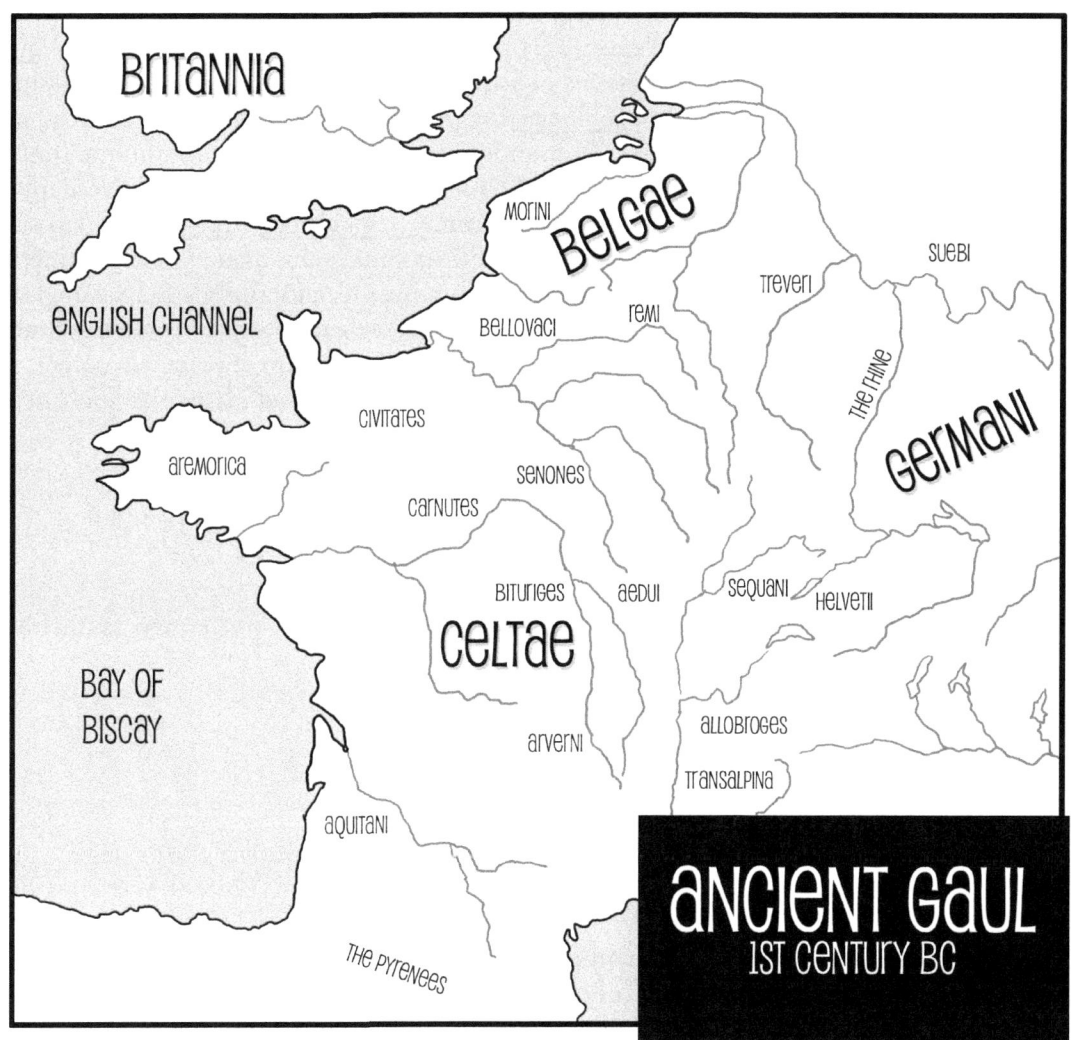

PLACES: Reading 1

Gallia, -ae, f.: Gaul, modern-day France

Garumna, -ae, m.: the river Garonne

Mātrōna, -ae, m.: the river Marne

Sēquana, -ae, m.: the river Seine

Rhēnus: the river Rhine

Rhodanus, -ī, m.: the river Rhone

Ōceanus, -ī, m.: the ocean (usually the Atlantic)

Pȳrēnaeī, -ōrum, m.: the Pyrenees Mountains (between Spain and France)

Hispānia, -ae, f.: the Spanish peninsula, Spain

About This Reading

The complete title of the work from which this chapter's readings are taken is *Commentāriī dē Bellō Gallicō*. The best translation of *commentāriī* is "memoirs"; however, most scholars simply call the work Caesar's *Commentaries*. The Gallic Wars took place approximately between 57 and 51 BC. Caesar composed his work in 52–51 BC. In 71 BC a German king, Ariovistus, had led 15,000 Germans into Gaul at the request of a tribe who wanted help against another tribe. More Germans, about 120,000, emigrated from their territory c. 58. About this same time, the Helvetians, a tribe living around Lake Geneva, set out 368,000 strong. Caesar, as governor of Cisalpine Gaul (mostly in what is today northern Italy, south of the Alps) realized that the Helvetians were going to come into the Province (i.e., Roman territory). Caesar "declared" war on Ariovistus and the Helvetians. Caesar conducted his war at his own expense and without the consent of the Senate, which he should have obtained. More than likely, he wrote his commentaries to justify his actions with the Senate and the Roman people.

I. Gallia est omnis dīvīsa in partēs trēs, quārum ūnam incolunt Belgae, aliam Aquitānī, tertiam quī ipsōrum lingua Celtae, nostrā Gallī appellantur. Hī omnēs linguā, īnstitūtīs, lēgibus inter sē differunt. Gallōs ab Aquitānīs Garumna flūmen, ā Belgīs Mātrōna et Sēquana dīvidit. Hōrum omnium fortissimī sunt Belgae, **proptereā quod** ā cultū atque hūmānitāte prōvinciae longissimē absunt, **minimē**que ad eōs mercātōrēs saepe commeant atque ea quae ad *effēminandōs* animōs pertinent important; proximīque sunt Germānīs, quī trāns Rhēnum incolunt, quibuscum *continenter* bellum gerunt. **Quā dē causā** Helvētiī quoque reliquōs Gallōs virtūte praecēdunt, quod ferē *cōtīdiānīs* proeliīs cum Germānīs contendunt, cum aut suīs fīnibus eōs prohibent aut ipsī in eōrum fīnibus bellum gerunt. Eōrum ūna, pars, quam Gallōs obtinēre dictum est, *initium* capit ā flūmine Rhodanō, continētur Garumnā flūmine, Ōceanō, fīnibus Belgārum, attingit etiam ab Sēquanīs et Helvētiīs flūmen Rhēnum, *vergit* ad septentriōnēs. Belgae ab *extrēmīs* Galliae fīnibus oriuntur, pertinent ad īnferiōrem partem flūminis Rhēnī, spectant in septentriōnem et orientem sōlem. Aquitānia ā Garumnā flūmine ad Pȳrēnaeōs montēs et eam partem Ōceanī quae est ad Hispāniam pertinet; spectat inter occāsum sōlis et septentriōnēs.

Phrases: Reading 1

proptereā quod – because

minimē – (governs the two following verbs connected by *atque*; the *-que* connects the following ideas to the previous, i.e., the larger structures)

Quā dē causā – for this reason

Glossary: Reading 1

Use your "eye" Latin to discern the meanings of the underlined words in the passage.

effēminō, -āre, -āvī, -ātum .... to make womanish, to weaken (Note the contrast here between *effēminō* [*fēmina*] and *virtūs* [*vir*] two lines down.)
continenter, adv. .... continuously
cōtīdiānus, -a, -um .... daily
initium, -ī, n. .... beginning
vergō, -ere .... incline (toward), face
extrēmus, -a, -um .... outermost

RESPONDĒ LATĪNĒ! READING 1

It is neither necessary nor advisable to answer these questions in complete sentences.

1. Quantās in partēs Caesar scrīpsit Galliam dīvidī?
2. Quantīs in rēbus inter sē differēbant Celtae, Belgae, Aquitānī?
3. Quī populus in Galliā erat fortissimus?
4. Quī fīnēs Belgārum saepe nōn inībant?
5. Quī gēns proxima Belgīs est?
6. Quōs Helvētiī virtūte praecēdēbant?
7. Quibuscum Helvētiī ferē cōtīdiānīs proeliīs contendunt?
8. Cūr Helvētiī ferē cōtīdiānīs cum Germānīs contendunt?
9. Cūius ager vergit ad septentriōnēs?
10. Quī fīnēs sunt proximī Hispāniae et Ōceanō?

Chapter Reading: Reading 2

Characters: Reading 2

Orgetorix, Orgetorigis, m.: the noblest and richest Helvetian, chosen to lead the migration

Marcus Messāla, Marcī Messālae, m.: Roman consul

Marcus Pīsō, Marcī Pīsōnis, m.: co-consul with Marcus Messala; an ancestor of Caesar's third wife, Calpurnia

Places: Reading 2

Iūra, -ae, m.: the Jura mountain range

Lacus Lemannus, -ī, m.: Lake Geneva

II. Apud Helvētiōs longē nōbilissimus fuit et *dītissimus* Orgetorix. Is **M. Messalā, [et] M. Pīsōne cōnsulibus** rēgnī cupiditāte inductus coniūrātiōnem nōbilitātis fēcit et cīvitātī persuāsit ut dē fīnibus suīs cum omnibus cōpiīs exīrent—*perfacile* esse, *cum* virtūte omnibus praestārent, tōtīus Galliae imperiō potīrī. Id hoc facilius iīs persuāsit, quod undique locī nātūrā Helvētiī continentur: ūnā ex parte flūmine Rhēnō lātissimō atque altissimō, quī agrum Helvētium ā Germānīs dīvidit; alterā ex parte monte Iūrā altissimō, quī est inter Sēquanōs et Helvētiōs; tertiā lacū Lemannō et flūmine Rhodanō, quī prōvinciam nostram ab Helvētiīs dīvidit. Hīs rēbus fīēbat **ut et minus lātē** *vagārentur* **et minus facile fīnitimīs bellum** *īnferre* **possent; quā ex parte** hominēs bellandī cupidī magnō dolōre *adficiēbantur*. Prō multitūdine autem hominum et prō glōriā bellī atque *fortitūdinis angustōs* sē fīnēs habēre arbitrābantur, quī in longitūdinem mīlia passuum CCXL, in lātitūdinem CLXXX patēbant.

Phrases: Reading 2

M. Messalā, [et] M. Pīsōne cōnsulibus – (Using an ablative absolute with the names of the consuls is a typical way of dating in ancient Roman historiography.)

ut . . . possent – (This is a noun clause that acts as the subject of the verb *fīēbat*): From these things it happened that they roamed not very widely and not very easily were able to bring war upon their neighbors.

quā ex parte – for this reason

Glossary: Reading 2

Use your "eye" Latin to discern the meanings of the underlined words in the passage.

dītissimus, -a, -um, adj. ....richest
perfacilis, -e, adj. ....very easy
cum, conj. ....since (with the subjunctive, *cum* takes on a new function, which will be introduced in section 38)
vagor, vagārī ....to wander
īnferō, -ferre, -tulī, -lātum ....to bring *x* (acc.) to/against *y* (dat.)
adficiō, -ficere, -fēcī, -factum ....to exert influence, to affect, to afflict
fortitūdō, fortitūdinis, f. ....strength, bravery
angustus, -a, -um, adj. ....narrow

RESPONDĒ LATĪNĒ! READING 2

It is neither necessary nor advisable to answer these questions in complete sentences.

1. Quis erat dītissimus apud Helvētiōs?
2. Quī sunt cōnsulēs in hāc fābulā?
3. Quārē facile persuāsit Orgetorix Helvetiīs ut fīnēs suōs exīrent?
4. Quō imperiō Helvētiī potīrī volēbant?
5. Quid dīvidit Helvētiōrum fīnēs ab fīnibus Rōmānōrum?

About the Author

GAIUS JULIUS CAESAR

Gaius Julius Caesar was probably one of the most complex and fascinating men who ever lived. He was born on July 13, 100 BC, and died on March 15, 44 BC. He was from an aristocratic but not wealthy family: although his family claimed descent from the goddess Venus through Aeneas's son Iulus, Caesar grew up in the Subura, one of the least fashionable neighborhoods in Rome. He married four times, his last wife being Calpurnia. He had one daughter, Julia, who was married to Pompey, later called "the Great." Caesar, Pompey, and Crassus had formed the first triumvirate. A brave man, perhaps reckless, Caesar crossed the Rubicon River with his troops in January, 49 BC. This crossing brought civil war to the Republic. He became dictator for life in 47 BC. On the feast of the Lupercal in 44, Marcus Antonius (Mark Antony), a distant cousin of Caesar, three times offered Caesar the royal diadem in public, which Caesar three times refused. In spite of Caesar's refusal of the crown, certain senators thought Caesar too ambitious to live. They murdered him in Pompey's Theater at the beginning of a senatorial session on the Ides of March in 44 BC. Plutarch says the assassins stabbed him twenty-three times. After Caesar's death, Antonius and Lepidus joined with Caesar's chief heir, Octavian—Caesar's great nephew and adopted son—to form the second triumvirate. These three soon had a falling out and civil war ensued again. After the forces of Octavian defeated the forces of Antony and Cleopatra at the Battle of Actium on September 2, 31 BC, Octavian became the sole ruler, later becoming the first emperor of Rome. He was known by the full name Gaius Julius Caesar Octavianus Augustus.

Bust of Gaius Julius Caesar

Derivative Detective

GEOGRAPHY

Typically, when we speak of derivatives we think of English words that derive from Latin origins. However, Latin has derivatives within its own language, too. This chapter introduces some fascinating Latin derivatives for direction. Knowing the origin of these words will help you better understand what they meant to the Romans.

Septentriōnēs (or Septemtriōnēs) = North

derivation: *septem* = seven, *triōnēs* = ploughing oxen

This word refers to the constellations known as *Ursa Maior* (the greater bear) and *Ursa Minor* (the smaller bear). The stars in this constellation resemble the form of a wagon and the oxen that pull it. This constellation is one of the polar constellations, a group of constellations that appear in the sky throughout the year revolving around the North Star. Today, the North Star is known as Polaris and is the tip of the handle of the Little Dipper or *Ursa Minor*. Thus, whenever a Roman looked northward at night, he would have seen the *septentriōnēs*. The name of this group of stars thus became the word for "north."

Oriēns = East

derivation: *orior, orīrī* = to rise

This word is the present participle of the Latin verb meaning "to rise." Thus, it literally means "the rising." It is often used as a substantive adjective meaning "the East," or "the place of the rising sun."

Occāsus = West

derivation: *occidō, occidere* = to fall

This noun is formed from the supine (fourth principal part) of *occidere* (to fall). It therefore literally means "a falling down." It often refers to the falling down or the descending of the heavenly bodies below the horizon. The heavenly bodies always descend to the west.

Auster = South

derivation: *austērus* = harsh, bitter

Auster was the personification of the South Wind in Roman mythology. This hot, dry wind originated in the desert climates of Africa. When the desert wind encountered cooler, wet climates, it could cause harsh storms across the Mediterranean Sea.

These words for the Roman compass have inspired several English derivatives as well. Using an English dictionary, see how many you can find. Remember that an English derivative will have both a similar spelling and a similar meaning to its Latin origin.

Scrībāmus!

Cartography is the science of mapmaking. You can imagine how important it was to Julius Caesar and other Roman generals to have well-drawn maps and excellent descriptions of the regions through which they planned to travel. Try your hand as a cartographer. Using Caesar's description of Gaul as an example, in Latin write up a description of the region in which you live.

Game Time!

NAME THAT COUNTRY

You may have recognized some of the names for the countries Caesar described in the first two chapters of his work about the Gallic Wars. Once upon a time, Rome ruled the entire civilized world. The map was covered with Latin names for all of the countries. For some, these names have carried down through the ages or changed only slightly. Others may seem completely foreign. Draw lines to match the modern country name with the ancient one. Then, locate the country on the map provided and write the correct corresponding letter in the blank provided.

1. Africa _____
2. Aegyptus _____
3. Anglia _____
4. Arabia _____
5. Armenia _____
6. Belgica _____
7. Bithynia _____
8. Bohemia _____
9. Scotia _____
10. Cilicia _____
11. Creta _____
12. Cyprus _____
13. Dacia _____
14. Galatia _____
15. Gallia _____
16. Germania _____
17. Graecia _____
18. Helvetia _____
19. Hibernia _____
20. Hispania _____
21. Hungaria _____
22. Illyricum _____
23. Italia _____
24. Iudaea _____
25. Lusitania _____
26. Macedon _____
27. Numidia _____
28. Persia _____
29. Phoenicia _____
30. Tripolitana _____

Spain
Belgium
Hungary
NE Algeria
NW Turkey
Crete
Arabian Peninsula
Central Turkey
Cyprus
England
Germany
Scotland
Iran
Israel, Palestine
Czech Republic
SE Turkey
Italy
France
Macedonia
Romania
Portugal
Greece
Lebanon
Armenia
Ireland
Tunisia
Switzerland
Egypt
Croatia, Bosnia, Serbia
Libya

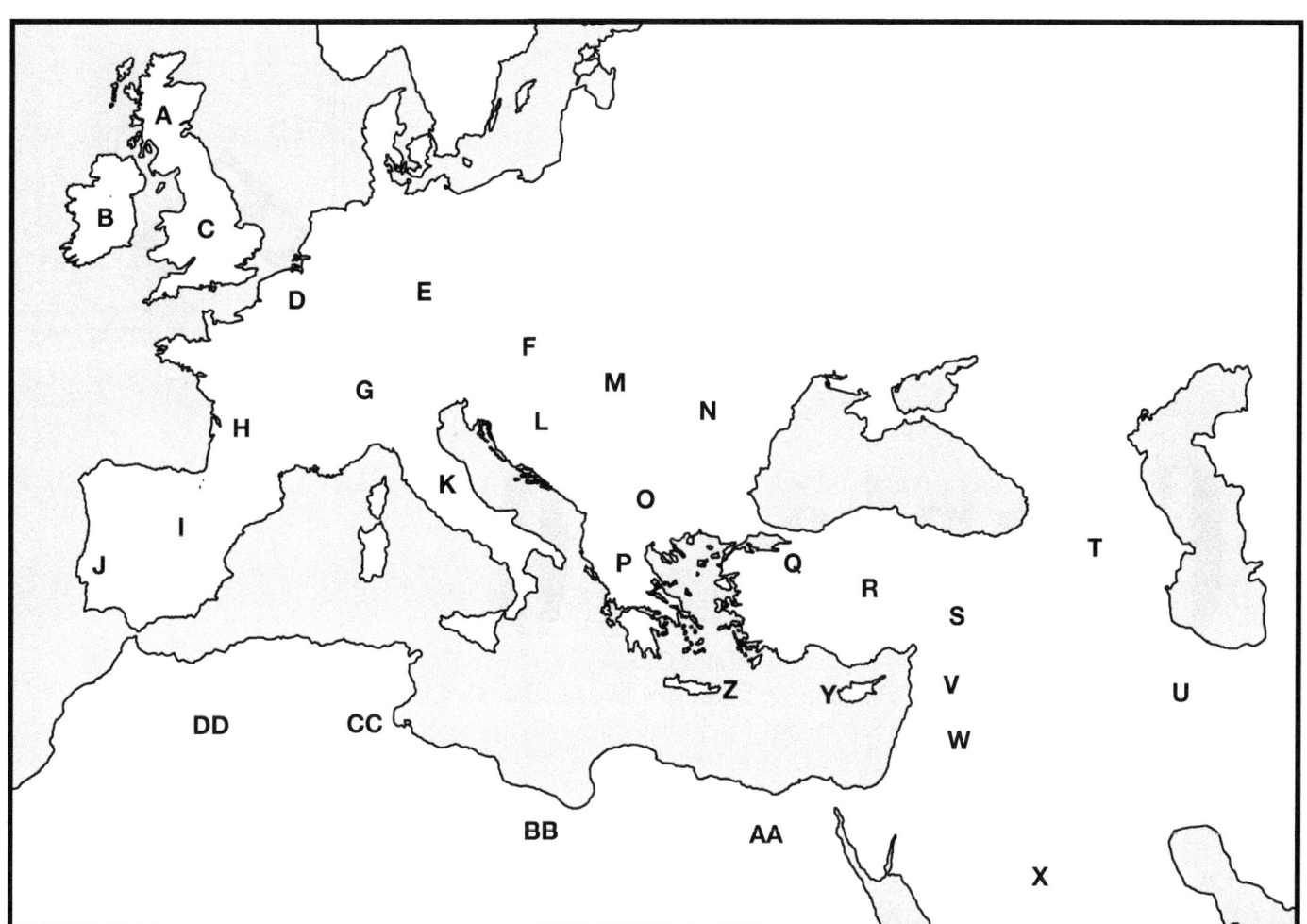

ANAGRAMS

See how many Latin words you can make from the letters in *Gaius Iulius Caesar*. Some examples have been provided to get you started. When you write down the Latin words, be sure to give the English meanings.

        es (you are)   si (if)   ius (law/gravy)   ager (field)   rus (the country)

Leges sine moribus vanae.

The University of Pennsylvania

The University of Pennsylvania's motto is excerpted from Horace (Book 3, Ode 24), "*Quid leges sine moribus vanae proficiunt?*"

Chapter 10

- Section 36. Result Clause
- Section 37. Purpose Clause vs. Result Clause
- Section 38. *Cum* Clauses
  - *Cum* Temporal
  - *Cum* Causal
  - *Cum* Concessive

VOCABULARY

LATIN	ENGLISH	DERIVATIVES
Nouns		
admīrātiō, admīrātiōnis, f.	admiration	(admiration)
clādēs, clādis, f.	destruction	
classis, classis, f.	(in military usage) all of the citizens called to fight; *hence*, the fleet, the army	(class)
cōnspectus, -ūs, m.	sight, view, range of sight	(conspectus)
fremitus, -ūs, m.	a dull, roaring sound	(fremitus)
interpres, interpretis, c.	interpreter, translator	(interpreter, interpretive)
lūdībrium, lūdībriī, n.	mockery	
quīlibet, quaelibet, quodlibet, indef. pro.	anyone you wish, no matter who, whoever	
sors, sortis, f.	a lot, a drawing of lots, casting of lots, fate	(sort, sortilege)
Verbs		
abōminor, abōminārī, abōminātus sum	to hate, to despise	(abomination)
appetō, -ere, -īvī, -ītum	to strive for, to seek	(appetite)
congredior, congredī, congressus sum	to come together	(congress)
conticēscō, conticēscere, conticuī	to be silent	
dīmicō, -āre, -āvī, -ātum	to fight, to contend, to struggle	

laetor, laetārī, laetātus sum (cf. laetus)	to rejoice	
opus est	there is a need, there is a necessity for *x* (dat.) of *y* (abl.); *x* (dat.) has need of *y* (abl.)	
summoveō, summovēre, summōvī, summōtum	to send away, to remove	
ADJECTIVES, ADVERBS, CONJUNCTIONS, etc.		
ēgregius, -a, -um, adj.	distinguished, excellent	(egregious)
inermis, -e, adj.	unarmed	
pār, paris, adj.	equal to, like (+ dat.)	(parity)
singulus, -a, -um, adj. (dis. num.)	separate, single, one at a time	(singular)
magis, CpAdv.	more, to a greater extent, rather	
paulisper, adv.	for a little while	
prope, adv.	nearly, almost	
totiēns, adv.	so often	

SECTION 36. Result Clause

A result clause, as the name implies, indicates the result or the consequence of an action or circumstance. Consider how English writers often express result.

    The students learned their lessons so well that they all excelled on their exam.

    The army fought with such great boldness that they defeated the enemy.

Often English will express result with a dependent clause introduced by "that" and followed by an *indicative* verb. Latin also uses a dependent clause to express result. The conjunction *ut* (often translated as "that") will often signal this dependent clause. While the main verb of the sentence is in the indicative mood, the verb in the result clause is in the *subjunctive* mood. This construction of *ut* with the subjunctive initially looks just like a purpose clause. As you read the examples, note that each main clause in both English and Latin contains an adverb or adjective of degree, such as "so," "so much," "such," and others (*adeō, ita, sīc, tālis, tam, tantus,* etc.). In Latin, result clauses follow the same sequence of tenses as the purpose clause and indirect command (see chapter 6, section 24).

    Exercitus **tālī** magnā cum audāciā pugnāvit **ut** hostem vinceret.

    The army fought with **such** great boldness **that** they defeated the enemy.

Exercise 1. Look carefully at the following sentences. Underline the main clause and double underline (===) the dependent clause in each one. Circle the adjective/adverb of degree in the result clauses.

  1. The students learned their lessons so well that they all excelled on their exam.

  2. The army fought with such great boldness that they defeated the enemy.

  3. Exercitus tālī magnā cum audāciā pugnāvit ut hostem vinceret.

Exercise 2. Underline the result clause in each of the following sentences. Circle any adjectives or adverbs of degree that you see in the main clause. Then translate.

1. Clādēs erat tam magna ut fremitūs in oppidō ūsque tollerentur.
2. Pater tuus est tam plēnus virtūte, māter est tam digna laude, et frāter est tam fortis, pār fortissimō mīlitum, ut laetēris magis quōque diē.
3. Puella totiēns conticēscit ut aliquī habeat eam nōn posse dīcere.
4. Adulēscēns in pugnā dīmicāvit tam fortiter ut cēpisset mox admīrātiōnem omnium quī eum scīvit.
5. Sōl sīc occiderat ut terram attingere vīsus esset.
6. Puer tāle malum fēcit ut nōn licēret eī domum amīcī commeāre.
7. Tantī senātōrēs inībant ut aedificium eōs habēre posset.
8. Sīc fit ut omnēs incolentēs urbem deō precentur.

SECTION 37. Purpose Clause vs. Result Clause

As mentioned previously, grammatically the purpose clause and result clause are very similar. Both use *ut* to introduce a subjunctive clause. Here are three tips to help you distinguish between these two clauses.

1. Purpose clauses will show the result *intended* by the subject in the main clause. Someone is intentionally doing something to bring about or cause a particular result. A result clause, on the other hand, is focused not on the intended, but on the *actual* occurrence. Consider the following sentence containing a result clause:

Exercitus tālī magnā cum audāciā pugnāvit ut hostem vinceret.

Contrast this with the purpose clause:

Exercitus pugnāvit ut hostem vinceret.

Notice the difference between the meaning of the result and the purpose clauses. Sometimes it can be difficult to discern the difference, but a purpose clause expresses *why* something is being done (intended outcome). A result clause, in contrast, expresses the actual outcome.

2. The main clause governing a result clause will usually contain an adverb or adjective of degree. A purpose clause will not. Consider again the following example:

Exercitus pugnāvit ut hostem vinceret.

Notice how this sentence is a purpose clause and thus does not have an adverb/adjective of degree. What key word in the contrasting sentence signals the result clause? What other words have you learned—adjectives and adverbs of degree—that could signal a result clause?

3. *Nē* introduces a negative purpose clause; *ut* + a negative introduces a negative result clause.

Exercitus tam paulā cum audāciā pugnāvit **ut nōn** hostem vinceret.

Exercitus pugnāvit **nē** ā hostibus vincerētur.

Exercise 3. Identify whether the following sentences are showing purpose or result and explain why. Then translate each sentence.

1. Interpres tam male dīxit ut intellegere nōn possēmus.
2. Deus sōlem in caelō posuit ut lūx omnem prōvinciam pertinēret.
3. Fremitus tempestātis tam magnus est ut nōn tē vocantem audīre possim.
4. Cōnspectus exercitūs tam timendus fuit ut fēminae fremitūs ad astra sufferrent.
5. Classis ad oppidum dēfendendum congressus est, nē hostis eōs vinceret.
6. There is a need for watchmen so that the gates may be defended at night.
7. The mother's concern is such that she forbids her son to fight.
8. The army contended against the enemy so that the citizens would not become slaves.
9. We have come together so that we may rejoice with the whole family.

Section 38. *Cum* Clauses

In *LA2*, you learned that dependent clauses can convey a number of ideas, including both time and condition. You have seen that, depending upon the context, these clauses may use either the indicative or the subjunctive mood. There are three such clauses introduced by the adverb *cum*: temporal, causal, and concessive. The subjunctive appears when there is some clear logical connection between the main clause and the subordinate clause (circumstantial, causal, or concessive; compare to the *ablative absolute*, which you learned about in *LA2*, section 60). When the author is only establishing the time, the indicative is used.

A. *Cum* Temporal: "when" (indicative or subjunctive)

When the clause establishes the time when the action takes place, then the indicative mood is used. Note that the time of the main verb and the time of the temporal clause are identical.

Cum nox est, is advenit.	When it is night, he comes.
Cum nox erit, is adveniet.	When it is night, he will come. (the subordinate clause uses a present for the future in English)
Cum nox erat, is advēnit.	When it was night, he came.

Notice how there is no logical connection between the *cum* clause and the main clause; the cum clause just tells you the time of the main action. When, however, this clause is describing the circumstances under which a past action has taken place, the subjunctive mood is used. There may still be an underlying sense of time, but the description of the circumstance will be of greater emphasis. Note carefully the contrast in the following examples.

Cum nox vēnerit, exercitūs discēssērunt.	When night came, the armies departed.
Cum imperātōrēs pācem potītī essent, exercitūs discēdērunt.	When generals had obtained peace, the armies departed.

Notice that the focus of the *cum* clause is on the circumstances surrounding the main verb, not the time.

Cum + present and perfect subjunctive is not called *cum* temporal by grammarians, but general temporal. See the following examples:

Cum nox veniat, dormiō.	When night comes, I sleep. Whenever night comes, I sleep.
Cum imperātōrēs pācem potītī sint, exercitūs discēdunt.	When generals have obtained peace, the armies depart. Whenever generals have obtained peace, armies depart.

Nota Bene: Some of these examples can be interpreted as *causal* or *concessive* (i.e., "Since the generals have obtained peace, the armies depart." See sections 38B and 38C.).

The following is a summary of the most important concepts regarding *cum* temporal:

- *Cum* + indicative indicates the *time* when the main verb has occurred.
- *Cum* + subjunctive can indicate the *circumstances* under which the main verb has occurred.

Exercise 4. Underline the temporal clause. Parse the verb in the temporal clause. Then translate each sentence.

1. Ego in amphitheātrō dīmicābō cum suēs volābunt!
2. Classis oppidum dēfendet cum opus erit.
3. Cum exercitus in prōvinciā illā dīmīcāvisset, cīvēs, quī erant inermēs, clādem urbis metuērunt.
4. Cum tū māiōrum admīrātiōnem accēperis, tum appellāre tē "ēgregium" licēbit.
5. Cum frūctus arbōrum esset parātus, ad torculārem ferēbātur/portābātur.
6. Cum abōmināre dēsistis, amāre vērum līberātus es.
7. Māter multum laetātur cum familia congregātur.
8. Servus suēs in stabulum ēgit cum nox vēnisset.

B. *Cum* Causal: "since" (subjunctive only)

Often *cum* will introduce a clause that is demonstrating the cause of a circumstance or event. In such cases, *cum* is best rendered as "since."

Māter multum laetātur **cum familia totiēns congrediātur**.

C. *Cum* Concessive: "although" (subjunctive only)

A concession (from *concedere*) means, in one sense of the word, "an acknowledgement or an admission." A concessive clause, therefore, will acknowledge or concede a circumstance while still maintaining that the information in the main clause is true. Thus the truth of the main clause is emphasized by this contrast.

Māter tamen multum laetātur **cum familia nōn totiēns congrediātur**.

Nota Bene:
- An adverb such as *tamen* in the main clause will often distinguish a *concessive* clause from a causal or temporal clause.
- A *cum* clause will always contain a subjunctive verb unless the clause is establishing the time when the main clause takes place.

Exercise 5. Underline the *cum* clause in each of the following sentences. Identify whether the clause is temporal, causal, or concessive. Then translate.

1. Cum Caesar vēnit, vīdit, tandem vīcit.
2. Cum vulgus conticēsceret, īra populī tamen maximē audīta est.
3. Ānserēs dominum excitāvērunt, cum fūr nocte appropinquāvit.
4. Cum lūdī in amphiteātrō essent, gladiātōrēs singulī dīmicābant.
5. Iūdex eum summōvit, cum iste iūdiciī lūdībrum fēcisset.
6. The citizen-army kept destruction from the town although the enemy was waging war in the province.
7. When the enemy will have come in sight of the town, attack!
8. Will you not strive for peace since you (pl) hate and fear that general?

Exercise 6. Read and discuss the meaning or significance of the following quotations.

1. Cum tacent, clamant. (Cicero)
2. Nec possum tecum vivere, nec sine te. (Martial)
3. Ut ameris, ama! (unknown)
4. Nullus est liber tam malus ut non aliqua parte prosit. (Pliny the Younger)
   Hint: *prosit* – it is profitable
5. Cum primi ordines concidissent, tamen acerrime reliqui resistebant. (Caesar)
6. Omnia mea mecum porto. (Cicero)
7. Credo ut intelligam. (Augustine)
8. Struit insidias lacrimis cum femina plorat. (Dionysius Cato)
9. In illo viro, tantum robur corporis et animi fuit, ut . . . fortunam sibi facturus videretur. (Livy)
10. Numquam imperator ita paci credit ut non se praeparet bello. (Seneca)
11. Nihil est miserum nisi cum putes. (Boethius)
12. Non ut edam vivo, sed ut vivam edo. (Quintilian)
13. Scripsit Cato . . . numquam se minus esse . . . solum quam cum solus esset. (adapted from Cicero)

Before You Read!

ABLATIVE ABSOLUTE

The ablative absolute, which you learned in *LA2* (see section 60), will appear in the chapter reading that follows. The ablative absolute often consists of a participle modifying a noun or pronoun, both in the ablative case. Because the participle is modifying the noun, it must agree with the noun in number and gender as well as in case. The ablative absolute is grammatically absolute or free from the rest of the sentence, but it is logically connected to the main sentence. It usually sets up or describes the circumstances for the main action of the sentence. There are two frequently used kinds of ablative absolute.

A. PRESENT ACTIVE PARTICIPLE

The present active participle should be translated as happening at a time concurrent with the main verb. The literal translation uses "with," but it is often better to change the participial phrase into a subordinate clause beginning with the conjunctions "when," "since," or "although."

> aurīgā agentī currum
> with the charioteer driving the chariot
> since the charioteer is driving the chariot
> when the charioteer is driving the chariot
> although the charioteer is driving the chariot

B. PERFECT PASSIVE PARTICIPLE

The perfect passive participle should be translated as time prior to the main verb. This means that the phrase "having been ____ed/en" is converted to a clause of its own, "had been ____ed/en" would be used when the main verb is past tense, and "has been ____ed/en" would be used when the main verb is in the present or future tense. The important point to remember is that the translation must clearly indicate that the action of the participle takes place before the action of the main verb. The adverbs "when," "since," and "although" are all acceptable introductions for this construction.

> currō actō ab aurīgā
> with the chariot having been driven by the charioteer
> since the chariot had been driven by the charioteer
> when the chariot had been driven by the charioteer
> although the chariot had been driven by the charioteer

Rewrite the following temporal clauses as ablative absolute phrases.

1. cum ducēs ēgregiī āmissī sint
2. cum sōl oriantur
3. cum cōnspectus appetītus esset
4. cum armātī summōtī essent
5. cum illa prōvincia vitāta erat

Chapter Reading

HANNIBAL SPEAKS TO SCIPIO

Titī Liviī *Ab Urbe Conditā*, XXX.xxx

Characters

Hannibal: a great Carthaginian general during the Second Punic War

Scipio: an up-and-coming Roman general who was much younger than Hannibal

Summōtīs parī spatiō armātīs, cum singulīs interpretibus [Hannibal et Scīpiō] congressī sunt, nōn suae modo aetātis maximī ducēs sed omnis ante sē memoriae omnium gentium cuīlibet rēgum imperātōrumve parēs. Paulisper alter alterīus cōnspectū, admīrātiōne <u>mūtuā prope</u> *attonitī*, conticuēre; tum Hannibal prior: "Sī hoc ita fātō datum erat ut quī prīmus bellum intulī populō Rōmānō, **quīque** totiēns prope in manibus victōriam habuī, **is** *ultrō* ad pācem petendam uenīrem, laetor tē mihi sorte potissimum datum ā quō peterem. Tibi quoque inter multa ēgregia nōn in ultimīs laudum hoc fuerit: Hannibalem cuī tot dē Rōmānīs ducibus victōriam dī dedissent tibi **cēssisse**, tēque huic bellō uestrīs *priusquam* nostrīs clādibus īnsignī fīnem imposuisse. Hoc quoque lūdībrium *cāsūs* ēdiderit fortūna ut cum patre tuō cōnsule cēperim arma, cum eōdem prīmum Rōmānō imperātōre **signa contulerim**, ad fīlium ēius inermis ad pācem petendam ueniam. **Optimum quidem fuerat** eam patribus nostrīs mentem datam ab dīs esse ut et uōs Ītaliae et nōs Āfricae imperiō **contentī essēmus**; neque enim nē uōbīs quidem Sicilia ac Sardinia satis digna pretia sunt prō tot classibus, tot exercitibus, tot tam ēgregiīs āmissīs ducibus; sed *praeterita* magis *reprehendī* possunt quam *corrigī*. Ita aliēna appetīvimus ut dē nostrīs dīmicārēmus **nec** in Ītaliā **sōlum** nōbīs bellum, uōbīs in Āfricā esset; **sed et** uōs in portīs uestrīs prope ac *moenibus* signa armaque hostium uīdistis et nōs ab Carthāgine fremitum castrōrum Rōmānōrum <u>exaudīmus</u>. Quod igitur nōs maximē abōminārēmur, uōs ante omnia optārētis, in meliōre uestrā fortūnā **dē pāce agitur**. Agimus **iī** quōrum et maximē <u>interest</u> pācem esse, et quī *quodcumque* ēgerimus **ratum** cīuitātēs nostrae **habitūrae sunt**: animō tantum nōbīs opus est nōn <u>abhorrente ā quiētīs</u> cōnsiliīs."

About This Reading

In the last two chapters, you read selections by authors writing near the end of the republican period about current events or events of the recent past in the republic. In this chapter, you will read a selection by a writer of the early Imperial period writing about an event near the beginning of the republican period.

Phrases

quīque – and who (not from *quisque*, but from *quī, quae, quod* and *-que*)

is – I am the one who (the repetition of the pronoun emphasizes the subject, which is first-person singular)

cēssisse – (infinitive in indirect statement with the noun *laudum*, which acts kind of like a verb of the head; notice the relative clause separating the two parts of the phrase *cuī . . . dedissent*)

signa contulerim – I have joined battle (lit., "I have brought standards together")

Optimum quidem fuerat – indeed it would have been best

contentī essēmus – (from either *contendō* or *contineō*; perhaps both were meant as a kind of play on words: "so that we would have been contained by/eager for the rule—of Italy for you all and of Africa for us")

nec . . . sōlum . . . sed et – and not only . . . but also

dē pāce agitur – it is being discussed about peace = peace is being discussed *or* we are discussing peace

iī – see the note on *is*

ratum . . . habitūrae sunt – they are about to consider ratified*

*Why do you think Livy used the future participle with *sunt* instead of the future form of *habeō*?

Glossary

Use your "eye" Latin to discern the meaning of the underlined words in the reading.

attonitus, -a, -um, adj.	thunderstruck, astonished
ultrō, adv.	willingly
dī	*deī*
priusquam, adv.	rather than
cāsus, -ūs, m.	event
praeterita, -ōrum, n.	past things
reprehendō, reprehendere, reprehendī, reprehēnsum	to blame
corrigō, corrigere, corrēxī, corrēctum	to set right, to repair
moenia, moenium, n. pl.	walls
quodcumque	whatsoever, whatever

RESPONDĒ LATĪNĒ!

Answer the following questions with the correct Latin word. Make sure that the grammar correctly matches the question.

1. Quid cum ducibus erant?
2. Quis locūtus est prior?
3. Secundum Hannibalem in hāc lectiōne (reading), quis prīmus bellum contrā Rōmānōs intulit?
4. Quis totiēns prope in manibus victōriam habuit?
5. Cūr Hannibal hūc vēnit?
6. Cēpitne Hannibal arma contrā patrem Scīpiōnis?
7. Gessitne Scīpiō arma cum locūtus esset cum Hannibale?
8. Quae rēs magis reprehendī quam corrigī possunt, secundum Hannibalem?
9. Nōnne Poenī (the Carthaginians) exaudīre fremitūs Rōmānōrum castrōrum possunt?
10. Num sunt Poenī quī vidēre arma sua in Rōmānīs castrīs poterant?

About the Author

TITUS LIVIUS

Titus Livius

Titus Livius, whom we call Livy, was born in Patavium, now called Padua, in 59 BC. (As Livy later said in *Ab Urbe Condita* and as Vergil said in the *Aeneid*, the Trojan Antenor had founded Patavium.) Livy studied, as did all Roman boys of his class, Greek and Latin literature and rhetoric. He went to Rome to live and study when he was more than likely in his early thirties. We know that he was a friend of the emperor Augustus, as he implied in Book IV of his great history, by 27 BC. Livy was married to a woman named Cassia, with whom he had at least two sons—Titus Livius Priscus and Titus Livius Longus—and at least one daughter.[1] Livy gloried in the republic, and his writings indicate that he had the same values as Augustus. His great history also appealed to and encouraged the patriotism Augustus was trying to instill in Roman hearts. Livy encouraged the young Claudius, grandnephew of Augustus, to write history. We know that, as an adult, Claudius was a great historian, and it is a pity that his writings have been lost.

Latin Alive! Book 1 featured readings that were inspired by Livy's *Ab Urbe Condita*. Among them was a reading entitled "The Summit Meeting at Zama" in chapter 21 of unit 5. The reading in this chapter is the original text upon which that piece was based. Compare that adaptation from *LA1* to the original text and see how far your reading skills have come. You may also wish to re-read many of the Culture Corner pieces from unit 5 of *LA1* to review the history behind the Punic Wars.

Scrībāmus et Colloquāmur!

AN EPIC SHOWDOWN

We do not know for certain what Scipio and Hannibal actually said in the final moments before the epic showdown at Zama. Livy is writing a historical narrative based on the information he had. Now it is your turn. Imagine two heroes, real or fictional, of equal caliber. If they were to have a conversation mere moments before their final showdown, what would they say? Write your own dialogue, then consider acting it out for your class with a partner. Be sure to include an example of a *cum* clause and a result clause.

The Battle of Zama was fought October 19, 202 BC. This epic battle, which signified a crucial turning point in history, has been the source of inspiration for artists and authors for centuries. Who would be the dominant power of the Mediterranean, Carthage or Rome? While there would be a third and final Punic War between these two powers, many historians consider this battle as the definitive answer to that question of power. Rome won. We know the course of history and the outcome that followed. But what if Hannibal and Carthage had won? What then would have been the outcome? Take this opportunity for a class discussion.

The Battle of Zama by Henri-Paul Motte, 1890

---

[1]. According to B.O. Foster in the introduction to the Loeb Classical Library edition of Livy's *History of Rome*, p. xiii, Seneca the Elder mentions a son-in-law of Livy's.

Terras irradient.
Amherst College, MA

Chapter 11

- Section 39. Conditional Review
  - Simple Present
  - Simple Past
  - Simple Future
  - Future Less Vivid
- Section 40. Contrary-to-Fact Conditionals
  - Present Contrary to Fact
  - Past Contrary to Fact
- Section 41. Doubting Clauses
  - Positive Doubt
  - Negative Doubt

VOCABULARY

LATIN	ENGLISH	DERIVATIVES
Nouns		
āra, ārae, f.	altar	
fortitūdō, fortitūdinis, f.	courage, strength	(fortitude)
obtrectātio, obtrectātiōnis, f.	envious detraction, disparagement	
prūdentia, -ae, f.	knowledge; wisdom, discretion, prudence	(prudent)
puerulus, puerulī, m.	a little boy	(puerile)
Verbs		
addūcō, addūcere, addūxī, adductus (cf. ad + ducere)	to lead to, to bring to, to convey to	(adduct)
cēlō, -āre, -āvī, -ātum	to hide or keep *x* secret	(conceal)
comperiō, comperīre, comperī, compertum	to find out	
dēstituō, dēstituere, dēstituī, dēstitutum	to lose, to leave behind (+ abl. sep.)	(destitute)
dēvincō, dēvincere, dēvīcī, dēvictum	to conquer completely, to overcome, to subdue	
dubitō, -āre, -āvī, -ātum	to doubt, to hesitate	(indubitably)

frūstrō, -āre, -āvī, -ātum (also dep.)	to deceive; to fail, to disappoint	(frustrate)
indigeō, indigēre, indiguī	to need, to want, to lack, to stand in need of (+ gen.)	(indigent)
īnfitior, īnfitiārī, īnfitiātus sum	to not confess, to deny	
proficīscor, proficīscī, profectus sum	to set out, to depart	
ADJECTIVES, ADVERBS, CONJUNCTIONS, etc.		
alius, alia, aliud, adj.	other, another	(alias)
dubius, -a, -um, adj.	doubtful, uncertain	(dubious)
imprūdēns, imprūdentis, adj.	unwise	(imprudent)
anteā, adv.	before, earlier	
velut, adv.	as if, just as if	
priusquam, conj.	before	
quin, conj.	(+ subj. after a negative main clause) that	

SECTION 39. Conditional Review

In chapter 5, we reviewed the form that simple conditions take in Latin. All simple conditions are dependent clauses that use the indicative because the likelihood of the condition taking place is not being questioned.

A. SIMPLE PRESENT: protasis and apodosis – present indicative

Sī studēs, tū bene agis.   If you are studying, you are doing well.
　　　　　　　　　　　　　If you study, you are doing well.
　　　　　　　　　　　　　If you study, you do well.

Nisi studēs, tū bene nōn agis.   If you are not studying, you are not doing well.
　　　　　　　　　　　　　　　If you do not study, you are not doing well.
　　　　　　　　　　　　　　　If you do not study, you do not do well.

B. SIMPLE PAST: protasis and apodosis – imperfect or perfect indicative

Sī studuistī, tū bene ēgistī.   If you studied, you did well.
Sī studēbās, tū bene agēbās.   If you were studying, you were doing well.
Sī nōn studistī, tū bene nōn ēgistī.   If you did not study, you did not do well.
Sī nōn studēbās, tū bene nōn agēbās.   If you were not studying, you were not doing well.

C. SIMPLE FUTURE (FUTURE MORE VIVID): protasis and apodosis – future indicative

Sī studēbis, tū bene agēs.   If you (will) study, you will do well.

Nota Bene: Remember that, in English, subordinate clauses that refer to the future usually use the present tense. This is why there are parentheses around the word "will."

In chapter 5, we also looked at another type of condition called the future less vivid. In contrast to the simple conditions, future less vivid means that there is less certainty about what *may* happen—in fact, it often suggests that the sequence of events will probably *not* happen. This conditional clause therefore uses the subjunctive mood.

D. FUTURE LESS VIVID: protasis and apodosis – present subjunctive

Translate: If ____ should/were to ____, then ____ would ____.

Caveant discipuli: While "then" is used in this sample translation, it may be omitted.

Sī studeās, tū bene agās.   If you should study, you would do well.
                            If you were to study, you would do well.

Now let us take this new idea of using the subjunctive mood in a conditional clause and apply it to two more conditional forms.

SECTION 40. Contrary-to-Fact Conditionals

A contrary-to-fact conditional describes a possibility that is contrary (or opposite) to what is happening now or what has happened in the past. In other words, the reality of the situation is not true. These conditions theorize about what would be happening or what would have happened if a situation were or had been different than it, in fact, is. There are two types of contrary-to-fact conditions: present and past.

A. PRESENT CONTRARY TO FACT: protasis and apodosis – imperfect subjunctive

Translate: "If ____ were ____ing, (then) ____ would be ____ing."

Notice that even though the action seems to have begun in the past, the implications affect the present time. Remember that the imperfect tense is often used to show an incomplete/unfinished action. Thus you will see an imperfect form in Latin (and what appears to be imperfect in English).

Sī studērēs, tū bene agerēs.   If you were studying, you would be doing well.

Implication: You obviously are *not* studying and therefore not doing well right now. The condition, therefore, is contrary to the present fact (that you are not doing well right now).

B. PAST CONTRARY TO FACT: protasis and apodosis – pluperfect subjunctive

Translate: "If ____ had ____ed, (then) ____ would have ____ed/en."

Notice that all of the action is contained in the past tense.

Sī studuissēs, tū bene ēgissēs.   If you had studied, you would have done well.

Implication: You did *not* study and therefore did not do well in the past. The condition, therefore, is contrary to the fact (that you did well). Notice both the condition and the result are completely contained in the past tense.

Nota Bene: There are variations on these conditional formulas at times. For example, the imperative mood is sometimes substituted for the apodosis of the verb. When labeling such sentences, just label the *protasis*.

Sī bene agere vīs, studē!   If you wish to do well, study!

Once you have learned the "formulas" for the conditional sentences, you will find that conditions can be mixed. For instance:

Sī studuissēs, tū bene agerēs.   If you had studied, you would be doing well.

Note how the protasis is *past CTF* (contrary to fact) and the apodosis is *present CTF*. You should be able to identify types of conditions not only at the sentence level but also at the clause level. Regular conditions will be identifiable with one label (e.g., past CTF). Mixed conditions will have to be given a label for each clause (e.g., protasis is past CTF; apodosis is present CTF).

Exercise 1. For each of the following sentences, first identify the tense and mood of the verbs, and then identify the type of conditional. Finally, translate each sentence.

1. Sī fundus oleās habēbit, tum torcular aedificābō.
2. Sī fundus oleās habet, tum torcular aedificābō.
3. Nēmō aurum tuum invēnisset, sī anteā id melius cēlāvissēs.
4. Aedificāre oporteat, sī agrum consitum habeat.
5. Sī amīcē dē Rōmānīs cōgitābis, nōn imprūdenter fēceris.
6. Hostēs istī nōs nōn dēvincerent, nisi exercitus noster fortitūdine et honōre et virtūte et copiīs indigēret.
7. Habeās multum frūctum, sī cōnsereās multās arborēs.
8. Habērēs multōs frūctūs, sī cōnsēvissēs multās arborēs.
9. Sī agricolae cōnsēverant multās arborēs, semper multum frūctum habēbant.
10. Nisi domī cīvium suōrum invidia fīnīvisset, Rōmānī superāre potuissent.
11. Sī hominēs veritātem dīxērunt, puerī eōrum in pāce vīxērunt.
12. Sī modo hominēs fortēs et iūstī terram hanc incolerent, tum nihil metuere necesse esset.

Exercise 2. For each of the following English sentences, identify the tense and mood required for each verb in Latin. Then translate the complete sentence into Latin.

1. If the little boy had hidden himself well, we would not have been able to find him.
2. It is necessary to act wisely, if you wish to be thought wise.
3. You would have certainly overcome, if only you had had a good plan.
4. If he were not ruling so unwisely, he would be the most powerful king of all.
5. If you should come at that time, we would be able to watch the setting of the sun together.
6. If you do not send him away now, the others will surely fight with him.
   Hint: Use *iam* for "now."
7. If you wish to live well, seek peace and despise hatred.

Exercise 3. Read and discuss the meaning or significance of the following quotations. Identify the type of conditional that appears in each quotation.

1. Sī Deus pro nobis [est], quis contra nos [esse potest]? (Romans 8:31)
2. Sī finis bonus erit, totum bonum erit.
3. Sī fractum non est, noli id reficere.
4. Sī minor plus est tum nihil sunt omnia.
5. Sī monumentum requiris, circumspice. (Michigan)
6. Sī post fata venit gloria, non propero.
7. Sī tacuisses, philosophus manisses. (Boethius)
8. Sī tu id aedificabis, ei venient.
9. Sī vis amari, ama. (Seneca)
10. Sī vis pacem, para bellum. (Vegetius)
11. Sī vīveret, verba eius audiretis. (Cicero)
12. Cenabis bene, mi Fabulle, apud me . . . si tecum attuleris bonam atque magnam cenam. (Catullus)

Section 41. Doubting Clauses

A. Positive Doubt

The verb *dubitāre*, when not accompanied by a negative (e.g., *nōn*), is usually followed by an infinitive of indirect statement or by an indirect question which uses the subjunctive mood.

Dubitō tē vērum dīcere.	I doubt that you are speaking the truth.
Dubitō an tū vērum dīcās.	I doubt whether you are speaking the truth.
Dubitāsne ā quō Sex. Roxcius occīsus sit? (adapted from Cicero)	Do you doubt who Sextus Roscius was murdered by?

B. Negative Doubt

When a negative does accompany the main verb (e.g., *nōn dubitō*, "I do not doubt"), *quin* + a subjunctive verb will follow.

| Nōn dubitō quin tū vērum dīcās. | I do not doubt that you are speaking the truth. |
| Nōn dubitō quin hic occīsus sit. | I do not doubt that this man was murdered. |

This same construction also applies to situations in which the negative is implied, though not directly expressed, with a doubting verb.

| Quis dubitat quin malus sīs? | Who doubts that you are evil? (implication is that *no one* doubts) |

Caveat Discipulus: The verb *dubitāre* can also mean "to hesitate." When translated as such, the phrase *nōn dubitō* will commonly be followed by an infinitive. There may be instances of *positive clauses* in which only context will tell you whether it means "doubt" or "hesitate."

Dubitō vērum dīcere.	I hesitate to tell the truth.
Nōn dubitō tibi crēdere.	I do not hesitate to believe you.
Dubitō vērum tē dīcere.	I doubt that you are telling the truth.
Dubitō vērum tibi dīcere.	I hesitate to tell you the truth.
Nōn dubio tē mihi crēdere.	I do not doubt that you believe me.

Exercise 4. Underline the doubting clause in each sentence, and then translate each sentence.

1. Dubitāsne vērum an fūr scelus in iūdiciō prō magistrātū īnfitiētur?
2. Nēmō dubitat quin populus Rōmānus omnēs gentēs virtūte superet.
3. Nōlī dubitāre quin tū vērum amēris.
4. Cīvēs quae ā prīncipe dīcta essent dubitābant.
5. Puerulus cēlāre factum nōn dubitāvit, sed pater omnia comperit.
6. Nōn dubium esse dēbet quin eādem mente sim futūrus.
7. Nōn est dubitāndum quin Hannibal multō cēterōs imperātōrēs prūdentiā praestiterit.
8. Ante āram sacram puer iūs iūrāre nōn dubitāvit, quod pater ēius velut imperātor imperāverat.

Before You Read!

Listed below are several English words with their meanings. Match them to some of the words underlined in the reading and try to determine the correct translations of those Latin words. (Not all words underlined in the reading are used in this exercise. Also, not all words in the exercise are new.)

clandestine = secret, hidden

cupidity = greed, desire

heredity = something left to someone, something inherited

host = victim

incense = a substance which will burn

invidious = jealous, envious

prudence = wisdom

remote = removed, moved away, set apart

segregate = set apart

As you read, you will see that several of the subordinating conjunctions are delayed from where you would expect them in English. Be on the lookout for them.

Chapter Reading

CORNELI NEPOTIS HANNIBAL

Characters

Hannibal: a Carthaginian general

Hamilcar: Hannibal's father

Philip: Philip V of Macedonia, who, according to Livy, formed an alliance with Hannibal in Italy in the summer of 215 BC

Antiochus: Antiochus III, the Great, the sixth ruler of the Seleucid Empire

Hannibal

Philip V of Macedonia

Antiochus III the Great

HANNIBAL, Hamilcaris filius, [erat] Carthāginiēnsis. Sī vērum est, quod nēmō dubitat, ut populus Rōmānus omnēs gentēs virtūte *superārit*, nōn est infitiandum Hannibalem **tantō** praestitisse cēterōs imperātōrēs prūdentiā, **quantō** populus Rōmānus antecēdat fortitūdine *cunctās* nātiōnēs. Nam *quotiēnscumque* cum eō congressus est in Ītaliā, semper discēssit superior. **Quod nisi** domī cīvium suōrum invidiā *dēbilitātus* esset, Rōmānōs vidētur superāre potuisse. Sed multōrum obtrectātiō dēvīcit ūnīus virtūtem. Hic autem velut *hērēditāte* relictum odium paternum *ergā* Rōmānōs sīc cōnservāvit, ut **prius** animam **quam** id dēposuerit, quī quidem, cum patriā pulsus esset et aliēnārum opum indigeret, numquam dēstiterit animō bellāre cum Rōmānīs.

Nam, **ut omittam Philippum**, quem absēns hostem *reddidit* Rōmānīs, omnium hīs temporibus potentissimus rēx Antiochus fuit. Hunc tantā cupidītāte incendit *bellandī* ut ūsque ā *rubrō* marī arma cōnātus sit īnferre *Ītaliae*. **Ad quem cum** lēgātī vēnissent Rōmānī, quī dē eius voluntāte explōrārent darentque *operam*, cōnsiliīs clandestīnīs ut Hannibalem in suspīciōnem rēgī addūcerent, tamquam **ab ipsīs corruptus alia atque** anteā sentīret, neque id frūstrā fēcissent idque Hannibal comperisset sēque ab interiōribus cōnsiliīs sēgregārī vīdisset, tempore datō adiit ad rēgem, eīque cum multa dē fidē suā et odiō in

Chapter 11

Rōmānōs *commemorāsset*, hōc adiunxit: "Pater meus," inquit "Hamilcar **puerulō mē**, *utpote* nōn **amplius**[1] IX **annōs** nātō, in Hispāniam imperātor proficīscēns Carthāgine, Iovī optimō maximō hostiās *immolāvit*. Quae dīvīna rēs dum cōnficiēbātur, quaesīvit ā mē, vellemne sēcum in castra proficīscī. Id cum libenter accēpissem atque ab eō petere *coepissem*, nē dubitāret dūcere [mē illūc], tum ille "Faciam," inquit "sī mihi fidem, quam postulō, dederis." Simul mē ad āram addūxit, apud quam sacrificāre īnstituerat, eamque cēterīs remōtīs tenentem iūrāre iussit numquam mē in amīcitiā cum Rōmānīs *fore*. Id ego iūs iūrandum patrī datum ūsque ad hanc aetātem ita conservāvī, ut nēminī dubium esse dēbeat, quīn reliquō tempore eādem mente sim futūrus. Quārē, **sī quid** amīcē dē Rōmānīs cōgitābis, nōn imprūdenter fēceris, sī mē *cēlāris*; cum quidem bellum parābis, tē ipsum *frūstrāberis*, sī nōn mē in eō prīncipem posueris."

Phrases

tantō . . . quantō – by so much . . . as much as; just as much . . . as

eō – them (This pronoun refers to *populus* and may therefore be translated as plural.)

Quod nisi – but if not, but unless (before conditions, *quod* often expresses a contrast: but)

prius . . . quam – *priusquam* (This is an example of tmesis, the placement of one or more words in between the parts of a compound word.)

prius animam quam id dēposuerit – literally, he put aside earlier his breath (i.e., died) than [he put aside] it (i.e., his hatred for the Romans)

ut omittam Philippum – to pass over Philip (sometimes the main clause governing the purpose clause may need to be supplied; in such cases, the English will often use the participle: passing over Philip)

Ad quem cum – *et cum ad eum* (Often the relative pronoun beginning a sentence is equivalent to a personal pronoun preceded by *et*. This is called a connective relative pronoun. These are often followed directly by another word of subordination, such as *cum*. The *cum* clause extends four lines to *vīdisset*. There are a few embedded subordinate clauses in this sentence, so be sure to distinguish between the different clauses. The verbs subordinated under *cum* can be translated by repeating "when" in order to keep the English sounding better and to help remember which verbs go with which clauses.)

ab ipsīs corruptus – having been seduced by they themselves (i.e., the Romans)

alia atque – other things than (with certain adjectives *atque* can mean "than, to, from")

puerulō mē – when I was a little boy (lit., "with me as a little boy")

amplius IX annōs – more than nine years [old] (Notice the lack of *quam* or the ablative case, to express the idea of "than." This often happens when a comparative is used with a word of number or measure. The word "than" is implied.)

sī quid – *sī aliquid*

Caveat Discipulus: The pronoun *aliquis* will drop its prefix when preceded by certain adverbs. Here is a helpful mnemonic to remember this rule of syntax: After *sī*, *nisī*, *num*, and *nē* all the *ali*'s go away!

Glossary

Use your "eye Latin" to discern the meanings of the words underlined in the passage.

superārit .... *superāverit* (syncopated perfect subjunctive)
cūnctus, -a, -um, adj. .... all
quotiēnscumque .... however often/as often
dēbilitō, dēbilitāre, dēbilitāvī, dēbilitātum .... to weaken, to lame (debilitating)
hērēditās, hērēditātis, f. .... inheritance
ergā + acc. .... against
omittō, omittere, omīsī, omissum .... to omit, to leave out; to let go
reddidit .... rendered, caused to be

---

[1]. The word *quam* is omitted with this comparative because *amplius* and a few other comparatives omit *quam* and keep the same case after the comparative as before the comparative with a word indicating number or measure.

bellō, bellāre	to wage war (cf. *bellum*)
ruber, rubra, rubrum	red
Ītaliae	to Italy (*īnferō* can take a dative of direction; ordinarily, for other verbs, the dative of direction is used only in poetry)
opera, -ae, f.	assistance, service
commemorāsset	had mentioned, had reminded of, had recounted (a syncopated form of *commemorāvisset*)
utpote	namely, in as much as, since, in so far as (justifies something about the main clause—here, the fact that he says he was a little boy)
immolō, -āre, -āvī, -ātum	to sacrifice
coepī*	begin
fore	*futūrum esse* (a future active infinitive of *sum* in indirect statement)
iūs iūrandum	an oath
nēminī	to nobody
cēlāris	*cēlāveris* (syncopated future perfect)
frūstror, frūstrārī, frūstrātus sum	to disappoint, deceive, trick (frustrate)

*Coepī is a defective verb. A defective has no Latin present system forms. Usually, then, the perfect tense *coepī* is translated with the English present tense.

RESPONDĒ LATĪNĒ!

Answer each question with a Latin word or phrase. Be sure that your answer is grammatically correct. The case of a noun in your answer may not be the same as it appears in the previous paragraphs.

1. Quis est pater Hannibalis?
2. Quid nēmō dubitat dē Rōmānīs virtūte?
3. Cum Hannibal ergā Rōmānōs pugnāvit, quis erat superior?
4. Quī invidiam ad Hannibalem habuērunt?
5. Ergā quōs cōnservābat Hannibal odium?
6. Quem absēns Hannibal hostem Rōmānōrum fēcit?
7. Quis erat tum potentissimus rēx?
8. Quis ā cēterīs sēgregātus clandestīnīs cōnsiliīs est?
9. Hamilcar dēsīderāvit Hannibalem ad quem locum proficīscī?
10. Quam rem tenet Hannibal cum iūs iūrandum patrī dat?
11. Quō Hannibal cum patre profectus est puerulus?

About the Author

CORNELIUS NEPOS

Cornelius Nepos, a biographer, was born in Hostilia, in Cisalpine Gaul, about 100 BC. This village is not far from modern-day Verona, the setting of William Shakespeare's *Romeo and Juliet*. Nepos was a friend of Catullus, who dedicated a book of his poems to him (see *Catullus* I:3). He was also friends with Cicero and Atticus. He is noted for the simplicity of his writing style. His only surviving work is the *Excellentium Imperatorum Vitae* (*Lives of Excellent Commanders*). He died in 24 BC.

Culture Corner

THIRD PUNIC WAR

Hannibal swearing hatred to Rome

The Third Punic War occurred between 149 and 146 BC. It was the last of the wars between the Romans and the Carthaginians, whom the Romans called *Poeni* because Carthage was originally a colony of Phoenicia, which was roughly where Lebanon is today. The first two Punic Wars were both longer and fiercer than the third; indeed, the only major battle of the third war was the Battle of Carthage, a battle resulting in the complete destruction of that city and in the sowing of the lands round about with salt so that the people could never again farm in that vicinity. At the end of the Third Punic War, Carthage no longer enjoyed an independent existence.

In reality, Carthage had enjoyed little, if any, independence between the Second and Third Punic Wars. The peace treaty at the conclusion of the Second Punic War stipulated that border disputes involving Carthage had to be decided by the Roman Senate. It was, incidentally, about this time that Cato the Elder kept ending speeches with *Carthago delenda est*. The Carthaginians were not able to retire their debt to the Romans until 151 BC. The Carthaginians believed that the payment in full of the debt meant that the peace treaty was no longer valid. The Romans disagreed. The Romans had, in fact, been keeping the peace so that there would be no interruptions in the payment of the debt. Rome was growing rapidly at this time, with a population of an estimated 400,000 people. All these people had to eat, and maintaining a food supply was both a problem and a burden. And so the Romans wanted the farmlands around Carthage.

In 151 the Numidians invaded Carthage and soundly defeated the Carthaginians, who then had to pay huge indemnities to Numidia for the next fifty years. Rome declared war on Carthage in 149. The Carthaginians tried to appease the Romans, even sending well-born children as hostages because the Romans said they would allow Carthage to keep its lands and independence if the Carthaginians would send hostages. Carthage and Utica had been allied against Rome; but, when Utica defected to Rome, 80,000 Roman soldiers came there to Utica. It was then that the Roman consuls demanded surrender of all weapons. They also insisted that the Carthaginians withdraw from Carthage and further told the Carthaginains that they would burn the city. When the Carthaginians heard this threat, they abandoned negotiations with the Romans. The Romans immediately besieged Carthage. The Third Punic War had begun. After three years of siege, during which the Carthaginians fought bravely, Scipio Aemilianus, later called Africanus because he had conquered Africa, took the city by storm.

Statue of Hannibal in Carthage

Est Vērum!

Hamilcar Barca and his sons established what became a thriving Carthaginian province in the land of Hispania (modern-day Spain). Hamilcar established the port city of Barcino, named for his Barcine clan, and the capital city of Carthago Nova (New Carthage). These cities remain today as Barcelona and Cartagena, respectively.

Major animi est voluptas quam corporis.
LaGrange College, GA.

Chapter 12

- Section 42. Clauses of Fearing
- Section 43. Genitive and Ablative of Quality (or Description)

VOCABULARY

LATIN	ENGLISH	DERIVATIVES
Nouns		
argūmentum, -ī, n.	indication, representation	(argument)
artifex, artificis, m.	workman, artisan	(artificer)
cacūmen, cacūminis, n.	extremity, peak	
cubitum, -ī, n.	elbow; cubit (distance in length from elbow to the end of the middle finger)	(cubit)
effigiēs, effigiēī, f.	symbol	(effigy)
latus, lateris, n.	side	(lateral)
longitūdō, longitūdinis, f.	length, height	(longitude)
obeliscus, -ī, m.	obelisk	(obelisk)
pondus, ponderis, n.	weight, burden	(ponder)
portus, portūs, m.	port, harbor	(port)
radius, -ī, m.	rod, ray	(radius)
Verbs		
adservō, -āre, -āvī, -ātum (cf. ad + servāre)	to watch over, to keep, to guard	
excīdō, excīdere, excīdī, excīsum (cf. ex + caedere)	to hew out, to cut out	(excise)
mergō, mergere, mērsī, mērsum	to plunge, to sink; to immerse, to submerge	(submerge)
timeō, timēre, timuī	to be afraid, to fear	(timid)
vehō, vehere, vexī, vectum	to carry, to convey	(vehicle)
vereor, verērī, veritus sum	to fear, to be afraid	
Adjectives, Adverbs, Conjunctions, etc.		
dīvus, -a, -um, adj.	divine	(divinity)
perpetuus, -a, -um, adj.	continuous, entire	(perpetual)

Section 42. Clauses of Fearing

When a verb of fearing introduces an action in which the subject does not want to be involved, a complementary infinitive is used. This is a simple construction, which you have seen many times before.

> Mīlitēs hostēs pugnāre nōn timent.
>
> Verēmur perīre.

Another construction of fear, the fear clause, introduces what one is concerned will happen (rather than what one does not want to do). Consider the difference between "I am afraid to do this" and "I am afraid that I will do this." In the first sentence, the person is hesitant to engage in an action (complementary infinitive). In the second, the person demonstrates concern that he/she may actually end up engaging in an action (fear clause). The fear clause does not express what someone is contemplating doing, but what may or may not happen. A fear clause is introduced by a word of fearing or danger (usually a verb) and begins with *nē* or *ut* plus a verb in the subjunctive mood. When introduced by *nē*, the clause is positive, stating what is to be feared. In such instances, *nē* is best rendered in English as "that" or "lest." The latter is often seen in English prose.

Timeō nē inimīcus tibi nocuerit.	I fear that the enemy has harmed you.
Timeō nē inimīcus tibi noceat.	I fear lest your enemy should harm you.
	I am afraid that your enemy will harm you.

When introduced by *ut* or by *nē nōn*, the fearing clause is negative, stating what is feared will *not* happen. These conjunctions are best rendered as "that not."

Timēbam ut inimīcus eī nocēret.	I was fearing that the enemy would not harm him.
Timuī nē nōn inimīcus eī nocuisset.	I feared that the enemy had not harmed him.

Exercise 1. Underline the fearing clause in each sentence. Then, identify whether it is positive or negative. Finally, translate each sentence.

Hint: There is not a future subjunctive. The future indicative is represented by the Latin present subjunctive in a fear clause.

1. Ōrātor timet nē argūmentum senātuī nōn persuādeat.
2. Nautae metuērunt nē aqua latera nāvis perfunderet.
3. Monte ērumpente populus verētur nē urbs incendiō cōnsumpta sit.
4. Vīlicus timuit ut servus gregem per noctem perpetuam adservāret.
5. Cum vīgilia oppidum adservāret, populus numquam metuēbat nē salūs in perīculō esset.
6. Nōlī timēre nē mōnstrum in cellā cēlet. Pāter tē adservābit!
7. Are you (s.) afraid that the ship may be immersed in the sea?
8. The artisan fears that the obelisk will not please the king.
9. We feared that the men would not sustain the weight of the obelisk.
10. Oh miserable me! I fear gravely lest the huge weight of the obelisk should fall onto the artisans!

Exercise 2. Underline the *ut* clause in each of the following sentences, and identify the type of clause. Translate each sentence.

1. Obeliscus tam altus erat ut vidēre cacūmen nōn possem.
2. Prīnceps iūssit ut nāvis magna aedificētur ut obeliscī Rōmam veherentur.
3. Artificēs aliquot per annōs labōrābunt ut monumentum ingēns rēgī faciant.
4. Cum tempestās sūrgat, nautae verentur ut nāvis salūtem portūs accēdāt.
5. Timet nē rēx suum fīlium in cacūmine obeliscī posuerit. Horribile dictū!
6. Radiī sōlis suprā terram Aegyptī ut artifex effigiem in lapide excīdat refulgent.
7. Rēx magnus et potēns timet ut memoria sua perpetuōs annōs maneat.
8. Interpretēs ut argūmenta multa in obeliscō vetere legerent congressī sunt.
9. Rēx imperāvit ut tū, ō artifex, effigiem in lapide rubrō obeliscī excīdās.
10. Cum eum dīcere vērē semper sciāmus, timēmus tamen ut haec fābula vēra sit.

Exercise 3. Read and discuss the meaning or significance of the following quotations.

1. Crudelius est quam mori semper timere mortem. (Seneca)
2. Cotidie damnatur qui semper timet. (Publilius Syrus)
3. Nemo timendo ad summum pervenit locum. (Publilius Syrus)
4. Multi famam, conscientiam pauci verentur. (Pliny the Younger)
5. Stultum est timere quod vitare non potes. (Publilius Syrus)
6. Illud utinam ne vere scriberem. (Cicero)
7. Quod sentimus, loquamur; quod loquimur, sentiamus: concordat sermo cum vita. (Seneca)
8. Timeo ne aliud credam atque aliud nunties. (Terence)
9. Qui dedit beneficium taceat; narret qui accepit. (Seneca)
10. Est autem fides credere quod nondum vides; cuius fidei merces est videre quod credis. (Augustine)

SECTION 43. Genitive and Ablative of Quality (or Description)

Another means to indicate character or quality is through the genitive or ablative of quality, sometimes called description. A noun and modifying adjective in one of these two cases may modify another noun in order to indicate character or quality. The ablative of description is commonly used when describing a physical trait. The genitive of quality often appears with numbers to describe measurement.

> Rēx erat vir pietātis magnae.
>
> Fīlium animō celerī habēs.

Exercise 4. Underline and then translate the descriptive phrase in each sentence. Include the genitive or ablative of description along with the noun it is describing.

e.g., Discipulī <u>magistrum maximae prūdentiae</u> habent.

  a teacher of greatest wisdom

1. Rōmae vīdimus obeliscum cubitōrum multōrum longitūdine.
2. Artifex statuam effigiē simillimā rēgī creābit.
3. Īra deae erat causa tantī dolōris Trōiānīs.
4. Gentēs Āfricae, populōs ferōcis artis bellō, magnopere timēmus.
5. In lapide octō radiōs trium cubitōrum excīdī.
6. The first obelisk with rays hewn out of the rock stood near the harbor.
7. A man of great wisdom we will deem worthy to rule our city.
8. We have established walls of greatest strength, which are able to defend us.
9. A citadel with very high walls cannot easily be overcome.

Exercise 5. Translate the following famous quotations into Latin.

1. We have nothing to fear, but fear itself. (Roosevelt)
2. Always do what you are afraid to do. (Emerson)
3. You need a bigger boat. (Martin Brody, paraphrased)
4. In time we hate that which we often fear. (Shakespeare)
   Hint: Translate "in time" as "finally."
5. A woman is the only thing I am afraid of that I know will not hurt me. (Lincoln)
   Hint: The indirect statement will need a future infinitive.
6. Why so serious? (the Joker)
7. I fear we have awakened a sleeping giant. (Admiral Isoroku Yamamoto, paraphrased)
8. Say "hello" to my little friend! (Tony Montana)

Before You Read!

DISTRIBUTIVE NUMBERS

In chapter 10, you learned the distributive number *singulī, -ae, -a*, meaning "single" or "one at a time." Distributive numbers decline as first and second declension adjectives, but in the plural only as they are always referring to a group. Poets often liked to use distributive numbers instead of the cardinal forms when talking about sets of numbers. Pliny will use them in the following passage when describing measurements. If you look carefully at the stem, you can usually discern the number signified. Use the number table in the reference section of this book (appendix B) to help you identify the following numbers.

quaternī (= quattuor)

quādrāgēnum = quādrāgēnōrum (= quādrāgintā)

octōnum = octōnōrum (= octō)

ūndēnīs (= ūndecim)

bīnum = bīnōrum (= duo)

Nota Bene: Poets also liked to use the ancient genitive plural ending *-um*, still seen in the third declension. Pliny makes a stylistic choice to use this same ending as well with his measurements. As you read, watch closely for the noun that the distributive adjective modifies. They will agree in case, number, and gender.

Chapter Reading

PLINY THE ELDER, *NATURALIS HISTORIA*

(With Some Emendations to Aid in Reading and Understanding)

Liber XXXVI, Caput XIV

Book 36, Chapter 14

Obeliscī Aegyptī

Trabēs ex eō <lapide>[1] fēcēre rēgēs quōdam certāmine, obeliscōs vocantēs Sōlis nūminī *sacrātōs*. Radiōrum ēius argūmentum in effigiē est, et ita significātur nōmine Aegyptō. Prīmus omnium id īnstituit *Mespheres*, quī rēgnābat in Sōlis urbe, somniō iussus; hoc ipsum <u>īnscrīptum</u> <est> in eō, *etenim sculptūrae* illae effigiēsque quās vidēmus Aegyptiae sunt litterae.

---

[1] The triangular brackets (<>) throughout the text indicate words that the editor has added to help you make sense of the text.

Posteā *et* aliī excīdēre rēgēs. Statuit eōs in suprā dictā urbe *Sesothes*, quattuor numerō, **quadrāgēnum octōnum** cubitōrum longitūdine. *Rhamsesis* autem, quō regante *Īlium* captum est, CXXXX cubitōrum <ūnum surrēxit>. Īdem, . . . <mōlientibus> *dīgrēssīs inde*, ubi fuit *Mnēvidis* rēgia, posuit alium, longitūdine quidem CXX cubitōrum, **sed <u>prōdigiōsā</u>** *crassitūdine*, **ūndēnīs per latera cubitīs**.

Opus id fēcisse dīcuntur [= $\overline{\text{CXX}}$ mīlia] hominum. Ipse rēx, cum surrēctūrus esset verērēturque nē <u>māchinae</u> ponderī nōn *sufficerent*, **quō māius** perīculum cūrae artificum *dēnūntiāret*, fīlium suum *adalligāvit* cacūminī, ut salūs ēius apud *mōlientēs prōdesset* et lapidī. **Hāc <u>admīrātiōne</u> operis** effectum est ut, cum oppidum id *expugnāret* Cambȳsēs rēx **ventumque esset** incendiīs ad *crepīdinēs* obeliscī, **extinguī iubēret** *mōlis* <u>reverentiā</u> quī nūllam <reverentiam> habuerat urbis.

. . . . .

Et aliī duo sunt Alexandrēae ad portum in Caesāris templō, quōs excīdit Mesphres rēx, **quadrāgēnum bīnum** cubitōrum. Super omnia accēssit <u>difficultās</u> marī Rōmam *dēvehendī*, spectātīs *admodum* nāvibus. Dīvus Augustus eam, quae *priōrem advexerat*, <u>mīrāculī</u> grātiā *Puteolīs* perpetuīs *nāvālibus dicāverat*; incendiō *cōnsumpta* ea est. Dīvus Claudius <alteram nāvem> aliquot per annōs adservātam, quā C. Caesar *inportāverat*, omnibus quae umquam in marī vīsa sunt mīrābiliōrem, in ipsā turribus *Puteolīs* ē pulvere *exaedificātīs*, perductam Ostiam portūs grātiā mērsit.[2]

Phrases

quadrāgēnum octōnum (genitive) – forty-eight

sed <u>prōdigiōsā</u> *crassitūdine* **ūndēnīs per latera cubitīs** – but [it was] of a marvelous girth/width/thickness (ablative of description) since there were eleven cubits on each side (ablative absolute; notice how this sentence is set up differently than the other measurements, such as *longitūdine* . . . CXX cubitōrum, which consist of an ablative of specification followed by a genitive of description/measure— "[an obelisk] of 120 cubits in length.")

quō māius – by which more . . . he might threaten (sometimes a purpose clause is introduced by a relative pronoun + subj.)

Hāc <u>admīrātiōne</u> operis – because of the admiration of this work *or* because the work was so admirable (abl. of cause)

ventumque esset – when they [the soldiers] had come (lit., "when it had been come"—Latin often uses the passive of certain intransitive verbs for a generic subject of a verb such as "they say," "they came," "they went" [*fertur, ventum est, itum est*]. English does not allow passives of intransitive verbs.)

effectum est ut . . . extinguī iubēret – it came about that . . . he ordered [it] to be extinguished (the *ut* clause is a noun clause that acts like the subject of the verb *effectum est*. It answers the question "What was effected?")

quadrāgēnum bīnum (genitive plural) – forty-two

Glossary

Use your "eye" Latin to discern the meaning of the underlined words in the reading.

trabs, trabis, f.	beam
sacrāre	*cōnsecrāre*
Mespheres	Mespheres, the name of a pharaoh of Egypt from the mid-second century BC.
etenim	*et enim*
sculptūra, -ae, f.	cutting, engraving
et	even (sometimes *et* is used as an adverb rather than a conjunction)

---

2. Pliny the Elder, *Naturalis Historia*, Liber XXXVI, Caput XIV, Book 36, Chapter 14, input by Bill Thayer, last modified July 2006, <http://penelope.uchicago.edu/Thayer/L/Roman/Texts/Pliny_the_Elder/36*.html>.

Sesothes	Sesothes, an ancient pharaoh of Egypt
Rhamsesis	Rhamses/Ramses, an ancient pharaoh of Egypt in the mid- to late second millenium BC.
Īlium, -ī, n.	Troy (cf. Iliad)
dīgredior, dīgredī, dīgressus sum	to depart
inde, adv.	from there, from the place
Mnēvis, Mnēvidis, m.	Mnevis, an Egyptian bull-deity worshipped at Heliopolis (Greek for Sun City)
crassitūdinō, crassitūdinis, f.	thickness
ūndēnī, -ae, -a, dis. num.	eleven
sufficiō, sufficere	to be sufficient
dēnūntiō, -āre, -āvī, -ātum	to threaten
adalligō, -āre, -āvī, -ātum	to bind, to fasten
mōlior, mōlīrī, mōlītus sum	to exert oneself, to labor, to strive, to work
prōsum, prōdesse	to benefit, to be of benefit or service
expugnō, expugnāre, expugnāvī, expugnātum	to take by assault, to storm (cf. *ex + pugnare*)
crepīdō, crepīdinis, f.	pedestal, base, foundation (of masonry)
extinguō	*exstinguō*
dēvehere	*dē + vehere*
admodum, adv.	to the limit, in a high degree (cf. *ad + modum*)
prior, priōris, CpAdj.	the former, first
advehere	*ad + vehere*
Puteolī, -ōrum, m.pl.	Puteoli, an important commercial city on the coast of Campania, considered a popular resort for the Romans
nāvālia, nāvālium, n.	dockyard, a place for construction and repair of ships
dicō, -āre, -āvī, -ātum	to proclaim, to dedicate (cf. *dīcere*)
inportō (also *importō*) *-āre, -āvī, -ātum*	to bring from abroad
exaedificō, -āre, -āvī, -ātum	to build up

RESPONDĒ LATĪNĒ!

1. Quō obeliscī esse sacrātōs dicitur?
2. Quis prīmum obeliscum instituit?
3. Quis Aegyptum regnābat cum Īlium captum est?
4. Cūr Cambȳsēs rēx nōn incendī obeliscum iussit?
5. Quōmodō Augustus duos obeliscōs Rōmam tulit?

About the Author

PLINY THE ELDER (GAIUS PLINIUS SECUNDUS, AD 23–79)

Pliny the Elder lived through some of the most turbulent of times for the Roman Empire. He witnessed firsthand the reign of terror under Caligula and then under Nero. During that time, he served in the Roman military, forming a lasting friendship with Vespasian, the future emperor. The German campaigns prompted him to write his first notable work, entitled *History of the German Wars*, but his *magnum opus* would come years later as a history of a different sort. His highly regarded *Historia Naturalis* thus became an encyclopedic work on astronomy, botany, geology, zoology, and other natural sciences. Pliny recorded not only the nature of these elements but also the purposes for which men used them. The passage contained in this chapter comes from his research on stones and their uses. The

Historia Naturalis is the first known work of its kind. For its vast wealth of knowledge, both historians and scientists are indebted to its author.

Pliny's extensive travels, first with the military and then through appointments made under Vespasian's rule, provided Pliny the opportunity to observe and record vast amounts of information regarding the natural world around him. Vespasian bestowed upon Pliny the office of Admiral of the Navy. In August of AD 79, he was stationed at Misenum, where he lived with his sister Plinia and her son Pliny the Younger, whom the elder adopted as a son in his will. On August 24, Mount Vesuvius erupted with devastating effect. Pliny the Elder boarded his ship and sailed out to the Bay of Naples in order to better observe the natural phenomena. While en route he received a plea for rescue from a friend. As the vessel approached Herculaneum, cinders and pumice began to fall. His helmsman advised Pliny to turn back, but Pliny responded, *"Fortes fortuna iuvat."* The crew pressed on. Pliny reached his friends, but the winds would not allow them to leave port for some time. Pliny died on that fateful day presumably from the toxicity of the fumes. His mission, however, was not in vain. Several of those he had come to rescue were eventually able to make the return voyage. It is by their account that Pliny the Younger was able to recount the event of his uncle's death to his friend Tacitus, the Roman historian, in one of his many well-known letters. You read a portion of that letter in *LA2*, in which Pliny describes his escape with his mother and the horrible nightmare of Vesuvius.

Culture Corner

ANCIENT OBELISKS IN MODERN TIMES

The work recorded by Pliny the Elder leaves us a marvelous record of the treasures of the ancient world, many of which can still be seen today. In this particular passage, Pliny recounts the manner in which the Caesars brought obelisks to Rome. The obelisk Caligula transported to Ostia and then up the Tiber to Rome was put in the great circus or race track which he built, later called the Circus of Nero. There the obelisk represented the power and might of Rome, which had extended so far south as to include the ancient empire of Egypt. On top of the apex of the obelisk was placed a gilded ball, which legend says contained the ashes of Julius Caesar.

In AD 1588, however, Rome was ruled by a new power: no longer the caesars, but the pope. Pope Sextus V ordered the obelisk to be moved from the Circus of Nero and erected anew in the square before St. Peter's Basilica. The gilded ball was removed and the legend discovered to be only dirt. In the ball's coveted position now stands a bronze sculpture of St. Peter. In this singular monument is displayed the transition of power: Egypt to Rome to Christendom.[3]

Rome was not the only nation, however, to covet the ancient treasures of Egypt. Pliny's records make reference to multiple obelisks which stood in Alexandria. Of these obelisks, Augustus transported two to Rome. The other two remained in Alexandria for centuries, but eventually made their way to London and New York in the nineteenth century AD. Today, this pair is known as Cleopatra's Needles. While Cleopatra herself had nothing to do with the construction or even inscription of these obelisks, their origin does lie with Egypt's greatest pharaohs.

The central column of inscriptions on the obelisk now standing in Central Park reveals that their origin lies with Thothmes III, whom Pliny calls Mesphres.[4] Thothmes III is the most famous and most powerful pharaoh of the eighteenth dynasty (c. 1600 BC). Thothmes brought great power and stability to Egypt and the surrounding region. In fact, some historians believe Thothmes is the very pharaoh with whom Joseph, son of Israel, found refuge and favor. Thothmes left many marvelous works behind, including the largest of the obelisks to survive antiquity, which now stands in the Basilica Laterna in Rome.

Cleopatra's Needle is not only dedicated to Thothmes, however. Three hundred years after the rule of Thothmes, Ramses II found plenty of room on the obelisks of his predecessor to add his own markings. These

---

3. Francios Lenormant and E. Chevallier, *A Manual of the Ancient History of the East to the Commencement of the Median Wars*, vol. 1 (Whitefish, MT: Kessinger Publishing, 2006), n.p.
4. Mesphres is the Greek transcription of the coronation name of Thothmes, Menkheperra.

Cleopatra's Needle in
New York's Central Park

are seen today on either side of the central column. Perhaps he intended to outdo his predecessor, perhaps he wanted those who had marveled at Thothmes to marvel at him as well—they certainly did. Ramses II is considered the greatest of the pharaohs of the nineteenth dynasty and erected many monuments of his own, such as the obelisk in the reading for this chapter. One of his most famous works is a colossus of himself called Ozymandias, for which Percy Bysshe Shelley wrote his famous poem. Ramses II may be the best known of Egypt's pharaohs to date, not only for his military and architectural triumphs but also as the pharaoh most often associated with the biblical hero Moses.

For thousands of years these obelisks stood in Heliopolis, the City of the Sun, as told by Pliny. The brass crabs at the base of the obelisks reveal through their inscriptions that the obelisks were indeed moved to Alexandria on the orders of Caesar Augustus in 12 BC. Pliny reveals the fate of those that traveled to Rome. Today you can gaze upon the records of ancient Egypt yourself while visiting New York's Central Park.[5]

Derivative Detective

ASSIMILATION

When two consonants come together in Latin, they tend to become alike; this is called assimilation. Although assimilation can occur almost anywhere in a word, our focus is on the assimilation occurring with prepositions used as prefixes and root words. In some cases, the letter at the end of the prefix truly becomes the same as the letter beginning the root word. In other cases, the final letter of the prefix changes so that its sound closely imitates the initial letter of the root word.

Although the preposition *in* does not always completely assimilate, it does become *im-* before *b*, *m*, and *p*. (This happens because *n* and *m* are similar in that they are pronounced through the nose—i.e., they are *nasals*. The letter *n* is pronounced at the teeth—*dental*—and *m* at the lips—*labial*. Since *b*, *m*, and *p* are also labials, the *n* tends to assimilate to *m*, keeping its nasal quality, but changing where it is pronounced—the point of articulation). The *n* is occasionally completely assimilated before *l* and *r*. Because these rules deal with sounds rather than meaning, they apply identically to the negative prefix *in*. These assimilations, as all assimilations, came about for ease in pronunciation. The same reason can cause omission. Examples of omission occur in *pāstor*, which was originally *pāsctor*, and in *lapis*, which was originally *lapids*.

Determine the Latin elements of each English word below. Then use an English dictionary to define each derivative.

import

immigrate

illiterate

imbibe

irresponsible

---

5. Charles Edward Moldenke, *New York Obelisk, Cleopatra's Needle* (New York: A.D.F. and Co., 1891), n.p. *and* Edouard Naville, *Bubastis (1887–1889)* (London: Kegan Paul, Trench, Trubner and Co., 1891), n.p.

Latin in Math

Latin is the language of the sciences, and that includes mathematics. Many of the terms you use every day in your math class are from Latin. You may have already recognized some of these terms in Pliny's description of the ancient obelisks. The Romans were masters of engineering. They carefully observed the accomplishments made by other cultures and sought to improve upon them. The works of men such as Pliny the Elder and Vitruvius preserved their amazing accomplishments for later men, such as DaVinci, Galileo, and Newton, to build upon.

Study the mathematical terms below. Use the Latin roots to discern the literal meaning of each word. Then, use a dictionary to learn the mathematical meaning of each word.

Exempli Gratia:

1. abscissa (ab + scindere), "to tear from."
   The x-coordinate of a point: its distance from the y-axis measured parallel to the x-axis.
2. acute (acūtus)
3. angle (angulus)
4. cardinal (cardinis)
5. concurrent (cum + currere)
6. dozen (duōdecim)
7. dodecahedron (duōdecim)
8. exponent (ex + pōnere)
9. fraction (frangere)
10. integer (integer)
11. obtuse (obtūsus)
12. plus (plūs)
13. radius (radius)
14. secant (secāre)
15. sequence (sequī)
16. subtract (sub + trahere)
17. tangent (tangere)
18. vector (vehere)

Unit 2 Reading

READING AND REVIEW FOR CHAPTERS 7–12

Pons Milvius

Christopher R. Schlect, New St. Andrew's College

The *Pons Milvius* spans the Tiber in northern Rome. Today it is the city's oldest bridge, built in 206 BC when Rome was fighting Carthage. Recently, city officials have waged a political battle over what to do about a mess of chains on the ancient bridge. Italian lovers have taken to padlocking a chain to the bridge and tossing the key into the river below. The locked chain symbolizes the couple's love, and losing the key indicates that the bonds of their love will endure forever. By 2007, the bridge became so burdened with locked chains that its structure was compromised. When a city official proposed cutting the chains and removing them, his political opponents chided him for waging a war—not on the Carthaginians, but on love.[1]

For twenty-two centuries, the *Pons Milvius* has displayed the mysterious link joining battle and love: whatever is loved—truly loved—must be fought for. It was love for Rome herself that inspired Gaius Claudius Nero (not Nero the emperor) to build the bridge in the first place. Following his victory over Hasdrubal Barca at the Battle of Metaurus in 207 BC, this Nero constructed the *Pons Milvius* to facilitate troop movements northward out of the city along the Flaminian Road, over the Apennine Mountains, and out to the Adriatic Sea. Again at this bridge, it was love for senatorial privilege that inspired Quintus Lutatius Catalus in 78 BC to repel the army of Lepidus, which was marching on Rome to put an end to Sulla's reforms.[2] Still later, Constantine claimed that it was love for Christ that inspired him to battle at this bridge, where his forces overtook Maxentius's retreating army in AD 312. Then Constantine legalized Christianity and ended generations of bloody persecution.[3]

Of all the acts of love and battle to occur at this bridge, perhaps the most intriguing is the discovery of Catiline's conspiracy to overthrow the government.[4] In 64 BC, Rome was a ferment of tension and unrest. Sulla's brutal dictatorship was still a fresh memory. He had turned back the clock on many of the political gains attained by the plebeians, especially when he curtailed the power of the people's representative, the Tribune. He placed the city's power squarely into the hands of an aristocratic Senate. Sulla's opponents were exiled, deprived of their property, or killed. But within ten years, most of Sulla's pro-aristocratic reforms had been repealed (ironically, during the consulship of two of Sulla's former lieutenants, Pompey and Crassus).

---

1. Ian Fischer, "Love Rite on a Bridge, but Is the Romance Fading?" *New York Times*, August 6, 2007, A4.
2. Lucius Cornelius Sulla Felix (c. 138–78 BC) was a Roman general and statesman. He is best known for his rule as dictator of Rome, which was a reign of terror for some. He became dictator during the struggle between the *optimates*, those who wanted to maintain an oligarchy, and the *populares*, who were populists.
3. Eusebius, *Vita Constantini*, I.27-31.
4. The details of Catiline's conspiracy are recorded in Sallust, *Bellum Catilinae*. See especially chapter 45.

So by 64 BC, both groups—the old-guard aristocrats and the common plebeians—had recently enjoyed fantastic political gains and suffered bitter disappointments, each at the other's expense.[5] Both groups sought greater privileges for themselves and intensified their loathing toward their opponents. A third group added to this ferment. This third group consisted of some plebeians of humble lineage who had recently gained unimaginable wealth by doing business in foreign markets that had opened to them in the wake of Rome's military exploits. Old-guard aristocrats wanted to curb the growing influence of these newly wealthy plebeians, and the ordinary plebeians worried that the wealthy plebeians would turn against them and join forces with the aristocracy. Into this storm of suspicion and fear stepped a wily Catiline.

Catiline aspired to the consulship in 65 BC, but he was not approved as a candidate. He succeeded in becoming a candidate two years later, but lost the election to Cicero and Antonius Hybrida. Unable to gain power by traditional means, Catiline then sought power outside the proper channels. He formed a secret coalition of people who, at the time, were politically frustrated, and led them in an elaborate plan to take over Rome. Catiline was joined by Publius Cornelius Lentulus, a former consul who was estranged from the Senate. Lentulus's involvement gave credibility to Catiline's plan and inspired others to join in. One of these was Manlius, who recruited an army in Etruria.[6] The conspirators also recruited the Allobroges, a Gallic people who resented their Roman governor. Catiline's plan was for various conspirators to plant themselves within the city, murder numerous senators, murder Cicero, set portions of the city afire, and stir up mobs of plebeians and slaves. After wreaking all this havoc within the city, they were to go out and join Manlius's army, march back into Rome, and take control of the city they had made chaotic and leaderless.

Catiline's plan might have succeeded had Cicero not found out about it. A friend tipped Cicero off in order to prevent his assassination. Cicero guarded himself against attack and also arranged to protect the threatened senators. Though Cicero had enough information to take these precautions, he did not have the hard evidence he required to put Catiline to trial and convict him of treason. Nonetheless, he stood up in the Senate and denounced Catiline, who was actually present at the time. Cicero's speech was so fierce that those seated near Catiline moved away from him while Cicero was speaking. Catiline left Rome, claiming to go into exile, but actually to join Manlius's army and proceed with his plan. Many of the conspirators remained within the city; Catiline's plan might yet have succeeded, but it unraveled at the *Pons Milvius*.

Cicero persuaded the Allobroges to turn against the conspiracy, unbeknownst to Catiline and his cohorts. Pretending to help the conspirators, the Allobroges came into possession of letters that revealed the conspiracy and implicated Catiline and Lentulus. Cicero arranged for several of his men to intercept these letters as the Allobroges carried them across the *Pons Milvius*. This gave Cicero the proof he needed—proof enough to overcome the doubts of any who did not want to believe that an ex-consul such as Lentulus could conspire to bring down the republic.

Catiline had devised a formidable plan to bring down the republic. The plan was formidable because it involved a coalition that drew participants from all social classes and all ranks of political influence. Love brought this conspiracy together—love of power and a zeal to wage war for what the conspirators loved. The chains that padlocked this conspiracy were cut at the *Pons Milvius*.

Before You Read!

You may notice some unusual spellings in this reading. In earlier Latin writings, the short letter *i* was written as a *u* in words such as the following:

> *maxumus* = *maximus*; *minumus* = *minimus*; *aestumāre* = *aestimāre*;
> *iūstissumō* = *iūstissimō*; *optumō* = *optimō*

The short *i* was often interchangeable with the short *e*, as in: *iīs* = *eīs*. And when what in classical Latin would be a short *u* was preceded by a *v* it would often be pronounced as a short *o*, as in: *voltum* = *vultum*.

---

5. The old-guard aristocrats were called patricians, a class of nobility who claimed descent from the original Senate founded by Romulus. The common plebeians were members of the *populares*.
6. Gaius Manlius was a former centurion under Sulla who aided Catiline in his conspiracy.

You may also find the following English derivatives with their English meanings helpful in interpreting the reading.

concord – peace, agreement
discord – disagreement
contagion – infection
avarice – greed
matériel – things needed to do a job, building materials

Also, be aware that there are many instances of ellipsis in this passage; so be on the lookout for missing forms of *sum* and the conjunction *et*. (This omission of a conjunction is called *asyndeton*).

BELLUM CATILĪNAE IX ET X, SALLUST

1 Domī **mīlitiaeque** bonī mōrēs *colēbantur*; Concordia maxuma, minuma
2 avāritia erat; iūs bonumque apud eōs nōn lēgibus magis quam nātūrā valēbat.
3 *Iūrgia*, discordiās, *simultātēs* cum hostibus exercēbant, cīvēs cum cīvibus dē
4 virtūte *certābant*. In *suppliciīs* deōrum magnificī, domī parcī, in amīcōs fidēlēs
5 erant. Duābus hīs artibus, **audāciā in bellō, ubi pāx ēvēnerat, aequitāte**, sēque
6 remque pūblicam cūrābant. Quārum rērum egō maxuma *documenta* haec habeō:
7 quod in bellō **saepius vindicātum est** in eōs, quī contrā imperium in hostem
8 pugnāverant quīque tardius revocātī proeliō excesserant, **quam** quī signa
9 relinquere aut pulsī locō cēdere ausī erant; in pāce vērō, quod beneficiīs magis
10 quam metū imperium *agitābant* et, acceptā iniūriā, ignōscere quam *persequī*
11 malēbant. Sed ubi labōre atque iūstitiā rēs pūblica crēvit, rēgēs magnī bellō
12 *domitī*, nationēs *ferae* et populī ingentēs vī *subāctī*, Carthāgō, *aemula* imperī
13 Rōmānī, **ab stirpe interiit** cūncta maria terraeque patēbant, *saevīre* fortūna ac
14 miscēre omnia *coepit*. **Quī labōrēs**, perīcula, dubiās atque *asperās* rēs facile
15 tolerāverant, iīs ōtium dīvitiaeque, optanda *aliās*, onerī miseriaeque fuēre.
16 Igitur prīmō imperī, deinde pecūniae cupīdō crēvit: ea quasi *materiēs* omnium
17 malōrum fuēre. Namque avāritia fidem, *probitātem* cēterāsque artīs bonās
18 subvertit; prō iīs superbiam, crūdēlitātem, deōs neglegere, omnia vēnālia
19 habēre *ēdocuit*. Ambitiō multōs mortālēs falsōs fierī *subēgit*, **aliud** clausum in
20 pectore, **aliud** in linguā prōmptum habēre, amīcitiās inimīcitiāsque nōn ex rē,
21 sed ex *commodō*, aestumāre magisque voltum quam *ingenium* bonum habēre.
22 Haec prīmō *paulātim* **crēscere**, interdum *vindicārī*; post, ubī *contāgiō* quasi
23 *pestilentia invāsit*, cīvitās *inmūtāta*, imperium ex iūstissumō atque optumō
24 crūdēle *intolerandumque* **factum**.

Phrases

mīlitiaeque – and on military campaign (a typical contrast between the peace and war—"at home and on military campaign")

audāciā in bellō, ubi pāx ēvēnerat, aequitāte = *audāciā in bellō [et], ubi pāx ēvēnerat, aequitāte* (ellipsis)

saepius ... quam – (*quam* goes with *saepius* and not with *tardius*)

vindicātum est – punishment was exacted (Latin uses the *impersonal* passive of verbs where we would use the personal; e.g., *bellātum est* "it was warred" = "war was waged")

ab *stirpe* interiit – perished root and all (lit., "perished from the root"; the point is that Carthage was destroyed for good and could never return, just as a tree whose roots have been taken up can no longer produce any shoots)

Quī labōrs – (*quī* acts as the subject of the clause and *labōrs* as one of the direct objects; the antecedent of *quī* is actually *iīs* on line 15, which you may want to translate first)

aliud . . . aliud – one thing . . . another thing

crēscere . . . vindicārī – they grew . . . they were punished (these are called *historical infinitives*; they are translated as though they were imperfect or perfect indicative forms)

factum = *factum est*

Glossary

Use your "eye" Latin to discern the meaning of the underlined words in the reading.

colō, colere, coluī, cultum	to cultivate, to tend
iūrgium, -ī, n.	quarrel
simultās, simultātis, f.	rivalry, feud
certō, -āre, -āvī, -ātum	to compete
supplicium, -ī, n.	supplication, prayerful entreaty
ēveniō, ēvenīre, ēvēnī, ēventum (*ex* + *venīre*)	to happen, to come about
aequitās, aequitātis, f.	fairness, justice
documentum, -ī, n.	proof
vindicō, -āre, -āvī, -ātum	to punish
agitō, -āre, -āvī, -ātum	to urge on, to accomplish
persequor, persequī, persecūtus sum	to prosecute, to pursue [the matter for punishment]
domitus, -a, -um, adj.	conquered, domesticated, tamed
ferus, -a, -um	wild, undomesticated, fierce (cf. *fera, -ae,* f.)
subigō, subigere, subēgī, subāctum (*sub* + *agere*)	to drive under, to subdue
aemulus, -a, -um, adj.	rival
stirps, stirpis, f.	root, source
intereō, interīre, interiī, interitum	to perish
saeviō, saevīre, saeviī, saevītum	to rage
coepī	to begin (defective verb with only a perfect stem)
asper, -a, -um, adj.	rough, hard, severe
aliās, adv.	previously, at other times, formerly
māteriēs, māteriēī, f.	building materials
probitās, probitātis, f.	integrity
vēnālis, -e, adj.	having a price, for sale
ēdoceō, ēdocēre, ēdocuī, ēdoctum	to teach
commodum, -ī, n.	advantage, interest
ingenium, -ī, n.	character
paulātim, adv.	gradually, little by little
contāgiō, contāgiōnis, f.	infection
pestilentia, -ae, f.	plague
invādō, invādere, invāsī, invāsum	to enter, to fall upon, to spread
inmūtātus, -a, -um, adj.	changed (= *immūtāta est*)
intolerandus, -a, -um, adj.	intolerable

Rhetorical Devices

CHIASMUS AND SYNCHYSIS

In *LA2*, you learned about synchysis. Synchysis is an arrangement of elements resulting in the pattern ABAB. It is sometimes called interlocking word order, and its effect is to tie elements together, to make a closer connection than another word order might bring about. Synchysis involves separating, artificially, words that belong together: e.g., *femina pulchra virum magnum amat* (without synchysis) *femina virum pulchra magnum amat* (with synchysis). This works in Latin because of the case endings, which clarify which word goes with which—an impossibility most of the time in English.

Chiasmus is a device in which elements of a phrase or sentence mirror each other (instead of interlocking as with synchysis). The reflection ends up with the structure ABBA and can be merely at the word level or can comprise an entire literary work. For our purposes, we will be focusing on chiasmus at the word and phrase level. It is called chiasmus after the Greek letter *chi*, which looks like our *X*, which you get if you connect the *A*s and *B*s when the structures are arranged one above the other.

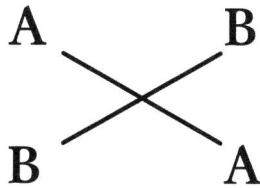

There are examples of chiastic lines in English; for example, John Keats in "Ode on a Grecian Urn" wrote "truth is beauty, beauty truth." This line from Keats is not typical of classical chiasmus, since it repeats the same words, something true chiasmus hardly, if ever, did in classical writing. Because English meaning comes from word order and not from inflections, chiasmus is much harder to produce in English than it is in Latin and Greek. An example of chiasmus in the Unit 2 Reading chapter is found on line 5: *audācia in bellō [et] ubi pāx ēvēnerat, aequitāte*. The phrase describes two virtues that are appropriate in two different circumstances: boldness is appropriate for war and equity in peace. Notice the chiasmus: (a) boldness (b) in war [and] (b) when peace had come about (a) justice. The parts of speech are not in chiasmus so much as the concepts. The parts of speech would be in chiasmus if the phrases *in bellō* and *ubi pāx ēvēnerat* had had the same structures (*in bellō* and *in pace*). However, the author chose to use another literary device called *variatio* to spice things up.

Here is an example of chiasmus of parts of speech rather than structure: *femina pulchra magnum virum amat*—"(a) the woman (b) beautiful (b) great (a) man loves." Because chiasmus can be employed on so many levels, be on the lookout for the creativity of different authors.

Enrichment Activity

Look up *chiasmus* on the Internet. In Wikipedia, for instance, you will find many examples of chiasmus; and, if you follow some links, you will learn what the device is called when the ABBA pattern is based on sentence elements other than words.

Question & Answer

In each of the following exercises, circle the letter of the correct answer.

1. What is the form of the first noun in the reading?
   a. nominative plural
   b. genitive singular
   c. vocative plural
   d. locative singular

2. What rhetorical device appears in lines 1 and 2?
   a. metonymy
   b. polysyndeton
   c. synchysis
   d. chiasmus

3. Which of the following line(s) contain an outstanding example of alliteration?
   a. 3 and 4
   b. 5 and 6
   c. 18
   d. 24

4. According to lines 3 and 4, Roman citizens _____.
   a. always got on well with hostile foreigners
   b. felt they had few, if any, national enemies
   c. competed with one another to achieve courage/virtue/excellence
   d. practiced very simple religious rites

5. Which of the following, according to Sallust, characterizes the Romans at home?
   a. extravagant
   b. cruel
   c. caring little for the republic
   d. frugal

6. By what two means did the Romans, according to Sallust, take care of themselves and the republic?
   a. daring in wartime and justice in peacetime
   b. frugality at home and extravagant spending for war
   c. good government and lavish religious practices
   d. faithfulness toward friends and maximum animosity toward enemies

7. In peacetime, according to lines 9–11, how did the Romans prefer to conduct their rule?
   a. through fear
   b. through kindnesses
   c. through fear and favors
   d. through neither fear nor favors

8. When the Romans received an injustice, they preferred to _____.
   a. execute the person who had brought the injustice about
   b. pardon the injustice
   c. ignore the injustice
   d. return a like injustice to the one guilty himself of injustice

9. Which of the following, according to the reading, did not happen as the republic grew?
   a. Great kings were conquered.
   b. The emperor was deposed.
   c. Carthage was destroyed.
   d. Land and sea were entirely open.

10. The Romans who had borne labors, danger, risk, and hard times eventually found leisure to be _____.
    a. unnecessary and unpleasant
    b. enjoyed only by the wealthiest Romans
    c. a burden and a misery
    d. more attractive than ever

11. Besides their feelings about leisure, many Romans had the same feelings about _____.
    a. literature and time to read
    b. wealth
    c. sumptuous clothing
    d. sumptuous meals

12. According to lines 16–18, what desire grew first for the Romans?
    a. a desire for a peace treaty with Carthage
    b. a desire for a return to a monarchy
    c. a desire for money
    d. a desire for rule/power

13. What did they desire secondly?
    a. rule
    b. a king
    c. a peace treaty with Carthage
    d. money

Unit 2 Reading

14. What undid the good faith and integrity of the Romans, according to the reading?
    a. laziness
    b. greed
    c. traitors to the republic
    d. an evil ruler

15. After the destruction of good faith and integrity, what did their fault bring about?
    a. arrogance
    b. cruelty
    c. neglect of the gods
    d. all of the above

16. Ambition drove many people to be deceitful.
    a. true
    b. false

17. According to lines 21 and 22, how did some evaluate friendship and enmities?
    a. on the basis of truth
    b. on the basis of advantage they might gain
    c. on economic status of other individuals
    d. none of the above

18. Upon what did some Romans place the most value?
    a. good appearance
    b. character
    c. wealth
    d. growth of the republic

19. What Nepos calls an "infection" spread like _____.
    a. wildfire
    b. a flood
    c. a plague
    d. gossip

20. After the "infection" had spread, how did the government change?
    a. It became tolerant of ill behavior.
    b. It changed from being just to being cruel.
    c. It did not change at all.
    d. It became supremely just.

Challenge Box

Search the reading to find further examples of chiasmus.

About the Author

Sallust

SALLUST

Gaius Sallustius Crispus was born into a plebeian family in 86 BC in Amiternum, a Sabine town. Sallust, as he is generally known, became quaestor in 55 BC and tribune of the people in 52 BC. He was a member of the *popularis* party and, as such, he always opposed Pompey and the aristocrats and favored Gaius Julius Caesar. His friendship with Caesar probably was the reason for his expulsion from the Senate in 50 BC. That same friendship was probably the same reason that he was reinstated as a senator in 49 BC. He was praetor in 46 BC. Having been with Caesar in Africa for the Battle of Thapsus, a battle that saw the defeat of the last of the Pompeian party, Sallust was rewarded with the governorship of the province of *Nova Africa*. His conduct in office was so filled with oppression and extortion that only the influence of Caesar allowed him to escape punishment. He returned to Rome and purchased lands on the Quirinal Hill, one of the Seven Hills of Rome. These lands became beautiful gardens, known as *Horti Sallusti*, upon which Sallust spent most of his wealth and which the emperors owned later. He retired from public life and devoted all his time to historical literature. The histories of Sallust were different from those of earlier historians, which were mere chronicles. His were explanations of events and studies of characters. His writings are of a high moral tone, perhaps because he reformed his own character. The ancients thought highly of Sallust's work, some saying that he was a better historian than Livy. Quintilian thought he was on the same level of excellence as Thucydides, famed author of *The History of the Peloponnesian War*.[7]

---

7. H.J. Rose, *A Handbook of Latin Literature* (Wauconda, IL: Bolchazy-Carducci Publishers, Inc., 1966), n.p.

Mens agitat molem.
University of Oregon

The University of Oregon adapted this motto from Vergil's *Aeneid* VI. 727.

Chapter 13

- Section 44. Latin Poetry: Meter and Scansion
- Section 45. Elision
- Section 46. Lyric Poetry
  - Hendecasyllabic
  - Sapphic

VOCABULARY

LATIN	ENGLISH	DERIVATIVES
Nouns		
columba, -ae, f.	dove	
lapillus, -ī, m.*	little stone, pebble; a precious stone or gem	(lapis lazuli)
libellus, -ī, m.*	little book	
mediocritās, mediocritātis, f.	moderation, the mean	(mediocrity)
passer, passeris, m.	sparrow	
penātēs, penātium, m. pl.	Penates (Roman household gods); *metonymy for* home, family	
prōlēs, prōlis, f.	offspring, descendent	
sordēs, sordis, f.	(often plural) dirt, filth; baseness (of rank or station)	(sordid)
Verbs		
dīligō, dīligere, dīlēxī, dīlēctum	to choose out; to prize, to love, to esteem highly	(diligent)
fundō, -āre, -āvī, -ātum	to lay a foundation, to found	(fundamental)
invideō, invidēre, invīdī, invīsum	to look upon with the evil eye, to envy, to begrudge	
lūgeō, lūgēre, lūxī, lūctum	to mourn, to be in mourning	
Adjectives, Adverbs, Conjunctions, etc.		
blandus, -a, -um, adj.	flattering, alluring	(blandishment)
lentus, -a, -um, adj.	slow	
pūrus, -a, -um, adj.	pure	(pure)
sōbrius, -a, -um, adj.	sober, not intoxicated; frugal, reasonable	(sobriety)

venustus, -a, -um, adj.	charming, delightful	
nimium, adv. (= nimis)	too much	
quārē *or* quā rē, inter. adv.	why? for what reason?	
sānē, adv.	utterly, completely, wholly	(sane)

Nota Bene: Notice how both *lapillus* and *libellus* have a double *ll* in the middle of the word. This *ll* indicates a diminutive, meaning it denotes smallness or affection. Thus we translate such words with the adjective "little."

Exempli Gratia:

librum – book, libellum – little book

lapis – stone, lapillus – little stone

SECTION 44. Latin Poetry: Meter and Scansion

In this chapter, we will take a brief hiatus from grammar studies to introduce Latin poetry. While you have read some poetry, such as the fragments from Ennius in chapters 2 and 3, most chapter readings have been prose selections. Poetry differs from prose in that it is written in meter. **Meter** is the arrangement of words into rhythmic verses. The metric rhythm in Latin (and Greek) poetry is created by carefully positioning long and short syllables into a pattern. The result is almost musical. In fact, ancient poetry was not meant to be read silently but to be performed aloud, often with musical accompaniment. Throughout this unit you will have the opportunity to read several poems in a variety of styles and meters from Rome's greatest poets.

Meter in Latin poetry is created by the arrangement of long and short syllables in order to create a verse or line of poetry. **Scansion** is the metrical analysis of a verse. In order to understand how to scan or analyze the meter of a verse, you must understand how to identify long and short syllables. Chapter 1 in *LA1* and *LA2* demonstrated how to identify these syllables. This same lesson is provided again in appendix A. Use this lesson to answer the questions in the following exercise.

Exercise 1. Answer the following questions about syllabication. (Hint: Use appendix A to help you answer the questions.)

1. Syllables can be either long by nature or by position. What are three rules for determining if a syllable is long?
2. List the diphthongs that can appear in Latin.
3. What letters are considered double consonants in Latin?
4. What letter does not count as a consonant when discussing syllabication because of its very soft, light sound?
5. What consonants are considered stops?
6. What consonants are considered liquids?
7. When a short vowel is followed by a stop + a liquid, is that syllable long or short?
8. List the three main rules for dividing a syllable.
9. List the three special rules for dividing a syllable.

Exercise 2. Mark the length of the syllables in the following words. When you scan Latin poetry, mark short syllables with the short mark you would use for an English word (˘) and long syllables with a macron (¯).

1. nefās
2. arma
3. libellī
4. aspexī
5. sōlēbās
6. labōriōsus
7. maneat
8. adversus
9. aevum
10. identidem
11. patrōna
12. lūmina
13. ausus
14. perdidit

When scanning poetry, there are a few more rules to keep in mind.

1. A syllable can be long when it contains a vowel followed by two or more consonants, **even if those consonants appear in a subsequent word**.
2. A vowel followed by the combination of a stop + a liquid **may or may not cause that syllable to be long**. This is a flexible syllable similar to the blank tile in a SCRABBLE game. The poet is allowed to use it as long or short depending upon what is needed for that metrical foot.
3. Remember that the combinations of *qu* and *gu* are **treated as a single consonant sound**, as are combinations involving the letter *h* (e.g., *th* and *ch*).

Exercise 3. Mark the length of the syllables in the following verses of poetry.

1. Auream quisquis mediocritātem

   dīligit, tūtus caret obsolētī

   sordibus tēctī, caret invidendā

   　　sōbrius aulā.

   　　　(Horace 2.10)
   Hint: *obsolētī* – worn out, poor　　*aula, -ae,* f. – inner court

2. Est sānē iocus iste, quod libellum

   mīsistī mihi, Grȳpe, prō libellō.

   　　　(Statius, *Silvae* 4.9)
   Hint: *iocus, -ī,* m. – joke

3. *Congratulations on the Birth of Your Son*

   sed damus lentō veniam, quod almā

   prōle fundāstī* vacuōs penātēs.

   ō diem laetum! venit ecce nōbīs

   　　Maximus alter.

   　　　(Statius, *Silvae* 4.7)

   Hint: *vacuus, -a, -um,* adj. – empty, void
   **fundāstī* = *fundāvistī* (This is an example of *syncope*, a contraction to reduce the number of syllables in a word. It can help the poet fit a word into the meter. There are also many examples of syncope in prose.)

Exercise 4. Read the verses in exercise 3 aloud with the meter or rhythm of the verses as the poet intended. Then translate.

SECTION 45. Elision

You have already seen examples of syncope, which is one instance of omission or contraction within a word. English poetry and song lyrics often omit syllables in order to make them fit the meter or rhythm used. Take, for example, the word "over," which is often contracted to "o'er," as in the following twelfth-century hymn:

> The strife is o'er, the battle done;
>
> The victory of life is won;
>
> The song of triumph has begun: Alleluia!
>
> from *Finita Iam Sunt Proelia*

A similar type of contraction that occurs between two words is known as elision. **Elision** is the omission of a vowel, consonant, or whole syllable between words when reading poetry aloud. In Latin, such an elision is a change only in pronunciation: there is no effect upon the written text. Elision, in addition to syncope, though a natural part of the Latin language, is utilized to make sure that the words of a verse fit the meter of the poem.

There are three rules about when and how a poet can elide two words.

1. **vowel – vowel** (or vowel preceded by *h*)

One word ends with a vowel or diphthong, and the following word begins with a vowel or diphthong. Remember that because of its light pronunciation, *h* does not count as a consonant in syllables or scansion.

> *quārē id* is read as *quārid*   *quār(ē) id*
>
> *quārē habē* is read as *quārabē*   *quār(ē h)abē*

2. **vowel *m* – vowel** (or vowel preceded by *h*)

One word ends with a vowel + *m*, and the following word begins with a vowel, diphthong, or the letter *h* + vowel.

> *quamquam animus* is read as *quamquanimus*   *quamqua(m a)nimus*

Nota Bene:

a. It is generally the last syllable or vowel sound of the first word that drops out or is elided into the following word.

b. An *h* does not prevent elision.

c. When elision, the vowel that remains retains its length.

3. **prodelision**

Prodelision is like elision, but involves the dropping of the last syllable of the first word and the retention of the first vowel sound of the following word. Prodelision occurs with *es* or *est*.

> *iacta est* is read as *iactast*
>
> *molestum est* is read as *molestumst*

Exercise 5. Mark the length of the syllables in the following verses of poetry. Watch carefully for examples of both elision and prodelision, and mark them with parentheses.

1. vīvāmus, mea Lesbia, atque amēmus (Catullus 5)

2. Lūgēte, Ō Venerēs Cupīdinēsque,
   et quantum est hominum venustiōrum:
   passer mortuus est meae puellae
   (Catullus 3)

3. Issa est passere nēquior Catullī,
   Issa est pūrior osculō columbae,
   Issa est blandior omnibus puellīs,
   Issa est cārior Indicīs lapillīs
   (Martial I.109)
   Hint: *indicus, -a, -um*, adj. – Indian

SECTION 46. Lyric Poetry

The ancient Greeks designed some poems to be accompanied by a lyre or other stringed instrument, thus the term *lyric* poetry. The poets would arrange syllables in different patterns to create a meter, or poetic rhythm, accompanied by this music. The Romans took many ideas about art and literature from the Greeks, and Roman poetry owes much, if not everything, to its Greek models and examples. Most meters are built around a **metrical foot**, or a specific pattern of syllables. You will learn a few of these metrical feet in this unit. The first is a choriamb. The **choriamb** consists of a long syllable, followed by two short syllables, and then one more long syllable.

choriamb: _ ᴗ ᴗ _   long – short – short – long

A. Hendecasyllabic

Classical hendecasyllabic verse consists of eleven syllables (*hendeca* is Greek for eleven). This particular style is also known as Phalaecean after the Greek poet Phalaeceus. The verse is built around a choriamb. The vertical lines indicate the division of the metrical feet.

x x | _ ᴗ ᴗ _ | ᴗ _ ᴗ _ x*

C͡uī** dōnō lepidum novum libellum (Catullus I)

__Nota Bene__: The variable *x* means that syllable could be either long or short.

**__Nota Bene__*: The curve mark over *cui* means that the two vowels are joined together to form one long vowel. This merging is called *synizesis*, from a Greek word meaning "collapse" or "compression."

B. Sapphic

This is a lyric stanza based on the hendecasyllabic verse. The choriamb now occurs in the very middle of the verse. This stanza is named for Sappho, an ancient Greek poetess who lived on the island of Lesbos. Each stanza contains three long verses (consisting of eleven syllables) followed by one short verse.

_ ᴗ _ x | _ ᴗ ᴗ _ | ᴗ _ x (first three verses)

_ ᴗ ᴗ _ | x (fourth verse)

     Ille mī pār esse deō vidētur,
       ille, sī fās est, superāre dīvōs,
         quī sedēns adversus identidem tē
           spectat et audit
             (Catullus 51)

Exercise 6. Scan the verses in exercises 3 and 5. Mark the metrical foot with the choriamb with vertical lines. The first line of #1 in exercise 3 is provided as an example. Then identify the meter for each one.

Example:

Exercise 3

1. (Horace 2.10) – sapphic stanza

_ ᴗ _ _ | _ ᴗ ᴗ _ | ᴗ _ ᴗ

Scan the remaining lines for exercise 3 and all of exercise 5. Note how the foot with the choriamb is marked.

Exercise 7. Read the verses in exercise 5 aloud with the meter or rhythm of the verses as the poet intended. Then translate the poetry in exercise 5.

Chapter Reading: Reading 1

Included in this chapter reading are two lyric poems written in two different meters by the poet Catullus. Catullus and Horace were the poets best known for lyric poetry in ancient Rome. While the Greeks intended for lyre to accompany such poems, the Romans would often simply recite them. Your class can choose to recite them with or without accompaniment.

CATULLUS I. AD CORNELIUM

In this poem, Catullus dedicates his book of poetry to Cornelius Nepos, the very same biographer whose work you read in chapter 11.

1 Cui dōnō *lepidum* novum *libellum*
2 *āridā* modo *pūmice expolītum*?
3 Cornēlī, tibi: namque tū solēbās
4 meās esse aliquid putāre *nūgās*.
5 Iam tum, cum ausus es ūnus Ītalōrum*
6 omne *aevum* tribus explicāre *cartīs*
7 doctīs, Iūppiter, et labōriōsīs!
8 Quārē habē tibi quidquid hoc *libellī*—
9 *quālecumque*, quod, ō *patrōna virgō*,
10 plūs ūnō maneat *perenne* saeclō!

*Cornelius Nepos' history of the Latin people was contained in three scrolls.

Glossary: Reading 1

lepidus .... *venustus*
āridus, -a, -um, adj. .... dry
pūmex, pūmicis, m. .... pumice stone (as used for polishing marble, books, etc.)
expoliō, expolīre, expolīvī, expolītum .... to smooth, to polish
nūgae, -ārum, f. pl. .... trifles, stuff
aevum, -ī, n. .... lifetime, age
carta, -ae, f. .... papyrus scroll
quāliscumque, quālecumque, adj. .... of whatever kind
patrōna, -ae, f. .... patroness, protectress
virgō, virginis, f. .... maiden
perennis, perenne .... lasting, remaining

Before You Answer the Questions

For this reading and, indeed, for all poetry readings, you will be seeing some questions of a different type than you have encountered previously while studying the Latin Alive! series. You will be required to tell in what line (*versus*) a certain feature appears. The word *quotus* means, among other things, "which one in a numbered series." Your answer would be a Latin ordinal number in the case appropriate to answering the question. You may state your answer with a Latin word, such as *prīmus* (in the correct case, of course) or with a Roman numeral with a superscript *o*: I°. The superscript *o* is like *nd*, *rd*, or *th* in English words such as "second," "third," and "seventh."

RESPONDĒ LATĪNĒ! READING 1

1. Quotō in versū poēta nōbīs dīcit quod dōnātur?
2. Quālis est libellus?
3. Quotō in versō poēta dīcit nōbis nōmen hominis cui libellus dēdicābit?
4. Quis solēbat carmina Catullī esse bona putāre et nōn modo nūgās?
5. Quantōs (How many) librōs scrīpsit Nepōs dē histōriā Ītalōrum?
6. Quotō in versū est dīvī nōmen?
7. Hōc in carmine quae rēs dēscrīptī sunt esse doctās labōriōsās?
8. Quotō in versū poēta suam spēm dēmōnstrāvit?

Chapter Reading: Reading 2

CATULLUS LI. AD LESBIAM

1 Ille mī pār esse deō vidētur,
2 ille, sī fās est, superāre *dīvōs*,
3 quī sedēns adversus *identidem* tē
4   spectat et audit
5 dulce rīdentem, miserō quod omnēs
6 *ēripit* sēnsūs mihi: nam simul tē,
7 Lesbia, *aspexī*, nihil **est super** mī
8   vōcis in ōre
9 lingua* sed *torpet, tenuis* sub *artūs*
10 flamma *dēmānat, sonitū suōpte*
11 *tintinant aurēs*, **gemina teguntur**
12   **lūmina nocte**.
13 ōtium, Catulle, tibī** *molestum* est:
14 ōtiō *exsultās* nimiumque *gestis*:
15 ōtium et rēgēs *prius* et beātās
16   perdidit urbēs.

*Remember that *gu* counts as a single consonant.
**The final vowel of *tibi*, *mihi*, and *sibi* can be either long or short.

PHRASES: Reading 2

est super – *superest*, remains

lūmina – Literally, this word means "lights." Poetically, it refers to "eyes," the lights of your soul.

geminā . . . lūmina nocte – This is an example of transferred epithet (also called hypallage). One would think that *gemina* should modify *lumina* (twin lights/eyes), but instead it must agree with *nocte*. This rhetorical device expands the emotional effect from Catullus's eyes to the night around him. Everything is dim and out of focus and with double vision because Lesbia is near.

GLOSSARY: Reading 2

dīvus, -a, -um	divine
adversus, prep (+ acc.)	opposite
identidem	repeatedly, again and again
ēripiō, ēripere, ēripuī, ēreptum	to snatch away *x* (acc.) from *y* (dat.) (cf. *ex* + *rapere*)
aspiciō, aspicere, aspexī, aspectum	to look at, to behold
torpeō, torpēre	to be stuck numb, to be paralyzed
tenuis, tenue	thin
artus, -ūs, m.	limb (of the body)
dēmānō, dēmānāre	to drip down
sonitus, -ūs, m.	sound
suōpte	*suō* + *pte*. The suffix *-pte* is emphatic. This word is best translated as "very own."
tintinō, -āre, -āvī, -ātum	to ring, to jingle (an example of onomatopoeia)
auris, auris, f.	ear
geminus, -a, -um	twin
tegō, tegere, tēxī, tēctum	to cover, to conceal
molestus, -a, -um	burdensome, annoying
exsultō, -āre, -āvī, -ātum	to leap up frequently, to rejoice exceedingly
gestiō, gestīre	to be excited, to rejoice
prius, adv.	earlier, before

RESPONDĒ LATĪNĒ! READING 2

1. Cui est aliquis par?
2. Quae rēs fās sit?
3. Secundum versūm tertium et quartum, quid agit homo quī sedet?
4. Quotō in versū rīdet aliquis?
5. Quae rēs hominī quī carmen dīcit ēreptae sunt?
6. Quis aspectus est—sedundum versum septimum?
7. Quot noctēs oculōs Catullī tegunt?
8. Quod nōmen est narrātor carminis?
9. Quotīs in versibus discimus dē exitiō rēgum?

About the Author

Gaius Valerius Catullus

CATULLUS

Gaius Valerius Catullus was one of the "new poets" of Rome, poets who modeled their work on that of learned Greek scholars and lyric poets at Alexandria during the Hellenistic Age. He was born in Verona c. 84 BC. According to St. Jerome, the author of the Latin Vulgate (the Latin version of the Bible), Catullus died around the age of thirty; so scholars generally agree that he died in 54 BC. He is best known for his passionate poems to "Lesbia," who was in real life probably named Clodia. She was a member of the aristocratic and outrageous clan of the Clodii. (*Clodius* is an old form of *Claudius*.) Catullus was not only a poet: in 57 BC he went to Bithynia on the staff of Memmius, Praetor (governor) of Bithynia. It was during this journey that he visited the grave of his brother to perform funeral rites. He wrote one of his most moving lyrics upon that visit to his brother's tomb. He stayed in Bithynia for a year. After returning to Italy, he probably spent the rest of his life at his villa in what is now Tivoli. Though Catullus's *Carmen XIII* attempts to portray Catullus as poor, or at least the speaker of the poem as poor, he very likely was more than a little well off. Although his life was brief, Catullus remains one of the most influential of Rome's poets, inspiring later poets long after his death. Latin students will enjoy recognizing the traces of his work in the poems of Tennyson, Frost, Watts, and even Kipling.

Culture Corner

Sappho

SAPPHO

Although Sappho influenced later poets such as Catullus, who in turn influenced still later poets, we know very little about her life, and what little we do know comes primarily from her poetry. Even that poetry consists more of fragments of poems than it does of whole poems, and those fragments may or may not be autobiographical. Most scholars believe that Sappho was born on Lesbos, a Greek island. She was probably exiled for a brief time of her life to Sicily. Most scholars believe that Sappho was either a teacher in or head of a girl's school. Though we know hardly anything about her life, we do know that she was an excellent writer of lyrical poetry. She was born about 620 BC and lived to an old age.

The Legacy of Catullus

As the poetry of Sappho inspired Catullus, so the poetry of Catullus has inspired many poets who lived after him. Take, for example, Sir Alfred Lord Tennyson (1809–1892). Tennyson greatly admired the work of Catullus. In the following poem, Tennyson sought to imitate the hendecasyllabic style that Catullus used in forty-three of his poems. The meter of English poetry will use a pattern of stressed and unstressed syllables instead of long and short syllables. Scan Tennyson's verses to identify the hendecasyllabic pattern. Then read the poem aloud with your class.

"Hendecasyllabics"
Alfred Lord Tennyson

O you chorus of indolent reviewers,
Irresponsible, indolent reviewers,
Look, I come to the test, a tiny poem
All composed in a metre of Catullus,
All in quantity, careful of my motion,
Like the skater on ice that hardly bears him,
Lest I fall unawares before the people,
Waking laughter in indolent reviewers.
Should I flounder awhile without a tumble
Thro' this metrification of Catullus,
They should speak to me not without a welcome,
All that chorus of indolent reviewers.
Hard, hard, hard it is, only not to tumble,
So fantastical is the dainty metre.
Wherefore slight me not wholly, nor believe me
Too presumptuous, indolent reviewers.
O blatant Magazines, regard me rather—
Since I blush to belaud myself a moment—
As some rare little rose, a piece of inmost
Horticultural art, or half-coquette-like
Maiden, not to be greeted unbenignly.

Est Vērum!

According to Aubrey Burl's book *Catullus: A Poet in the Rome of Julius Caesar* (New York: Carroll and Graf Publishers, 2004), Gaius Valerius Catullus was half Celtic. He was from a wealthy family, and he was born c. 84 BC in Verona. Verona is in the area once called Cisalpine Gaul, a region bounded by the Alps on the north and the Rubicon River on the south. You will remember that Caesar's crossing of the Rubicon in 49 BC led to civil strife in Italy.

Centuries after the life of Catullus, William Shakespeare set his tragedy *Romeo and Juliet* in Verona. The events of that play are more than likely based on two families that actually lived in Verona prior to Shakespeare's time. We do not really know how Shakespeare learned of the situation he dramatized.

et docere et rerum exquirere causas
University of Georgia, GA

The motto for the University of Georgia is reminiscent of this famous line from the Roman poet Vergil: *"Felix, qui potuit rerum cognoscere causas."* (*Georgics*, Book 2, line 490)

Chapter 14

- Section 47. Relative Clause of Characteristic
- Section 48. Dative of Direction
- Section 49. Dactylic Hexameter

VOCABULARY

LATIN	ENGLISH	DERIVATIVES
Nouns		
arx, arcis, f.	stronghold, fortress	
fōrma, -ae, f.	form, beauty; shape, stature	(formation)
genus, generis, n.	race, nation, kind, type	(genus)
īra, -ae, f.	anger, wrath	(irate)
lītus, lītoris, n.	shore	(littoral)
moenia, moeniōrum, n. pl.	walls, fortifications of a city	(munitions, cf. munīre, to fortify)
mōles, mōlis, f.	great difficulty, burden	
nūmen, nūminis, n.	divinity, godhead	
Verbs		
contingō, contingere, contigī, contāctum	to come into contact with, to touch	(contact)
dignor, dignārī, dignātus sum	to deem worthy *or* deserving	(dignify)
errō, -āre, -āvī, -ātum	to wander, to sin	(error)
impellō, impellere, impulī, impulsum	to drive on	(impulse)
patior, patī, passus	to suffer, to experience; to allow, to permit	(patience, passion)
rapiō, rapere, rapuī, raptum	to snatch, to tear away, to seize	(rapture)
vertō, vertere, vertī, versum	to turn	(revert)
volvō, volvere, volvī, volūtum	to roll, to tumble	(revolve, convoluted)

Adjectives, Adverbs, Conjunctions, etc.		
antīquus, -a, -um, adj.	ancient, earlier, former, old	(antique)
īnsignis, -e, adj.	marked, distinguished, prominent	(insignia, cf. signum, sign)
memor, memoris, adj.	mindful, remembering	(memorable)
tot, indec. adj.	so many	

SECTION 47. Relative Clause of Characteristic

You have already learned the relative clause with the verb in the indicative. This dependent clause is always introduced by the relative pronouns *quī, quae, quod*. The clause in the indicative always states, or indicates, a reported fact about the antecedent. The antecedent is a noun or pronoun that comes before the relative pronoun, just as the Latin verb *antecēdere* (to come before) implies.

> Aenēās erat prīnceps quī multōs Trōiānōs ad Ītaliam addūxit.
>
> **relative pronoun** – quī
>
> **antecedent** – prīnceps
>
> **reported fact** – multōs Trōiānōs ad Ītaliam addūxit

Relative clauses may also appear with a verb in the subjunctive mood. Sometimes these clauses show purpose or result. In such cases, the clause follows the same pattern as the *ut* clauses you have already learned. The only difference is that a relative pronoun introduces the clause instead of the adverb *ut*.

When the relative clause contains a subjunctive verb and does *not* show purpose or result, it is called a **relative clause of characteristic**. The relative clause of characteristic is used to define the character of the antecedent. There are a number of ways in which Latin introduces clauses of characteristic.

1. This clause may often indicate the character of the antecedent, especially if that antecedent is an undefined or unspecified person/thing.

> Est prīnceps quī tot virtūtēs demonstrāverit.
>
> Quis est quī hanc fābulam dubitet?

2. The clause may indicate the existence or non-existence of something or someone.

> sunt quī = there are those who . . .
> quis est quī = who is there who . . .
>
> Sunt quī hanc fābulam crēdant.
> Nēmō est quī omnia sciat.

3. Certain adjectives may also introduce a characteristic clause with a relative pronoun: *dīgnus, indīgnus, aptus* (as well as *ūnus, sōlus*, though these last two actually more often introduce clauses of existence).

> Prīnceps est dīgnus quī honōrem recipiat.

Exercise 1. Underline the relative clause in each sentence; parse the verb in the clause. Then, translate the entire sentence.

1. Arcem aedificēmus, cūius moenia sunt magna fortitūdine et magnitūdine.
2. Quī ā vērō erret, in falsīs āmittētur.
3. Ūnum, quī tot labōrēs prō patriā patiātus erit, laudārī dignor.
4. Trōia, ā quā Aenēās vēnerat, erat antīqua īnsignisque urbs.
5. Sunt quī memorēs īrae ad pācem vertant.
6. Dīcitur moenia Trōiae, quae nēmō vī superāre poterat, aedificāta esse nūmine.
7. Erat imprūdēns quī illum saxum dē scopulō volvisset.

Exercise 2. Underline the relative clause in each English sentence. Determine whether it should be an indicative clause or a subjunctive clause (clause of characteristic). Translate the sentence into Latin.

1. The little boy who is rolling rocks down from the roof might kill the pigs!
2. He who turns his cart from the road will fall down the cliff.
3. The geese that have come into the house are snatching fruit from the table.
4. He alone who is able to snatch the sword from the stone will be king.
5. Those who are mindful of the teacher's anger will not wander in their studies.
6. Always do what you are afraid to do. (Emerson)

Section 48. Dative of Direction

In Latin, prose authors often use the accusative of place to which to express direction toward a place. For most nouns, this construction uses a preposition such as *ad* or *in* + the accusative case.

    Nōs ad Ītaliam nāvigēmus.   Let us sail to Italy.

There is a special group of nouns that we use without a preposition to indicate place to which. We simply express the destination in the accusative case. This group consists of the names of cities; towns; small islands in the Mediterranean; and the nouns *domus*, *humus*, and *rūs*.

Caveat Discipulus: Remember that this same group of nouns also uses the ablative case without a preposition for place from which and the locative case for place where.

    Nōs domum nāvigēmus.   Let us sail home.

Latin poets, however, often used the dative case to express a direction or final destination. Perhaps this practice came about because many modeled their poetry on that of the ancient Greeks, who used the dative case for direction toward a place in their poetry. The omission of the preposition gave the poet greater flexibility as he tried to fit the meter of the poem. Whatever the reason, the dative of direction appears often in poetry, but rarely in Latin prose.

    Nōs Ītaliae nāvigēmus.   Let us sail to Italy.

Exercise 3. Underline the accusative direction phrase in each sentence. Rewrite the accusative phrase using the dative of direction, then translate the entire sentence. To help you with this exercise, the following is a list of place names that will occur in the chapter reading.

Karthāgō, Karthāginis, f. .... Carthage
Ītalia, -ae, f. .... Italy
Latium, -ī, n. .... Latium (region of Italy in which Rome is located)
Libya, -ae, f. .... Libya (region of North Africa in which Carthage is located)
Samos/Samus, -ī, f. .... Samos (an island in the Mediterranean Sea famous for its worship of Juno)
Trōia, -ae, f. .... Troy
Tyrus, -ī, f. .... Tyre (a city in Phoenicia whose people settled Carthage)

Here's an example of what your answers should look like for this exercise:

<u>Ad Ītaliam</u> aestāte nāvigāre volō!
Accusative Direction Phrase: Ad Ītaliam
Dative of Direction: Ītaliae
Translation: I want to sail to Italy in the summer!

1. Colōnī ad Libyam ut urbem novam fundārent Tyrō nāvigāverant.
2. Cum ab Trōiā profectī essent, Aenēās puerulum et patrem et multōs Trōiānōs aliōs ad Ītaliam addūxit.
3. Propter īram deae, quae sit nūllīus parvae magnitūdinis, Trōiānī Karthāginem impulsī erunt.
4. Et populī Trōiae et Tyriī ad lītora Libyae errāverant, appetentēs locum in quō urbem conderent.
5. Properēmus ad agrum Samī ut currum antīquum in templō videāmus.
6. Fāta prīncipem ut et generem et deōs ad Latium īnferret hortantur.
7. Ōlim Aenēās per multōs labōrēs perīculōsōs ad Latium accēderit, sed numquam Trōiam redet.

Section 49. Dactylic Hexameter

Dactylic hexameter is the meter of epic poetry. Homer used this meter in writing both the *Iliad* and the *Odyssey*. Romans later adapted the meter to their own language for their great masterpieces. Instead of the choriamb, this meter will use a combination of the following:

1. Dactyl ➔ | _ ᴗ ᴗ | long – short – short

Dactyl comes from the Greek word meaning "finger." Take a close look at your fingers and note that each one has three segments. The segment closest to your palm is longer than the two that follow. Thus comes the pattern: long – short – short.

2. Spondee ➔ | _ _ | long – long

Spondee comes from the Greek word meaning "libation." A libation was a drink offering to the gods. The spondee was a rhythm often used in the music that accompanied such rituals.

3. Trochee ➔ | _ ᴗ | long – short

Trochee comes from the Greek word meaning "a running foot." Perhaps this refers to the short, quick nature of this rhythm.

Each verse of dactylic hexameter (from the Greek *hex*, meaning "six") consists of six metrical feet, most of which are dactyls. A spondee may be substituted for any foot but the fifth one (with rare exception). The last foot is either a trochee or a spondee.

$$|\_\underset{\smile}{\smile}|\_\underset{\smile}{\smile}|\_\underset{\smile}{\smile}|\_\underset{\smile}{\smile}|\_\smile\smile|\_x|$$

Nota Bene: Don't let that new symbol confuse you. The symbol $\underset{\smile}{\smile}$ simply indicates that that syllable can either be two short syllables or one long syllable. You don't see that symbol in the fifth foot because it can only have one long and two short syllables in it.

Arma virumque canō, Trōiae quī prīmus ab ōrīs (Vergil, *Aeneid*)
_ ∪ ∪ | _ _ ∪ ∪ | _   _ | _   _ | _ ∪ ∪ | _ _

Another element of dactylic hexameter is the caesura. A **caesura** (from the Latin *caedō, caedere, caesī, caesum*, "to cut") is a word break appearing in the middle of a foot. Since there is often more than one word break in a line, the principal caesura occurs near the middle of the verse. This caesura allows the reader a break to breathe, and may also provide him a pause for dramatic effect. In dactylic hexameter, the caesura usually appears in the third or fourth foot, but may also appear in the second foot of the verse. As with English poetry or music, such pauses often come in a logical place where a natural break in speaking would occur (but such a pause is not necessary).

Nota Bene: A caesura will most often come in the middle of the foot between two words.

The (principal) caesura is marked by the symbol //.

Exempli Gratia:

Arma virumque canō, Trōiae quī prīmus ab ōrīs (Vergil, *Aeneid*)
_ ∪ ∪ | _ _ ∪ ∪ | _ // _ | _   _ | _ ∪ ∪ | _ _

I sing of arms and the man // who first from the shores of Troy . . .

As noted by the comma (in the Latin), the caesura is a natural place to take a breath or pause. When provided by the editors (not the poet, since the Romans had no punctuation marks), punctuation can provide great clues for a caesura. The reader should also note that following the comma is a relative clause. The beginning or end of such clauses is another logical place to find a caesura.

Exercise 4. Scan the following verses, making sure to include the principal caesura if the meter is hexameter. Then indicate the style of meter for each: dactylic hexameter or hendecasyllabic. Read the verses aloud in Latin and then in English.

Caveat Discipulus: Watch for elisions!

1. quae rēgiō in terrīs nostrī nōn plēna labōris? (Vergil, *Aeneid*)
   Hint: *Rēgiō in*—the *i* in *rēgiō* is read as a consonant = *rēgj(ō) in*.

2. hunc tegit obscūrus subter praecordia veprēs
   nec vērō, tōtō spīrāns dē corpore flammam,
   aestiferōs ualidīs ērumpit flātibus ignēs. (Cicero, *Aretea*)

   Vocabulary Hints:

   tegō, -ere .... to cover
   obscūrus, -a, -um, adj. .... dark
   subter, prep. (+ acc.) .... under
   praecordia, -ōrum, n. pl. ..... underbelly, midriff, stomach, breast
   veprēs, vepris, m. .... thornbush
   spīrō, -āre .... to breath out
   aestiferus, -a, -um, adj. .... heat-bearing
   ērumpō, -ere .... to burst forth, to spew
   flātus, -ūs .... blowing, breeze, strong wind

3. Dī magnī, horribilem et sacrum libellum! (Catullus, 14)

4. quem nēmō ferrō potuit superāre nec aurō (Ennius, *Annales*)

5. Sēlēctōs nisi dās mihī libellōs,
   admittam tineās trucēsque blattās. (Martial, *Apophoreta*)

   Vocabulary Hints:
   sēlēctus, -a, -um ....choice, chosen, something selected
   admittō, -ere ....to admit, give an audience to
   tinea, -ae, f. ....worm
   trux, trucis ....savage, ferocious
   blatta, -ae, f. ....cockroach

6. Quārē nec tālīs dignantur vīsere coetūs,
   nec sē contingī patiuntur lūmine clārō. (Catullus, 64: 407–408)

   Vocabulary Hints:
   coetus, -ūs, m. .... meeting, interaction

Before You Read!

REVIEW: ELLIPSIS IN POETRY

You have already learned that poets sometimes use elision or syncope to shorten words or phrases to fit the meter being used. Authors of both prose and poetry will also shorten a line with the use of an ellipsis, the omission of a word. There are two types of ellipsis that often occur in poetry:

1. Omission of linking verbs.

   quae rēgiō in terrīs nostrī (est) nōn plēna labōris?

2. Omission of prepositions. Often a prepositional phrase, particularly those used in place expressions, will drop the preposition.

   (ad) Lāvīniaque vēnit lītora

Chapter Reading: Reading 1

AENEID I.I–XXXIII

I.I–VII

1 Arma virumque *canō*, <u>Trōiae</u> quī prīmus ab ōrīs
2 <u>Ītaliam</u>, fātō *profugus*, *Lāvīnia*que vēnit
3 lītora; multum ille et terrīs iactātus et altō*
4 vī *superum* saevae memorem Iūnōnis ob īram;
5 multa quoque et bellō passus, dum conderet urbem,
6 īnferretque deōs Latiō, genus unde *Latīnum*,
7 *Albānī*que patrēs, atque altae moenia Rōmae.

*Notice how the caesura in line 3 does not lend itself to a pause.

GLOSSARY: **Reading 1**

Use your "eye" Latin to discern the meaning of the underlined words in the reading.

canō, canāre .... *cantō, cantāre*
profugus, -a, -um, adj. .... fugitive, banished, driven
Lāvīnius, -a, -um, adj. .... Lavinian, region of Italy that would be named for Lavinia, a Latin princess and future wife of Aeneas
superus, -a, -um, adj. .... high; (as a plural noun) the gods; (*superum* = *superōrum*, an archaic form of the genitive plural)
Latīnus, -a, -um, adj. .... Latin
Albānī, Albānōrum, m. pl. .... Albans, *gēns in Ītaliā*

Chapter Reading: Reading 2

I. VIII–XI

8 Mūsa, mihī causās memorā, quō nūmine *laesō*,
9 quidve *dolēns*, rēgīna *deum* tot volvere cāsūs
10 īnsignem pietāte virum, tot *adīre* labōrēs
11 impulerit. Tantaene animīs *caelestibus* īrae?

GLOSSARY: **Reading 2**

laedō, laedere, laesī, laesum .... to hurt, to offend
dolēns (pres. part.), *doleō, dolēre* .... to suffer, to grieve (cf. *dolor*)
deum .... *deōrum* (archaic genitive)
adeō, adīre .... *ad + īre*
caelestis, caeleste, adj. .... heavenly, celestial (cf. *caelum*)

Chapter Reading: Reading 3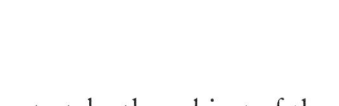

I. XII–XVIII

12 Urbs antīqua fuit, (*Tyriī* tenuēre *colōnī*)
13 Karthāgō, Ītaliam contrā *Tiberīna*que longē
14 *ōstia*, dīves opum studiīsque *asperrima* bellī;
15 quam **Iūnō fertur** terrīs magis omnibus ūnam
16 *posthabitā coluisse* Samō; hīc illius arma,
17 hīc currus fuit; **hoc rēgnum** dea gentibus **esse**,
18 **sī quā** *fāta sinant*, iam tum *tendit*que *fovet*que.

PHRASES: **Reading 3**

Iūnō fertur – It is said that Juno *or, literally* Juno is said (In Latin it is common to take the subject of the indirect statement as the subject of the passive verb. A literal translation sounds odd.)

hoc rēgnum ... esse – [she intends] this [city] to be a kingdom (*hoc* refers back to *urbs* but is attracted into the gender of *rēgnum*, which is its predicate)

sī quā = *sī quā viā* – if in any way (remember that after *sī*, *aliquā* loses its *ali-*)

GLOSSARY: Reading 3

Use your "eye" Latin to discern the meaning of the underlined words in the reading.

Tyrius, -a, -um, adj.	Tyrian, of Tyre (Tyre was a region of Phoenicia whose people settled the town of Carthage in Libya.)
Tiberina, -ae, f.	Tiber River, which runs through the city of Rome and down to the Mediterranean Sea
ōstium, -ī, n.	mouth, delta of a river
asperrima	*saevissima, durissima*
posthabeō, posthabēre, posthabuī, posthabitum	to esteem less
colō, colere, coluī, cultum	to cultivate, to attend to, to cherish (cf. *colōnus*)
sinō, sinere, sīvī, situm	to place, to put down, to allow
tendō, tendere, tetendī, tentum	to intend, to aim
foveō, fovēre, fōvī, fōtum	to hope for

Chapter Reading: Reading 4

I.XIX–XXII

19 <u>Prōgeniem</u> sed enim <u>Trōiānō</u> ā *sanguine* dūcī
20 audierat, *Tyriās* ōlim quae verteret arcēs;
21 hinc populum lātē rēgem bellōque superbum
22 ventūrum excidiō <u>Libyae</u>: sīc volvere *Parcās*.

GLOSSARY: Reading 4

Use your "eye" Latin to discern the meaning of the underlined words in the reading.

sanguis, sanginis, m.	blood
Tyrius, -a, -um, adj.	Tyrian
Parcae, Parcārum, f. pl.	the Fates (Clotho, Lachesis, and Atropos are known together as the Fates, three goddesses who determined the fate of all)

Chapter Reading: Reading 5

I.XXIII–XXVIII

23 Id metuēns, *veteris*que memor *Sāturnia* bellī,
24 prīma quod ad Trōiam prō cārīs gesserat Argīs—
25 *necdum* etiam causae īrārum saevīque dolōrēs
26 *exciderant* animō: manet altā mente *repostum*
27 iūdicium *Paridis* sprētaeque iniūria fōrmae,
28 et genus invīsum, et raptī *Ganymēdis* honōrēs.

GLOSSARY: Reading 5

veteris, vetere	*antīquus*
Sāturnia	*fīlia Sāturnī, Iūnō*

Argī, Argōrum, m. .... Argos, an important city in southern Greece (the Peloponnesus)
necdum .... *neque dum* (and not yet)
excidō, excidere, excidī .... to fall out, to fall (from *ex* + *cadere*)
repostum = repositum; *repositus, -a, -um*, adj. .... stored up
Paris, Paridis, m. .... *Paris, princeps Troiae*
spernō, spernere, sprēvī, sprētum .... to spurn, to reject
Ganymēdis, gen. sing. .... Ganymede (According to mythology, Ganymede was a handsome young youth whom Jupiter, transformed into an eagle, snatched from earth and carried off to Olympus. There he "snatched" the honor of being cupbearer to the gods from Hebe, daughter to Jupiter and Juno, and gave the honor to Ganymede. The case of *raptī* is ambiguous. It could modify Ganymede or the honors. Both items were "snatched" in one sense or the other. A wonderful play on words and wonderful use of word order by Vergil.)

Chapter Reading: Reading 6

I.XXIX–XXXIII

29 Hīs *accēnsa* super, iactātōs aequore tōtō

30 *Trōas, relliquiās Danaum* atque *immītis* Achillī,

31 *arcēbat* longē *Latiō*, multōsque per annōs

32 errābant, āctī fātīs, maria omnia circum.

33 Tantae mōlis erat Rōmānam condere gentem!

Glossary: Reading 6

Use your "eye" Latin to discern the meaning of the underlined words in the reading.
accendō, accendere, accendī, accensum .... to set on fire, to kindle
Trōas .... *Trōiānōs*
relliquia, -ae, f. .... leftovers, scraps
Danaum .... *Graecōrum*
immītis, immīte .... *crūdēlis*
arceō, arcēre, arcuī .... to hinder, to prevent, to keep from
Latium, Latiī, n. .... Latium, region in Italy

RESPONDĒ LATĪNĒ! READINGS 1–6

1. Praeter virum quās rēs cantāvit poēta?
2. Unde vēnerat vir?
3. Quotīs in versibus poēta nōbis dīxit quō vir venīret?
4. Cūius īra erat contrā virum?
5. Quās rēs inferet vir Latiō?
6. Quem adloquitur poēta octāvō in versū?
7. Quis erat pietāte īnsignis?
8. Cui aut quibus magna īra erat?

9. Quī urbem antīquam tenēbant?
10. Quōrum erat Karthāgō dīves?
11. Quem urbem Iūnō amābat, secundum versum XII ūsque ad (up to) versum XVI?
12. Quā in urbe erant Iūnōnis arma?
13. Quotō in versū scrīpsit poēta dē populō quī Karthāginem vastāret?
14. In versū XXIIIo cūius erat Iūnō memor?
15. Ubi vetus bellum pugnātum erat?
16. Quī prīnceps Trōiānus fōrmae deae iniūriās tūlerat?
17. Quī populus erat reliquus ā Graecīs?
18. Quis arcēbat Trōiānōs longē Latiō?
19. Quotō in versū scrīpsit Vergilius Aenēan et Trōiānōs magnā cum difficultāte gentem Rōmānam conditūrōs esse?
20. Quotīs in versibus scrīpsit Vergilius Karthāginem longē ab Ītaliā esse?

A bust of Vergil from his tomb in Naples
(Image courtesy of A. Hunter Wright)

About the Author

PUBLIUS VERGILIUS MARO

Publius Vergilius Maro, whom we call Vergil, was born on the Ides of October in 70 BC in Andes, a town in Cisalpine Gaul. Vergil's father was wealthy enough to provide his son with a good education in such places as Milan, Rome, and Naples. Young Vergil considered law as a career, but turned his interest to poetry at a young age. His poetry followed the sequence of genres common to poets in the ancient world: pastoral poetry (which is lyrical), didactic poetry, and epic poetry. His major works are the *Eclogues* (or *Bucolics*), the *Georgics*, and the *Aeneid*.

Tradition tells us that Vergil was not strong and healthy. After finishing the *Aeneid*, the poet traveled to Greece (*circa* 19 B C), where he intended to edit his epic. He met Augustus in Athens and decided to return to Italy. He completed the journey across the sea, but he was ill with a fever. He died in the harbor of Brundisium on September 21, 19 BC. Vergil had wanted the *Aeneid* burned if he should die before he finished editing the epic; however, Augustus ordered Vergil's literary executors, Lucius Varius Rufus and Plotius Tucca, to disregard Vergil's wish that the work be burned. Augustus ordered the work to be published with as few changes as possible. This order may be the reason that there are several unfinished lines, called hemistiches, in the poem. Vergil, Rome's greatest poet and surely one of the greatest poets in all of literary history, influenced Ovid and other later Roman poets, as well as Dante, Milton, Keats, and Shakespeare.

CHARACTERISTICS OF EPIC POETRY

Epic poetry has many characteristics. The most obvious characteristic of an epic is that it is long. The second most obvious is that an epic is a poem. While books and movies such as *Gone with the Wind* are often termed "epic," they are not truly epic because they are not poems. An epic is also national in scope: it is about the founding of a society or a hero whose activities and life affect a society or both. The epic also contains the following:

- an invocation to a muse
- long ceremonial speeches
- epic similes*
- descriptions of armor and weapons

- scenes of battle, athletic contests, or both
- intervention of the gods into the affairs of men
- a beginning *in medias res* (This means that the poem begins in the middle of the basic plot and has flashbacks to earlier important events. After the flashback, the plot continues in a straightforward manner.)
- an adventurous journey, often to the underworld

***Nota Bene**: Epic similes are also called Homeric similes. These epic similes are long and involved. While a regular simile makes simple comparisons, such as "she ran like a gazelle," an epic simile makes extended comparisons, such as this passage from *Odyssey* XIII line 28-35:

> But Odysseus often turned his head towards the all-shining sun, eager for it to set. For indeed he earnestly desired to go. But as when a man longs for supper, whose pair of oxen all day long have dragged a well-constructed plow along a fallow-field, and therefore, gladly, does the light of the sun set for him to head for his supper, and his knees fail him as he goes, thus welcome was the sun's setting light welcome to Odysseus. (translated by Edward J. Kotynski)

There are two types of epic: folk epic and literary epic. The folk epic is in the oral tradition—it was composed orally over a long period of time and handed down to succeeding generations. The *Iliad* and the *Odyssey*, along with the Anglo-Saxon epic *Beowulf*, are the prime examples of the folk epic. Folk epics must have had more than one "author." The literary epic is an effort by one author-poet to imitate the folk epic. Vergil imitated Homer, and John Milton imitated Vergil. The closest thing to true epic in American literature is *John Brown's Body* by Stephen Vincent Benét.

Derivative Detective

-*MEN* WORDS

You have by now learned several nouns whose nominative singular ends in -*men*. Look carefully over the following list. Consider what elements all of these words have in common.

        certāmen   crīmen   flūmen   lūmen   nōmen   nūmen

The suffix -*men* basically means "thing." Many of these words are contractions (or examples of syncope) that occur when this suffix is attached to another word. With this in mind, discern the meanings of the following Latin words. Then use your detective skills to see how many English derivatives you can find. **Hint:** Remember that the -*men* changes to -*min* for the noun's stem. Also, not all of the words will have English derivatives.

agmen	fulmen	nōmen
certāmen	grāmen	nūmen
crīmen	līmen	strāmen
flūmen	lūmen	tegmen

Colloquāmur

DESCRIPTIVE DISCUSSIONS

To further practice the lessons in this chapter, write positive descriptions of your classmates or teachers using the relative clause of characteristic. Then, as a class, practice speaking Latin by sharing these descriptive phrases and guessing the person whom each one is meant to describe.

Exempli Gratia:

    Putō dē puellā quae sit benignissima.

The Legacy of Vergil

Vergil, inspired by the epic poems of Homer, wrote the *Aeneid*, his *magnum opus*. This epic tale recounts in artful hexameter the adventures of Aeneas as he brings the Trojan remnant to Italy, a remnant that would, in time, give birth to the Roman nation. Vergil's work, along with the epic poems of Homer, would continue to inspire later authors to try their own hand at such a masterful work. One who succeeded in such a task was John Milton. The following are two excerpts from Milton's epic *Paradise Lost*. The first passage contains the opening lines to the poem. The second passage is taken from Book VI, about halfway through the epic. Milton chose iambic pentameter, a verse commonly used by Shakespeare, over dactylic hexameter. Hexameter is notoriously difficult to work with in English. As you read the excerpt, however, you will notice several elements of epic poetry and observe the influence of Homer and Vergil. Read the poem and then discuss these similarities with your classmates.

> Of Man's first disobedience, and the fruit
> Of that forbidden tree whose mortal taste
> Brought death into the World, and all our woe,
> With loss of Eden, till one greater Man
> Restore us, and regain the blissful seat,
> Sing, Heavenly Muse, that, on the secret top
> Of Oreb, or of Sinai, didst inspire
> That shepherd who first taught the chosen seed
> In the beginning how the heavens and earth
> Rose out of Chaos: or, if Sion hill
> Delight thee more, and Siloa's brook that flowed
> Fast by the oracle of God, I thence
> Invoke thy aid to my adventurous song,
> That with no middle flight intends to soar
> Above th' Aonian mount, while it pursues
> Things unattempted yet in prose or rhyme.
> And chiefly thou, O Spirit, that dost prefer
> Before all temples th' upright heart and pure,
> Instruct me, for thou know'st; thou from the first
> Wast present, and, with mighty wings outspread,
> Dove-like sat'st brooding on the vast Abyss,
> And mad'st it pregnant: what in me is dark
> Illumine, what is low raise and support;
> That, to the height of this great argument,
> I may assert Eternal Providence,
> And justify the ways of God to men.
>
> *Paradise Lost* I.1–26

> He, in celestial panoply all armed
> Of radiant Urim, work divinely wrought,
> Ascended; at his right hand Victory
> Sat eagle-winged; beside him hung his bow

Challenge Box:

Can you find a line in *Paradise Lost* which Milton borrows from the *Aeneid* lines 1-33?

And quiver with three-bolted thunder stored;
And from about him fierce effusion rolled
Of smoke, and bickering flame, and sparkles dire:
Attended with ten thousand thousand Saints,
He onward came; far off his coming shone;
And twenty thousand (I their number heard)
Chariots of God, half on each hand, were seen;
He on the wings of Cherub rode sublime
On the crystalline sky, in sapphire throned,
Illustrious far and wide, but by his own
First seen, them unexpected joy surpris'd,
When the great Ensign of Messiah blaz'd
Aloft by Angels borne, his Sign in Heav'n:
Under whose Conduct Michael soon reduc'd
His army, circumfus'd on either Wing,
Under their Head imbodied all in one.
Before him Power Divine his way prepar'd;
At his command the uprooted Hills retir'd
Each to his place, they heard his voice and went
Obsequious, Heav'n his wonted face renew'd,
And with fresh Flow'rets Hill and Valley smil'd.
This saw his hapless Foes, but stood obdur'd,
And to rebellious fight rallied their Powers
Insensate, hope conceiving from despair.
In heavn'ly Spirits could such perverseness dwell?
Paradise Lost VI.760–788

A scene from Book II of the *Aeneid*: Aeneas carries his father, Ancises, upon his shoulders from the burning city of Troy as Aeneas's son Ascanius follows.

Est Vērum!

Vergil was dubbed by Christians of the medieval era as "the virtuous pagan." This is largely because of a poem known as the "Fourth Eclogue" in which Vergil seems to foretell of the birth of Christ. Historians today largely believe Vergil's intent in this poem was to glorify the birth of a new heir for Augustus Caesar. Nonetheless, this title has been attached to Vergil since that time. For this reason, the Italian poet Dante Alighieri places Vergil as a guide for the hero of his epic poem *The Divine Comedy*. Vergil's task in this epic is to serve as a guide and interpreter through the various levels of hell. Because of his standing as a "virtuous pagan," Vergil himself is not condemned to the sentences of his fellow Romans, but he is instead elevated to a state of semi-grace.

Palma non sine pulvere
Wesleyan University, Kansas

Wesleyan University adapted this motto from line 51 of Horace's First Epistle: *"Cui sit condicio dulcis sine puluere palmae?"*

Chapter 15

- Section 50. Compound Verbs and the Dative Case
- Section 51. Objective Genitive
- Section 52. More on Meter
  - Alcaic Meter

VOCABULARY

LATIN	ENGLISH	DERIVATIVES
Nouns		
aes, aeris, n.	bronze	
coma, -ae, f.	the hair of the head	(comet)
ēnsis, ēnsis, m.	sword	(ensiform)
grex, gregis, m./f.	herd, flock	(congregation)
imber, imbris, m.	rain, shower	
meritum, meritī, n.	merit	(meritocracy)
mulier, mulieris, f.	woman, female	(muliebrity)
rēmus, -ī, m.	oar	(trireme)
ruīna, -ae, f.	ruins, that which has fallen down	(ruin)
venēnum, -ī, n.	poison	(venom)
Verbs		
adsurgō, adsurgere, adsurrēxī, adsurrēctum	to surge ahead	
cingō, cingere, cīnxī, cīnctum	to bind, to encircle	(cincture)
conbibō, conbibere, conbibī, conbibitūrum	to drink together; to drink in excess	
dēdūcō, dēdūcere, dēdūxī, dēductum	to draw off, to lead off	(deduce)
minuō, minuere, minuī, minūtum	to lessen, to diminish	(minute)
quaerō, quaerere, quaesīvī, quaesītum	to seek, to look for; to question	(inquire)
Adjectives, Adverbs, Conjunctions, etc.		
āter, ātra, ātrum, adj.	dull black (not shiny), flat black	(atrabilious)
citus, -a, -um, adj.	swift	
ēbrius, -a, um, adj.	drunk	(inebriated)

latēns, latentis, adj.	hiding, hidden	(latent)
tacitus, -a, -um, adj.	silent	(tacit)
quidlibet, adv.	whatever you like, anything whatsoever	
scīlicet, adv.	naturally, certainly, undoubtedly	

SECTION 50. Compound Verbs and the Dative Case

You have already learned that a number of verbs, called special intransitives, will govern the dative case instead of the accusative (see *LA1*, section 44; *LA2*, section 12). Among these are verbs such as:

placeō, placēre – to please (to be pleasing to)

faveō, favēre – to favor (to be favorable to)

serviō, servīre – to serve (to be of service to)

In addition to this special group, there are many compound verbs that also govern an object in the dative case. A compound verb consists of a root verb to which a preposition has been added as a prefix.

Exercise 1. Look carefully at the following list of compound verbs. Using the alphabetical glossary at the back of the book, write out the prefix and root word that form each compound verb. Then write the meaning of the compound verb.

Caveat Discipulus: Remember that prefixes and root words often change their spelling slightly when forming compound words.

Example: impellere – in + pellere = to drive on, to strike; to incite, to urge on

1. dēprōmere
2. expavēscere
3. conbibere
4. antecēdere
5. reparāre
6. dēdūcere
7. contingere
8. adsurgere
9. invidēre
10. revertere

Not every compound verb takes an object in the dative case. Typically, those that take a dative use as prefixes the prepositions *ad, ante, circum, cum, in, inter, ob, post, prae, prō, sub,* and *super*. Compounds using these prepositions often, but not always, are followed by a dative direct object, especially when the meaning of the resulting word is significantly different from the meaning of the two parts put together. The use of a dative or accusative with such compound verbs will vary depending upon the author. Therefore, it is best to keep in mind that a compound verb might take a dative instead of an accusative.

Exercise 2. Look again at the list of verbs in exercise 1. Based on what you have just learned about compound verbs that govern the dative, which of these verbs might take a dative object?

Exercise 3. Underline the verbs in each of the following sentences and circle their objects. Then translate each sentence. Remember that these objects may be accusative, dative, or even ablative.

1. Mīles aere saevō sē cingit.
2. Rēgīna nāvibus citīs ātrīs, quae sē domō dēdūcerent, invīdit.
3. Imber perīculum ignis, cum diū nūllus fuerit, scīlicet minuet.
4. Rēmīs adsurgendī causā celeriter ad orās ūtēbāmur.
5. Hostibus ēnsibus antecēdēmus, et urbs eōrum in ruīnīs relicta erit.
6. Fruēris carmine mulierum et fābulā poētae.
7. Columbam mollem grex sedentem tacitam in agrīs cīnxit.
8. Perīre quaerēns in modō nōn similī mulierī, rēgīna ēnsem cēpit.
9. Mulierēs comās flōribus cingunt et manibus contingunt dum in templum prōcēdunt.
10. Quaerite quidlibet, sed meritum bonum scelerī numquam succēdet.

SECTION 51. Objective Genitive

The **objective genitive** is a genitive that acts as the direct object of the verbal idea implied in certain types of nouns.

Exempli Gratia:

Amor patriae eum movet.   Love of the fatherland moves him.
(i.e., He loves the fatherland.)

Exercise 4. Read and discuss the meaning or significance of the following quotations.

1. Salus populi suprema lex. (motto of Missouri)
2. Caelum non animum mutant qui trans mare currunt. (Horace)
3. Crescit amor nummi, quantum ipsa pecunia crevit. (Juvenal)
4. Quod cibum est aliis, aliis est venenum. (proverb)
5. Praestat honesta mors turpi vitae. (Nepos)
6. Felix qui potuit rerum cognoscere causas. (Vergil)

SECTION 52. More on Meter

ALCAIC METER

Alcaic meter is used for lyric stanza. A **stanza** is a set of four lines of poetry that follow a particular pattern. This meter is named for Alceus, a Greek poet from the island of Lesbos. It is the meter which the poet Horace used most often in his *Odes*. You will read two selections from Horace's *Odes* in the chapter's reading.

First two verses: x _ ᴗ _ _ // _ ᴗ ᴗ _ | ᴗ x

Third verse: x _ ᴗ _ _ _ ᴗ ᴗ x

Fourth verse: _ ᴗ ᴗ _ ᴗ ᴗ _ | ᴗ _ x

There is *almost always* a caesura after the fifth syllable in the first two verses. Any exceptions to this rule should be taken as significant.

Exercise 5. Scan the following lines of poetry. These are taken from the first stanza of chapter reading 1.

Nunc est bibendum, nunc pede līberō

pulsanda tellus, nunc Saliāribus

ōrnāre pulvīnar deōrum

tempus erat dapibus, sodālēs.

(Horace, I.37)

Chapter Reading: Reading 1

A POET'S THOUGHTS ON CLEOPATRA AFTER THE BATTLE OF ACTIUM

(Horace, Ode I.xxxvii)

1 Nunc est bibendum, nunc pede līberō
2 pulsanda *tellūs*, nunc *Saliāribus*
3 ōrnāre *pulvīnar* deōrum
4 tempus erat *dapibus*, sodālēs.
5 <u>Antehāc</u> nefās dēprōmere Caecubum
6 *cellīs avītīs*, dum *Capitōliō*
7 rēgīna <u>dēmentīs</u> ruīnās
8 *fūnus* et imperiō parābat
9 <u>contāminātō</u> cum grege turpium
10 morbō virōrum, **quidlibet impotēns**
11 **spērāre** fortūnāque dulcī
12 ēbria. Sed minuit furōrem
13 vix ūna *sōspes* nāvis ab ignibus,
14 mentemque *lymphātam Mareōticō*
15 *redēgit* in vērōs timōrēs
16 Caesar, ab Ītaliā volantem
17 rēmīs *adurgēns*, *accipiter* velut
18 mollīs columbās aut *leporem* citus
19 *vēnātor* in campīs <u>nivālis</u>
20 *Haemoniae*, daret ut *catēnīs*
21 <u>fātāle</u> <u>mōnstrum</u>. Quae generōsius
22 perīre quaerēns nec <u>muliebriter</u>
23 *expāvit* ēnsem nec latentīs
24 classe citā *reparāvit ōrās*,
25 ausa et iacentem vīsere rēgiam
26 *voltū* <u>serēnō</u>, fortis et asperās
27 *tractāre* <u>serpentēs</u>, ut ātrum
28 corpore conbiberet venēnum;
29 *dēlīberātā* morte, ferōcior,
30 saevīs *Liburnīs* scīlicet invidēns
31 prīvāta dēdūcī superbō—
32 nōn humilis mulier—triumphō.

Cleopatra

Phrases: Reading 1

quidlibet impotēns spērāre – unbridled in her expectations/hope of whatever she wanted/wished (*impotēns* has two meanings, "powerless" and "unable to be controlled"; perhaps this is intended as a pun to show that in reality she was powerless in her hopes)

GLOSSARY: Reading 1

Use your "eye" Latin to discern the meaning of the underlined words in the reading.

tellūs, tellūris, f.	earth, ground
Saliāris, -e, adj.	sumptuous, magnificent (This word is derived from *Saliī*. The Salii, priests of Jupiter Gravidus, were a group founded by King Numa Pompilius. The name means "jumpers" or "leapers." They made solemn processions through Rome on the Kalends of March. After the processions, they held sumptuous feasts; therefore, the word *saliārius* came to mean "sumptuous" or "magnificent.")
pulvīnar, pulvīnāris, n.	couch, highly decorated couch
daps, dapis, f.	banquet
sodālis, sodālis, m./f.	friend, mate, companion
dēprōmō, dēprōmere, dēprōmpsī, dēprōmptum	to draw forth, to bring forth, to fetch
Caecubum, -ī, n.	Caecuban wine, a fine wine from the district of Caecubus in Latium
cella, -ae, f.	cellar, wine cellar
avītus, -a, um, adj.	of or belonging to a grandfather, ancestral, of ancestors
Capitōlium	the Capitoline Hill, the tallest but smallest of the seven Roman hills
fūnus, fūneris, n.	funeral, burial, death
sōspes, sōspitis, adj.	saved, safe (This word is usually a noun meaning "saver.")
lymphātus, -a, -um, adj.	driven mad, maddened
Mareōticum, -ī, n.	Mareotic, a type of fine wine from Mareotis, a district in Egypt; (sometimes) Egyptian (notice the contrast between the *Latin* wine and the *Egyptian* wine in this poem)
redigō, redigere, redēgī, redāctum	to redirect
adurgeō, adurgēre	to pursue closely, to give a close chase to
accipiter, accipitris, m.	hawk (cf. *accipio*)
lepus, leporis, m.	hare
vēnātor, vēnātōris, m.	hunter
Haemoniae	Thessaly
catēna, catēnae, f.	chain (Spanish *cadena*, chain)
expavēscō, expavēscere, expavī	to be struck with fear
reparō, reparāre, reparāvī, reparātum	to get, to acquire; to renew, to repair
ōra, -ae, f.	shore
voltus, -ūs	*vultus, -ūs*
tractō, -āre, -āvī, -ātum	to handle, to manage (related to *trahō*)
dēlīberō, -āre, -āvī, -ātum	to deliberate, to plan ahead
Liburnus, -a, -um, adj.	Liburnian, from Liburnus; (masc. plur.) the Liburnī (who lived along the Adriatic coast in what is today Croatia and were known for their naval prowess); (fem.) Liburnian warships; swift galley warships used by the Romans and as part of Octavian's fleet

Challenge Box

What is the dominant rhetorical figure in the first stanza? What is its effect?

Challenge Box

Where and how does the tone of Horace's poem change toward Cleopatra?

RESPONDĒ LATĪNE! READING 1

As you answer these questions, you will notice that you will not always be able merely to pull an answer directly from the reading: you will need to answer the questions using correct Latin grammar that fits the question. For example, if a question for the first line of the poem were *Quid nunc necesse est agere?* (What now is necessary to do?), you would answer *bibere* (to drink). Notice how the infinitive in the questions informs you that you will need an infinitive in the answer.

1. Quae rēs tellūrem pulsābit?
2. Quālis pēs est?
3. Quōrum est pulvīnar?
4. Quis parābat Capitōliō ruīnās?
5. Quālēs sunt virī quī cum rēgīnā erant?
6. Ā quō vix ūna nāvis sōspes erat?
7. Quis rēgīnam in vērōs timōrēs dūxit?
8. Quis erat similis accipitrī?
9. Quis erat similis mollī columbae?
10. Quis erat fātāle mōnstrum?
11. Quās rēs ausa est Cleopatra tractāre?

Chapter Reading: Reading 2

THE POET BELIEVES HE WILL ACHIEVE IMMORTALITY

Horace's *Odes* III.xxx

This poem is written in a meter called lesser Asclepiad, which you have not learned. It is built around two choriambs. Scan the first three lines to find the choriamb and discern the metrical pattern.

1 *Exēgī* monumentum aere *perennius*
2 rēgālīque sitū pyramidum *altius,*
3 quod nōn imber *edāx,* nōn *Aquilō* impotēns
4 possit *dīruere* aut innumerābilis
5 annōrum series et fuga temporum.
6 Nōn omnis moriar **multaque pars** meī
7 vītābit *Libitīnam*; ūsque ego *posterā*
8 crēscam laude *recēns,* dum Capitōlium
9 *scandet* cum tacitā virgine pontifex.
10 Dīcar—*quā* violēns *obstrepit Aufidus*
11 et quā pauper aquae *Daunus agrestium*
12 rēgnāvit populōrum—ex humilī potēns
13 prīnceps *Aeolium* carmen ad *Ītalōs*
14 dēdūxisse modōs. Sūme superbiam
15 quaesītam meritīs et mihi *Delphicā*
16 *laurō* cinge volēns, *Melpomenē,* comam.

PHRASE: Reading 2

multaque pars – and a great part (lit., "and a much part")

GLOSSARY: Reading 2

Use your "eye" Latin to discern the meaning of the underlined words in the reading.

exigō, exigere, exēgī, exāctum	to complete
perennis, -e, adj.	lasting
edāx, edācis, adj.	gnawing
Aquilō, Aquilōnis, m.	the north wind (*aquilo* seems to be derived from *aqua*: the north wind brings rain)
dīruō, dīruere, dīruī, dīrutum	to tear asunder, to overthrow, to demolish
Libitīna, -ae, f.	the goddess of the dead and of corpses. Her temple was the repository of items needed for funerals and for death certificates.
posterus, -a, -um, adj.	coming after
recēns, recentis, adj.	fresh, recent
scandō, scandere, scandī, scānsum	to climb
quā, adv.	where
obstrepō, obstrepere, obstrepuī, obstrepitum	to roar
Aufidus, -ī, m.	The Aufidus is the main river in Apulia in southern Italy. This river is notable for its swift and violent course. Today it is called the River Ofonto.
Daunus, -ī, m.	a legendary king over part of Apulia and the father-in-law of Diomedes
agrestis, -e, adj.	having to do with fields and the countryside, rural (cf. *ager*)
Aeolius, -a, -um, adj.	Aeolian, describing a) a group of Greeks speaking with a particular dialect, b) an area composed of islands off the coast of Sicily (In the *Aeneid*, it is the home of Aeolus, the king of the winds.)
Delphicus, -a, -um, adj.	Delphian, of or from Delphi (a small town in Phocis, an area just west of Athens)
laurus, laurī, f.	laurel
Melpomenē, -ēs, f.	Melpomene, the muse of lyric poetry and tragedy

RESPONDĒ LATĪNE! READING 2

1. Quid poēta aedificāvit?
2. Quae rēs est altior sitū pyramidum?
3. Quid aut quis Libitīnam vītābit?
4. Quis scandet Capitōlium cum pontifice?
5. Quis corōnābit poētam?
6. Quotō in versū dīxit poēta sē aliquid aedificāvisse?
7. Quotīs in versibus scrīpsit poēta sē mortem vītātūrum esse?

Challenge Box

Find and explain an example of metonymy and an example of synecdoche in the poem.

Derivative Detective

Prepositions, when compounded with other words, often change their forms. If one can recognize which preposition is being compounded, it will be easier to recognize the parts of a compound word and find its definition both in English and in Latin.

- *Ab* becomes *ā* before *m* or *v* and in the word *āfuī*. It sometimes becomes *au* as in *auferō*.
- *Ab* becomes *abs* before *c* or *t*, as in *abcīdō*, an alternate form of *abscīdō*.
- *Ad* is assimilated before *c*, *g*, *l*, *p*, *r*, *s*, and *t*.
- *Cum* appears as *com* before *b*, *m*, and *p* and as *con* before *c*, *d*, *f*, *g*, *i*, *q*, *s*, and *v* and as *co* before *gn* or *n*.

Using all of the information above, determine the original Latin form from which the following English derivatives have been formed. Use the Latin to try to derive English definitions. Then, use an English dictionary to check your derivations and write out the meanings of the English words.

cognate	commotion
abstain	aggravate
corrupt	allocate
colloquial	incorrigible
corroborate	attain

About the Author

QUINTUS HORATIUS FLACCUS

Quintus Horatius Flaccus, whom we call Horace, was a lyric poet who flourished during the reign of Augustus Caesar. He was born in Venusia (near Apulia) on December 8, 65 BC. His father was a freedman and farmed in Venusia for a time. Later he moved to Rome and made enough money to give his son a good education, first in Rome and then in Athens. After the death of Gaius Julius Caesar on March 15, 44 BC, Quintus joined the army of Brutus and fought in the Battle of Phillipi. He later claimed that he saved himself by throwing away his shield and running. He returned to Italy after Octavian declared an amnesty for the soldiers of Brutus's army. At one time he was a treasury official, and the income from this job enabled him to pursue his career as a poet. He was in the literary circle that included Vergil and Maecenas, who was a friend and confidant of Augustus. After an admirable career, which created some of the greatest poetry of the ancient world, he died in Rome on November 27, 8 BC.

Quintus Horatius Flaccus

Culture Corner

THE NINE MUSES

You have now seen Catullus, Vergil, Milton, and Horace reference their muses. Perhaps you have heard other authors reference a muse as well. Often authors and artists of all art forms will talk of seeking their muse as a metaphor for inspiration. But who are the Muses? And why are they associated with inspiration in the creative arts?

The Muses are the nine daughters of Zeus and Mnemosyne, his first wife. Mnemosyne was a goddess of memory and is also said to be the mother of Athena, goddess of wisdom. For the ancient Greeks, the nine Muses embodied the creative arts. It was the Muses who held knowledge of ancient tales and the Muses whose grace could inspire the beauty of song and meter and all art. So it came about that each of

Mnemosyne's daughters, who frolicked on Mount Helicon, became associated with a particular form of art held dear to the Greeks. You can find them called upon by name and invoked through images in literature and art created throughout the ages.

Calliope: Muse of epic poetry, represented by a writing tablet

Clio: Muse of history, represented by a scroll

Erato: Muse of love poetry, represented by a cithara (lyre)

Euterpe: Muse of lyric poetry and of music, represented by an aulos (flute-like instrument)

Melpomene: Muse of music and later of tragedy, represented by a tragic mask

Polyhymnia: Muse of sacred poetry or hymns, represented by a veil

Terpsichore: Muse of dance, represented by a lyre

Thalia: Muse of comedy, represented by a comedic mask

Urania: Muse of astronomy, represented by a globe or compass

Plato once called Sappho the tenth Muse. Since then, the term "muse" has often been applied to talented female poets, and occasionally to women who offer inspiration. Can you guess which muse each of our poets thus far might have invoked and why?

The Legacy of Horace

As was the case with both Catullus and Vergil, Horace is another of Rome's poets whose work has continued to inspire poets long after his death. The following are samples of poetry by two of England's greatest poets, which pay homage to Horace. Perhaps the monument of his work has lasted even longer than he might possibly have imagined.

The first great English poet is the incomparable William Shakespeare, who is perhaps best known for his wonderful plays and numerous sonnets. His preferred meter is the iambic pentameter, a popular choice for his times. In the following sonnet, his theme echoes that of Horace in *Ode* III.xxx. Read through Shakespeare's sonnet and then again through Horace's piece *Ode* III.xxx (see p. 161). Discuss with your teacher and your class how the ideas and imagery in these two poems compare.

Sonnet LV

William Shakespeare

Not marble, nor the gilded monuments
Of princes, shall outlive this powerful rhyme;
But you shall shine more bright in these contents
Than unswept stone besmear'd with sluttish time.
When wasteful war shall statues overturn,
And broils root out the work of masonry,[1]
Nor Mars his sword nor war's quick fire shall burn
The living record of your memory.
'Gainst death and all-oblivious enmity
Shall you pace forth; your praise shall still find room
Even in the eyes of all posterity
That wear this world out to the ending doom.[2]
So, till the judgment that yourself arise,
You live in this, and dwell in lovers' eyes.

---
1. Broils are violent quarrels.
2. Doom means judgment and does not have a negative connotation here (i.e., the end of time).

A poet of the late nineteenth century, Alfred Lord Tennyson was distinguished as a Poet Laureate of the United Kingdom under the reign of Queen Victoria. He is today one of the most popular of English poets. Tennyson loved the classical authors to the extent that he not only studied them himself, but insisted that his sons read classical poetry even at a very young age—Horace in particular; in Latin, of course. Tennyson not only sought to imitate the themes of these poets, but their style and meter as well. Such was the case with his poem "Hendecasyllabics," featured in chapter 13 (see p. 144). Tennyson also wrote a number of poems in Alcaic meter. While acknowledging the difference of writing an Alcaic rhythm in English instead of Latin or Greek, Tennyson's desire was to emulate his predecessors. Tennyson writes,

> My Alcaics are not intended for Horatian Alcaics, nor are Horace's Alcaics the Greek Alcaics, nor are his Sapphics, which are vastly inferior to Sappho's, the Greek Sapphics. The Horatian Alcaic is perhaps the stateliest metre in the world except the Virgilian hexameter at its best; but the Greek Alcaic, if we may judge from the two or three specimens left, had a much freer and lighter movement: and I have no doubt that an old Greek if he knew our language would admit my Alcaics as legitimate, only Milton must not be pronounced Milt'n. Is that very Horatian?[3]

How Horatian it is we may leave for scholars to debate, but what is not in doubt is the legacy that has been passed down from Alceus to Horace to Tennyson and others: a love for the beauty of lyric stanza as set down by a classical muse.

Scan the lines of Tennyson's poem extolling John Milton. Remember that English poets will use a pattern of stressed and unstressed syllables in lieu of Latin's long and short syllables. Read the poem aloud together as a class and compare to Horace's Alcaic.

MILTON

Alfred, Lord Tennyson

Written in Alcaic Meter

O mighty-mouth'd inventor of harmonies,
O skilled to sing of Time or Eternity,
God-gifted organ-voice of England,
Milton, a name to resound for ages;

Whose Titan angels, Gabriel, Abdiel,
Starr'd from Jehovah's gorgeous armouries,
Tower, as the deep-domed empyrean
Rings to the roar of an angel onset—

Me rather all that bowery loneliness,
The brooks of Eden mazily murmuring,
And bloom profuse and cedar arches
Charm, as a wanderer out in ocean,

Where some reflulgent sunset of India
Streams o'er a rich ambrosial ocean isle,
And crimson-hued the stately palm-woods
Whisper in odorous heights of even.[4]

---

3. Alfred, Lord Tennyson, *The Works of Alfred, Lord Tennyson* (London: Macmillan, 1908), 378.
4. Alfred Baron Tennyson, *The Works of Tennyson* (London: Macmillan, 1913), n.p.

Virtus tentamine gaudet.
Hillsdale College, Michigan

Chapter 16

- Section 53. Proviso Clause
- Section 54. *Dum* Clauses
- Section 55. Poetry Review
  - Metrical Feet
  - Meter
  - Elision

VOCABULARY

LATIN	ENGLISH	DERIVATIVES
Nouns		
carmen, carminis, n.	tune, song; poem	
frōns, frontis, f.	forehead, brow	(front)
genetrīx, genetrīcis, f.	mother	
labor, labōris, m.	work, labor, toil	(labor)
lympha, -ae, f.	water	(lymph node)
nāta, -ae, f.	daughter	
sēdēs, sēdis, f.	chair, seat	(sedentary)
sīdus, sīderis, n.	group of stars, constellation, heavenly body	
Verbs		
adsum, adesse, adfuī, adfutūrum (ad + esse)	to be near, to be present	
attollō, attollere	to lift up, to raise up	
auferō, auferre, abtulī, ablātum (ab + ferre)	to carry off, to take away	
inpleō/impleō, inplēre, inplēvī, inplētum (cf. plēnus)	to fill up	(implement)
mereō, merēre, meruī, meritum (cf. meritum)	to deserve, to merit	(merit)
reperiō, reperīre, repperī, repertum	to find again, to find	
Adjectives, Adverbs, Conjunctions, etc.		
nūbilus, -a, -um, adj.	cloudy, gloomy, troubled	
adhūc, adv.	still, yet, up to this point	
dummodo, adv. (cf. dum + modo)	provided that	

Section 53. Proviso Clause

In English, a proviso is a clause in a contract that stipulates a condition. For example:

I will give you a thousand pieces of gold, provided that you defeat the enemy.

The term "proviso" comes from the Latin word *prōvideō*, meaning "to look ahead." This idea of planning with forethought is seen in the dependent clause in the sentence directly above. You can even see a derivative of *prōvideō* in the key phrase "provided that," which introduces the clause.

This idea is carried over from the use of the **proviso clause** in Latin, which is a type of conditional. As such, the proviso is a subordinate clause using the subjunctive mood. It is most often introduced by the word *dummodo* or the two words *dum* and *modo* separately, but occasionally by *dum* alone. *Dummodo* is a compound word formed from *dum* + *modo*, which literally means "only while." Thus the apodosis can happen only while the condition of the protasis is accomplished.

Tibi mīlle aureōs dabō, dummodo hostem vincās.
I will give a thousand gold pieces to you, provided that you conquer the enemy.

The negative proviso clause will use *nē* (or, in later authors, *nōn*).

Tibi mīlle aureōs dabō, dummodo hostem nē iuvēs.
I will give a thousand gold pieces to you, provided that you don't help the enemy.

Exercise 1. Underline the proviso clause in each sentence and parse the verb in the clause. Then translate the sentence.

1. Dummodo sīdera caelum nocte inpleant, lūx semper erit.
2. Habēbimus satis lymphae, dummodo caela nūbila sint.
3. Dummodo opus sit, labor fit.
   Hint: See chapter 9.
4. Genetrīx erit miserrima, dummodo nātam reperīre nē possit.
5. Nēmō ēbrius fiet, dummodo multum lymphae cum vīnō bene misceātur.
6. You will not be able to see, provided that your hair is in your eyes.
7. You deserve honor, provided that you live with honor.
8. Provided that the dogs watch over the flock, it will be safe.

Section 54. *Dum* Clauses

Although the conjunction *dum* may also be used to introduce a proviso clause with a subjunctive verb, it most often is used with an indicative verb in a temporal sense. With the indicative, *dum* is best rendered as "while" or "as long as." *Dum* with the subjunctive may also be translated "until," expressing the idea of anticipation (not an actual fact).

Exercise 2. Read and discuss the meaning or significance of the following quotations.

1. Dummodo sit dives, barbarus ipse placet. (Ovid)
2. Oderint dum metuant. (Seneca)
3. Dum inter homines sumus, colamus humanitatem. (Seneca)
4. Sedit qui timuit ne non succederet. (Horace)
5. Dum vivimus, vivamus. (Epicurean philosophy)
6. Sit divus, dummodo non sit vivus! (attributed to Caracalla before the murder of his brother Geta)
7. Quidquid vis esto, dummodo nil recites! (Martial)
   Hint: *esto* – be! (future imperative)
8. Dum excusare credis, accusas. (St. Jerome)
9. Dummodo morata recte veniat, dotata est satis. (Plautus)
10. Multi honesta neglegunt dummodo potentiam consequantur. (adapted from Cicero)

Exercise 3. Translate these famous quotations into Latin.

1. It ain't over 'til the fat lady sings.
2. while you were sleeping
3. I am prepared to go anywhere, provided it be forward. (David Livingstone)
   Hint: anywhere – *usquam*; forward – *porro*
4. I can believe anything provided that it is quite incredible. (Oscar Wilde)
5. He is really not so ugly after all, provided that one shuts his eyes and does not look at him. (Oscar Wilde)
   Hint: Translate "one" as "you."
6. I love it when a plan comes together. (Hannibal Smith)

SECTION 55. Poetry Review

This unit has introduced several fundamental principles for Latin poetry. Before looking at our last poem from the golden age of literature let's review what you have learned.

A. METRICAL FEET

Each line of poetry consists of a combination of metrical feet. You have learned or seen most of the following: choriamb, dactyl, spondee, and trochee. Identify the metrical foot for each pattern below.

1. | _ _ | long – long
2. | _ ᴗ | long – short
3. | _ ᴗ ᴗ _ | long-short-short-long
4. | _ ᴗ ᴗ | long – short – short

B. METER

Meter is the arrangement of metrical feet in order to create a certain rhythm desired by the poet. There are numerous meters in Latin poetry, most of which the Romans borrowed from the Greek poets who had come before. In this book, we have looked closely at hendecasyllabic, dactylic hexameter, and Alcaic. Identify each metrical pattern below. Notice how, of the meters we've learned, only the dactylic hexameter is actually analyzed in terms of feet.

1. _ ᴗ ᴗ | _ ᴗ ᴗ | _ ᴗ ᴗ | _ ᴗ ᴗ | _ ᴗ ᴗ | _ x
2. _ _ | _ ᴗ _ | ᴗ _ _ ᴗ _ ᴗ
3. x _ ᴗ _ _ // _ ᴗ ᴗ _ | ᴗ x
4. _ ᴗ _ x | _ ᴗ ᴗ _ | ᴗ _ x
   _ ᴗ ᴗ _ | x

C. ELISION

Often, for the sake of meter, an elision occurs between two words. Elision is the omission of a vowel at the end of a word before a vowel at the beginning of the next word when pronouncing Latin, especially Latin poetry. Recall the two rules for when poets will elide two words. Provide an example for each one from your past readings.

1. _____
   vowel – vowel (or vowel preceded by *h*)
2. _____
   vowel *m* – vowel (or vowel preceded by *h*)

Exercise 4. Scan the following lines of poetry from the reading for this chapter. Identify the meter.

paene simul vīsa est dīlectaque raptaque Dītī:

ūsque adeō est properātus amor. Dea territa maestō

et mātrem et comitēs, sed mātrem saepius, ōre

clāmat, et ut summā vestem laniārat ab ōrā,

Before You Read!

Often poets substitute a plural word for the singular. Sometimes this is for metrical reasons—a certain quantity of syllable was required to fit the meter. Sometimes the substitution is made for a style preference—the poet thought it more fashionable to use a plural form instead of a singular one. In such instances, it is acceptable for you as the interpreter to translate the plural word as singular. Watch the context of the phrase carefully and let it guide you as you read.

One such example of this substitution of number in English is called the royal we. Occasionally, the pronoun "we" is substituted for "I," especially when royalty are concerned.

Exempli Gratia:

> "So, thanks to all at once and to each one,
>
> Whom we invite to see us crown'd at Scone."
>
> *Macbeth* (V.viii. 74-75)

Chapter Readings: Reading 1

OVID'S *METAMORPHOSES*, LIBER V

Prologue

According to Ovid in *Metamorphoses V*, the giant Typhoeus aspired to reach the heavens. As punishment for those aspirations, he was being crushed beneath the weight of the whole island of Sicily. His struggles to escape caused earthquakes. Fearing that cracks in the earth's crust would allow light into the Underworld and frighten the dead, Pluto came to the upper earth in his chariot to examine the situation. Having found the foundations of the earth secure, he was no longer afraid. While Pluto was on the earth, Venus persuaded Cupid to wound him with one of his arrows. After the wound, Pluto saw Proserpina.

Reading 1

1 " 'Haud *procul Hennaeis* lacus est ā moenibus altae,
2 nōmine Pergus, <u>aquae</u>: nōn illō plūra *Caÿstros*
3 carmina *cycnōrum lābentibus* audit in undīs.
4 silva <u>corōnat</u> aquās cingēns latus omne suīsque
5 <u>frondibus</u> ut *vēlō Phoebēōs* submovet *ictūs*;
6 frīgora dant *rāmī*, *Tyriōs* humus *ūmida* flōrēs:
7 perpetuum *vēr* est. **Quō** dum <u>Prōserpina</u> *lūcō*
8 <u>lūdit</u> et aut *violās* aut candida <u>līlia</u> carpit,
9 dumque <u>puellārī</u> studiō *calathōs*que sinumque
10 inplet et aequālēs *certat* superāre legendō,
11 paene simul vīsa est dīlectaque raptaque *Dītī*:
12 ūsque *adeō* est properātus amor. Dea territa *maestō*
13 et mātrem et comitēs, sed mātrem saepius, ōre
14 clāmat, et ut summā vestem *laniārat* ab *ōrā*,
15 *collectī* flōrēs <u>tunicīs</u> cecidēre *remissīs*,
16 tantaque <u>simplicitās</u> <u>puerīlibus</u> adfuit annīs,

17 haec quoque <u>virgineum</u> mōvit *iactūra* dolōrem.
18 *Raptor* agit currūs et **nōmine** *quemque* **vocandō**
19 <u>exhortātur</u> equōs, quōrum per colla *iubās*que
20 *excutit* <u>obscūra</u> tīnctās ferrūgine habēnās,
21 perque lacūs altōs et *olentia* <u>sulphure</u> fertur
22 *stagna Palīcōrum ruptā ferventia* terrā
23 et *quā Bacchiadae*, <u>bimarī</u> gēns orta *Corinthō*,
24 inter <u>inaequālēs</u> posuērunt moenia <u>portūs</u>.' "

PHRASES: Reading 1

Quō – and by this (lit., "by which"; remember that sometimes a relative pronoun is used as a connector meaning *et eō*)

nōmine *quemque* **vocandō** – calling each by name (this could be taken one of two ways: 1) with *quemque* in apposition with *equōs* and *nōmine vocandō* as a gerundive phrase in the ablative: "he exhorted the horses each with a name being called"; 2) *vocandō* is taken as a gerund with *quemque* as object and *nōmine* as an ablative of agent: "calling each by name." Whichever option is taken, the meaning is the same.)

GLOSSARY: Reading 1

Use your "eye" Latin to discern the meaning of the underlined words in the reading.

procul, adv.	far
Hennaeus, -a, -um, adj.	Hennaean, of Henna (city in the middle of Sicily)
Caӯstros, -ī, m.	a river in Lydia (Lydia is a country in Asia Minor. Its capital is Sardis. This is from where some scholars believe the Etruscans originated.)
cycnus, -ī, m.	swan
lābor, lābī, lāpsus sum	to slide, to glide
vēlum, -ī, n.	cover
Phoebēus, -ī, m.	Apollo
ictus, -ūs, m.	shot, blow
rāmus, -ī, m.	branch
Tyrius, -a, -um, adj.	Tyrian, of Tyre (city in Phoenicia)
ūmidus, -a, -um, adj.	moist
vēr, vēris, n.	spring
lūcus, lūcī, m.	grove
viola, -ae, f.	violet
calathus, -ī, m.	handbasket (for flowers), wicker basket
certō, -āre, -āvī, -ātum	to compete
Dīs, Dītis, m.	a name for Pluto or Hades, the god of the Underworld (meaning "rich," probably derived from the Greek word *plouton*, from which we get Pluto, meaning "wealth-giver")
adeō, adv.	so, to such a degree
maestus, -a, -um, adj.	sad, mournful
laniārat	*laniāverat* (syncopated); *laniō, -āre, -āvī, -ātum* – to tear
ōra, -ae, f.	edge, border
colligō, colligere, collēgī, collēctum	to collect
remittō, remittere, remīsī, remissum	to let go of
iactūra, -ae, f.	a letting go, a throwing down
raptor, raptoris, m.	snatcher, the one seizing (cf. *rapere*)

quemque	(from *quisque*, a compound word in which the first element, *quis-*, is declined, but the second element, *-que*, is not); *quisque*, *quidque* – each
iuba, -ae, f.	mane
excutiō, excutere, excussī, excussum	to shake about
tīnctus, -a, -um, adj.	dyed
ferrūgō, ferrūginis, f.	iron-rust (cf. *ferrum*)
habēna, -ae, f.	rein, halter
olēns, olentis, adj.	smelling of (+ abl.)
stagnum, -ī, n.	pool, swamp
Palīcī, -ōrum, m.	the Palici, sons of Jupiter, worshiped in Sicily by the town of Palica
rumpō, rumpere, rūpī, ruptus	to break, to burst, to tear
ferveō, fervēre	to be boiling, to be boiling hot
quā, adv.	where
Bacchiadae	an ancient Corinthian family descended from Bacchus
Corinthus, -ī, m.	Corinth, an isthmus connecting the southern part of Greece to the northern part (on the left is the gulf of Corinth, on the right the Aegean Sea)

RESPONDĒ LATĪNĒ! READING 1

1. Quōrum carmina audiēbant aquae Pergī?
2. Secundum (according to) quartum versum quae rēs corōnābat lacum?
3. Secundum sextum versum, quae rēs frīgora dedērunt?
4. Quae dea iuvenis, fīlia deae agricultūrae, ludēbat et carpēbat flōrēs?
5. Quī deus Prōserpinam simul vīdit et amāvit?
6. Quam saepius clamāvit puella?
7. Ubi laniāverat Prōserpina suum vestem?
8. Quis equōs exhortābātur?
9. Quārē stagna olent?
10. Secundum ultimum versum quālēs sunt portūs?

Chapter Readings: Reading 2

FIRST INTERLUDE

Pluto has kidnapped Proserpina and taken her to the Underworld. Her grieving mother, Ceres, not knowing at all what has happened to her daughter and knowing only that she is missing, is seeking her daughter as this reading begins.

READING 2

1 "'*Intereā* **pavidae** *nēquīquam* fīlia **mātrī**
2 **omnibus est terrīs omnī quaesīta** *profundō*.
3 Illam nōn *ūdīs* veniēns *Aurōra capillīs*
4 *cēssantem* vīdit, nōn *Hesperus*; illa duābus
5 *flammiferās pīnūs* manibus *succendit* ab *Aetnā*
6 perque *pruīnōsās* tulit *inrequiēta* tenēbrās;

7 rūrsus ubī alma diēs *hebetārat* sīdera, nātam
8 sōlis ab occāsū sōlis quaerēbat ad <u>ortūs</u>.
9 Fessa labōre *sitim* concēperat, ōraque nūllī
10 *conluerant* <u>fontēs</u>, cum <u>tēctam</u> *strāmine* vīdit
11 forte casam parvāsque forēs pulsāvit; *at inde*
12 *prōdit anus* dīvamque videt lymphamque rogantī
13 dulce dedit *tostā* quod *tēxerat* ante *polentā*.
14 Dum <u>bibit</u> illa dātum, dūrī puer ōris et <u>audāx</u>
15 *cōnstitit* ante deam rīsitque *avidam*que vocāvit.
16 **Offēnsa est neque adhūc *ēpōtā* parte loquentem**
17 **cum <u>liquidō</u> mixtā perfūdit dīva *polentā*:**
18 conbibit ōs *maculās* et, quae modo bracchia gessit,
19 *crūra* gerit; cauda est mūtātīs *addita* <u>membrīs</u>,
20 inque brevem fōrmam, nē sit vīs magna nocendī,
21 *contrahitur*, parvāque <u>minor</u> *mēnsūra lacertā* est.' "

Phrases: Reading 2

pavidae ... mātrī – by her frightened mother (dative of agent is often used with the perfect passive)

omnibus est terrīs omnī quaesīta *profundō* – (read as though *quaesīta est omnibus terrīs [et] omnī profundō*; the lack of *et* is called asyndeton and occurs again in line 13)

Offēnsa ... polentā – (read as though the order were *Dīva offēnsa est et perfūdit loquentem parte nōn adhūc ēpōtā—polentā cum liquidō mixtā*)

Glossary: Reading 2

Use your "eye" Latin to discern the meaning of the underlined words in the reading.

intereā, adv.	meanwhile
nēquīquam, adv.	in vain
profundum, -ī, n.	depth of the sea
ūdus, -a, -um, adj.	damp, moist, wet (cf. humid)
Aurōra, -ae, f.	Aurora, goddess of the dawn; dawn
capillus, -ī, m.	*coma*
cēssō, -āre, -āvī, -ātum	to cease, to leave off
Hesperus, -ī, m.	Hesper, god of the evening; evening
flammifer, flammifera, flammiferum, adj.	*ferēns flammam*
pīnus, -ūs, f.	pine
succendō, succendere, succendī, succēnsum	to kindle, to light on fire
Aetna, -ae, f.	Mount Etna in Sicily
pruīnōsus, -a, -um, adj.	frosty
inrequiētus, -a, -um, adj.	unquiet, restless
hebetārat	*hebetāverat* (syncopated); *heberō, -āre, -āvī, -ātum* – to blunt, to make dull (in this context, "dim")
sitis, sitis, f.	thirst (*sitim = sitem*)
conluō, conluere, conluī	to moisten, to wet
strāmen, strāminis, n.	straw, litter
at, conj.	but, but look!, behold!
inde, adv.	from there, thence
prōdeō, prōdīre, prōdiī, prōditum	to come forth

anus, -ūs, f.	old woman, matron
torreō, torrēre, torruī, tostus	to dry up, to bake (cf. toast)
tegō, tegere, tēxī, tēctum	to cover
polenta, -ae, f.	peeled barley
cōnstō, cōnstāre, cōnstitī, cōnstātus	to stand
avidus, -a, -um, adj.	greedy, gluttonous
ēpōtus, -a, -um, adj.	drunk off, drained (perfect passive participle *ēpōtō*)
macula, -ae, f.	spot, mark, stain
crūs, crūris, n.	leg
addō, addere, addidī, additum	to put to, to place upon
contrahō, contrahere, contraxī, contractum	to draw together, to compress
mēnsūra, -ae, f.	a measuring, measurement
lacerta, -ae, f.	lizard

RESPONDĒ LATĪNĒ! READING 2

1. Quis est pavida?
2. Ubi māter fīliam suam quarēbat?
3. Cuī sunt capillae ūdae?
4. Quālēs stellae hebetātae erant diē?
5. Quis ē parvā casā vēnit?
6. Quis dulce aliquid dedit?
7. Quālis est puer quī deam rīsit?
8. Quae facta sunt bracchia puerī?
9. Quae rēs in ōre puerī erant?
10. Quantus nunc est audāx puer mēnsūrā?

Chapter Readings: Reading 3

SECOND INTERLUDE

Ceres continued to wander over many lands. When she had searched all the lands, she came back to Sicily, her starting point and the place from which Proserpina had disappeared. (Since Proserpina was gathering flowers there when Hades kidnapped her, even today Sicily is known as Persephone's Island because of the abundance of wildflowers in the spring.) Ceres met the nymph Cyane, who had been turned to water; and, thus even though she might have wanted to, she could not speak to tell Ceres where Proserpina was; however, in reflections in the surface of her pool Cyane showed Ceres evidence of Proserpina. It was only then that Ceres knew that her daughter had been kidnapped, but she still did not know where Proserpina was. She cursed all the lands and continued to wander and to search.

READING 3

1 " 'Tum caput *Ēlēis Alphēias* <u>extulit</u> undīs
2 *rōrantēs*que comās ā fronte remōvit ad *aurēs*
3 atque āit "Ō tōtō quaesītae virginis orbe
4 et *frūgum* genetrīx, *inmēnsōs siste* labōrēs
5 nēve tibī *fīdae* <u>violenta</u> *īrāscere* terrae.
6 Terra nihil meruit patuitque *invīta rapīnae*,

7 nec sum prō patriā *supplex*: hūc *hospita* vēnī.
8 *Pīsa* mihī patria est et **ab** *Ēlide* **dūcimus** <u>ortūs</u>,
9 *Sīcaniam peregrīna colō*, sed grātior omnī
10 haec mihi terra *solō* est: hōs nunc *Arethūsa* penātēs,
11 hanc habeō *sēdem*. **Quam** tū, *mītissima*, **servā**.
12 *Mōta locō* cūr sim tantīque per aequoris undās
13 *advehar Ortygiam*, veniet <u>nārrātibus</u> hōra
14 *tempestīva* meīs, cum tū cūrāque *levāta*
15 et vultūs meliōris eris. Mihi *pervia* tellūs
16 *praebet* iter, *subterque* <u>imās</u> ablāta <u>cavernās</u>
17 hīc caput attollō *dēsuēta*que sīdera cernō.
18 *Ergō* dum *Stygiō* sub terrīs *gurgite labor*,
19 vīsa tua est oculīs *illīc* Prōserpina nostrīs:
20 illa quidem *tristis* neque adhūc *interrita* vultū,
21 sed rēgīna tamen, sed *opācī* maxima mundī,
22 sed tamen *infernī pollēns mātrōna* tyrannī!"
23 'Māter ad audītās *stupuit ceu saxea* vōcēs
24 *attonitae*que diū <u>similis</u> fuit, utque dolōre
25 pulsa gravī gravis est āmentia, curribus <u>ōrās</u>
26 <u>exit</u> in *aetheriās*: ibi tōtō nūbila vultū
27 ante Iovem passīs stetit invidiōsa *capillīs*
28 "prō" que "meō vēnī *supplex* tibi, Iuppiter," inquit
29 "sanguine prōque tuō: sī nūlla est grātia mātris,
30 nāta patrem moveat, neu sit tibi cūra, precāmur,
31 vīlior **illīus**, quod **nostrō** est *ēdita partū*.
32 *Ēn* quaesīta diū tandem mihi nāta reperta est,
33 **sī reperīre vocās āmittere certius, aut sī**
34 **scīre, ubi sit, reperīre vocās. Quod rapta ferēmus,**
35 dummodo reddat eam!"''

Ceres

PHRASES: Reading 3

ab *Ēlide* **dūcimus** <u>ortūs</u> – from Elis we take [our] arisings (She is saying that she had her origins in Pisa of Elis. Now, however, she inhabits an area near Syracuse, in Sicily.)

Quam . . . servā – and preserve it . . . (lit., "which preserve," but remember that a relative pronoun beginning a clause can be translated like *et* + personal pronoun)

illīus – (depends on the noun *cūra* on the previous line)

nostrō *partū* – since she was my child [and not Juno's] (lit., "our birth," but it means "since I gave birth," not "since I was born")

sī reperīre vocās āmittere certius, aut sī scīre, ubi sit, reperīre vocās – if you call "losing more certainly" finding, or if you call "knowing where she is" finding

Quod rapta [est] ferēmus – I can put up with the fact that she has been kidnapped (lit., "we will bear that she has been snatched")

Glossary: Reading 3

Use your "eye" Latin to discern the meaning of the underlined words in the reading.

Ēlēis, Ēlēidis, f. adj.	from Elis, Elean
Alphēias, Alphēiadis, f.	"Daughter of Alpheus," the nymph and fountain, Arethusa, a fountain near Syracuse in Sicily
rōrō, -āre, -āvī, -ātum	to scatter dew, to be dripping with dew
auris, auris, f.	ear
frūx, frūgis, f.	fruit
inmēnsus, -a, -um, adj.	boundless, without measure, vast, large
sistō, sistere, stitī, status	to cause to stand, to place
fīdus, -a, -um, adj.	*fidēlis*
īrāscor, īrāscī, īrātus sum	to be angry at, to be in a rage against (+ dat.)
invītus, -a, -um, adj.	unwilling, reluctant
rapīna, -ae, f.	robbery, plunder (cf. *rapere*)
supplex, supplicis, adj.	suppliant, kneeling in entreaty, entreating
hospita, -ae, f.	stranger
Pīsa, -ae, f.	Pisa, a city in the area of Elis
Ēlis, Ēlidis, f.	Elis, an area in the Peloponnesus where the Olympic games were held
Sīcania, -ae, f.	Sicily
peregrīna	a sojourner
colō, colere, coluī, cultus	to till, to cultivate
solum, -ī, n.	ground, soil; country
Arethūsa, -ae, f.	a fountain near Syracuse in Sicily
sēdēs, sēdis, f.	seat, centre of power, home base
mītis, mīte, adj.	mild, mellow
advehar	*ad + vehere*
Ortygia, -ae, f.	Ortygia, an island that forms part of the city of Syracuse
tempestīvus, -a, -um, adj.	at the right time, proper time
levō, -āre, -āvī, -ātum	to lift, to raise, to elevate
pervius, -a, -um, adj.	passable, able to be crossed (cf. *per + via*)
praebeō, praebēre, praebuī, praebitum	to hold forth, to offer
subter, prep. (+ acc.)	below, beneath
īmus, -a, -um, adj.	lowest, deepest
dēsuētus, -a, -um, adj.	disused, laid aside
Stygius, -a, -um, adj.	of the Styx, Stygian, of the lower world
gurges, gurgitis, m.	raging abyss, whirlpool
lābor, lābī, lāpsus sum	to slip
illīc, adv.	there, at that place
tristis, triste, adj.	sad, gloomy
interritus, -a, -um, adj.	unperturbed
opācus, -a, -um, adj.	shady, in the shade
īnfernus, -a, -um, adj.	lower, under
pollēns, pollentis	*potēns, potentis*
mātrōna, -ae, f.	married woman, wife
stupeō, stupēre, stupuī	to be struck senseless, to be stunned, to be stupefied
ceu, adv.	as, like, just as
saxeus, -a, -um, adj.	stone, made of stone
attonitus, -a, -um, adj.	thunderstruck, stunned
ōra, -ae, f.	shore
aetherius, -a, -um, adj.	heavenly
capillus, -ī, m.	*coma*
ēdō, ēdere, ēdidī, ēditum	to produce, to send forth
partus, partūs, m.	birth
ēn, interj.	behold, look!

RESPONDĒ LATĪNĒ! READING 3

1. Quis ex undīs caput suum extulit?
2. Quem adloquitur (speak to, address) Alphēias dīcēns, "siste labōrēs?"
3. Quotō in versū aliquis dīxit sē velle deam sēdem servāre?
4. Quālia erant sīdera quae nympha cernit?
5. Quis erat maxima regīna opācī?
6. Quotō in versō stat aliquis ante rēgem deōrum?
7. Quis patrem moveat?

About the Author

PUBLIUS OVIDIUS NASO

Publius Ovidius Naso, whom we call Ovid, was born in Sulmo in 41 BC. He studied as a young man in Rome. He was a public servant who devoted himself to poetry and also enjoyed an active social life. Perhaps his best known work is the *Metamorphoses*, a series of mythological stories in which characters are transformed. Late in his career he offended the emperor, Augustus, through his writings and through some other unknown action. He became an exile and lived the rest of his life at Tomis, a remote settlement on the Black Sea.

Ovid's work has been a great source of inspiration to artists throughout the ages. Chaucer's *Canterbury Tales* pays homage to every genre known in the English Middle Ages, but there are more references to Ovid in this classic work than any other source. The twelfth century has been referred to as the *aetās Ovidiāna* (Ovidian age) because of the great number of poets who wrote on Ovidian themes and imitated Ovidian hexameter. During the Renaissance, Ovid was arguably the most influential of all the classical poets. He inspired numerous painters and sculptors; writers of all kinds translated and adapted his work.

With your parents' help, search for a painting or sculpture that depicts the abduction of Proserpina. Learn something about the artist who created the work. Consider carefully how the artist's work interprets Ovid's story.

The Legacy of Ovid

Ovid's *Metamorphoses* may have inspired more pieces of fine art and literature than any other work from the Classical Age. His poem tells incredible tales of strange transformations for god and man alike. These tales have captivated readers for centuries and inspired their imaginations. One cannot visit a museum without beholding some piece inspired by Ovid. Much of literature reflects this classical masterpiece as well. Besides Chaucer, John Milton pays homage in *Paradise Lost*, comparing the loss of Eden to the loss of Proserpine.

> . . . that fair field
>
> Of Enna, where Proserpine gath'ring flow'res
>
> Herself a fairer Flow'r by gloomy Dis
>
> Was gather'd, which cost Ceres all that pain
>
> To seek her through the world . . .
>
> (*Paradise Lost*, IV. 268-271)

Perhaps the Renaissance author most influenced by Ovid was the great bard himself, William Shakespeare. His numerous sonnets and plays, all written in iambic pentameter, reveal an intimate knowledge of Ovid. Proserpine herself makes several appearances in Shakespeare's works. Some critics have compared Oberon and Titania of *A Midsummer Night's Dream* to Pluto and Proserpine. The dark lord and his lady make a fitting model for the dueling King and Queen of the nightly fairie realm. Shakespeare makes a more direct reference to the abduction of Proserpine in *The Winter's Tale*, c. 1610.

> . . . O Proserpina,
> For the flow'rs now, that, frighted, thou let'st fall
> From Dis's waggon! daffodils,
> That come before the swallow dares, and take
> The winds of March with beauty; violets, dim,
> But sweeter than the lids of Juno's eyes,
> Or Cytherea's breath; pale primroses,
> That die unmarried, ere they can behold
> Bright Phoebus in his strength (a malady
> Most incident to maids); bold oxlips, and
> The crown imperial; lilies of all kinds
> (The flow'r-de-luce being one). O these I lack.
>
> (4.4.116-120)

Ovid

Classical influence did not die with the Renaissance. In the nineteenth century it flourished anew with several well-known writers. In grand style, Alfred, Lord Tennyson composed a long rendition of the woeful tale titled *Demeter and Persephone*, after the goddesses' Greek names. Mary Shelley, best known for her novel *Frankenstein: or, The Modern Prometheus*, co-authored a children's play with her husband, Percy Bysshe Shelley, titled *Proserpine*. The short play was written in poetic verse, meaning it was a play written in verse and meant to be performed aloud. The couple wrote poems on this same subject as well as other tales from Ovid.

Proserpine's story has, in fact, inspired many female poets for its strong portrayal of women as mother, daughter, and reluctant queen. Another such poetess is Sarah Helen Whitman, one-time fiancée of Edgar Allan Poe and an excellent poet in her own right. Ms. Whitman wrote a love poem to Poe titled, "Proserpine to Pluto in Hades." While the poem gives Proserpine more favorable feelings to her one-time captor than Ovid might have done, much of the imagery found in the poem comes directly from his portrayal in the *Metamorphoses*. Read Whitman's poem and you will find references to familiar characters, places, flowers, and other elements in the Latin poem you have just read. Clearly she had more than a passing familiarity with Ovid, but with her own love now gone, Ms. Whitman had obtained a different perspective on Pluto and his realm.

Artists of this age, such as Dante Gabriel Rossetti, became known for a medieval revivalism, both in art and in literature. Rossetti is known not only for his paintings but also for the sonnets he wrote to accompany them. Such a coupling focused on Proserpine follows this article. Even in the twentieth century, poets such as Robert Graves ("Escape") continue to reveal inspiration from Ovid's first-century work.

Ask for the definition of "classic" and this is the response that will be given: a work of highest quality and enduring excellence that serves as a model or guide. The corpus of work from AD 1–2000 reveals that Ovid and his colleagues fit that description. Not only were Ovid, Horace, Vergil, and Catullus seen as providing the highest form of excellence in poetry in their own day, but for centuries poets have used these classic bards as a guide, striving to listen to the same muse who whispered in their ears so many centuries ago.

"Proserpine to Pluto in Hades"

Sarah Helen Whitman (1803–1878)

Ms. Whitman puts a new perspective on Ovid's story. It is intended as a reflection of her own feelings for Edgar Allan Poe to whom she was engaged. Her mother did not approve of the match and Poe later blamed the would-be mother-in-law for the failure of their engagement. Whitman wrote this poem to Poe in the years following his tragic death. The poetess also alludes to Proserpine in a poem titled "The Raven" written for Poe on Valentine's Day, as a response to his poem of the same title.[1]

---

1. Information taken from Caroline Ticknor's *Poe's Helen* and from the preface of Brett Rutherford's *Last Flowers: The Romance and Poetry of Edgar Allen Poe and Sarah Helen Whitman.*

Nec repetita sequi curet Proserpina matrem
                    —Virgil, Georgics, I. 39

I think on thee amid these spring-time flowers,
    On thee, my emperor, my sovran lord,
Dwelling alone in dim Tartarean towers
    Of thy dark realm, by earth and heaven abhorred,
Wandering afar by that Avernian river
Where dead kings walk and phantoms wail forever.

I think on thee in that stern palace regnant,
    Where no sweet voice of summer charms the air,
Where the vast solitude seems ever pregnant
    With some wild dream of untold despair.
Thy love, remembered, doth heaven's light eclipse;
I feel thy lingering kisses on my lips.

I languish for the late autumnal showers,
    The cool, cool plashing of the autumn rain,
The shimmering hoar-frost and fast-fading flowers,
    That give me back to thy dark realm again:
To thee I'll bring Sicilia's starry skies
And all the heaven of summer in my eyes.

When from the earth's noontide beauty borne away
    To the pale prairies of that under world,
A mournful flower upon thy breast I lay
    Till round thy heart its clinging tendrils curled—
A frightened dove, that tamed its fluttering pinion
To the dear magic of thy love's dominion.

For thou wert grandly beautiful as night,
    Stern Orcus, in thy realm of buried kings;
And thy sad crown of cypress in my sight
    Fairer than all the bright and flowery rings
Of wreathĕd poppies and of golden corn
By Ceres on her stately temples worn.

I sat beside thee on Hell's dusky throne,
    Nor feared the awful shadow of thy fate;
Content to share the burden of thy crown,
    And all the mournful splendors of thy state;
Bending my flower-like beauty to thy will,
Seeking with light thy lonely dark to fill.

Wondering, I think how thy dear love hath bound me
    In a new life that half forgets the old;
All day I haunt the meadows where you found me,
    Knee-deep in daffodils of dusky gold,
Or sit by Cyane's sad fountain, dreaming
Of the red lake by thy proud palace gleaming.

When, in her car by wingĕd dragons borne,
    Pale Ceres sought me through the shuddering night,
With angry torches and fierce eyes, forlorn,
    Slaying the dark that screened me from her sight,
Like a reft lioness that rends the air
Of midnight with her perilous despair,

Jove, pitying the great passion of her woe,
    Gave back thy queen-bride to the mother's grief—
To Ceres gave—through summer's golden glow
    And all the crescent months, from spear to sheaf:
Alas, how sadly in Sicilian bowers
I pass this lonely, lingering time flowers!

In the long silence of the languid noons,
    When all the panting birds are faint with heat,
I wander listless by the blue lagoons
    To hear their light waves rippling at my feet
Through the dead calm, and count the lingering time
By the slow pulsing of their silver chime.

I languish for the late autumnal showers,
    The cool, cool plashing of the autumn rain,
The shimmering hoar-frost and fast-fading flowers,
    That give me back to thy dark realm again;
I have no native land from thee apart,
And my high heaven of heavens is in thy heart.

Proserpine, an oil painting by Dante Gabriel Rossetti, 1874

Proserpine

Dante Gabriel Rossetti, 1874

Mr. Rossetti was so inspired by the tale of Proserpine that he not only penned a poem about the woeful goddess, but painted her portrait as well. Consider carefully the words chosen by the poet to paint a verbal portrait of the goddess. Discuss how they are reflected in the oil painting.

Afar away the light that brings cold cheer
Unto this wall,—one instant and no more
Admitted at my distant palace—door.
Afar the flowers of Enna from this drear
Dire fruit, which, tasted once, must thrall me here.
Afar those skies from this Tartarean grey
That chills me: and afar, how far away,
The nights that shall be from the days that were.

Afar from mine own self I seem, and wing
Strange ways in thought, and listen for a sign:
And still some heart unto some soul doth pine,
(Whose sounds mine inner sense is fain to bring,
Continually together murmuring,)—
"Woe's me for thee, unhappy Proserpine!"

Est Vērum!

In his magnum opus, *The Canterbury Tales*, Geoffrey Chaucer invoked every literary genre known to the English Middle Ages. Of these genres, however, he calls upon Ovid significantly more than any other author. Many tales from the *Metamorphoses* appear in some shape or form throughout Chaucer's tale. Pluto and Proserpine themselves appear in the "The Merchant's Tale."

Unit 3 Reading

READING AND REVIEW FOR CHAPTERS 13–16

The Latin Poetry of John Milton

Grant Horner, Professor of Renaissance and Reformation Studies

The Master's College

John Milton is known as perhaps the greatest genius of the seventeenth century, which is known as the "century of genius." This is the age of Shakespeare, of Francis Bacon—inventor of the scientific method—and of the King James Bible. One of the greatest poets in the English language, ranked alongside Shakespeare himself, Milton was also a theologian and was heavily involved in politics. Milton was a Puritan, meaning that he wished for the English Protestant Church to remove itself fully from Roman Catholic doctrine and practice.

Milton was known for his incredible capacities in all areas related to the humanities, particularly languages. Friends said he had the Bible essentially memorized and, according to Cyriack Skinner's seventeenth-century biography, Milton's daughters said he "had his Homer by heart." His study of languages began early and at home; he was introduced to classical Latin around age five, Greek at ten, Hebrew at twelve, and other languages as he grew older. By age twelve he was writing beautiful Latin poetry, and by the age of fifteen he was translating Hebrew psalms into English verse. Milton was formally educated starting at age seven at Saint Paul's School in the heart of London; his teachers there included Alexander Gil, who was famously strict with whippings of lazy students, but nonetheless beloved. Young Milton had as a private tutor the brilliant scholar Thomas Young. Both Young and Gil were widely known as Christian Humanist scholars of great learning and erudition and were among the leading Latinists in all England. At the time of Milton's education, all academic instruction and conversation was actually carried on in Latin. This means that a young English boy would be learning Greek and Hebrew with lessons given in the ancient Roman tongue!

All told, Milton eventually was fluent in upwards of two dozen languages, including tongues rarely studied in the seventeenth century, such as Syriac and Anglo-Saxon. In his forties he became Secretary of Foreign Tongues, also called Latin Secretary, for the English government—one of the highest positions for a scholar, which involved handling foreign correspondence and negotiations.

But of all the languages he knew, Latin was his most beloved, and functionally he was more bilingual than primarily a user of English. Milton was writing complex Latin poetry and prose in his teens, and his work was so polished that when he visited Italy at age twenty, the greatest Italian scholars and poets wrote poems praising him and saying he had outdone Homer, Vergil, and Dante with his linguistic mastery of Greek, Latin, and Italian. His work is marvelously populated by a variety of classical tropes and figures of speech, such as anaphora, antithesis, metonymy, periphrasis, synecdoche, and zeugma, and like all great Renaissance authors, Milton sought to imitate the Greek and Latin classics in both style and content.

Because of these tropes and figures of speech, Milton's Latin is extraordinarily "classical" even for a Renaissance Englishman. His Latin (and his English) reads more like Cicero or Catullus than it does like John Donne or William Shakespeare. Most of the scholars of the fifteenth through the seventeenth centuries adapted Latin in various ways and modernized it. Classical Latin had divided over the centuries into a very precise literary language, such as we see with Cicero, and a simple "vulgar Latin" variation, spoken by the man on the street. Later on, medieval Latin shifted to being used mostly by the Catholic Church, while the remnants of vulgar Latin evolved into the Romance languages of Europe. Written Latin—first in manuscript, then in print after the middle of the fifteenth century—had developed a series of abbreviations to save time and space on the expensive parchment and paper. *Quemadmodum*, for example, would look like *Quemadm*, and *Epistolarum* might be shortened to *Epstlm*. Abbreviations varied from scribe to scribe and had to be learned—not only did you need to know the endings, but you also had to learn their varying abbreviations. These writing shortcuts are part of the reason that Latin endings started to drop off as Latin turned into the various Romance languages, which are not as highly inflected; this is why medieval manuscripts are very hard to read (except to experts). Knowing Latin is not enough. Imagine parsing nouns or conjugating verbs if the endings are trimmed or simply missing! Milton, however, kept strictly to a severely Roman and even Ciceronian "pure" Latin, which was fully inflected, precise, ornate, and modeled after the greatest classical authors. For him, medieval Latin was an impure, barbaric style ruined by the Church, and was merely a bridge that led toward the development of the Romance languages.

Milton was probably one of the greatest Latinists in all of Europe during his lifetime, having been steeped from his earliest years in the works of Ovid, Catullus, Vergil, Persius, Horace, Seneca, Claudian, Petronius, Prudentius, Lucan, Tibullus, Statius, and many others. Milton set out in his early twenties on a six-year project of reading entirely through all the works of classical antiquity. Can you imagine what that must have been like? And apparently he did just that, as his own work cites thousands of poets and authors from Greece and Rome. Indeed, Milton's works quote or allude to over 1,500 Greek and Latin authors from classical antiquity. Most good libraries today don't even contain that many books in the ancient languages. Milton wrote (but did not publish) a massive Latin thesaurus which became the basis of one of the most important Latin dictionaries ever created, Adam Littleton's *Dictionarium Latino-Barbarum* (1677).[1] Milton was entirely fluent in both writing and speaking Latin, which at that time was the international scholarly language.

Milton was particularly fond of Ovid's poetry, which was incredibly popular during the Renaissance. Ovid's *Metamorphoses*, written in the epic meter of dactylic hexameter, is constantly quoted or alluded to by Milton, perhaps more than by any other Latin writer. Milton often imitates Ovid's humor, his irony, and his extraordinary linguistic complexity. For example, in Ovid's story of Narcissus and Echo, the poet plays elaborate and very funny language games in the conversation between the two characters. Milton imitates this playfully but precisely in his story of Eve seeing her reflection in a pond right before meeting Adam in *Paradise Lost*, Book IV. He carefully reproduces the wordplay from highly inflected Ovidian Latin to seventeenth-century syntactical English, which is quite a feat.

For John Milton, like most great poets before him, the big question was fame. The great classical poets wrote openly about their desire for immortality through literature. Milton knew that his ability to write great Latin poetry would bring him, in his own words, only into the "second rank among the Latines."[2] Who could compete against Vergil and Ovid, really? No one! So Milton's goal was to be the greatest poet in the English language. His method was to write precisely controlled, richly figurative poetic English, modeled carefully on the classics of Greece and Rome, but opening up new poetic vistas in the comparatively young language of England. Four hundred years later, the consensus is that Milton achieved his goal. His imitative mastery of great Latin poetry is surely a major reason his greatness is so universally acknowledged. Milton may be the definitive example of a writer whose poetic imaginative power is directly linked to his love of Latin.

---

1. According to Milton's biographer W.R. Parker in his book *Milton: A Biography* (Oxford University Press, 1968), Milton collected three volumes full of Latin definitions over his lifetime. These notebooks were probably passed to his nephew Edward Phillips, who was a lexicographer, and from Phillips the manuscript likely passed to Littleton, who based his work directly on Milton's. Littleton's famous dictionary was widely circulated and reprinted many times and became a major source for many Latin/English dictionaries that followed it.
2. Milton, *The Reason of Church-Government Urg'd against Prelaty*, Book II, 1642, accessed October 3, 2012, <http://www.dartmouth.edu/~milton/reading_room/reason/book_2/index.shtml>.

Before You Read!

Notice Milton's age when he wrote the poem that is this unit's reading (see the title). Think about how knowing his age may or may not affect your appreciation of the poem. The occasion of the composition of the poem is the death of a beadle at Cambridge University, where Milton was a student. Originally, a beadle was a minor lay church official who ushered and otherwise assisted the priest. In medieval universities, and indeed in some British universities today, a beadle may assist in reporting attendance, securing the grounds of a college, and giving information to the public about the college. He often wears a special uniform to represent the institution and carries the mace of the college or university in processions (see the word *baculō* in the first line of the elegy). In Victorian England, beadles were also functionaries of the city and acted as heralds. The most famous beadle in fiction is Mr. Bumble in Charles Dickens's *Oliver Twist*.

ELEGIA SECUNDA, ANNO ÆTATIS 17.

In obitum Præconis Academici Cantabrigiensis.*

*You see in the title a digraph: æ. The word "digraph" comes from Greek words meaning "double" and "writing." A digraph is used to show that two letters make one meaningful sound, or phoneme, such as *sh* or *wh* in English. The poem as published in Milton's time would have had digraphs throughout the text; however, we have, for reasons of simplicity, used digraphs in our text only for the title so that you can see and learn about them.

Characters

Iovis, Iovis: Jupiter, also called Jove, king of the gods

Corōnīdēs, Corōnīdae: Aesclepius, son of Coronis (human) and Apollo (god); Aesclepius was a famous healer who later became a god. One of his most famous temples was in Epidauros in the southern part of Greece. (The Greek ending *-īdēs* means "son of.")

Phoebus, Phoebī: Phoebus, one of the titles of Apollo

Cyllēnius: Cyllenius, a title of Hermes referring to his birthplace on Mt. Cyllene

Eurybatēs, Eurybatis: Eurybates, herald of the Greeks during the Trojan War

Achillēus, Achillēī: Achilles, greatest of the Greek warriors in the Trojan War

Pallas, Pallados: Pallas, a title for Athena; *Palladi* is dative so the *i* would be expected to be long, but this is a Greek word, and in Greek, the dative *i* of the third declension is short. This line refers to the time one of the Muses told a story about Proserpina to Pallas Athena (Minerva). You read about this event in chapter 16.

Ātrīdae: *Atridae . . . ducis* – Agamemnon

Mūsae, -ārum: Muses, the goddesses of the arts

1 Tē, quī <u>cōnspicuus</u> *baculō* <u>fulgente</u> solēbās
2   *Palladium* totiēs** ōre *ciēre* gregem,
3 Ultima *praecōnum praecōnem* tē quoque saeva
4   Mors rapit, officiō nec favet ipsa suō.
5 Candidiōra **licet** fuerint tibi *tempora plūmīs*
6   Sub quibus accipimus *dēlituisse* Iovem,
7 Ō dignus tamen *Haemoniō iuvenēscere succō*,
8   Dignus in *Aesōniōs* vīvere posse diēs,
9 Dignus quem *Stygiīs* <u>medicā</u> <u>revocāret</u> ab undīs
10   Arte Corōnīdēs, saepe rogante <u>deā</u>.

11 Tū sī iūssus erās aciēs *accīre* <u>togātās</u>,

   12 Et celer ā Phoebō nūntius īre tuō—

13 Tālis in *Īliacā* stābat Cyllēnius *aulā*

   14 *Ālipēs*, <u>aethereā</u> missus ab arce*** Patris.

15 Tālis & Eurybatēs ante ōra *furentis* Achillēī

   16 Rettulit Ātrīdae iūssa <u>sevēra</u> ducis.

17 Magna <u>sepulchrōrum</u> rēgīna, *satelles Avernī***

   18 Saeva nimis Mūsīs, Palladī saeva nimis,

19 *Quīn* illōs rapiās **quī pondus <u>inūtile</u> terrae**—

   20 Turba quidem est tēlīs ista petenda tuīs.

21 Vestibus hunc igitur *pullīs*, Acadēmia lūgē,

   22 Et *madeant lachrymīs*** <u>nigra</u> *feretra* tuīs.

23 *Fundat & ipsa modōs querebunda*** Elegēia tristēs*,

   24 *Personet &* **tōtīs** *naenia moesta**** **scholīs**.

**totiēs = totiēns
<u>sepulchrōrum</u> = <u>sepulcrōrum</u>
lachrymīs = lacrimīs
querebunda = queribunda
moesta = maesta

***These words recall line 356, Book IV, of Vergil's *Aeneid*: "*Iove missus ab ipso....*"

John Milton

Phrases

licet + perfect subjunctive = although

quī pondus <u>inūtile</u> terrae – (*est* is implied in this relative clause)

tōtīs . . . scholīs – in all the schools/throughout all the schools and colleges (ablative of place where; the preposition is missing because it is a poem)

Glossary

Use your "eye" Latin to discern the meaning of the underlined words in the reading.

baculum, baculī, n.	rod, stick (perhaps here, mace)
Palladius, -a, -um, adj.	of Pallas, of the goddess Athena, Palladian
cieō, ciēre, cīvī, citum	to arouse, to shake, to stir up, to cause to move, to urge
praeco, praecōnī, m.	herald, messenger (i.e., beadle)
tempora	temples (at the sides of the head) (This word literally means "times." Named after the Greek τὰ καίρια [*ta kairia*], the right time or place; hence the vital spot for one to get hit and die; related to the Greek word for "time" and "opportunity," therefore translated *tempora*.)
plūma, plūmae, f.	down
dēlitēscō, dēlitēscere, dēlituī	to lie in hiding, to conceal oneself, to hide
Haemonius, -a, -um, adj.	Thessalian, from Thessaly, Haemonian
iuvenescō, iuvenescere, iuvenuī	to grow up; to grow young again (Ovid)
succus, succī, m.	juice, moisture, sap, potion (usually seen as *sūcus* and sometimes with the genitive *sūcūs*)
Aesōnius, -a, -um, adj.	Aesonian, pertaining to Jason's father, who drank a potion made by Medea that was supposed to make him young again (of the famed Jason and the Argonauts)

Stygius, -a, -um, adj.	Stygian, infernal, pertaining to the lower world (the Styx is a river running through the lower world)
acciō, accīre, accīvī, accitum	to summon, to call, to recall, to fetch
Īliacus, -a, -um, adj.	pertaining to Troy, of Troy (also known as Ilium)
aula, -ae, f.	courtyard
Ālipēs, ālipidis, f.	wing-footed, a title for Hermes
&	*et* (This symbol is called an "ampersand," a word meaning originally "*and* through itself *and*." In other words, the symbol itself makes the Latin word *et* itself. The word was probably originally "andperseand," a word difficult to pronounce. We have left the lines in which the ampersand appears exactly as they would have been printed in Milton's day.)
furēns, furentis, adj.	mad, raging (cf. *furor*)
satelles, satellitis, c.	attendant
Avernus, Avernī, m.	Avernus, a place considered to be an entrance to the Underworld, the Underworld
quīn, adv.	why not? wherefore not?
pullus, -a, -um, adj.	black, mournful
academīa, -ae, f.	Academy, Acedēmia (*acadēmīa* properly has a long *i* but there is classical precedent for scanning it short)
madeō, madēre	to be wet, to be soaked
lachrymīs	*lacrimīs* – tears
feretrum, feretrī, n.	bier
fundō, fundere, fūsī, fūsum	to pour out, to shed (not to be confused with *fundō, fundāre*)
querebundus, -a, -um, adj.	mournful, complaining
elegēia	usually scanned ĕlĕgīă, but in Ovid ĕlĕgēīă
tristis, triste, adj.	sad
personō, personāre, personuī	to resound, to sound about
naenia, -ae, f.	funeral song, dirge
maestus, -a, -um, adj.	sad, sorrowful
schola, -ae, f.	school, college (*Schola* originally meant "leisure." It then also meant "time given to learning or pleasant disputation." How many of us have heard that our school days are the best days of our lives and the easiest ones, too?)

More on Meter

THE ELEGIAC COUPLET

In this unit, you have learned a few of the more common meters, such as hendecasyllabic and dactylic hexameter, used by Latin authors. These meters were invariably adopted from earlier forms of Greek poetry, and were in turn handed down to later generations of poets who would seek to imitate their Latin predecessors. One of the more common metrical styles was the elegiac couplet, used here by Milton. Ennius, whom you read in chapters 2 and 3, was the first to adapt the elegiac couplet to Latin. Catullus and Ovid both used this meter regularly. Having now learned dactylic hexameter, you will be able to pick up this meter easily.

The poem is arranged in couplet verses. The first verse in the couplet is written in dactylic hexameter, the second in dactylic pentameter. The word "pentameter" derives from the Greek word *penta* (five). It has only five feet as opposed to the six found in hexameter.

Study the following patterns.

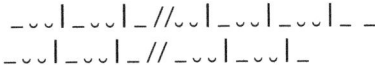

Note how the first line follows the traditional pattern of a dactylic hexameter. Any of the first four feet may still substitute a spondee for a dactyl. The third foot often contains a caesura. In the second line, the first two feet are also dactyls. Then half a spondee appears with a caesura. This half-spondee is followed by two more dactyls and then a final long syllable. It is almost as if the spondee split in half and placed one syllable in the middle and the other at the end. You should also notice that in the second line there are only four dactyls possible instead of five. This rearrangement of dactyls and spondees produces the shorter pentameter. Now try your own hand at scanning the first couplet of Milton's poem.

Tē, quī cōnspicuus baculō // fulgente solēbās

Palladium totiēs ōre ciēre gregem,

Question & Answer

In each of the following exercises, circle the letter of the correct answer.

1. *Tē* in line 1 is _____.
   a. an imperative
   b. the object of *rapit* in line 4
   c. the subject of *ciēre* in line 2
   d. the subject of *solēbās* in line 1

2. *Palladium . . . gregem* in line 2 refers to which of the following?
   a. cows
   b. a temple
   c. the walls of Cambridge
   d. students

3. According to this elegy, who or what is the final messenger?
   a. education
   b. death
   c. Apollo
   d. Mercury

4. Scan the first four feet of line 5.
   a. _ ∪ ∪ | _ ∪ ∪ | _ ∪ ∪ | _ ∪ ∪
   b. _ ∪ ∪ | _ _ | _ ∪ ∪ | _ ∪ ∪
   c. _ ∪ ∪ | _ _ | _ ∪ ∪ | _ _
   d. _ ∪ ∪ | _ ∪ ∪ | _ _ | _ ∪ ∪

5. What deity mentioned hid beneath feathers?
   a. Proserpina
   b. Mercury
   c. Jupiter
   d. Minerva

6. Line 8 indicates that _____.
   a. the herald was not respected while he live
   b. the herald is worthy to live again or anew
   c. the herald of the gods is related to Aeson
   d. Aeson is Jason's descendant

7. According to lines 8–10, _____.
   a. the healing art of the son of Coronis could bring people back to life
   b. the Styx can never be recrossed
   c. the goddess Coronis would never ask her son for a favor
   d. none of the above

8. *Togātās* in line 11 is a way of describing what?
   a. the ancient Romans
   b. the strong walls of Cambridge University
   c. the Cambridge students in their academic caps and gowns
   d. all of the above

9. Which of the following, according to the poem, did Eurybates do?
   a. made announcements to Agamemnon on behalf of Achilles
   b. made announcements to Achilles on behalf of Agamemnon
   c. acted as a messenger from Jupiter
   d. stood on the high citadel of his father

10. Rather than the herald, whom should death have claimed?
    a. worthless and useless people
    b. the Cambridge students
    c. both of the above
    d. none of the above

11. What things in the poem are dark or black?
    a. clothing
    b. the herald's bier
    c. both of the above
    d. none of the above

12. Scan the first four feet of line 21.
    a. _ ᴗ ᴗ | _ ᴗ ᴗ | _ ᴗ ᴗ | _ ᴗ ᴗ
    b. _ ᴗ ᴗ | _ _ | _ ᴗ ᴗ | _ ᴗ ᴗ
    c. _ ᴗ ᴗ | _ _ | _ _ | _ ᴗ ᴗ
    d. _ ᴗ ᴗ | _ ᴗ ᴗ | _ _ | _ ᴗ ᴗ

About the Author

JOHN MILTON

John Milton was born in London, England, on Friday, December 9, 1608. As a child, he attended St. Paul's School, which was attached to St. Paul's Cathedral, of which John Donne was the dean. Milton would have heard him preach. Milton's parents encouraged him to be a good student, and he learned Latin, Greek, Hebrew, French, and Italian. These languages would serve him well when, as an adult during the Commonwealth (or republican period) in England, he was Latin secretary, analogous to secretary of state in the United States today. When older, he attended Christ's College at Cambridge University. After graduation from Cambridge as *magister artium*, he embarked on a grand tour of Europe.

Milton was much involved with government during the tumultuous years of the English Civil War and the republican period of English history, when royal rule and the monarchy were replaced by the government of Oliver Cromwell. The monarchy was restored in 1660.

By 1648 John Milton realized he was going blind. He became permanently blind by 1652, the same year in which his second of three wives died, leaving him to care for several children. After he was blind and severely hampered by domestic problems and by the enmity of the restored monarchy because of his work on behalf of the Commonwealth, Milton wrote his greatest poem, the epic *Paradise Lost*, as well as other great poems.

Glossaries
Vocabulary by Chapter

Chapter 1

LATIN	ENGLISH	DERIVATIVES
Nouns		
colōnus, colōnī, m.	farmer, (sometimes) a tenant farmer	(colonize)
cornū, -ūs, n.	horn; wing (of an army)	(cornet)
frūctus, -ūs, m.	fruit; profit, benefit	(fructose)
fūr, fūris, m./f.	thief (used as a term of reproach to slaves)	(furtive)
iniūria, -ae, f.	wrong, injury; insult, offense	(injury)
lacus, -ūs, m.	lake, pond, large body of water	(loch)
lēx, lēgis, f.	law	(legislate)
māiōrēs, māiōrium, m./f. pl. (cf. the comparative form of magnus)	ancestors	
mercātor, mercātōris, m.	merchant	(commercialize)
opus, operis, n.	work	(operative)
praedium, praediī, n.	farm, landed estate	(praedial)
sapientia, -ae, f. (cf. sapiens)	wisdom	(sapient)
silva, -ae, f.	woods, forest	(Pennsylvania)
vīs, vīs, f.	force, power; (pl.) strength, troops, forces	(vis)
Verbs		
invītō, -āre, -āvī, -ātum (cf. vitare, "to avoid")	to invite, entertain, summon	(invite)
nesciō, -īre, -īvī, -ītum	to not know, to be ignorant of	(nescience)
Adjectives, Adverbs, Conjunctions, etc.		
vetus, veteris, adj.	old, ancient	(veteran)

Chapter 2

	LATIN	ENGLISH	DERIVATIVES
Nouns			
	fremitus, -ūs, m.	a roaring, murmuring	(fremitus)
	secūris, secūris, f.	axe, hatchet	
Verbs			
	caedō, caedere, cecīdī, caesum (cf. caedes)	to cut down, to kill	(caesarian)
	cavō, -āre, -āvī, -ātum	to make hollow, to hollow out	(excavate)
	cōgitō, -āre, -āvī, -ātum	to think, to consider	(cogitate)
	existimō, -āre, -āvī, -ātum	to judge a thing according to its value	(estimate)
	licet, licēre, licuit *or* licitum est	it is allowed for *x* (dat.) to *y* (inf.); *x* (dat.) may *y* (inf.)	
	oportet, oportēre, oportuit	it is proper/right for *x* (acc.) to *y* (inf.); *x* (acc.) should *y* (inf.)	
	praestō, praestāre, praestitī, praestitum	to place before, to present; to be outstanding, to be distinguished; to prevail; to overcome; to stand before	
	prōmittō, prōmittere, prōmīsī, prōmissum	to let go forward, to send forth; to promise	(promise)
	sonō, sonāre, sonuī, sonitum	to sound, to resound, to make a noise	(sonic)
	vīsō, vīsere, vīsī, vīsum	to look at carefully, to contemplate	(visage)
Adjectives, Adverbs, Conjunctions, etc.			
	frondōsus, -a, -um, adj.	full of leaves, leafy	(frond)

Chapter 3

	LATIN	ENGLISH	DERIVATIVES
Nouns			
	ōrātor, ōrātōris, m. (cf. ōrātiō, ōrāre)	orator, speaker	(orator)
Verbs			
	circumeō, circumīre, circumīvī/circumiī, circuitum	to go around; to enclose	(circuit)
	cōnsequor, cōnsequī, cōnsecūtus sum (cf. sequor)	to follow, to go after; to obtain	(consequence)
	cunctor, cunctārī, cunctātus sum (cf. cunctātiō)	to delay; to hesitate (+ inf.)	
	faeneror, faenerārī, faenerātus sum	to lend [money] at interest; to drain by extortion	
	gignō, gignere, genuī, genitum	to beget, to bear, to bring forth	(genitive)
	gradior, gradī, grēssus sum	to walk, to step	(grade)
	habeō, habēre, habuī, habitum	to have, to hold; to consider	(habit)
	hortor, hortārī, hortātus sum	to encourage, to exhort	(exhortation)
	misceō, miscēre, miscuī, mixtum	to mix, to mingle	(miscellaneous)
	morior, morī/morīrī, mortuus sum (cf. mortuus)	to die	(mortuary)
	nītor, nītī, nīsum sum/nīxum sum (cf. nīsus)	to strive, to exert oneself, to make an effort	

Latin	English	Derivatives
pōnō, pōnere, posuī/posīvī, positum	to put, to place	(deposit)
redeō, redīre, rediī/redīvī, reditum	to go back, to come back, to return	
Adjectives, Adverbs, Conjunctions, etc.		
perīculōsus, -a, -um, adj. (cf. perīculum)	dangerous	(perilous)
hinc, adv.	from this, from here	
quom (archaic form of cum, conj.), adv.	when	

Chapter 4

LATIN	ENGLISH	DERIVATIVES
Nouns		
duplum, -ī, n.	a double amount	(duplex)
mercātūra, -ae, f.	trade, buying and selling (used disparagingly)	(mercantile)
quadruplum, -ī, n.	a quadruple amount	(quadruplets)
Verbs		
existimō, -āre, -āvī, -ātum	to estimate, count	
fruor, fruī, frūctus/fruitus sum (+ abl.)	to have the benefit of, to enjoy	(fruit)
īnstituō, īnstituere, īnstituī, īnstitūtum	to undertake, to begin, to decide to do; to put in place	(institute)
sustineō, sustinēre, sustinuī, sustentum	to hold up, to support, to sustain	(sustenance)
Adjectives, Adverbs, Conjunctions, etc.		
amplus, -a, -um, adj.	large, wide, spacious, ample, grand; distinguished	(amplify)
invidiōsus, -a, -um, adj.	envious; hateful, spiteful, seething	(invidious)
stabilis, -e, adj.	stable, firm, steady	(stable, stability)
strēnuus, -a, -um, adj.	brisk, prompt, active, vigorous	(strenuous)
studiōsus, -a, -um, adj.	eager to (+ inf.); eager for (+ gen.)	(studious)
interdum, adv.	sometimes, occasionally, now and then	
item, adv. (cf. īdem)	likewise, in the same way	
suprā, adv.	above	(superior)
tam, adv.	so	
vērum, adv.	truthfully	(verily)
nisi, conj.	if not, unless; except	

Chapter 5

LATIN	ENGLISH	DERIVATIVES
Nouns		
adulēscentia, -ae, f.	youth	(adolescent, adolescence)
aetās, aetātis, f.	age, lifetime (*Aetās* is the contracted form of *aevitās*, which in turn is from *aevum*, meaning "eternity," "time," or "lifetime.")	(coeval, medieval)
aqua, -ae, f.	water	(aquatic)

Latin	English	Derivatives
dōlium, -ī, n.	a large jar for storing wine	
fundus, -ī, m.	farm, estate (cf. praedium) (This word originally meant "soil" or "ground." The meaning "farm," then, is a type of synecdoche.)	(fundamental)
olea, -ae, f.	olive, olive tree	
tempestās, tempestātis, f.	storm	(tempest, temper)
torcular, torculāris, n. (i-stem)	a wine press, an oil press	(torque, torture)
Verbs		
accēdō, accēdere, accēssī, accēssum	to approach, to come near	(accede)
cōnserō, cōnserere, cōnsēvī, cōnsitum	to sow, to plant	
dēiciō, dēicere, dēiēcī, dēiectum	to throw down, to hurl down (cf. dē + iaciō)	(dejected)
expediō, expedīre, expedīvī/ expediī, expedītum	to set free; to be useful	(expedite)
soleō, solēre, solitus sum (semi-deponent)	to be accustomed	
Adjectives, Adverbs, Conjunctions, etc.		
oleārius, -a, -um, adj.	of oil, for oil	
vīnārius, -a, -um, adj.	of wine, for wine	
continuō, adv.	immediately	
diū, adv.	for a long time	
nē, adv.	not (used to introduce a negative purpose; often translates as "so that not" or "lest")	
quotannīs, adv.	every year	
nēve, conj.	and not, or not (an alternate form is neu.)	
ut *or* utī, conj.	(with the indicative) as; when; (with the subjunctive) in order that, to	

Chapter 6

LATIN	ENGLISH	DERIVATIVES
Nouns		
ānser, ānseris, m.	goose	
arvum, -ī, n.	plowed land, field (cf. arāre, "to plow")	
dīum, -ī, n.	open air, open sky	
faenum, -ī, n.	hay	
frīgus, frīgoris, n.	cold, coolness	(frigid)
hiems, hiemis, f.	winter	(hiemal)
pābulum, -ī, n.	food, fodder for animals	(pabulum)
plaustrum, -ī n.	wagon, cart	
stabulum, -ī, n.	standing room, quarters, a stable	(stable)

LATIN	ENGLISH	DERIVATIVES
sūs, suis, c.	pig, sow, hog	
tēctum, -ī, n.	roof, house (by synecdoche)	
vīlicus, -ī, m.	overseer of a villa	
Verbs		
cōnficiō, cōnficere, cōnfēcī, cōnfectum	to put together, to finish	
mācerō, -āre, -āvī, -ātum	to soften	(macerate)
perfundō, perfundere, perfūdī, perfūsum	to pour over	
saliō, salīre, saluī, saltum	to spring, to leap, to jump	
vetō, vetāre, vetuī, vetitum	to forbid, to prohibit	(veto)
Adjectives, Adverbs, Conjunctions, etc.		
aliquot, indec. adj.	some, several	
plānus, -a, -um, adj.	flat, level, even	(plane)
pluvius, -a, -um, adj.	rainy, of rain	(pluviometer)
praesertim, adv.	especially, chiefly	

Chapter 7

	LATIN	ENGLISH	DERIVATIVES
Nouns			
	molestia, -ae, f.	trouble, annoyance	(molest)
	pausa, -ae, f.	pause, end	(pause)
	prex, precis, f.	prayer	(imprecation)
	quisquam, quaequam, quicquam/quidquam, indef. pro. (cf. quis, quid)	anyone, anything	
	senecta, -ae, f. (cf. senex)	old age	(senectitude)
	sententia, -ae, f.	opinion, feeling	(sentiment, sentence)
	vīta, -ae, f.	life	(vital)
Verbs			
	adversor, adversārī, adversātus sum	to oppose, to resist (+ dat.)	(adversary)
	lubet/libet, lubēre, lubuit	(impersonal) it is pleasing	
	opitulor, opitulārī, opitulātus sum (cf. ops)	to bring aid, to help, to assist	
	pudeō, pudēre, puduī (cf. pudendus)	to make ashamed, to shame	(pudency)
	tolerō, -āre, -āvī, -ātum	to bear, to endure, to tolerate, to sustain	(tolerate)
Adjectives, Adverbs, Conjunctions, etc.			
	dēnique, adv.	and then, finally	
	ecquandō, inter. adv. (cf. ec- [in the word ecce] + quandō)	ever, at any time (often carries an attitude of indignation)	
	praeterquam, adv. (cf. praeter)	except for, other than	
	adversum/adversus, prep. (+ acc.)	against	(adverse)

Chapter 8

LATIN	ENGLISH	DERIVATIVES
Nouns		
audācia, -ae, f.	boldness, audacity (cf. audax)	(audacious)
coniūrātiō, coniūrātiōnis, f.	conspiracy	
cūra, -ae, f.	care, concern	(curator)
iūssus, iūssūs, m.	an order (cf. iubeō)	(jussive)
patientia, -ae, f.	patience, experience	(patient)
vigilia, vigiliae, f.	a watching for the security of a place; sentinels, soldiers keeping watch (cf. vigilō)	(vigilant)
Verbs		
abūtor, abūtī, abūsus sum	to use fully, to abuse (cf. utor)	(abuse)
arbitror, arbitrārī, arbitrātus sum	to think, to judge (cf. arbiter, arbitrium)	(arbitration)
dēsum, dēesse, dēfuī, dēfutūrum	to lack, to fail	
ēlūdō, ēlūdere, ēlūsī, ēlūsum	to ward off, to evade, to elude; to mock	(elusive)
iactō, -āre, -āvī, -ātum	to throw repeatedly or energetically, to throw about, (with the reflexive) to gesticulate	
precor, precārī, precātus sum	to pray, to entreat	
properō, -āre, -āvī, -ātum	to hurry, to hasten	
vītō, -āre, -āvī, -ātum	to avoid	
Adjectives, Adverbs, Conjunctions, etc.		
ācer, ācris, ācre, adj.	sharp, eager; severe, fierce	(acrid)
perniciōsus, -a, -um, adj.	destructive, ruinous	(pernicious)
praeclārus, -a, -um, adj.	very famous, excellent	
nimis, adv.	too much	
tandem, adv.	finally, at last, in the end; I ask, I pray (in urgent questioning)	
ac *or* atque, conj.	and	

Chapter 9

LATIN	ENGLISH	DERIVATIVES
Nouns		
occāsus, -ūs, m.	the setting of the heavenly bodies; the west; fall, destruction (cf. occidō)	
prōvincia, -ae, f.	province	(provincial)
septentriōnēs, septentriōnum, m. pl. (also spelled septemtriōnēs)	the seven ploughing oxen (a constellation); the north	(septentrional)
Verbs		
attingō, attingere, attigī, attāctum	to touch	
commeō, -āre, -āvī, -ātum	to go up and down, to come and go, to visit frequently	
contineō, continēre, continuī, contentum	to hold together, to keep together; to keep in, to surround, to contain	(content)
fīō, fierī, factus sum	to occur, to happen; to be made, to be done	

Latin	English	Derivatives
incolō, incolere, incoluī	to inhabit, to dwell (in) (cf. incola)	
occidō, occidere, occidī, occāsum	to fall, to fall down	(occasion)
orior, orīrī, ortus sum	to rise	(Orient)
pertineō, pertinēre, pertinuī	to reach, to extend (to)	(pertinent)
praecēdō, praecēdere, praecēssī, praecēssum	to go before, to precede, to surpass	(precedent)
ADJECTIVES, ADVERBS, CONJUNCTIONS, etc.		
fīnitimus, -a, -um, adj.	neighboring, adjacent	(finite)
longus, -a, -um, adj.	long	(long)
longē, adv.	by far	
minus, CpAdv.	less; not very (comparative form of parvus)	
proptereā, adv.	on that account, therefore	
saepe, adv.	often	
undique, adv.	from/on all sides, from everywhere, everywhere	

Chapter 10

Latin	English	Derivatives
NOUNS		
admīrātiō, admīrātiōnis, f.	admiration	(admiration)
clādēs, clādis, f.	destruction	
classis, classis, f.	(in military usage) all of the citizens called to fight; *hence*, the fleet, the army	(class)
cōnspectus, -ūs, m.	sight, view, range of sight	(conspectus)
fremitus, -ūs, m.	a dull, roaring sound	(fremitus)
interpres, interpretis, c.	interpreter, translator	(interpreter, interpretive)
lūdībrium, lūdībriī, n.	mockery	
quīlibet, quaelibet, quodlibet, indef. pro.	anyone you wish, no matter who, whoever	
sors, sortis, f.	a lot, a drawing of lots, casting of lots, fate	(sort, sortilege)
VERBS		
abōminor, abōminārī, abōminātus sum	to hate, to despise	(abomination)
appetō, -ere, -īvī, -ītum	to strive for, to seek	(appetite)
congredior, congredī, congressus sum	to come together	(congress)
conticēscō, conticēscere, conticuī	to be silent	
dīmicō, -āre, -āvī, -ātum	to fight, to contend, to struggle	
laetor, laetārī, laetātus sum	to rejoice	
opus est	there is a need, there is a necessity for *x* (dat.) of *y* (abl.); *x* (dat.) has need of *y* (abl.)	
summoveō, summovēre, summōvī, summōtum	to send away, to remove	
ADJECTIVES, ADVERBS, CONJUNCTIONS, etc.		
ēgregius, -a, -um, adj.	distinguished, excellent	(egregious)
inermis, -e, adj.	unarmed	

Latin	English	Derivatives
pār, paris, adj.	equal to, like (+ dat.)	(parity)
singulus, -a, -um, adj. (dis. num.)	separate, single, one at a time	(singular)
magis, CpAdv.	more, to a greater extent, rather	
paulisper, adv.	for a little while	
prope, adv.	nearly, almost	
totiēns, adv.	so often	

Chapter 11

LATIN	ENGLISH	DERIVATIVES
Nouns		
āra, ārae, f.	altar	
fortitūdō, fortitūdinis, f.	courage, strength	(fortitude)
obtrectātio, obtrectātiōnis, f.	envious detraction, disparagement	
prūdentia, -ae, f.	knowledge; wisdom, discretion, prudence	(prudent)
puerulus, puerulī, m.	a little boy	(puerile)
Verbs		
addūcō, addūcere, addūxī, adductus (cf. ad + ducere)	to lead to, to bring to, to convey to	(adduct)
cēlō, -āre, -āvī, -ātum	to hide or keep x secret	(conceal)
comperiō, comperīre, comperī, compertum	to find out	
dēstituō, dēstituere, dēstituī, dēstitutum	to lose, to leave behind (+ abl. sep.)	(destitute)
dēvincō, dēvincere, dēvīcī, dēvictum	to conquer completely, to overcome, to subdue	
dubitō, -āre, -āvī, -ātum	to doubt, to hesitate	(indubitably)
frūstrō, -āre, -āvī, -ātum (also dep.)	to deceive; to fail, to disappoint	(frustrate)
indigeō, indigēre, indiguī	to need, to want, to lack, to stand in need of (+ gen.)	(indigent)
īnfitior, īnfitiārī, īnfitiātus sum	to not confess, to deny	
proficīscor, proficīscī, profectus sum	to set out, to depart	
Adjectives, Adverbs, Conjunctions, etc.		
alius, alia, aliud, adj.	other, another	(alias)
dubius, -a, -um, adj.	doubtful, uncertain	(dubious)
imprūdēns, imprūdentis, adj.	unwise	(imprudent)
anteā, adv.	before, earlier	
velut, adv.	as if, just as if	
priusquam, conj.	before	
quin, conj.	(+ subj. after a negative main clause) that	

Chapter 12

LATIN	ENGLISH	DERIVATIVES
Nouns		
argūmentum, -ī, n.	indication, representation	(argument)
artifex, artificis, m.	workman, artisan	(artificer)
cacūmen, cacūminis, n.	extremity, peak	
cubitum, -ī, n.	elbow; cubit (distance in length from elbow to the end of the middle finger)	(cubit)
effigiēs, effigiēī, f.	symbol	(effigy)
latus, lateris, n.	side	(lateral)
longitūdō, longitūdinis, f.	length, height	(longitude)
obeliscus, -ī, m.	obelisk	(obelisk)
pondus, ponderis, n.	weight, burden	(ponder)
portus, portūs, m.	port, harbor	(port)
radius, -ī, m.	rod, ray	(radius)
Verbs		
adservō, -āre, -āvī, -ātum (cf. ad + servāre)	to watch over, to keep, to guard	
excīdō, excīdere, excīdī, excīsum (cf. ex + caedere)	to hew out, to cut out	(excise)
mergō, mergere, mērsī, mērsum	to plunge, to sink; to immerse, to submerge	(submerge)
timeō, timēre, timuī	to be afraid, to fear	(timid)
vehō, vehere, vexī, vectum	to carry, to convey	(vehicle)
vereor, verērī, veritus sum	to fear, to be afraid	
Adjectives, Adverbs, Conjunctions, etc.		
dīvus, -a, -um, adj.	divine	(divinity)
perpetuus, -a, -um, adj.	continuous, entire	(perpetual)

Chapter 13

LATIN	ENGLISH	DERIVATIVES
Nouns		
columba, -ae, f.	dove	
lapillus, -ī, m.	little stone, pebble; a precious stone or gem	(lapis lazuli)
libellus, -ī, m.	little book	
mediocritās, mediocritātis, f.	moderation, the mean	(mediocrity)
passer, passeris, m.	sparrow	
penātēs, penātium, m. pl.	Penates (Roman household gods); *metonymy for* home, family	
prōlēs, prōlis, f.	offspring, descendent	
sordēs, sordis, f.	(often plural) dirt, filth; baseness (of rank or station)	(sordid)

VERBS		
dīligō, dīligere, dīlēxī, dīlēctum	to choose out; to prize, to love, to esteem highly	(diligent)
fundō, -āre, -āvī, -ātum	to lay a foundation, to found	(fundamental)
invideō, invidēre, invīdī, invīsum	to look upon with the evil eye, to envy, to begrudge	
lūgeō, lūgēre, lūxī, lūctum	to mourn, to be in mourning	
ADJECTIVES, ADVERBS, CONJUNCTIONS, etc.		
blandus, -a, -um, adj.	flattering, alluring	(blandishment)
lentus, -a, -um, adj.	slow	
pūrus, -a, -um, adj.	pure	(pure)
sōbrius, -a, -um, adj.	sober, not intoxicated; frugal, reasonable	(sobriety)
venustus, -a, -um, adj.	charming, delightful	
nimium, adv. (= nimis)	too much	
quārē *or* quā rē, inter. adv.	why? for what reason?	
sānē, adv.	utterly, completely, wholly	(sane)

Chapter 14

LATIN	ENGLISH	DERIVATIVES
NOUNS		
arx, arcis, f.	stronghold, fortress	
fōrma, -ae, f.	form, beauty; shape, stature	(formation)
genus, generis, n.	race, nation, kind, type	(genus)
īra, -ae, f.	anger, wrath	(irate)
lītus, lītoris, n.	shore	(littoral)
moenia, moeniōrum, n. pl.	walls, fortifications of a city	(munitions, cf. munīre, to fortify)
mōles, mōlis, f.	great difficulty, burden	
nūmen, nūminis, n.	divinity, godhead	
VERBS		
contingō, contingere, contigī, contāctum	to come into contact with, to touch	(contact)
dignor, digārī, dignātus sum	to deem worthy *or* deserving	(dignify)
errō, -āre, -āvī, -ātum	to wander, to sin	(error)
impellō, impellere, impulī, impulsum	to drive on	(impulse)
patior, patī, passus	to suffer, to experience; to allow, to permit	(patience, passion)
rapiō, rapere, rapuī, raptum	to snatch, to tear away, to seize	(rapture)
vertō, vertere, vertī, versum	to turn	(revert)
volvō, volvere, volvī, volūtum	to roll, to tumble	(revolve, convoluted)

ADJECTIVES, ADVERBS, CONJUNCTIONS, etc.		
antīquus, -a, -um, adj.	ancient, earlier, former, old	(antique)
īnsignis, -e, adj.	marked, distinguished, prominent	(insignia, cf. signum, sign)
memor, memoris, adj.	mindful, remembering	(memorable)
tot, indec. adj.	so many	

Chapter 15

	LATIN	ENGLISH	DERIVATIVES
NOUNS			
	aes, aeris, n.	bronze	
	coma, -ae, f.	the hair of the head	(comet)
	ēnsis, ēnsis, m.	sword	(ensiform)
	grex, gregis, m./f.	herd, flock	(congregation)
	imber, imbris, m.	rain, shower	
	meritum, meritī, n.	merit	(meritocracy)
	mulier, mulieris, f.	woman, female	(muliebrity)
	rēmus, -ī, m.	oar	(trireme)
	ruīna, -ae, f.	ruins, that which has fallen down	(ruin)
	venēnum, -ī, n.	poison	(venom)
VERBS			
	adsurgō, adsurgere, adsurrēxī, adsurrēctum	to surge ahead	
	cingō, cingere, cīnxī, cīnctum	to bind, to encircle	(cincture)
	conbibō, conbibere, conbibī, conbibitūrum	to drink together; to drink in excess	
	dēdūcō, dēdūcere, dēdūxī, dēductum	to draw off, to lead off	(deduce)
	minuō, minuere, minuī, minūtum	to lessen, to diminish	(minute)
	quaerō, quaerere, quaesīvī, quaesītum	to seek, to look for; to question	(inquire)
ADJECTIVES, ADVERBS, CONJUNCTIONS, etc.			
	āter, ātra, ātrum, adj.	dull black (not shiny), flat black	(atrabilious)
	citus, -a, -um, adj.	swift	
	ēbrius, -a, um, adj.	drunk	(inebriated)
	latēns, latentis, adj.	hiding, hidden	(latent)
	tacitus, -a, -um, adj.	silent	(tacit)
	quidlibet, adv.	whatever you like, anything whatsoever	
	scīlicet, adv.	naturally, certainly, undoubtedly	

Chapter 16

	LATIN	ENGLISH	DERIVATIVES
Nouns			
	carmen, carminis, n.	tune, song; poem	
	frōns, frontis, f.	forehead, brow	(front)
	genetrīx, genetrīcis, f.	mother	
	labor, labōris, m.	work, labor, toil	(labor)
	lympha, -ae, f.	water	(lymph node)
	nāta, -ae, f.	daughter	
	sēdēs, sēdis, f.	chair, seat	(sedentary)
	sīdus, sīderis, n.	group of stars, constellation, heavenly body	
Verbs			
	adsum, adesse, adfuī, adfutūrum (ad + esse)	to be near, to be present	
	attollō, attollere	to lift up, to raise up	
	auferō, auferre, abtulī, ablātum (ab + ferre)	to carry off, to take away	
	inpleō/impleō, inplēre, inplēvī, inplētum (cf. plēnus)	to fill up	(implement)
	mereō, merēre, meruī, meritum (cf. meritum)	to deserve, to merit	(merit)
	reperiō, reperīre, repperī, repertum	to find again, to find	
Adjectives, Adverbs, Conjunctions, etc.			
	nūbilus, -a, -um, adj.	cloudy, gloomy, troubled	
	adhūc, adv.	still, yet, up to this point	
	dummodo, adv. (cf. dum + modo)	provided that	

Glossaries

Alphabetical Glossary

Nota Bene:
- Latin phrases appear in *italics*.
- Explanations of English translations appear in parentheses.

Latin	English	Book: Chapter
-ne, enclitic	(introduces a yes/no question)	2:13
-que, enclitic	and	2:13
-ve, enclitic	or	2:13
ā, ab, prep. (+ abl.)	from, away from; by	1:11
Aarōn, Aarōnis, m.	Aaron (brother of Moses)	
abhorreō, abhorrēre	to shrink back	
abiciō, abicere, abiēcī, abiectum	to cast away, to cast down, to throw down	
ablātīvus, -ī, m.	ablative case; *ablātīvus casus* – same meaning	
abōminor, abōminārī, abōminātus sum	to hate, to despise	3:10
absēns, absentis, adj.	being absent, away	
absum, abesse, āfuī, āfutūrum	to be away from (+ abl.)	
abundāns, abundantis	abundant, overflowing	
abūtor, abūtī, abūsus sum	to use fully, to abuse (cf. ūtor)	3:08
ac *or* atque, conj.	and	3:08
accēdō, accēdere, accessī, accessum	to approach, to come near	2:22/3:05
accipiō, accipere, accēpī, acceptum	to receive, to accept (ad + capere); to hear (in a story or report)	1:16/2:19
acclāmātiō, acclāmātiōnis, f.	acclamation, cheering	
accūsātīvus, -ī, m.	accusative case; *accūsātīvus casus* – same meaning	
accūsātor, accūsātōris, m.	accuser, prosecutor	
accūsō, -āre, -āvī, -ātum	to accuse	
ācer, ācris, ācre, adj.	sharp, eager; severe, fierce	1:15/3:08

acerbus, -a, -um, adj.	bitter, harsh; severe	2:14
Achillēs, Achillis, m.	Achilles	
aciēs, aciēī, f.	sharp edge or point; battle line (military)	2:19
āctiō, āctiōnis, f.	action	
āctīvus, -a, -um	(in grammar) active voice	
acūtus, -a, -um, adj.	sharp, pointed	2:05
ad, prep. (+ acc.)	to, toward, near, at, against	1:11
adamō, -āre, -āvī, -ātum	to fall in love with	1:19
addō, -dere, -didī, -ditum	to add	
addūcō, addūcere, addūxī, adductus (cf. ad + dūcere)	to lead to, to bring to, to convey to	3:11
adferō, adferre, attuli, adlātum/allātum	to bring (ad + ferre)	2:21
adfīgō, adfīgere, adfīxī, adfīxum	to fasten to, to fix onto	
adhortātus, -ūs, m.	exhortation, encouragement	2:04
adhūc, adv.	still, yet, up to this point	3:16
adiectīvum, -ī, n.	adjective; *adiectīvum nōmen* – same meaning	
adiungō, adiungere, adiūnxī, adiūnctum	to attach (acc.) to (dat.)	
adiuvō, adiuvāre, adiūvī, adiūtum	to help	
administrō, -āre, -āvī, -ātum	to manage	1:17
admīrātiō, admīrātiōnis, f.	admiration	3:10
admīror, admīrārī, admīrātus sum	to admire	2:26
admoneō, admonēre, admonuī, admonitum	to bring to mind	
adōrō, -āre, -āvī, -ātum	to worship, to adore	
adportō, -āre, -āvī, -ātum	to carry, to carry toward	2:22
adservō, -āre, -āvī, -ātum (cf. ad + servāre)	to watch over, to keep, to guard	3:12
adsum, adesse, adfuī, adfutūrum (ad + esse)	to be near, to be present	3:16
adsurgō, adsurgere, adsurrēxī, adsurrēctum	to surge ahead	3:15
adulēscēns, adulēscentis, adj.	young, growing up; (as a noun) young man, young woman	
adulēscentia, -ae, f.	youth, age of growing up	3:05
adūnō, -āre, -āvī, -ātum	to make one, to unite	2:27
adveniō, advenīre, advēnī, adventum	to arrive, to arrive at (+ ad + acc.)	1:28
adverbium, -ī, n.	adverb	
adversor, adversārī, adversātus sum	to oppose, to resist (+ dat.)	3:07
adversum/adversus, prep. (+ acc.)	against	3:07
advolō, -āre, -āvī, -ātum	to fly to	
aedificium, -ī, n.	building	
aedificō, -āre, -āvī, -ātum	to build	1:05
aedīlitās, aedīlitātis, f.	office of an aedile, aedileship	
aeger, aegra, aegrum	sick, ill; troubled, distressed	
Aegyptus, -ī, f.	Egypt	
Aenēās/Aenēa (nom.), Aenēae/Aenēā (gen.), Aenēae (dat.), Aenēan/Aenēam (acc.), Aenēā (abl.), Aenēa (voc.)	Aeneas (son of Anchises)	

aēneus, -a, -um, adj.	bronze	1:07
aequālis, -e, adj.	even, equal; (as a noun) equals, peers	2:21
aequālitas, aequālitatis, f.	equality, proportion	
aequor, aequoris, n.	sea, the sea	2:06
aequus, -a, -um, adj.	equal, level	
aes, aeris, n.	bronze	3:15
aestās, aestātis, f.	summer	2:20
aestimō, -āre, -āvī, -ātum	to judge the value of, to appraise	
aestumō	(*see* aestimō)	
aetās, aetātis, f.	age, lifetime	2:15/3:05
aetherius, -a, -um, adj.	ethereal, heavenly	
affectiō, affectiōnis, f.	affection, good will	
afficiō, afficere, affēcī, affectum	to treat; to affect, to influence, to move	2:14
Āfrica, -ae, f.	Africa	
ager, agrī, m.	field; land, territory	1:06
agnōscō, agnōscere, agnōvī, agnitum	to know, to identify, to understand, to recognize	1:25
agō, agere, ēgī, āctum	to do, to act; to drive	1:29/2:19
agricola, -ae, m.	farmer	1:04
albus, -a, -um, adj.	white, dull white	2:20
ālea, -ae, f.	die, game of chance	
Alexandrēa, -ae, f.	Alexandria (a city built by Alexander the Great off the coast of Egypt)	
aliēnus, -a, -um, adj.	of another, belonging to another, strange	
aliquī, aliquae, aliquod, indef. adj.	any, some	
aliquis, aliquid, pro.	anyone, someone, somebody; anything, something	1:25/2:16
aliquot, indec. adj.	some, several	3:06
aliter, adv.	otherwise, in another manner	2:10
alius, alia, aliud, adj.	other, another; *alius . . . alius* ; *alii . . . alii* – one . . . another; some . . . others	1:21/2:18/3:11
almus, -a, -um, adj.	nourishing; kind	2:06
alter, -a, -um, adj.	the other (of two); *alter . . . alter* = one . . . the other; the second (in a series)	1:21/2:18
altus, -a, -um, adj.	high, tall, deep	1:23
ambitiō, ambitiōnis, f.	ambition	
ambulō, -āre, -āvī, -ātum	to walk	1:03
āmentia, -ae, f.	foolishness, insanity	2:15
amīca, -ae, f.	friend (female friend)	1:05
amīcitia, -ae, f.	friendship	2:24
amīcus, -a, -um, adj.	friendly	1:17
amīcus, -ī, m.	friend (male friend)	1:06
amita, -ae, f.	father's sister, paternal aunt	
āmittō, āmittere, āmīsī, āmissum	to send away, to let go; to lose	1:18
amō, -āre, -āvī, -ātum	to love, to like	1:02
amor, amōris, m.	love	1:19

amphitheātrum, -ī, n.	amphitheater (a circular theater with seats on all sides)	
amplius, adv.	more; more than	2:14
amplus, -a, -um, adj.	large, wide, spacious, ample, grand; distinguished	2:14/3:04
an, conj.	whether, or	2:08
ancilla, -ae, f.	maidservant	1:05
angelus, -ī, m.	angel	
anima, -ae, f.	life, breath	2:15
animal, animālis, n.i.	animal	1:14
animātiō, animātiōnis, f.	spirit	
animus, -ī, m.	soul, mind; courage	2:11
annus, -ī, m.	year	1:15
ānser, ānseris, m.	goose	3:06
ante, prep. (+ acc.)	before; (adv.) before	1:22
anteā, adv.	before, earlier	3:11
antecēdō, antecēdere, antecessī, antecessum	to come before, to precede; to surpass	1:25
antehāc, adv.	before this, previously	
antequam, conj.	before	1:26
antīquus, -a, -um, adj.	ancient, earlier, former, old	3:14
apertus, -a, -um, adj.	open	2:12
Apollō, Apollinis, m.	Apollo (son of Jupiter and Latona and twin brother of Diana)	
apostolus, -ī, m.	apostle	
appellō, -āre, -āvī, -ātum	to call, to name; to address, to speak to	1:14
appetō, -ere, -īvī, -ītum	to strive for, to seek	3:10
appropinquō, -āre, -āvī, -ātum	to approach	
aptus, -a, -um, adj.	fitting, proper, apt, suitable for/fit for (+ dat.)	1:15
apud, prep. (+ acc.)	among, near, at the house of	1:18
aqua, -ae, f.	water	3:05
āra, ārae, f.	altar	2:07/3:11
arbiter, arbitrī, m	arbiter, eyewitness, judge	2:08
arbitrātus, -ūs, m.	decision	
arbitrium, -ī, n.	judgment, decision; power of deciding	2:03
arbitror, arbitrārī, arbitrātus sum	to think, to judge (cf. arbiter, arbitrium)	3:08
arcus, -ūs, m.	arch, triumphal arch; bow	2:12
ārdeō, ārdēre, ārsī, ārsūrum	to be on fire, to burn	2:10
argentum, argentī, n.	silver	2:11
argūmentum, argūmentī, n.	indication, representation	3:12
āridus, -a, -um, adj.	dry	
arma, armōrum, n. pl.	weapons, arms	1:09
armō, -āre, -āvī, -ātum	to arm, to equip with weapons	2:19
arō, -āre, -āvī, -ātum	to plow	1:03

ars, artis, f.	art, skill, method	
artifex, artificis, m.	workman, artisan	3:12
arvum, -ī, n.	plowed land, field (cf. arāre, "to plow")	3:06
arx, arcis, f.	stronghold, fortress	3:14
as, assis, m.	a small coin	
ascendō, ascendere, ascendī, ascēnsum	to climb, to go up	1:13
aspērsus, -a, -um, adj.	sprinkled	2:27
asȳlum, -ī, n.	place of refuge, sanctuary	
āter, ātra, ātrum, adj.	dull black (not shiny), flat black (cf. niger)	3:15
atque	(*see* ac)	
ātrium, -ī, n.	hall of a house, the main room of a house; the house	
atrōx, atrōcis, adj.	horrible	2:08
attingō, attingere, attigī, attāctum	to touch	3:09
attollō, attollere	to lift up, to raise up	3:16
attractiō, attractiōnis, f.	attraction	
auctor, auctōris, m.	originator, author	
auctōritās, auctōritātis, f.	authority	1:27
audācia, -ae, f.	boldness, audacity (cf. audax)	3:08
audāx, audācis, adj.	daring, bold; reckless, audacious	
audeō, audēre, ausus sum	to dare	2:26
audiō, audīre, audīvī/audiī, audītum	to hear, to listen	1:27
auferō, auferre, abtulī, ablātum (ab + ferre)	to carry off, to take away; to lead away	3:16
augeō, augēre, auxī, auctum	to increase, to make greater	2:27
augmentum, -ī, n.	an increase, growth	2:27
Augustus, -ī, m.	Augustus, the name given to Octavian; a title that was given to subsequent emperors	
aureus, -a, -um, adj.	made of gold, golden	
aureus, -ī, m.	a gold coin worth 25 denarii or 100 sestertii; *nummus aureus* – same meaning	
aurīga, aurīgae, m.	charioteer	2:20
aurum, -ī, n.	gold	1:14
aut, conj.	or	1:03
autem, conj.	however; now	2:11
autumnus, -ī, m.	autumn, fall	
auxilium, auxiliī, n.	aid, help	1:06
avāritia, -ae, f.	greed, avarice	2:16
avārus, -a, -um, adj.	greedy	2:11
avia, -ae, f.	grandmother	
avunculus, -ī, m.	mother's brother, maternal uncle	
avus, -ī, m.	grandfather; ancestor	
balneum, -ī, n.	bath, bathhouse	2:21
baptīzō, -āre, -āvī, -ātum	to baptize	
barba, -ae, f.	beard	

barbarus, -ī, m.	barbarian	
basilica, -ae, f.	basilica (a public building with double colonnades)	
beātus, -a, -um, adj.	blessed, happy	2:16
bellō, -āre, -āvī, -ātum	to wage war	
bellum, -ī, n	war	1:06
bene, adv.	well	1:17
benīgnus, -a, -um, adj.	kindhearted, mild	2:07
bēstia, -ae, f.	beast, wild animal	2:02
bimaris, -e, adj.	of two seas, lying between two seas	
bis mīllēsimus, -a, -um, adj.	two thousandth	
bis, adv.	twice	
blandus, -a, -um, adj.	flattering, alluring	3:13
bonitās, bonitātis, f.	goodness, kindness	2:09
bonus, -a, -um, adj.	good	1:07
bōs, bovis, m.	ox	2:08
brevis, -e, adj.	short, brief	1:15
cacūmen, cacūminis, n.	extremity, peak	3:12
cadāver, cadāveris, n.	dead body, corpse	
cadō, cadere, cecidī, cāsum	to fall	2:13
caecus, -a, -um, adj.	blind	2:19
caedēs, caedis, f.i.	a cutting, cutting down; killing, slaughter	2:27
caedō, caedere, cecīdī, caesum	to cut down, to kill	3:02
caelestis, -e, adj.	heavenly, from heaven	
caelum, -ī, n.	sky, heaven; weather	1:14
caeruleus, -a, -um, adj.	blue, sky blue	2:20
Caesar, Caesaris, m.	Caesar (the general and statesman); a title of the Roman emperors	
calamitās, calamitātis, f.	damage, harm, disaster	
calamitōsus, -a, -um, adj.	disastrous, destructive	
caldus, -a, -um, adj.	(*see* calidus)	
caleō, calēre, caluī, calitūrum	to be *or* become warm *or* hot	2:16
calidus, -a, -um, adj.	warm, hot; fiery	
cālīgō, cālīginis, f.	vapor; gloom, darkness	2:13
calor, calōris, m.	heat, warmth	2:21
Cambȳses, Cambȳsis, m.	Cambyses (son of Cyrus the elder and king of Persia)	
camera, -ae, f.	room; vault	1:16
campus, -ī, m.	plain, field (of battle)	
candidātus, -ī, m.	a candidate for office	
candidus, -a, -um, adj.	shining white, glittering white	2:06
canis, canis, m/f.	dog	2:07
cantō, -āre, -āvī, -ātum	to sing	1:02
cānus, -a, -um, adj.	white, gray; (as a noun) gray hair	2:27
capillus, -ī, m.	hair (of the head)	

capiō, capere, cēpī, captum	to take, to seize; to capture; *capere cōnsilium* – to make a plan	1:16
Capitōlium, -ī, n.	the Capitol at Rome; the temple of Jupiter on the Mons Tarpeius	
captīvitās, captīvitātis, f.	state of being in slavery, bondage, captivity	
captīvō, -āre, -āvī, -ātum	to capture	
captīvus, -a, -um, adj.	caught, taken prisoner, captive	
captīvus, -ī, m.	captive, prisoner of war	1:18
capulus, -ī, m.	coffin	2:02
caput, capitis, n.	head	1:10
cardinālis, -e, adj.	that on which something turns, depends; cardinal	1:22
careō, carēre, caruī, caritūrum (+ abl.)	to be without, to lack, to be in need of; to be deprived of; to want; to be free from	1:09
carmen, carminis, n.	tune, song; poem	3:16
carpō, carpere, carpsī, carptum	to seize, to pluck	1:28
carrus, -ī, m.	wagon, cart; chariot	1:09
Carthāgō, Carthāginis, f.	Carthage (a city in North Africa); *see also* Karthāgō, Karthāginis	
cārus, -a, -um, adj.	dear, expensive, costly; (+ dat.) dear to	1:11/1:17/2:09
casa, -ae, f.	hut, cottage, cabin	
castellum, -ī, n.	castle, fort, stronghold	
castra, castrōrum, n.pl.	camp	1:11
cāsus, cāsūs, m.	a fall; event; (in grammar) case	
Catilīna, -ae, m.	Catiline (a man who conspired against the Roman Republic)	
causa, -ae, f.	cause, reason; (causā + gen.) for the sake of	2:16
caverna, -ae, f.	cavern, cave	
cavō, -āre, -āvī, -ātum	to make hollow, to hollow out	3:02
cēdō, cēdere, cēssī, cēssum,	to withdraw; to give up ground, to yield	2:03
celebrō, -āre, -āvī, -ātum	to crowd; to celebrate	
celer, celeris, celere, adj.	swift, quick, rapid	1:15
cella, -ae, f.	storeroom	
cēlō, -āre, -āvī, -ātum	to hide or to keep *x* secret	3:11
cēna, -ae, f.	dinner	1:05
cēnō, -āre, -āvī, -ātum	to dine, to eat	
centēsimus, -a, -um, adj.	one hundredth	
centēsimus, -a, -um; prīmus, -a, -um, adj.	one hundred and first	
centum ūnus, -a, -um, adj.	one hundred and one	
centum, adj.	one hundred	
centum, indec.	one hundred	
Cerēs, Cereris, f.	Ceres (daughter of Saturn and Ops, mother of Proserpina, goddess of agriculture)	
cernō, cernere, crēvī, crētum	to discern	
certāmen, certāminis, n.	conflict, contest	2:03

certē, adv.	certainly	2:15
certus, -a, -um, adj.	certain	2:15
cervus, -ī, m.	stag, deer	
cēssō, -āre, -āvī, -ātum	to cease	
cēterī, -ōrum, adj.	the rest	1:12
charta, -ae, f.	paper	
Chrīstiānus, -a, -um, adj.	Christian	
Chrīstus, -ī, m.	Christ	
Cicerō, Cicerōnis, m.	Cicero (a Roman senator, speaker, and lawyer, who helped uncover the Catilinian conspiracy)	
cingō, cingere, cīnxī, cīnctum	to bind, to encircle	3:15
cinis, cineris, m.	ashes, ruin; death	2:13
circā, adv.; prep. (+ acc.)	around, about	
circueō, circuīre, circuivi/circuiī, circuitum	(see circumeō)	
circuitus, circuitūs, m.	circuit, going around	
circulāris, -e, adj.	circular	
circum, prep. (+acc.)	around	1:12
circumdō, circumdare, circumdedī, circumdatum	to surround	1:11
circumeō, circumīre, circumīvī/circumiī, circuitum	to go around; to enclose	3:03
circumscrībō, circumscrībere, circumscripsī, circumscriptum	to draw a line around	1:19
cista, -ae, f.	box; money box	2:02
citus, -a, -um, adj.	swift	3:15
cīvilis, -e, adj.	civil	1:29
cīvis, cīvis, m.	citizen	2:03
clādēs, clādis, f.	destruction	3:10
clam, adv.	secretly	2:14
clāmō, -āre, -āvī, -ātum	to shout; to cry out for	1:08
clāmor, clāmōris, m.	shout	2:13
clandestīnus, -a, -um, adj.	secret, hidden	
classis, classis, f.	(in military usage) all of the citizens called to fight; *hence*, the fleet, the army	1:26/3:10
claudō, claudere, clausī, clausum	to shut, to close; to close off	1:13
clausus, -a, -um, adj	closed	2:12
clēmentia, clēmentiae, f.	mercy	2:09
clipeum, -ī, n.	bronze disk, shield	2:21
coerceō, -ēre	to enclose, to confine	
cōgitō, -āre, -āvī, -ātum	to think, to consider, to ponder	3:02
cognitiō, cognitiōnis, f.	learning, acquisition of knowledge; understanding	2:11
cognōscō, cognōscere, cognōvī, cognitum	to learn, to perceive, to understand	2:12
cōgō, cōgere, coēgī, coāctum	to force	2:20

cohors, cohortis, f.	a cohort, a tenth part of a legion	
collum, collī, n.	neck	1:14
colō, colere, coluī, cultum	to cultivate, to serve	
colōnus, colōnī, m.	farmer, (sometimes) a tenant farmer	3:01
color, colōris, m.	color, complexion	2:20
colossus, -ī, m.	a giant statue	
columba, -ae, f.	dove	3:13
coma, -ae, f.	the hair of the head	3:15
comes, comitis, m.	companion	2:03
comētēs, comētae, f.	comet	
commemorō, -āre, -āvī, -ātum	to commemorate, to bring to mind	
commeō, -āre, -āvī, -ātum	to go up and down, to come and go, to visit frequently	3:09
commīsceō, commīscēre, commīscuī, commīxtum	to mix together	2:14
commissiō, commissiōnis, f.	celebration of games	
committō, committere, commīsī, commissum	to entrust, to commit	
comparō, -āre, -āvī, -ātum	to bring together, to compare	
comperiō, comperīre, comperī, compertum	to find out	3:11
compraehendō, compraehendere, compraehēnsī, compraehēnsum	to lay hold of, to grasp, to comprehend	
conbibō, conbibere, conbibī, conbibitūrum	to drink together; to drink in excess	3:15
concēdō, concēdere, concēssī, concēssum	to yield, to admit, to concede; to depart, to withdraw; to hand down/over	
concēssiō, concēssiōnis, f.	concession	
concipiō, concipere, concēpī, conceptum	to take in, to recognize, to gain	2:09
concordia, -ae, f.	unity of feeling	
concordō, -āre, -āvī, -ātum	to agree, to be in harmony	
condemnō, -āre, -āvī, -ātum	to condemn	
condō, condere, condidī, conditum	to found, to establish	1:19
cōnfessiō, cōnfessiōnis, f.	confession	
cōnfessiōnāle, cōnfessiōnālis, n.	confessional	
cōnficiō, cōnficere, cōnfēcī, cōnfectum	to put together, to finish	3:06
congredior, congredī, congressus sum	to come together	3:10
coniugātiō, coniugātiōnis, f.	(in grammar) conjugation	
coniūnctiō, coiūnctiōnis, f.	(in grammar) conjunction	
coniungō, coniungere, coniūnxī coniūnctum	to unite, to join together	1:23/2:19
coniūnx, coniugis, m./f.	spouse, husband, wife	2:12
coniūrātiō, coniūrātiōnis, f.	conspiracy	3:08
cōnor, cōnārī, cōnātus sum	to try	2:27
cōnscientia, -ae, f.	knowledge, conscience	2:08
cōnscrībō, cōnscrībere, cōnscripsī, cōnscriptum	to enlist, to enroll; to write up	1:27

cōnsecrō, -āre, -āvī, -ātum	to dedicate as holy, to consecrate	2:18
cōnsentiō, cōnsentīre, cōnsēnsī, cōnsēnsum	to agree	1:27
cōnsequor, cōnsequī, cōnsecūtus sum	to follow, to go after (cf. sequor); to obtain	3:03
cōnserō, cōnserere, cōnsēvī, cōnsitum	to sow, to plant	3:05
cōnservō, -āre, -āvī, -ātum	to conserve, to preserve	
cōnsīderō, -āre, -āvī, -ātum	to look at carefully, to consider	
cōnsōbrīna, -ae, f.	female first cousin	
cōnsōbrīnus, -ī, m.	male first cousin	
cōnsōlor, cōnsōlārī, cōnsōlātus sum	to encourage, to strengthen, to comfort	
cōnspectus, -ūs, m.	sight, view, range of sight	3:10
cōnspiciō, cōnspicere, cōnspexī, cōnspectum	to catch sight of	1:16
cōnspicuus, -a, -um, adj.	visible, remarkable, striking	
cōnsuēscō, cōnsuēscere, cōnsuēvī, cōnsuētum	to be accustomed	2:18
cōnsuētūdō, cōnsuētūdinis, f.	custom, habit; usage; customary law	
cōnsul, cōnsulis, m.	consul	
cōnsulātus, -ūs, m.	consulship, office of consul	2:04
cōnsulō, cōnsulere, cōnsuluī, cōnsultum	to ask advice of, to consult	2:07
cōnsūmō, cōnsūmere, cōnsūmpsī, cōnsūmptum	to consume, to eat	1:16
contāgiōsus, -a, -um, adj.	contagious	
contāminātus, -a, -um, adj.	polluted, impure, defiled	
contemptibilis, -e, adj.	contemptible, worthless	
contendō, contendere, contendī, contentum	to stretch; to hasten; to exert oneself	2:14
conticēscō, conticēscere, conticuī	to be silent	3:10
contineō, continēre, continuī, contentum	to hold together, to keep together; to keep in, to surround, to contain	3:09
contingō, contingere, contigī, contāctum	to come into contact with, to touch	3:14
continuō, adv.	immediately	3:05
contrā, prep. (+ acc.)	against; (adv.) in return, opposite	1:19/2:24
convertō, convertere, conversī, convertum	to convert	
convocō, -āre, -āvī, -ātum	to call together	
cōpia, -ae, f.	supply, abundance; (pl. military) troops	1:09/2:24
cor, cordis, n.	heart	2:16
cōram, prep. (+ abl.)	in front of, before the face of	2:11
corium, coriī, n.	skin, hide	1:19
cornū, -ūs, n.	horn; wing (of an army)	1:28/3:01
corōna, -ae, f.	wreath, crown of leaves	
corōnātiō, corōnātiōnis, f.	coronation, crowning ceremony	
corōnō, -āre, -āvī, -ātum	to crown	
corpus, corporis, n.	body	1:10
cōtīdiē, adv.	daily, every day	
crēdō, crēdere, crēdidī, crēditum, (+ dat. of person, + acc. of thing)	to believe, to trust in	1:19

cremō, -āre, -āvī, -ātum	to burn	2:05
creō, -āre, -āvī, -ātum	to create, to make	1:07
crēscō, crēscere, crēvī, crētum	to grow, to increase	2:24
crīmen, crīminis, n.	accusation; crime	
crucifīgō, crucifīgere, crucifīxī, crucifīxum	to crucify	
crūdēlis, -e, adj.	hard-hearted, cruel	1:19
crūdēlitās, crūdēlitātis, f.	cruelty	
crūstulum, -ī, n.	small pastry, cookie	
cubitum, -ī, n.	elbow; cubit (distance in length from elbow to the end of the middle finger)	3:12
culīna, -ae, f.	kitchen	1:05
culpa, -ae, f.	fault, blame; sin	2:20
culpō, -āre, -āvī, -ātum	to blame	2:13
cultus, -ūs, m.	agriculture; culture, sophistication	2:04
cum, adv.	when	2:12
cum, prep. (+ abl.)	with	1:11/2:10
cunctātiō, cunctātiōnis, f.	delay, hesitation, doubt	2:15
cunctor, cunctārī, cunctātus sum	to delay; to hesitate (+ inf.) (cf. cunctātiō)	3:03
cūnctus, -a, -um, adj.	all	2:10
cupiditās, cupiditātis, f.	desire	2:02
cupīdō, cupīdinis, m.	desire	
Cupīdō, Cupīdinis, m.	Cupid (god of love, son of Venus)	
cupidus, -a, -um, adj.	desirous	2:02
cupiō, cupere, cupīvī/cupiī, cupītum	to desire, to long for	
cūr, adv.	why	2:17
cūra, -ae, f.	care, concern	3:08
cūrātiō, cūrātiōnis, f.	cure	
cūriōsitās, cūriōsitātis, f.	desire for knowledge, curiosity	
cūrō, -āre, -āvī, -ātum	to care for, to give attention to	
currō, currere, cucurrī, cursum	to run; to hurry	1:11
currus, -ūs, m.	chariot	2:20
damnātiō, damnātiōnis, f.	condemnation	
damnō, -āre, -āvī, -ātum	to condemn	2:16
datīvus, -ī, m.	(in grammar) dative case; *casus datīvus* – same meaning	
dē, prep. (+ abl.)	from, down from; about, concerning	1:11
dēbeō, dēbēre, dēbuī, dēbitum	to owe; ought, must	1:18
decem, adj.	ten	
decem, indec.	ten	
decimus, -a, -um, adj.	tenth	
dēcipiō, dēcipere, dēcēpī, dēceptum	to deceive	1:21
dēclārō, -āre, -āvī, -ātum	to declare	
dēcrētum, -ī, n.	decision, resolution, decree	

dēdicō, -āre, -āvī, -ātum	to consecrate, to dedicate; to declare	1:14
dēdūcō, dēdūcere, dēdūxī, dēductum	to draw off, to lead off	3:15
dēfendō, dēfendere, dēfendī, dēfēnsum	to defend, to protect	
dēferō, dēferre, dētulī, dēlātum	to bring down, to report; to offer, to confer, to grant	2:04
dēficiō, dēficere, dēfēcī, dēfectum	to loosen, to remove (oneself); to die	2:25
dēiciō, dēicere, dēiēcī, dēiectum	to throw down, to hurl down (cf. dē + iaciō)	3:05
deinde, adv.	then	1:08
dēlectō, -āre, -āvī, -ātum	to delight	2:20
dēleō, dēlēre, dēlēvī, dēlētum	to destroy	1:10
dēmēns, dēmentis, adj.	insane, crazy, mindless	
dēmentia, -ae, f.	mindlessness	
dēmittō, dēmittere, dēmīsī, dēmissum	to send down, to let down, to lower	
dēmōnstrō, -āre, -āvī, -ātum	to point out, to show, to demonstrate	1:20
dēnique, adv.	and then, finally	3:07
dēns, dentis, m.	tooth	
dēnsus, -a, -um, adj.	dense, crowded together	
dēpōnō, dēpōnere, dēposuī, dēpositum	to lay down, to set aside	2:03
dēscendō, dēscendere, dēscendī, dēscēnsum	to descend, to go down	
dēscrībō, dēscrībere, dēscrīpsī, dēscriptum	to describe, to show	
dēserō, dēserere, dēseruī, dēsertum	to leave, to abandon	2:23
dēsertor, dēsertōris, m.	deserter	2:03
dēsertum, -ī, n.	desert	
dēsīderō, -āre, -āvī, -ātum	to desire, to wish	1:08
dēsignō, -āre, -āvī, -ātum	to designate, to appoint	
dēsistō, dēsistere, dēstitī, dēstitum	to cease	
dēstituō, dēstituere, dēstituī, dēstitutum	to lose, to leave behind (+ abl. sep.)	3:11
dēsum, dēesse, dēfuī, dēfutūrum	to lack, to fail	3:08
dētrahō, dētrahere, dētraxi, dētractum	to drag down, to pull down, to draw away; to diminish	
deus, -ī, m./dea, -ae, f.	god/goddess	1:07
dēvincō, dēvincere, dēvīcī, dēvictum	to conquer completely, to overcome, to subdue	3:11
dexter, dextra, dextrum, adj.	right; (f. noun) right hand	1:11
dīcō, dīcere, dīxī, dictum	to speak, to say, to tell; to mention	1:11
diēs, diēī, m/f.	day (feminine used for an appointed or set day)	1:29
differō, differre, distulī, dīlātum	to be different	
difficilis, -e, adj.	difficult	
digitus, -ī, m.	digit; finger or toe	
dignor, dignārī, dignātus sum	to deem worthy or deserving	3:14
dignus, -a, -um, adj.	worthy; (+ abl.) worthy of	1:29
dīligēns, dīligentis, adj.	careful	
dīligō, dīligere, dīlēxī, dīlēctum	to choose out; to prize, to love, to esteem highly	3:13
dīmicō, -āre, -āvī, -ātum	to fight, to contend, to struggle	2:03/3:10
dīmittō, dīmittere, dīmīsī, dīmissum	to send away, to dismiss	1:29

Dīs, Dītis, m.	Pluto (god of the underworld)	
discēdō, discēdere, discessī	to go away, to depart	1:22
disciplīna, -ae, f.	teaching, doctrine	
discō, dīscere, didicī	to learn	1:15
discordia, -ae, f.	discord, disharmony	
discors, discordis, adj.	discordant, unharmonious	2:09
discrīmen, discrīminis, n.	difference, distinction	
dispergō, dispergere, dispērsī, dispērsum	to scatter, to disperse	2:18
dissimilis, -e, adj.	unlike	1:17
distinguō, distinguere, distīnxī, distīnctum	to distinguish	
distribuō, distribuere, distribuī, distribūtum	to distribute, to hand out	
diū, adv.	for a long time	2:07/3:05
dīum, -ī, n.	open air, open sky	3:06
diūtius, CpAdv.	for a longer time (*see* diū)	
dīversus, -a, -um, adj.	diverse, different, unlike	
dīves, dīvitis, adj.	rich; (as a noun) a rich person	1:24
dīvidō, dīvidere, dīvīsī, dīvīsum	to divide	2:23
dīvīnitās, dīvīnitātis, f.	divinity	
dīvitiae, -ārum, f.	riches, wealth	
dīvus, -a, -um, adj.	divine	3:12
dō, dare, dedī, datum	to give	1:06
doceō, docēre, docuī, doctum	to teach	1:15
doctus, -a, -um, adj.	learned, experienced	
doleō, dolēre, doluī, dolitum	to feel pain (physical or mental); to grieve	
dōlium, -ī, n.	a large jar for storing wine	3:05
dolor, dolōris, m.	pain, suffering	2:13
domus, -ūs, f.	house, home	1:28
dōnec, adv.	until	2:14
dōnum, -ī, n.	gift	1:06
dormiō, -īre, -īvī/iī, -ītum	to sleep, to be asleep	
dōtātus, -a, -um, adj.	endowed, dowried	
dubitō, -āre, -āvī, -ātum	to doubt, to hesitate	2:15/3:11
dubius, -a, -um, adj.	uncertain, doubtful	3:11
ducentēsimus, -a, -um, adj.	two hundredth	
ducentī, -ae, -a, adj.	two hundred	
dūcō, dūcere, dūxī, ductum	to lead; *dūcō uxōrem (in mātrimōnium)* – to lead into marriage, to marry	
dulcis, -e, adj.	sweet	2:06
dum, adv.	while	1:07
dummodo, adv.	provided that (cf. dum + modo)	3:16
duo mīlia, adj.	two thousand	
duo, duae, duo, adj.	two	1:22

duodecim	twelve	
duodecim, adj.	twelve	
duodecimus, -a, -um, adj.	twelfth	
duodētricesimus, -a, -um, adj.	twenty-eighth	
duodēvīcēsimus, -a, -um, adj.	eighteenth	
duodēvīgintī, adj.	eighteen	
duplum, -ī, n.	a double amount	3:04
duplus, -a, -um, adj.	double	
dūrātiō, dūrātiōnis, f.	duration	
dūrō, -āre, -āvī, -ātum	to make hard, to be hard; to endure	
dūrus, -a, -um, adj.	hard, rough, stern, unfeeling	
dux, ducis, m./f.	leader	1:12
ē, ex, prep. (+ abl.)	out of, from	1:11
ēbrius, -a, -um, adj.	drunk	3:15
ecquandō, inter. adv.	ever, at any time (often carries an attitude of indignation) (cf. ec- [in the word ecce] + quandō)	3:07
ēdō, ēdere, ēdidī, ēditum	to give out, to put forth, to bring forth, to raise, to set up	2:07
ēducātiō, ēducātiōnis, f.	upbringing, rearing; education	1:15
ēducō, -āre, -āvī, -ātum	to raise up (a child), to rear, to educate	2:11
efferrō, efferre, extulī, ēlātum	to bring out, to lift up	
efficiō, efficere, effēcī, effectum	to make, to bring to pass, to effect	2:25
effigiēs, effigiēī, f.	symbol	3:12
effugiō, effugere, effūgī	to run away, to escape, to flee from	1:19
ego, meī, pro.	I, me	1:19
ēgregius, -a, -um, adj.	distinguished, excellent	3:10
ēlegantia, -ae, f.	elegant	
elegīa, -ae, f.	an elegy (song or poem expressing sorrow)	
elephantus, -ī, m.	elephant	
ēloquēns, ēloquentis, adj.	eloquent	
ēloquentia, -ae, f.	eloquence	
ēlūdō, ēlūdere, ēlūsī, ēlūsum	to ward off, to evade, to elude; to mock	3:08
ēmittō, ēmittere, ēmīsī, ēmissum	to send forth, to let out	
emō, emere, ēmī, emptum	to buy, to procure	1:22
enim, adv.	indeed	2:15
ēnsis, ēnsis, m.	sword	3:15
eō, īre, iī/īvī, ītum	to go	1:18
epidēmicus, -a, -um, adj.	prevalent; epidemic	
epīscopātus, -ī, m.	office of bishop, bishopric	2:25
epistula, -ae, f.	letter	1:22
equus, equī, m.	horse	1:06
ergō, conj.	therefore	2:10

errō, -āre, -āvī, -ātum	to wander, to sin	3:14
error, errōris, m.	a wandering, uncertainty; error, sin	2:19
ērumpō, ērumpere, ērūpī, ēruptum	to erupt, to burst forth	
ēsuriō, ēsurīre, ēsurīvī, ēsurītum	to hunger, to be hungry	
et, conj.; adv.	and; even	1:03
etenim, conj.	and indeed (= et enim)	
etiam, adv.	also, even	1:10
ēvādō, ēvādere, ēvāsī, ēvāsum	to come out, to escape	1:13
ēvangelicus, -a, -um, adj.	evangelical	
ēventum, -ī, n.	event, occurence	
ēvolō, -āre, -āvī, -ātum	to fly out	
exaltō, -āre, -āre, -ātum	to exalt, to raise up	
exaudiō, exaudīre, exaudīvī, exaudītum	to hear clearly	
excēdo, excēdere, excēssi, excēssus	to exceed	
excerpō, excerpere, excerpsī, excerptum	to take out	
excidium, -ī, n.	destruction	2:13
excīdō, excīdere, excīdī, excīsum (cf. ex + caedere)	to hew out, to cut out	3:12
excipiō, excipere, excēpī, excaptum	to take out, to except	
excitō, -āre, -āvī, -ātum	to wake, to rouse	
exclūdō, exclūdere, exclūsi, exclūsum	to shut out, to exclude	2:21
excolō, excolere, excoluī, excultum	to tend	2:14
excūsō, -āre, -āvī, -ātum	to excuse	
exemplum, -ī n.	example	2:17
exerceō, exercēre, exercuī, exercitum	to train, to exercise	1:08
exercitus, -ūs, m.	army; military expedition	1:28
exhālō, -āre, -āvī, -ātum	to breathe, to exhale	
exhibeō, exhibēre, exhibuī, exhibitum	to grant, to exhibit, to show	
exhortor, exhortārī, exhortātus sum	to encourage strongly, to urge	
existimō, -āre, -āvī, -ātum	to estimate, to count, to judge a thing according to its value	3:02/3:04
exitium, -ī, n.	ruin, destruction	2:23
expediō, expedīre, expedīvī/expediī, expedītum	to set free; to be useful	3:05
experientia, -ae, f.	experience	
expiō, -āre, -āvī, -ātum	to propitiate, to appease; to make amends to (a person or deity); to purify, to cleanse, to atone for (a sin or fault)	2:22
explicō, -āre, -āvī, -ātum	to unfold, to reveal, to explain	2:19
explōrātor, explōrātōris, m.	searcher, explorer	
explōrō, -āre, -āvī, -ātum	to search out, to investigate, to explore	
exspectātus, -a, -um, adj.	awaited, wished for, welcome; (+ dat. of the person interested) awaited for by, wished for by, welcome to	2:22

exspectō, -āre, -āvī, -ātum	to wait for; to see, to expect	1:20
exstinguō, exstinguere, exstinxī, exstīnctum	to put out, to extinguish	1:24
extendō, extendere, extendī, extēnsum	to extend, to stretch out	
externus, -a, -um, adj.	outside, external, foreign	
exterreō, exterrēre, exterruī, exterritum	to terrify	
extrā, prep. (+ acc.)	outside, outside of	2:24
extulit	(see efferō)	
fābula, -ae, f.	story, tale; play	1:05
faciēs, faciēī, f.	face; appearance	1:29
facilis, -e, adj.	easy	2:06
faciō, facere, fēcī, factum	to do, to make	1:16
factio, factiōnis, f.	political party, faction	1:24
factum, -ī, n.	deed	1:22
faenerātor, faenerātōris, m.	moneylender	
faeneror, faenerārī, faenerātus sum	to lend [money] at interest; to drain by extortion	3:03
faenum, -ī, n.	hay	3:06
fallāx, fallācis, adj.	deceitful, deceptive	2:05
fāma, -ae, f.	rumor, saying; fame	
familia, -ae, f.	family	1:12
fās, indec., n.	right, divine right; *fas est* – it is right, it is lawful	2:27
fātālis, fātāle, adj.	deadly, fatal, fated	
fātum, -ī, n.	fate	1:19
faveō, favēre, fāvī, fautum + dat.	to favor, to show favor to; to support	1:17/2:03
fēlēs, fēlis, f.	cat	
fēlīcitās, fēlīcitātis, f.	happiness, good fortune	2:04
fēlīx, fēlīcis, adj.	happy	1:16
fēmina, -ae, f.	woman	1:04
fēneror	(see faeneror)	
fenestra, -ae, f.	window	2:21
ferē, adv.	almost, approximately, closely	2:07
ferō, ferre, tulī, lātum	to bring, to carry; to bear	1:18
ferōx, ferōcis, adj.	fierce	
ferrum, -ī, n.	iron; sword (by metonymy)	1:10
fessus, -a, -um, adj.	tired	1:29
festīnō, -āre, -āvī, -ātum	to hurry	
fidēlis, -e, adj.	faithful, loyal to	1:17
fidēs, fideī, f.	faith, trust; faithfulness, loyalty	1:29
fīlia, -ae, f.	daughter	1:05
fīniō, -īre, -īvī, -ītum	to finish	
fīnis, fīnis, m.i.	end, boundary	1:14
fīnitimus, -a, -um, adj	neighboring, adjacent	3:09
fīō, fierī, factus sum	to occur, to happen; to be made, to be done	3:09
firmiter, adv.	firmly	

firmō, -āre, -āvī, -ātum	to make firm, to strengthen	2:11
firmus, -a, -um, adj.	firm, strong, stable	
flamma, -ae, f.	flame	1:07
flammeus, -a, -um, adj.	fiery; flame covered; (as a neuter noun) bridal veil	1:16
flāvus, -a, -um, adj.	yellow	
fleō, flēre, flēvī, flētum	to weep	2:26
flōridus, -a, -um, adj.	flowery, made of flowers	2:06
flōs, flōris, m.	flower, blossom	1:16
flūmen, flūminis, n.	river	1:12
foenerātor	(*see* faenerātor)	
foeneror	(*see* faeneror)	
foetidus, -a, -um	stinky, smelly	
fōns, fontis, m.	natural spring	
foris, foris, f.	door (usually pl.)	2:22
fōrma, -ae, f.	form, beauty; shape, stature	3:14
fōrmō, -āre, -āvī, -ātum	to shape, to form	
fortis, -e, adj.	strong, brave	1:15
fortiter, adv.	bravely	
fortitūdō, fortitūdinis, f.	courage, strength	1:26/3:11
fortūna, ae, f.	fortune, luck	1:21
forum, -ī, n.	marketplace; public space	
frangō, frangere, frēgī, frāctum	to break	2:09
frāter, frātris, m.	brother	1:19
fremitus, -ūs, m.	a roaring, murmuring; a dull, roaring sound	3:02/3:10
frequēns, frequentis, adj.	frequent	
frequentō, -āre, -āvī, -ātum	to visit repeatedly; to crowd	
frīgidus, -a, -um, adj.	cold, cool	
frīgus, frīgoris, n.	cold, coolness	3:06
frondōsus, -a, -um, adj.	full of leaves, leafy	3:02
frōns, frondis, f.	leafy branch	
frōns, frontis, f.	forehead, brow	3:16
frūctus, -ūs, m.	fruit; profit, benefit	1:28/3:01
frūgālitās, frūgālitātis, f.	thriftiness	
frūmentum, -ī, n.	grain	1:09
fruor, fruī, frūctus/fruitus sum (+ abl.)	to have the benefit of, to enjoy	2:26/3:04
frūstrā, adv.	in vain	2:08
frūstrō, -āre, -āvī, -ātum (also dep.)	to deceive; to fail, to disappoint	3:11
frūstror	(*see* frūstrō)	
fuga, -ae, f.	flight, rapid movement, swift passing	
fugiō, fugere, fūgī, fugitum	to flee, to run away	2:02
fulgeō, fulgēre, fūlsī	to flash, to glitter, to shine	
fūmus, -ī, m.	smoke	2:13
fundō, -āre, -āvī, -ātum	to lay a foundation, to found	3:13

fundus, -ī, m.	farm, estate (cf. praedium)	2:23/3:05
fūr, fūris, m./f.	thief (used as a term of reproach to slaves)	3:01
furor, furōris, m.	rage, madness; frenzy	2:04
futūrum exactum, -ī, n.	(in grammar) future perfect tense; *tempus futūrum exactum* – same meaning	
futūrum, -ī, n.	(in grammar) future tense; *tempus futūrum* – same meaning	
Gāia, -ae, f.	Gaia (used in wedding ceremonies to represent the bride)	
Gāius, -ī, m.	Gaius (a Latin praenomen; often referring to some generic person, as in "Tom, Dick, or Harry;" used in wedding ceremonies to represent the groom)	
Galīlaea, -ae, f.	Galilee	
gaudeō, gaudēre, gāvīsus sum	to rejoice, to rejoice at	2:26
gaudium, gaudiī, n.	joy	1:09
geminus, -a, -um, adj.	twin	
generōsus, -a, -um, adj.	noble	
genetrīx, genetrīcis, f.	mother	3:16
genitīvus, -ī, m.	genitive case; *casus genitīvus* – same meaning	
gēns, gentis, f.	tribe, nation	1:27
genū, -ūs, n.	knee	1:28
genus, generis, n.	race, nation, kind, type; (in grammar for nouns) gender; (in grammar for verbs) voice	3:14
Germānus, -a, -um, adj.	German	
germānus, -ī, m.	brother	1:06
gerō, gerere, gessī, gestum	to wear, to carry on; *bellum gerere* – to wage war	1:11/2:24
gignō, gignere, genuī, genitum	to beget, to bear, to bring forth	3:03
gladiātor, gladiātōris, m.	swordsman; gladiator	
gladiātōrius, -a, -um	belonging to gladiators, gladiatorial	
glōria, -ae, f.	glory, fame, renown; pride	
gradior, gradī, grēssus sum	to walk, to step	2:26/3:03
Graecia, -ae, f.	Greece	1:04
grammaticus, -ī, m.	grammarian, grammar teacher	2:26
grandē, adv.	very	
grandis, -e, adj.	large, great	
grātia, grātiae, f.	grace, favor, thanks, gratitude; grace, kindness	2:16
grātus, -a, -um, adj.	pleasing, welcome, agreeable	2:03
gravis, -e, adj.	serious, important, weighty	1:15
gravitās, gravitātis, f.	heaviness, weight; (later) gravity	
grex, gregis, m./f.	herd, flock	3:15
gubernātor, gubernātōris, m.	governor	1:27
gustō, -āre, -āvī, -ātum	to taste	2:12
habeō, habēre, habuī, habitum	to have, to hold; to consider	1:08/3:03

habitō, -āre, -āvī, -ātum	to live, to dwell	1:03
haesitō, -āre, -āvī, -ātum	to hesitate	2:15
harēna, -ae, f.	sand; arena	
hasta, -ae, f.	spear	
haud, adv.	by no means, hardly	2:10
hauriō, haurīre, hausī, haustum	to draw out; to drink up, to drain	2:12
hercle!	by Hercules! (like the English "Oh my gosh!")	
hesperius, -a, -um, adj.	western	2:12
Hibernia, -ae, f.	Ireland	
hīc, adv.	here	2:02
hic, haec, hoc, dem. pro./adj.	this, (pl.) these	1:20
hiems, hiemis, f.	winter	1:28/3:06
hinc, adv.	from this, from here	3:03
historia, -ae, f.	history	
historicus, -ī, m.	historian	2:14
homō, hominis, m.	human, man	1:14
honestus, -a, -um, adj.	honorable, honest	2:02
honor, honōris, m.	honor	1:17
honōrō, -āre, -āvī, -ātum	to honor	
hōra, hōrae, f.	hour	1:23
horrendus, -a, -um, adj.	horrible, terrible	
horrēns, horrentis, adj.	shivering	2:16
horribilis, -e, adj.	terrifying	
horridus, -a, -um, adj.	frightful	
hortor, hortārī, hortātus sum	to encourage, to exhort	3:03
hortus, -ī, m.	garden	2:10
hostia, hostiae, f.	sacrificial victim (usually a large animal)	
hostis, hostis, m.i.	enemy	1:20
hūc, adv.	here, to this place, hither	2:24
hūmānitās, hūmānitātis, f.	humanity, human kindness; culture, refinement	
hūmānus, -a, -um, adj.	human	
hūmidus, -a, -um, adj.	wet, moist; dewy	
humilis, -e, adj.	humble, lowly	
humus, -ī, f.	ground	1:06
iaceō, iacēre, iacuī	to lie down; to lie dead	2:08
iaciō, iacere, iēcī, iactum	to throw	1:16
iactō, -āre, -āvī, -ātum	to throw repeatedly or energetically, to throw about; (with the reflexive) to gesticulate	3:08
ibi, adv.	there	2:25
īdem, eadem, idem, inten. adj.	the same	2:24
īdōlolatrīa, -ae, f.	idolatry, worship of idols	
idōneus, -a, -um, adj.	fitting, suitable	
igitur, conj.	therefore	1:21

ignis, ignis, m.i.	fire	1:16
ignōscō, ignōscere, ignōvī, ignōtum (+dat.)	to grant pardon to, to forgive, to overlook	2:03
illacrimō, -āre, -āvī, -ātum	to weep over	
ille, illa, illud, dem. pro./adj.	that, those	1:20
illūc, adv.	there, to that place, thither	2:24
imāgō, imāginis, f.	imitation, copy, image	
imber, imbris, m.	rain, shower	3:15
imbuō, imbuere, imbuī, imbūtum	to wet, to steep, to saturate	2:26
imitō, -āre, -āvī, -ātum	to imitate	
immēnsus, -a, -um, adj.	immeasurable, boundless	
immineō, imminēre	to project over or toward a thing (+ dat.); to draw near	2:24
immortālitās, immortālitātis, f.	immortality	
impediō, -īre, -iī, -ītum	to impede, to obstruct	
impellō, impellere, impulī, impulsum	to drive on, to strike; to incite, to urge on	3:14
imperātor, imperātōris, m.	general; emperor	
imperfectum, -ī, n.	(in grammar) imperfect tense; *tempus imperfectum* – same meaning	
imperium, imperiī, n.	power, command; an order; empire	1:26
imperō, -āre, -āvī, -ātum (+ dat. of person, + acc. of thing)	to order, to command	2:03
impetus, -ūs, m.	attack, charge; impulse, vigor, energy	1:28
impius, -a, -um, adj.	impious	2:18
impōnō, impōnere, imposuī, impositum	to put, to place upon	2:22
importō, -āre, -āvī, -ātum	to bring in, to import	
impossibilis, -e, adj.	impossible	
impotēns, impotentis, adj.	powerless; out of control	2:09
imprimō, imprimere, impressī, impressum	to press upon, to enforce	2:18
imprisonō, -āre, -āvī, -ātum	to imprison	
imprūdēns, imprūdentis, adj.	unwise	3:11
īmus, -a, -um, adj.	bottom	2:21
in, prep. (+ abl.)	in, on	1:11
in, prep. (+ acc.)	into, to, toward; against; for	1:11/2:03
inaequālis, -e, adj.	unequal, uneven	
incendium, -ī, n.	fire, heat	2:14
incipiō, incipere, incēpī, inceptum	to begin	1:16
incola, -ae, m./f.	inhabitant, resident, settler	1:04
incolō, incolere, incoluī	to inhabit, to dwell (in) (cf. īncola)	3:09
incrēdulitās, incrēdulitātis, f.	unbelief	
indicō, -āre, -āvī, -ātum	to show, to point out, to indicate	
indifferēns, indifferentis, adj.	unconcerned, indifferent	
indigeō, indigēre, indiguī	to need, to want, to lack, to stand in need of (+ gen.)	3:11
indignātiō, indignātiōnis, f.	displeasure, indignation	2:08

induō, induere, induī, indūtum	to put on	1:13
ineō, inīre, inīvī, initum	to enter, to begin	2:09
inermis, -e, adj.	unarmed	3:10
īnfandus, -a, -um, adj.	unspeakable, shocking	2:13
īnfāns, īnfantis, m/f.i.	baby	1:14
īnfantia, -ae, f.	infancy, early childhood	
īnferior, īnferius, CpAdj.	lower	
īnferō, īnferre, intulī, inlātum	to bring in; to bring to (+ dat.)	2:03
īnfīnītīvus, -a, -um, adj.	unlimited, indefinite	
īnfīrmitās, īnfīrmitātis, f.	weakness	
īnfitior, īnfitiārī, īnfitiātus sum	to not confess, to deny	3:11
īnflexibilis, -e, adj.	inflexible, unbending	
īnflō, -āre, -āvī, -ātum	to blow, to puff up	2:08
īnfōrmis, -e, adj.	having no shape, shapeless, formless	
īnfundō, īnfundere, īnfūdī, īnfūsum	to pour into, to infuse	
ingēns, ingentis, adj.	huge	1:15
ingrātus, -a, -um, adj.	ungrateful	
inhumātus, -a, -um	unburied	
inimīcitia, -ae, f.	enmity, hostility	
inimīcus, -a, -um, adj.	unfriendly	1:17
inimīcus, -ī, m.	personal enemy	1:24
iniūria, -ae, f.	wrong, injury; insult, offense	1:20/3:01
iniūstus, -a, -um, adj.	unjust	2:18
innocēns, innocentis, adj.	innocent	
innocentia, -ae, f.	innocence	
innumerābilis, -e, adj.	countless, innumerable	
innumerus, -a, -um, adj.	countless, unnumbered	
inops, inopis, adj.	weak, poor, needy	2:08
inpleō/impleō, inplēre, inplēvī, inplētum	to fill up (cf. plēnus)	3:16
inquam	I say (*see* inquit)	
inquīrō, inquīrere, inquīsīvī, inquīsītum	to begin an investigation, to examine, to look into	
inquit	he/she says	
īnsāniō, īnsānīre, īnsānīvī/īnsāniī, īnsānītum	to be insane, to be crazy	
īnsānus, -a, -um, adj.	insane	2:22
īnscrībō, īnscrībere, īnscrīpsī, īnscrīptum	to inscribe, to engrave	
īnsignis, -e, adj.	marked, distinguished, prominent	3:14
īnspiciō, īnspicere, īnspexī, īnspectum	to look at, to examine	
īnstituō, īnstituere, īnstituī, īnstitūtum	to undertake, to begin, to decide to do; to put in place	2:09/3:04
īnstitūtum, -ī, n.	custom, institution	
īnstrūmentum, -ī, n.	equipment, instrument, utensil	
īnstruō, īnstruere, īnstruxī, īnstructum	to instruct	2:15
īnsula, -ae, f.	island	1:04

intāctus, -a, -um, adj.	intact, untouched, unharmed	
integer, integra, integrum, adj.	untouched, whole, complete; upright	1:26
intellēctus, -ūs, m.	intellect, understanding, comprehension	
intellegō, intellegere, intellexī, intellectum	to understand	1:21
intendō, intendere, intendī, intentum	to stretch, to extend	2:08
inter, prep. (+ acc.)	between, among; (of an event or time period) during	2:12
intercēdō, intercēdere, intercēssī, intercēssum	to intercede	
interdum, adv.	sometimes, occasionally, now and then	3:04
intereō, interīre, interiī, interitum	to go away; to die	
interest	it is of interest to (takes the gen. of the person who is interested; e.g. *imperium Caesaris interest* – "command is of interest to Caesar"); it is of interest to *someone* that . . . (instead of taking a subject, *interest* can introduce an indirect statement; e.g. *Caesaris interest populum Rōmānum sibi parēre* – "it is of interest to Caesar that the Roman people obey him")	
interficiō, interficere, interfēcī, interfectum	to kill	1:24/2:19
interim, adv.	in the meantime	
interiōribus, adj.	inner, interior, middle	
intermittō, intermittere, intermīsī, intermissum	to leave, to leave off; to interrupt	2:02
interpres, interpretis, c.	interpreter, translator	3:10
interrogātiō, interrogātiōnis, f.	question	
interrogō, -āre, -āvī, -ātum	to ask a question	
intolerābilis, -e, adj.	intolerable, unbearable	
introeō, -īrī, -īvī, -itum	to enter	
intus, adv.	within, inside	2:26
inūtilis, -e, adj.	useless	
inveniō, invenīre, invēnī, inventum	to find, to discover	
inventor, inventōris, m.	author, inventor	
invideō, invidēre, invīdī, invīsum	to look upon with the evil eye, to envy, to begrudge	3:13
invidia, -ae, f.	envy, jealousy	2:08
invidiōsus, -a, -um, adj.	envious; hateful, spiteful, seething	3:04
invīsibilis, -e, adj.	invisible	
invīsus, -a, -um, adj.	hated	2:10
invītō, -āre, -āvī, -ātum	to invite, to entertain, to summon (cf. vitare, "to avoid")	3:01
invocō, -āre, -āvī, -ātum	to invoke, to call upon	
Iovis	(*see* Iuppiter)	
ipse, ipsa, ipsum, inten. pro.	himself, herself, itself; themselves	1:20/2:24
īra, -ae, f.	anger, wrath	3:14

īrātus, -a, -um, adj.	angry	
irrevocābilis, -e, adj.	irrevocable, unchangeable	
is, ea, id, dem. pro./adj.	that; he, she, it	1:19
Isrāhēl, Isrāhēlis, m.	Israel (usually spelled Isrāēl)	
iste, ista, istud, dem. pro./adj.	that (of yours/near you)	1:20
Ītalia, -ae	Italy	
item, adv. (cf. īdem)	likewise, in the same way	3:04
iter, itineris, n.	journey; path	1:10
iterum, adv.	again	1:17
iubeō, iubēre, iūssī, iūssum	to order, to command	1:14
Iūdaeus, -a, -um, adj.	Jewish; Jew	
iūdex, iūdicis, m.	judge, juror	
iūdicium, -ī, n.	court of law; trial, legal proceeding	2:04
iugum, iugī, n.	yoke	2:09
iungō, iungere, iūnxī, iūnctum	to join, to unite	1:28
Iuppiter, m.	Jupiter (Zeus)	
iūrō, -āre, -āvī, -ātum	to swear, to take an oath	1:20
iūs, iūris, n.	law; right	1:24
iūssus, iūssūs, m.	an order (cf. iubeō)	3:08
iūstitia, -ae, f.	justice; righteousness; declaration of righteousness, justification	2:27
iuvenis, iuvenis, adj.	young, youthful	1:15
iuvenis, iuvenis, m./f.	youth, young man	1:10
iuvō, iuvāre, iūvī, iūtum	to help	1:07
Kalendae, -ārum, f. pl.	the first day of the Roman month	
Karthāgō, Karthāginis, f.	Carthage; *see also* Carthāgō, Carthāginis, f.	
labor, labōris, m.	work, labor, toil	3:16
labōrō, -āre, -āvī, -ātum	to work	1:02
lābrum, -ī, n	washbasin, tub	2:21
lacrima, -ae, f.	tear	
lacus, -ūs, m.	lake, pond, large body of water, reservoir	3:01
laetitia, -ae, f.	happiness, gladness, joyfulness	2:05
laetor, laetārī, laetātus sum	to rejoice	3:10
laetus, -a, -um, adj.	happy	1:08
lapillus, -ī, m.	little stone, pebble; a precious stone or gem	3:13
lapis, lapidis, m.	stone	2:18
lascīvus, -a, -um, adj.	playful, frolicsome	2:06
latēns, latentis, adj.	hiding, hidden	3:15
Latīnē, adv.	in Latin	
lātitūdō, lātitūdinis, f.	width	
Latium, -ī, n.	Latium (the name of the geographical area in which Rome is located)	
lātrīna, -ae, f.	lavatory, bathroom	
lātrō, -āre, -āvī, -ātum	to bark	2:07

lātus, -a, -um, adj.	wide, broad	
latus, lateris, n.	side	3:12
laudō, -āre, -āvī, -ātum	to praise	
lavō, -āre, -āvī, lavātum/lautum	to wash	2:21
lectus, -ī, m.	couch, bed; bier	1:16
lēgātus, -ī, m.	officer, lieutenant	1:12
legiō, legiōnis, m.	legion (up to 6,000 men); (pl) troops, army	1:20
lēgitimus, -a, -um	allowed by law	
legō, legere, lēgī, lēctum	to choose, to pick; to collect, to gather; to read, to recite	1:12
lentus, -a, -um, adj	slow	3:13
lēx, lēgis, f.	law	1:22/3:01
libellus, -ī, m.	little book	3:13
libenter, adv.	gladly, willingly; (in conversation) you're welcome	
līber, lībera, līberum, adj.	free	1:12
liber, librī, m.	scroll, book	
līberālis, -e, adj.	of a free person; liberal arts (the skills a free person has time to pursue)	
līberī, līberōrum, m. pl.	children	1:06
līberō, -āre, -āvī, -ātum	to free, to set free	1:09
lībertus, -ī, m.	freed slave, freedman	1:22
Libya, -ae, f.	Libya, Northern Africa	
licet, licēre, licuit *or* licitum est	it is allowed for *x* (dat.) to *y* (inf.); *x* (dat.) may *y* (inf.)	3:02
līlium, līliī, n.	lily	
lingua, -ae, f.	tongue; language	
līnum, -ī, n.	line, rope; thread	1:19
liquidum, -ī, n.	liquid, water	
littera, -ae, f.	letter of the alphabet; (pl.) literature, epistle	1:22/2:17
lītus, lītoris, n.	shore	3:14
locus, -ī, m.	place; passage (in literature)	2:05
longē, adv.	by far	3:09
longitūdō, longitūdinis, f.	length, height	3:12
longus, -a, -um, adj.	long	3:09
loquor, loquī, locūtus sum	to speak, to converse	2:26
lubet/libet, lubēre, lubuit	(impersonal) it is pleasing	3:07
lucrum, -ī, n.	wealth, gain	2:11
lūdībrium, lūdībriī, n.	mockery	3:10
lūdificō, -āre, -āvī, -ātum	to fool	1:09
lūdō, lūdere, lūsī, lūsum	to play	
lūdus, -ī, m.	school, game	1:15
lūgeō, lūgēre, lūxī, lūctum	to mourn, to be in mourning	3:13
lūmen, lūminis, n.	light, lamp, torch	2:10
lūna, -ae, f.	moon	2:20

lupīnum, -ī, n.	lupine plant	
Lutherānus, -a, -um, adj.	Lutheran	
lūx, lūcis, f.	light	2:21
lympha, -ae, f.	water	3:16
mācerō, -āre, -āvī, -ātum	to soften	3:06
māchina, -ae, f.	machine	
magis, CpAdv.	more, to a greater extent, rather	3:10
magister, magistī, m.	master; teacher	
magistrātus, -ūs, m.	magistrate	2:04
magnificus, -a, -um, adj.	grand, great	
magnitūdō, magnitūdinis, f.	greatness	
magnopere, adv.	greatly, especially	1:26/2:07
magnus, -a, -um, adj.	big, great	1:07
māior, māius, CpAdj. (from magnus)	bigger, older; māiōrēs (by itself) ancestors	
māiōrēs, māiōrum, m./f. pl.	ancestors (cf. comparative form of magnus)	3:01
male, adv.	badly	
malignitās, malignitātis, f.	harm, malignity	
malignus, -a, -um, adj.	harmful, malignant	
mālō, mālle, māluī	to prefer, to want more	2:10
malus, -a, -um, adj.	bad, evil	
mandātum, -ī, n.	mandate, order	2:19
mandō, mandāre, mandāvī, mandātum	to entrust something (acc.) to someone (dat.); to give an order to (+ dat.)	
maneō, manēre, mānsī, mānsum	to stay, to remain	1:18
manifestus, -a, -um, adj.	clear, manifest	
manus, -ūs, f.	hand; band (of men)	1:28
mare, maris, n.i.	sea	1:14
marītus, -ī, m.	husband	1:13
massa, -ae, f.	lump, mass, whole (from Greek μᾶζα)	
māter, mātris, f.	mother	1:10
mātertera, -ae, f.	mother's sister, maternal aunt	
Matthaeus, -ī, m.	St. Matthew (the evangelist)	
maximē, adv.	especially	
maximus, -a, -um, SpAdj. (from magnus)	greatest, very great	
mediātor, mediātoris, m.	a mediator	
medicāmen, medicāminis, n.	medicine, remedy	
mēdicus, -a, -um, adj.	of healing, healing, medical	
mediocritās, mediocritātis, f.	moderation, the mean	3:13
mediocriter, adv.	moderately	
medius, -a, -um, adj.	middle, middle of	2:21
melior, melius, CpAdj. (from bonus)	better	
membrum, -ī, n.	limb, member (of the body)	
meminī, meminisse	to remember	

memor, memoris, adj.	mindful, remembering	3:14
memoria, -ae, f.	memory, memorial; place of remembrance	
memorō, -āre, -āvī, -ātum	to mention, to tell	
mēns, mentis, f.	mind	2:15
mēnsa, -ae, f.	table, course of a meal	1:15
mēnsis, mēnsis, m.	month	1:23
mēnsūra, -ae, f.	measuring, measurement	
mercātor, mercātōris, m.	merchant	3:01
mercātūra, -ae, f.	trade, buying and selling (used disparagingly)	3:04
mercēs, mercēdis, f.	wage, reward	
mereō, merēre, meruī, meritum	to deserve, to merit (cf. meritum)	3:16
mergō, mergere, mērsī, mērsum	to plunge, to sink; to immerse, to submerge	2:06/3:12
meritum, meritī, n.	merit	3:15
metuō, metuere, metuī, metūtum	to fear	1:21/2:22
metus, -ūs, m.	fear	2:13
meus, -a, -um, adj.	my, mine; my own	1:24/2:25
mī = mihi	to me, for me	
mīles, mīlitis, m.	soldier; (medieval Latin) knight	1:11
mīlia	(*see* mīlle)	
mīlitō, -āre, -āvī, -ātum	to serve as a soldier, to campaign	1:22
mīlle passūs, mīlia passuum	a mile (1,000 paces)/miles (thousands of paces)	1:28
mīlle, (pl. mīlia), adj.	thousand	1:23
mīlle, adj.	a thousand	1:23
mīllēsimus, -a, -um, adj.	a thousandth	
minimus, -a, -um, adj.	least, very little	1:23
ministerium, -ī, n.	ministry, attendance (in the sense of waiting upon), service	
minor, minus, CpAdj.	less, smaller	
minuō, minuere, minuī, minūtum	to lessen, to diminish	3:15
minus, CpAdv.	less; not very (comparative form of parvus)	3:09
minūtus, -a, -um, adj.	small, minute	
mīrābilis, -e, adj.	wonderful, extraordinary, strange	2:27
mīrāculum, -ī, n.	marvel, great sight	
misceō, miscēre, miscuī, mixtum	to mix, to mingle	3:03
miser, -a, -um, adj.	unhappy, wretched, miserable	1:19
miseria, -ae, f.	misery, distress (due to poverty)	
misericordia, -ae, f.	compassion, mercy	
misericors, misericordis, adj.	compassionate, merciful	
miseror, -ārī, -ātus sum	to pity	
mītis, mīte, adj.	gentle	1:24
mittō, mittere, mīsī, missum	to send	1:11
mōbilis, -e, adj.	movable; agile; changeable, inconstant	2:06
modestia, -ae, f.	temperance; humility	1:26

modestus, -a, -um, adj.	well-behaved; humble, modest; disciplined	1:26
modicus, -a, -um, adj.	little, moderate, of modest size	2:19
modo, adv.	only, presently, just	1:13
modus, -ī, m.	method, way; limit	2:15
moenia, moeniōrum, n. pl.	walls, fortifications of a city	3:14
mōles, mōlis, f.	great difficulty, burden	3:14
molestia, -ae, f.	trouble, annoyance	3:07
mollis, molle, adj.	soft, tender	2:16
mōmentum, -ī, n.	importance	2:17
monastērium, monastēriī, n.	a monastery	
moneō, monēre, monuī, monitum	to warn	1:08
mōns, montis, m.	mountain	1:20
mōnstrō, -āre, -āvī, -ātum	to show	1:06
mōnstrum, -ī, n.	portent; monster	
monumentum, -ī, n.	monument, memorial; tomb	
mōrātus, -a, -um, adj.	mannered	
morbus, morbī, m.	disease, illness	2:07
mordeō, mordēre, momordī, mōrsum	to bite; to bite into, to grip	2:07
morior, morī/morīrī, mortuus sum	to die (cf. mortuus)	2:26/3:03
mors, mortis, f.	death	1:23
mortālis, -e, adj.	mortal	2:22
mortuus, -a, -um, adj.	dead	1:09
mōs, mōris, m.	custom, habit; (pl.) morals, character	2:17
moveō, movēre, mōvī, mōtum	to move, to set in motion	
mox, adv.	soon	1:08/2:07
Mōȳsēs, Mōȳsis/Mōȳsī, m.	Moses (man who led the Israelites out of Egypt)	
muliebris, -e, adj.	feminine, womanly	
muliebriter, adv.	(see muliebris)	
mulier, mulieris, f.	woman, female	3:15
multitūdō, multitūdinis, f.	great number, multitude	
multus, -a, -um, adj.	much; many	1:07
mundus -ī, m.	world, earth	2:12
mūniō, mūnīre, mūnīvī, mūnītum	to fortify, to protect	2:23
mūnus, mūneris, n.	favor, gift, reward; service, duty	2:20
mūrus, -ī, m.	wall	
Mūsa, -ae, f.	a Muse (one of the nine goddesses of art and skill—music, poetry, etc.)	
mūsica, -ae, f.	music; poetry; high art	
mūtātiō, mūtātiōnis, f.	change	
mūtuus, -a, -um, adj.	borrowed	
nam, conj.	for, indeed; on the other hand	2:04
nārrātor, nārrātōris, m.	narrator	
nārrātus, -ūs, m.	story, narrative	

nārrō, -āre, -āvī, -ātum	to tell	1:06
nāsus, -ī, m	nose	2:27
nāta, -ae, f.	daughter	3:16
natio, nationis, f.	nation, people	
nātīvitās, nātīvitātis, f.	birth	2:11
natō, -āre, -āvī, -ātum	to swim	1:10
nātūrālis, -e, adj.	natural	
nātus, -ūs, m.	birth	2:12
nauta, -ae, m.	sailor	1:04
nāvigō, -āre, -āvī, -ātum	to sail	1:02
nāvis, nāvis, f.i.	ship	1:14
nē, adv.	not (used to introduce a negative purpose); don't; lest, so that not	3:05
nebula, -ae, f.	cloud	2:13
nec (*or* neque), conj.	and not, not; *nec* . . . *nec* – neither . . . nor	2:15
necō, -āre, -āvī, -ātum	to kill	1:08
nefās, indec., n.	against divine law, crime, evil deed	2:27
neglego, neglegere, neglexi, neglectus	to neglect, to disregard, to ignore	
negō, -āre, -āvī, -ātum	to deny, to say no	2:08
negōtium, -ī, n.	business, occupation	2:22
nepōs, nepōtis, m.	grandson, descendant	2:07
neque	(*see* nec)	
nēquius, -a, -um, adj.	wicked, depraved; worthless	
nesciō, -īre, -īvī, -ītum	to not know, to be ignorant of	3:01
neu	(*see* nēve)	
neuter, neutra, neutrum, adj.	neither	1:21/2:18
neutrālis, -e, adj.	(in grammar) neuter	
nēve, conj.	and not, or not (an alternate form is neu)	3:05
niger, nigra, nigrum, adj.	shiny black, black	
nihil, indec.	nothing (nil—contracted form)	2:03
nil	(*see* nihil)	
nimbus, -ī, m.	cloud	
nimis, adv.	too much	3:08
nimium, adv.	(*see* nimis)	3:13
nisi, conj.	if not, unless; except	3:04
nīsus, -ūs, m.	pressure, effort	2:08
nītor, nītī, nīsum sum/nīxum sum	to strive, to exert oneself, to make an effort (cf. nīsus)	3:03
nivālis, nivāle, adj.	snowy	
niveus, -a, -um, adj.	of snow, snowy	2:05
nix, nivis, f.	snow	1:28
nōbilitās, nōbilitātis, f.	nobility	
noceō, nocēre, nocuī + dat.	to harm, to be harmful to	1:17
noctū	at night	

nocturnus, -a, -um, adj.	nocturnal, by night	
nōlō, nōlle, nōluī	to not wish, to not want, to be unwilling; (impv. + inf.) don't	1:21/2:10
nōmen, nōminis, n.	name; title; (in grammar) noun	1:14
nōminātīvus, -ī, m.	nominative case; *casus nōminātīvus* – same meaning	
nōn, adv.	not	1:02
nōnāgēsimus, -a, -um, adj.	ninetieth	
nōnāgintā, adj.	ninety	
nōndum, adv.	not yet	
nōngentēsimus, -a, -um, adj.	nine hundredth	
nōngentī, -ae, -a, adj.	nine hundred	
nōnne, inter. adv.	introduces a question expecting the answer "yes"	2:17
nōnus, -a, -um, adj.	ninth	
nōs, nostrī/nostrum, pron.	we	
nōscitō, -āre, -āvī, -ātum	to try to recognize	2:13
noster, nostra, nostrum, adj.	our	2:25
nōtitia, -ae, f.	knowledge, being known	2:19
notō, -āre, -āvī, -ātum	to mark, to designate with a mark	2:24
nōtus, -a, -um, adj.	known	1:13
novem, adj.	nine	
nox, noctis, f.	night; darkness	1:14
nūbēs, nūbis, f.	cloud	
nūbilus, -a, -um, adj.	cloudy, gloomy, troubled	3:16
nūllus, -a, -um, adj.	no, none, not any	1:21/2:18
num, inter. adv.	introduces a question expecting the answer "no"	2:17
nūmen, nūminis, n.	divinity, godhead	3:14
numerus, -ī, m.	number	
numquam, adv.	never	1:21
nunc, adv.	now	1:09
nūntium, -ī, n.	news	
nūntius, -ī, m.	messenger; message	1:13
nux, nucis, f.	nut; nut tree	1:16
ō!	Oh!, O!	
ob, prep. (+ acc.)	in front of, before; because of, on account of	1:21
obeliscus, -ī, m.	obelisk	3:12
obēsus, -a, -um, adj.	fat, stout, thick	
obiectum, -ī, n.	object	
oblīquus, -a, -um, adj.	(in grammar) indirect	
oblīviōsus, -a, -um, adj.	forgetful, oblivious	2:26
oboediēns, oboedientis, adj.	obedient	
obscūrō, -āre, -āvī, -ātum	to obscure, to hide	2:21
obscūrus, -a, -um, adj.	dark, gloomy	
observō, -āre, -āvī, -ātum	to observe	

obses, obsidis, m.	hostage	1:12
obstinātiō, obstinātiōnis, f.	determination; stubbornness	
obtineō, obtinēre, obtinuī, obtentum	to hold on, to possess; to obtain, to be true	1:23
obtrectātiō, obtrectātiōnis, f.	envious detraction, disparagement	3:11
obtruncō, -āre, -āvī, -ātum	to slaughter	1:22
occāsiō, occāsiōnis, f.	occasion, opportunity	2:11
occāsus, -ūs, m.	the setting of the heavenly bodies; the west; fall, destruction (cf. occidō)	3:09
occidō, occidere, occidī, occāsum	to fall, to fall down	3:09
occīdō, occīdere, occīdī, occīsus	to cut down, to kill	2:18
occupō, -āre, -āvī, -ātum	to seize, to occupy, to take possession of	2:25
octāvus, -a, -um, adj.	eighth	
octingentēsimus, -a, -um, adj.	eight hundredth	
octingentī, -ae, -a, adj.	eight hundred	
octō, adj.	eight	
octō, cardinal number	eight	
Octōber, Octōbris, m.	month of October, October	
octōgēsimus, -a, -um, adj.	eightieth	
octōgintā, adj.	eighty	
oculus, -ī, m.	eye	2:09
ōdī, ōdisse	to hate	
odium, odiī, n.	hatred, hate	1:20/2:06
odor, odōris, m.	smell, odor	
offerō, offerre, obtulī, oblātum	to offer	2:10
officium, -ī, n.	office, duty	1:17
olea, -ae, f.	olive, olive tree	3:05
oleārius, -a, -um, adj.	of oil, for oil	3:05
oleum, -ī, n.	oil	
ōlim, adv.	one day, one time, once upon a time	2:12
Olympus, -ī, m.	Mount Olympus	
omnis, omne, adj.	all, every	1:15
onerōsus, -a, -um, adj.	heavy, burdensome	2:26
onus, oneris, n.	burden	2:09
opīniō, opīniōnis, f.	opinion	
opitulor, opitulārī, opitulātus sum	to bring aid, to help, to assist (cf. ops)	3:07
oportet, oportēre, oportuit	it is proper/right for x (acc.) to y (inf.); x (acc.) should y (inf.)	3:02
oppidum, -ī, n.	town	1:06
opprimō, opprimere, oppressī, oppressum	to overwhelm, to press down, to press down on	2:13
oppugnō, -āre, -āvī, -ātum	to attack	1:02
ops, opis, f.	aid, help; (pl.) riches, resources	2:10
optimus, -a, -um, adj.	best, very good	1:09
optō, -āre, -āvī, -ātum	to wish for, to desire	1:07

opus, operis, n.	work; *opus est* – there is a need, there is a necessity for *x* (dat.) of *y* (abl.); *x* (dat.) has need of *y* (abl.)	2:04/3:01/3:10
ōrātiō, ōrātiōnis, f.	speech, oration; prayer	1:22
ōrātor, ōrātōris, m.	orator, speaker (cf. ōrātiō, ōrāre)	3:03
orbis, orbis, m.	circle, ring, orbit; world, universe	2:04
ōrdō, ōrdinis, n.	order, series	2:05
orīgō, orīginis, f.	origin, source	2:08
orior, orīrī, ortus sum	to rise	3:09
ōrnō, -āre, -āvī, -ātum	to decorate, to adorn	1:16
ōrō, -āre, -āvī, -ātum	to pray, to entreat, to beg	2:25
ortus, -ūs, m.	rising	
ōs, ōris, n.	mouth	1:24
os, ossis, n.	bone	2:02
ōsculum, -ī, n.	kiss	
ostendō, ostendere, ostendī, ostentus	to show, to expose to view	2:16
ōtium, -ī, n.	leisure	2:22
pābulum, -ī, n.	food, fodder for animals	3:06
pācātus, -a, -um, adj.	peaceful, tranquil	2:04
pācātus, -ūs, m.	pacification, peace, quiet	
pācificus, -a, -um, adj.	peacemaking, peaceful	
pactum, -ī, n.	agreement, deal	
paedagōgus, -ī, m.	guide, warden; slave teacher of children	
paene, adv.	almost	2:19
palam, adv.	openly	
pār, paris, adj.	equal to, like (+ dat.)	1:17/2:21/3:10
parātus, -a, -um, adj.	prepared	1:20
parcō, parcere, pepercī, parsum (+ dat.)	to spare	2:12
parcus, -a, -um, adj.	modest, thrifty	2:07
parēns, parentis, m/f.	parent	1:14
pāreō, pārēre, pāruī, pāritum (+ dat.)	to obey, to be obedient to	1:17
parliamentārius, -a, -um, adj.	parliamentary	
parō, -āre, -āvī, -ātum	to prepare, to get ready	1:08
parricīdium, -ī, n.	parricide, murder of parent or close relative	2:27
pars, partis, f.	part, piece	1:14
participātiō, participātiōnis, f.	participation	
parvus, -a, -um, adj.	little, small	1:14
passer, passeris, m.	sparrow	3:13
passīvus, -a, -um, adj.	(in grammar) passive voice	
pāssus, -ūs, m.	pace, footstep	1:28
pateō, patēre, patuī	to stand open, to lie open	2:16
pater, patris, m.	father	1:10
paternus, -a, -um, adj.	paternal, of a father	2:11

patiēns, patientis, adj.	(in grammar) acting as a direct object	
patientia, -ae, f.	patience, experience	3:08
patior, patī, passus	to suffer, to experience; to allow, to permit	3:14
patria, patriae, f.	fatherland, country	1:04
Pātricius, -ī, m.	Patrick	
patrius, -a, -um, adj.	of a father, fatherly	2:05
patruus, -ī, m.	paternal uncle, father's brother	2:27
paucī, paucae, pauca, pl. adj.	few, a few	1:23
paulisper, adv.	for a little while	3:10
pauper, pauperis, adj.	poor; (as a noun) a poor man	1:23
pausa, -ae, f.	pause, end	3:07
paveō, pavēre, pāvī	to quake, to tremble with fright, to be scared, to become afraid	
pavidus, -a, -um, adj.	pale, fearful	2:23
pāx, pācis, f.	peace	1:12
peccō, -āre, -āvī, -ātum	to sin; to blunder, to make a mistake	2:22
pectus, pectoris, n.	breast, chest	2:04
pecūnia, -ae, f.	money	1:23
pēior, pēius, CpAdj. (from malus)	worse	
pellis, pellis, f.	skin, hide	2:08
pellō, pellere, pepulī, pulsum	to strike at, to beat; to drive back	2:25
penātēs, penātium, m. pl.	Penates (Roman household gods); *metonymy for* home, family	3:13
pendeō, pendēre, pependī	to hang, to suspend	2:23
penna, -ae, f.	feather; quill, pen	
per, prep. (+ acc.)	through, throughout	1:11
perdō, perdere, perdidī, perditum	to waste, to destroy, to ruin	2:16
pereō, peīre, perīvī/periī, peritum	to die, to perish	1:23
perfectum, -ī, n.	(in grammar) perfect tense; *tempus perfectum* – same meaning	
perfectus, -a, -um, adj.	finished, complete, perfect	
perferō, perferre, pertulī, perlātum	to bear through, to carry on; to endure patiently	2:02
perficiō, perficere, perfēcī, perfectum	to finish, to complete	2:11
perfundō, perfundere, perfūdī, perfūsum	to pour over	3:06
perīculōsus, -a, -um, adj.	dangerous (cf. perīculum)	3:03
perīculum, -ī, n.	danger	1:12
permaneō, permanēre, permānsī, permānsum	to continue, to persist, to last	
permittō, permittere, permīsī, permissum	to permit, to allow	1:29
perniciēs, perniciēī, f.	destruction	2:09
perniciōsus, -a, -um, adj.	destructive, ruinous	3:08
perpetuō, adv.	continuously, perpetually	
perpetuus, -a, -um, adj.	continuous, entire; *in perpetuum* – continuously, forever, in perpetuity	3:12

Alphabetical Glossary

persecūtiō, persecūtiōnis, f.	prosecution; persecution	
persevērō, -āre, -āvī, -ātum	to persevere in (+ acc.), to continue	
persōna, -ae, f.	mask; (in grammar) person; (in a play) character, role	
persuādeō, persuādēre, persuāsī, persuāsum (+ dat.)	to make sweet to, to persuade	2:03
pertineō, pertinēre, pertinuī	to reach, to extend (to); to pertain (to), to apply (to)	3:09
perturbō, -āre, -āvī, -ātum	to throw into confusion	
perveniō, pervenīre, pervēnī, perventum	to arrive	2:25
pēs, pedis, m.	foot	2:21
pessimus, -a, -um, SpAdj. (from malus)	worst, very bad	
pestilēns, pestilentis, adj.	pestilential, destructive	
petō, petere, petīvī/petiī, petītum	to aim at, to aim for, to attack; to look for, to seek	1:11/2:06
pietās, pietātis, f.	piety, duty (to gods, family, country); dutiful conduct	2:17
pīrāta, -ae, m.	pirate	
piscīna, -ae, f.	fish pond; swimming pool	
pius, pia, pium, adj.	pious, devout (god-fearing)	1:07
placeō, placēre, placuī, placitus (+ dat.)	to please, to be pleasing to	1:17
planēta, -ae, f.	planet	
plānus, -a, -um, adj.	flat, level, even	3:06
plaustrum, -ī, n.	wagon, cart	3:06
plēbēs, plēbeī, f.	commoner, plebeian (as a group, not as individuals)	2:05
plēnus, -a, -um, adj.	full, full of (+ abl./gen.)	1:25
plōrō, -āre, -āvī, -ātum	to lament, to wail, to cry	2:26
plūrāliter, adv.	in the plural	
plūrimus, -a, -um, adj.	most, very much	1:23
plūs quam perfectum, -ī, n.	(in grammar) pluperfect; *tempus plūs quam perfectum* – same meaning	
plūs, plūris, Cp. noun/adj. (from multus)	more	
pluvius, -a, -um, adj.	rainy, of rain	3:06
pōculum, -ī, n.	cup	2:11
poēma, poēmatis, n.	poem	
poena, -ae, f.	penalty, punishment; *poenam dare* – to pay a penalty	2:25
poenālis, -e, adj.	of or belonging to punishment; penal	2:26
poēta, -ae, m.	poet	1:04
polliceor, pollicērī, pollicitus sum	to promise	
pondus, ponderis, n.	weight, burden	3:12
pōnō, pōnere, posuī/posīvī, positum	to put, to place; to embody	1:11/3:03
pōns, pontis, m.	bridge	2:24
porrō, adv.	forward; *ire porro* – to go forward	
porta, -ae, f.	gate	2:24
portō, -āre, -āvī, -ātum	to carry	1:03

portus, portūs, m.	port, harbor	3:12
positiō, positiōnis, f.	position	
possideō, possidēre, possēdī, possessum	to possess	
possum, posse, potuī	to be able, can	1:18
post, prep. (+ acc.); adv.	after; afterward	1:19
posteā, adv.	afterward	1:13
posthāc, adv.	after this	
postquam, conj.	after	1:25
postulō, -āre, -āvī, -ātum	to demand	1:24
potēns, potentis, adj.	able, capable; powerful	1:18
potentia, -ae, f.	power	
potestās, potestātis, f.	power, strength	2:27
potior, potīrī, potītus sum (+ gen., abl., or acc.)	to get hold of, to acquire	2:26
pōtō, -āre, -āvī, -ātum	to drink	2:11
praecēdō, praecēdere, praecessī, praecessum	to go before, to precede, to surpass	3:09
praecipuus, -a, -um, adj.	special; principal	1:14
praeclārus, -a, -um, adj.	very famous, excellent	3:08
praedicō, -āre, -āvī, -ātum	to proclaim, to assert, to preach (*see* medieval definition of *praedīcō*)	
praedispositiō, praedispositiōnis, f.	predisposition, prearrangement	
praedium, praediī, n.	farm, landed estate	3:01
praefectus, -ī, m.	magistrate, official, ruler	2:23
praemium, -ī, n.	reward; booty, loot	1:24
praepositiō, praepositiōnis, f.	(in grammar) preposition	
praesēns, praesentis, adj.	present; (in grammar) present tense; *tempus praesēns* – same meaning	
praesertim, adv.	especially, chiefly	3:06
praesidium, -ī, n.	defense, protection, escort	
praestō, praestāre, praestitī, praestitum	to place before, to present; to be outstanding, to be distinguished; (impersonally) it is beneficial; to do, to accomplish, to make good; to prevail; to overcome; to stand before	2:04/3:02
praeter, prep. (+ acc.)	except, besides; past; *praeter quod* – except that	2:03
praeterquam, adv.	except for, other than (cf. praeter)	3:07
prasinus, -a, -um, adj.	green, leek-green	2:20
prātum, -ī, n.	meadow, meadow grass	2:06
precātiō, precātiōnis, f.	prayer	
precor, precārī, precātus sum	to pray, to entreat	3:08
premō, premere, pressī, pressum	to press	
pressio, pressionis, f.	a pressing, a pressing down, pressure	
pretium, -ī, n.	price	1:23
prex, precis, f.	prayer	3:07
prīdem, adv.	long ago	

prīmus, -a, -um, adj.	first	
prīmus, -a, -um, adj.	first	
prīnceps, prīncipis, m.	prince, leader	1:19
prīncipium, -ī, n.	beginning	2:11
prīstinus, -a, -um, adj.	former, early; original	2:11
prius, adv.	before, earlier	
priusquam, conj.	before	3:11
privātus, -a, -um, adj.	private, non-public	
prīvō, -āre, -āvī, -ātum	to bereave, to deprive, to rob	2:25
prō, prep. (+ abl.)	in front of, before; on behalf of, for; instead of; in proportion to; in return for, in payment for	1:11
probō, -āre, -āvī, -ātum	to approve, to prove	1:11
prōcēdō, prōcēdere, prōcessī, prōcessum	to advance, to proceed	1:18
prōcrāstinō, -āre, -āvī, -ātum	to put off, to defer, to delay	
prōcūrātor, prōcūrātōris, m.	administrator, procurator	
prōdigiōsus, -a, -um, adj.	unnatural, marvelous	
proelium, -ī, n.	battle	1:18
prōferō, prōferre, prōtulī, prōlātum	to bring forward; to produce	
proficīscor, proficīscī, profectus sum	to set out, to depart	3:11
profundō, profundere, profūdī, profūsum	to pour forth, to gush forth	
prōgeniēs, prōgeniēī, f.	progeny, descendants, race	
prōgressum, -ī, n.	progress	
prohibeō, prohibēre, prohibuī, prohibitum	to keep (back), to prevent, to hinder	1:09
prōiciō, prōicere, prōiēcī, prōiectum	to fling forth or away	
prōiectile, prōiectilis, n.	projectile	
prōlēs, prōlis, f.	offspring, descendent	3:13
prōmittō, prōmittere, prōmīsī, prōmissum	to let go forward, to send forth; to promise	3:02
prōmō, prōmere, prōmpsī, prōmptum	to bring forth, to bring out; to produce	
prope, adv.	nearly, almost; nearby	3:10
prope, prep. (+ acc.)	near	1:12
properō, -āre, -āvī, -ātum	to hurry, to hasten	3:08
prophēta, prophētae, m.	a prophet	
propitia, -ōrum, n.pl.	means of propitiation	2:10
propitius, -a, -um, adj.	favorable, gracious	
propius, CpAdv.	nearer	
prōpōnō, prōpōnere, prōposuī, prōpositum	to put before; to propose	1:12
prōportiōnālis, -e, adj.	proportional	
proprius, -a, -um, adj.	its own, particular	2:19
propter, prep. (+ acc.)	near; on account of	
proptereā, adv.	on that account, therefore	3:09
Proserpina, -ae, f. (*also* Prōserpina)	Proserpine, Persephone (daughter of Ceres and wife of Pluto)	
prosperus, -a, -um, adj.	favorable	

prōtector, prōtectōris, m.	bodyguard, guard	
prōvehō, prōvehere, prōvexī, prōvectum	to carry forth, to conduct	2:20
prōvideō, prōvidēre, prōvīdī, prōvīsum	to provide	
prōvincia, -ae, f.	province	3:09
proximum, prep. (+ acc.)	next to	
proximus, -a, -um, adj.	next, near	1:23
prūdentia, -ae, f.	knowledge; wisdom, discretion, prudence	3:11
psalmus, -ī, m.	psalm	
pūblicus, -a, -um, adj.	public	1:15
pudendus, -a, -um, adj.	shameful	2:10
pudeō, pudēre, puduī	to make ashamed, to shame	3:07
puella, -ae, f.	girl	1:04
puellāris, -e, adj.	girlish	
puer, puerī, m.	boy	1:06
puerīlis, -e, adj.	childlike, childish	
pueritia, -ae, f.	childhood	2:14
puerulus, puerulī, m.	a little boy	3:11
pugna, -ae, f.	battle	
pugnō, -āre, -āvī, -ātum	to fight	1:06
pulcher, pulchra, pulchrum, adj.	beautiful	1:04
pulsō, -āre, -āvī, -ātum	to strike, to beat	2:05
pultō, -āre, -āvī, -ātum	to knock *or* strike a door	2:22
pulvis, pulveris, m.	dust	2:13
pūniceus, -a, -um, adj.	reddish, rosy	
pūniō, pūnīre, pūnīvī, pūnītum	to punish	2:15
pūpa, -ae, f.	doll	1:05
purgātōrium, -ī, n.	purgatory	
pūrgō, -āre, -āvī, -ātum	to cleanse	
purpureus, -a, -um, adj.	purple	
pūrus, -a, -um, adj.	pure	3:13
putō, -āre, -āvī, -ātum	to think	2:20
pȳramis, pȳramidis, f.	pyramid	
quadrāgēsimus, -a, -um, adj.	fortieth	
quadrāgintā, adj.	forty	
quadringentī, -ae, -a, adj.	four hundred	
quadruplum, -ī, n.	a quadruple amount	3:04
quaerō, quaerere, quaesīvī, quaesītum	to seek, to look for; to question	2:15/3:15
quaestus, -ūs, m.	way of making money, occupation; gain, profit	
quālis, -e, rel. or inter. adj.	of what sort, what kind	
quamquam, adv.	although, however	2:13
quandō, inter. and rel. adv. and conj.	when; *sī quandō* – if ever	2:16/2:17
quandringentēsimus, -a, -um, adj.	four hundredth	
quantitās, quantitātis, f.	amount, quantity	

quantus, -a, -um, adj.	how great, how much	2:06
quārē *or* quā rē, inter. adv.	why? for what reason?	3:13
quartus, -a, -um, adj.	fourth	
quārtus, -a, -um, adj.	fourth	
quārtus, -a, -um; decimus, -a, -um, adj.	fourteenth	
quasi, adv.	as if, as it were	2:13
quattuor, adj.	four	
quattuor, indec. adj.	four	
quattuordecim, adj.	fourteen	
quercus, -ūs, f.	oak tree	2:02
quī, quae, quod, rel. pro.	who, what, which, that	1:25/2:16
quia, adv.	since, because	2:15
quīdam, quaedam, quiddam, pro./adj.	a certain . . .	2:24
quidem, adv.	indeed, even, certainly, of course; *nē . . . quidem . . .* – not even	2:24
quidlibet, adv.	whatever you like, anything whatsoever	3:15
quidquid, adv.	whatever	2:16
quiētus, -a, -um, adj.	quiet, calm	
quīlibet, quaelibet, quodlibet, indef. pro.	anyone you wish, no matter who, anyone who comes, whoever	3:10
quīlubet	(*see* quīlibet)	
quin, conj.	(+ subj. after a negative main clause) that	3:11
quīnārius, -ī, m.	coin worth five asses or half a denarius	
quīndecim, adj.	fifteen	
quīngentēsimus, -a, -um, adj.	five hundredth	
quīngentī, -ae, -a, adj.	five hundred	
quīnquāgēsimus, -a, -um, adj.	fiftieth	
quīnquāgintā, adj.	fifty	
quīnque, adj.	five	
quīnque, indec. adj.	five	
quīntus decimus, -a, -um, adj.	fifteenth	
quīntus, -a, -um, adj.	fifth	
quis, quid, inter. adj, inter. pro.	who, what, which	1:25/2:17
quisquam, quaequam, quicquam/quidquam, indef. pro.	anyone, anything (cf. quis, quid)	3:07
quisque, quidque, pro.	each	
quō, adv.	to what place	2:17
quod, conj. (+ ind.; + subj.)	because; that, the fact that	1:12
quom (archaic form of cum, conj.), adv.	when	3:03
quōmodo, adv.	in what way, how	2:17
quoque, conj.	also	1:07/2:02
quot, indecl. adj.	how many, as many as	2:17
quotannīs, adv.	every year	3:05

quotiēnscumque, adv.	however often	
quotus, -a, -um, adj.	in what number . . . ?	
radius, -ī, m.	rod, ray	3:12
rapiō, rapere, rapuī, raptum	to snatch, to tear away, to seize	3:14
rārus, -a, -um, adj.	sparse, scattered	2:13
ratiō, ratiōnis, f.	reason, ration	1:21
reāctiō, reāctiōnis, f.	reaction	
reciprocus, -a, -um, adj.	reciprocal	
recitō, -āre, -āvī, -ātum	to recite, to read aloud	
recūsō, -āre, -āvī, -ātum	to refuse	2:02
reddō, reddere, reddidī, redditum	to give back, to return	1:18
redeō, redīre, rediī/redīvī, reditum	to go back, to come back, to return	3:03
redūcō, redūcere, redūxī, reductum	to lead back	
referō, referre, rettulī, relātum	to bring back, to carry back, to return; to report; to announce	1:25
reficiō, reficere, refēcī, refectum	to repair, to remake	
reflectō, reflectere, reflexī, reflexum	to bend back	1:24
refulgeō, refulgēre, refulsī	to gleam back, to shine brightly, to glitter	2:06
rēgālis, -e, adj.	regal	2:05
rēgia, -ae, f.	palace	1:09
regimen, regiminis, n.	regimen, course of treatment	
rēgīna, -ae, f.	queen	1:04
regiō, regiōnis, f.	place, region, province	
rēgnātor, rēgnātōris, m.	ruler	2:23
rēgnō, rēgnāre, rēgnāvī, rēgnātum	to rule	1:03
rēgnum, -ī, n.	kingdom; rule, power	2:25
regō, regere, rēxī, rēctum	to rule, to keep in order	
relinquō, relinquere, relīquī, relictum	to leave behind	1:19
reliquus, -a, -um, adj.	the remaining	
remedium, ī, n.	cure, remedy	
removeō, removēre, remōvī, remōtum	to withdraw	
rēmus, -ī, m.	oar	3:15
renovō, -āre, -āvī, -ātum	to renew	2:13
renūntiātiō, renūntiātiōnis, m/f.	report	2:18
repellō, repellere, reppulī, repulsum	to drive back; to refuse	2:04
reperiō, reperīre, repperī, repertum	to find again, to find	3:16
reportō, -āre, -āvī, -ātum	to bring back	
rēs pūblica, reī pūblicae, f.	state, republic, government	1:29
rēs, reī, f.	thing; matter, affair; state; *novae rēs* – revolution	1:29
resistentia, -ae, f.	resistance	
resistō, resistere, restitī	to resist, to withstand	
respondeō, respondēre, respondī, respōnsum	to reply, to respond	1:13
restituō, restituere, restituī, restitūtum	to set up again, to restore	2:04

retardō, -are, -āvī, -ātum	to retard, to slow down, to slow, to impede	
retrahō, retrahere, retraxī, retractum	to draw back, to drag	
rētribūtiō, rētribūtiōnis, f.	retribution, repayment	
retrō, adv.	in the past	2:20
revēlō, -āre, -āvī, -ātum	to uncover, to unveil	
reveniō, revenīre, revēnī, reventum	to come back, to return	1:27
reverendus, -a, -um, adj.	revered, respected (render with the title Reverend)	
reverentia, -ae, f.	fear, awe, reverence for (+ gen.)	
revertō, revertere, revertī, reversum	to turn back, to cause to return	1:12
revocō, -āre, -āvī, -ātum	to recall, to call back	
revolvō, revolvere, revolvī, revolūtum	to roll back	
rēx, rēgis, m.	king	1:10
Rhodus, -ī, f.	Rhodes (an island off the south coast of Asia Minor)	
rīdeō, rīdēre, rīsī, rīsum	to laugh	2:05
rigidus, -a, -um, adj.	stiff, unbending, stubborn	2:06
rīpa, -ae, f.	riverbank, shore	1:10
rīvus, -ī, m.	river, brook, small stream	1:10
rogō, -āre, -āvī, -ātum	to ask	1:03
Rōma, -ae, f.	Rome	
Rōmānus, -a, -um, adj.	Roman	
rosa, -ae, f.	rose	1:05
rotō, -āre, -āvī, -ātum	to rotate, to roll	
rotundus, -a, -um, adj.	round, circular	
ruber, rubra, rubrum, adj.	red	
rūgōsus, -a, -um, adj.	wrinkled	2:08
ruīna, -ae, f.	ruins, that which has fallen down	3:15
rūmor, rūmōris, m.	hearsay, rumor; reputation	
rūrsus, adv.	again, backwards	2:08
rūs, rūris, n.	country (as opposed to city)	1:28
russeus, -a, -um, adj.	red, russet	2:20
rūsticus, -a, -um, adj.	country, rural, rustic	
sacer, sacra, sacrum, adj.	sacred, holy	1:07
sacerdōs, sacerdōtis, m./f.	priest/priestess	2:14
sacrāmentālis, -e, adj.	sacramental	
sacrāmentum, sacrāmentī, n.	sacrament	
sacrificō, -āre, -āvī, -ātum	to sacrifice	
sacrilegus, -a, -um, adj.	sacrilegious	
saepe, adv.	often	3:09
sacvitia, -ae, f.	cruelty, savagery	2:09
saevus, -a, -um, adj.	fierce	2:06
sāl, salis, m.	salt; salary (military)	2:19
saliō, salīre, saluī, saltum	to spring, to leap, to jump	3:06
saltō, -āre, -āvī, -ātum	to dance	1:07

salūs, salūtis, f.	health, safety; greetings	2:20
sānē, adv.	utterly, completely, wholly	3:13
sanguineus, -a, -um, adj.	blood red, bloody	
sanguis, sanguinis, m.	blood	
sapiēns, sapientis, adj.	wise	2:17
sapientia, -ae, f.	wisdom (cf. sapiens)	3:01
satiō, -āre, -āvī, -ātum	to satisfy, to appease	2:11
satis (*or* sat), indec. adj.	enough (often accompanied by a partitive genitive)	2:19
satisfactiō, satisfactiōnis, f. (satis + facere)	satisfaction, reparation	
satura, -ae, f.	satire	
saturō, -āre, -āvī, -ātum	to fill, to satiate	
scelus, sceleris, n.	crime, evil deed	2:23
scīlicet, adv.	naturally, certainly, undoubtedly	3:15
sciō, scīre, scīvī/sciī, scītum	to know	1:27
scopulus, -ī, m.	rock, crag, cliff (esp. rock in the sea)	2:06
scrība, -ae, m.	clerk; scribe	1:11
scrībō, scrībere, scripsī, scriptum	to write	1:15
scrīptor, scrīptōris, m.	writer	2:23
scūtum, -ī, n.	shield	1:07/2:24
sēcrētō, adv.	secretly	
secundus, -a, -um, adj.	second; following; favorable	
secundus, -a, -um, adj.	second	
secūris, secūris, f.	axe, hatchet	3:02
secūrus, -a, -um, adj.	secure (cf. sine + cūra)	
sēdecim, adj.	sixteen	
sēdēs, sēdis, f.	chair, seat	3:16
sēditiōsus, -a, -um, adj.	rebellious, seditious	2:09
sēgregō, -āre, -āvī, -ātum	to separate	
semper, adv.	always	1:20
senātor, senātōris, m.	senator, member of the Roman Senate	1:18
senātus, -ūs, m.	senate; body of elders	1:28
senecta, -ae, f.	old age (cf. senex)	3:07
senex, senis, adj.	old, aged; (as a noun) old man	1:15
senior, seniōris, adj.	older, elder	1:24
sententia, -ae, f.	opinion, feeling; sentence	3:07
sentiō, sentīre, sēnsī, sēnsum	to perceive, to feel, to sense	1:27/2:21
sēparō, -āre, -āvī, -ātum	to separate	
septem, adj.	seven	
September, Septembris, m.	month of September, September	
septendecim, adj.	seventeen	
septentriōnēs, septentriōnum, m.pl. (also spelled septemtriōnēs)	the seven ploughing oxen (a constellation); the north	3:09
septimus decimus, -a, -um, adj.	seventeenth	

septimus, -a, -um, adj.	seventh	
septingentēsimus, -a, -um, adj.	seven hundredth	
septingentī, -ae, -a, adj.	seven hundred	
septuāgēsimus, -a, -um, adj.	seventieth	
septuāgintā, adj.	seventy	
sepulchrum, -ī, n.	burial place, grave, tomb, sepulchre	
sequor, sequī, secūtus sum	to follow	2:26
serēnus, -a, -um, adj.	fair, bright, cloudless; serene	
seriēs, seriēī, f.	chain, row, succession	
serpēns, serpentis, c.	snake, serpent	
serviō, -īre, -īvī, -ītum (+dat.)	to be a slave to, to serve	2:03
servō, -āre, -āvī, -ātum	to guard, to save, to take care of, to protect	1:06/1:10
servus, -ī, m.	servant, slave	
sescentēsimus, -a, -um, adj.	six hundredth	
sescentī, -ae, -a, adj.	six hundred	
sēstertia, -ōrum, n.	1,000 sēstertiī	
sēstertius, -ī, m.	a coin worth two-and-a-half asses; sēstertium – 1,000 sēstertiī	
sevērus, -a, -um, adj.	grave, serious, strict, stern, severe	
sex, adj.	six	
sex, indec. adj.	six	
sexāgēsimus, -a, -um, adj.	sixtieth	
sexāgintā, adj.	sixty	
sextus decimus, -a, -um, adj.	sixteenth	
sextus, adj.	sixth	
sī, conj.	if	1:14
sīc, adv.	thus, so; in this way	1:20
siccus, -a, -um, adj.	dry, thirsty	2:26
sīcut, adv.	just as	1:21/2:05
sīdus, sīderis, n.	group of stars, constellation, heavenly body	3:16
significō, -āre, -āvī, -ātum	to indicate, to signify, to mean	2:14
signum, -ī, n.	sign; meaning	1:07
silēns, silentis, adj.	silent	
silentium, -ī, n.	silence	
silva, -ae, f.	woods, forest	3:01
similis, -e, adj.	like, similar (to)	1:17
simplex, simplicis, adj.	simple, plain	2:16
simplicitās, simplicitātis, f.	simplicity	
simul, adv.	at the same time, together, as soon as, at once	2:05
simulācrum, -ī, n.	image, likeness	2:10
sincērē, adv.	honestly	1:26
singulāriter	(in grammar) in the singular	
singulus, -a, -um, adj. (dis. num.)	separate, single, one at a time	3:10

sinus, sinūs, m.	fold, pocket	2:16
sitiō, sitīre, sitīvī/sitiī	to be thirsty	
situs, -ūs, m.	site, position	2:11
sōbrius, -a, -um, adj.	sober, not intoxicated; frugal, reasonable	3:13
socius, sociī, m.	ally	1:06
sōl, sōlis, m.	sun	2:20
soleō, solēre, solitus sum (semi-deponent)	to be accustomed	3:05
solidus, -a, -um, adj.	firm, solid	
sōlitūdō, sōlitūdinis, f.	loneliness, solitude, being alone	
sōlum, adv.	alone, only	
sōlus, -a, -um, adj.	alone, only	1:21/2:18
somnium, -ī, n.	dream	2:24
sonō, sonāre, sonuī, sonitum	to sound, to resound, to make a noise	3:02
sōpiō, -īre, -īvī, -ītum	to put to sleep	2:04
sordēs, sordis, f.	(often pl.) dirt, filth; baseness (of rank or station)	3:13
sordidus, -a, -um, adj.	dirty, filthy	
soror, sorōris, f.	sister	1:19
sors, sortis, f.	a lot, a drawing of lots, casting of lots, fate	2:09/3:10
spatiōsus, -a, -um, adj.	spacious	2:21
spatium, -ī, n.	space	2:21
speciēs, speciēī, f.	sight, outward appearance; kind	2:05
spectāculum, -ī, n.	show, entertainment	2:10
spectō, -āre, -āvī, -ātum	to look at, to watch	1:05
spēlunca, -ae, f.	cave	2:14
spērō, -āre, -āvī, -ātum	to hope	1:27
spēs, speī, f.	hope	1:29
spīrituālis, -e, adj.	spiritual	
spīritus, spīritūs, m.	breath, breath of life, spirit; wind	2:03
spolium, -ī, n.	spoil, booty	2:26
squālidus, -a, -um, adj.	dirty	1:13
stabilis, -e, adj.	stable, firm, steady	3:04
stabulum, -ī, n.	standing room, quarters, a stable	3:06
statua, -ae, f.	statue	1:12
statūra, -ae, f.	stature, size	
status, -ūs, m.	state, condition	2:09
stella, -ae, f.	star	1:05
stō, stāre, stetī, statum	to stand; (price + dat.) to cost	1:17/1:23
strēnuus, -a, -um, adj.	brisk, prompt, active, vigorous	3:04
studeō, studēre, studuī (+ dat)	to study, to direct one's zeal to	1:17
studiōsus, -a, -um, adj.	eager to (+ inf.); eager for (+ gen.)	3:04
studium, -ī, n.	zeal, eagerness	1:09
stultus, -a, -um, adj.	foolish	
suādeō, suādēre, suāsī, suāsum	to urge, to recommend, to advise	

sub	(+ acc.) up to; (+ abl.) under	1:11
subdō, subdere, subdidī, subditum	to place, to lay, *or* to set (acc.) under (dat.)	2:27
subiciō, subicere, subiēcī, subiectum	to throw up, to bring up; to suggest	2:14
subitō, adv.	suddenly	
submoveō	(*see* summoveō)	
subter	below, beneath	
subvertō, subvertere, subvertī, subversum	to upset, to overthrow, to overturn	2:23
succēdō, succēdere, successī, successum	to advance, to come next; to succeed	2:12
successīvē, adv.	successively	
sufferō, sufferre, sustulī, sublātum	to raise up, to support	
suffrāgium, -ī, n.	vote, right to vote, decision, judgment	
suī, sibi, sē, sē, refl pro.	himself, herself, itself, (pl.) themselves	
sulfur, sulfuris, n.	sulfur	
sum, esse, fuī, futūrum	to be	1:07
summoveō, summovēre, summōvī, summōtum	to send away, to remove	3:10
summus, -a, -um, SpAdj. (from superus)	highest, top	
sūmō, sūmere, sūmpsī, sūmptum	to take up	2:14
super, adv.	besides, in addition	
superbia, -ae, f.	pride, haughtiness	
superbus, -a, -um, adj.	proud, haughty	2:05
superior, superius, CpAdj. (from superus)	higher, superior; above, earlier	
superō, -āre, -āvī, -ātum	to surpass, to outdo, to be above and beyond; to overcome; to be outstanding; to remain, to be left (over)	1:18
superstitiō, superstitiōnis, f.	superstition, unreasonable belief or fear	
superus, -a, -um, adj.	upper	
suprā, adv., prep. + acc.	above	3:04
suprēmus, -a, -um, SpAdj. (from superus)	highest	
surgō, surgere, surrēxī, surrēctum	to rise, to arise	1:16
sūs, suis, c.	pig, sow, hog	3:06
suspīciō, suspīciōnis, f.	suspicion	
sustineō, sustinēre, sustinuī, sustentum	to hold up, to support, to sustain	3:04
suus, -a, -um, adj.	his own, her own, its own, their own	1:24/2:25
symptōma, symptōmatis, n.	symptom	
tabula, -ae, f.	table, tablet	
tacitus, -a, -um, adj.	silent	3:15
tālis, -e, adj.	such, of such a kind	2:18
tam, adv.	so	1:25/3:04
tamen, adv.	nevertheless, however	1:26/2:02
tamquam (or tanquam), adv.	just as, as if	2:15
tandem, adv.	finally, at last, in the end; I ask, I pray (in urgent questioning)	2:06/3:08

tangō, tangere, tetigī, tāctum	to touch, to handle	2:15
tantus, -a, -um, adj.	so much, so great, of such a . . .	2:07
tarditās, tarditātis, f.	slowness, sluggishnes; dullness	
tardus, -a, -um, adj.	slow	2:21
tēctum, -ī, n.	roof, house (by synecdoche)	3:06
tēctus, -a, -um, adj.	covered	
tellūs, tellūris, f.	the earth; land, country	
tēlum, -ī, n.	thrown or cast weapon (i.e., arrow, spear, javelin, etc.)	
tempestās, tempestātis, f.	storm; season	3:05
templum, -ī, n.	temple	1:07
temptō, -āre, -āvī, -ātum	to try, to attempt	1:10
tempus, temporis, n.	time, opportunity; (in grammar) tense	1:17
tenāx, tenācis, adj.	holding on, tenacious	2:07
tendō, tendere, tetendī, tentum/tēnsum	to stretch, to strain	
tenēbrae, -ārum, f.	shadows, darkness	2:12
teneō, tenēre, tenuī, tentum	to hold	1:11
tenuō, -āre, -āvī, -ātum	to thin out, to lessen	2:12
tepidus, -a, -um, adj.	lukewarm	
ter, adv.	three times	
tergum, -ī, n.	back, backside	2:10
terra, -ae, f.	earth, land	1:04
terreō, terrēre, terruī, territum	to scare, to frighten	1:08
tertius decimus, -a, -um, adj.	thirteenth	
tertius, -a, -um, adj.	third	
tertius, -a, -um, adj.	third	
testimōnium, testimōnii, n.	testimony	
thesis, thesis, f.	proposal, thesis	
timeō, timēre, timuī	to be afraid, to fear	1:10/3:12
timidus, -a, -um, adj.	afraid	1:10
toga, -ae, f.	toga	1:11
togātus, -a, -um, adj.	wearing a toga	
tolerō, -āre, -āvī, -ātum	to bear, to endure, to tolerate, to sustain	3:07
tollō, tollere, sustulī, sublātum	to lift, to raise	2:13
torcular, torculāris, n. (i-stem)	a wine press, an oil press	3:05
tot, indec. adj.	so many	3:14
totidem, indec. adj.	that same amount	
totiēns, adv.	so often	3:10
tōtus, -a, -um, adj.	whole, entire	1:21/2:18
trādō, trādere, trādidī, trāditum	to hand over; to surrender	2:14
trahō, trahere, traxī, tractum	to drag, to draw	2:11
trāns, prep. (+ acc.)	across	1:11
trānseō, trānsīre, trānsiī, trānsitum	to go across, to pass over	

trecentēsimus, -a, -um, adj.	three hundredth	
trecentī, -ae, -a, adj.	three hundred	
trēcentī, indec. adj.	thirty	
tredecim, adj.	thirteen	
trēs, tria, adj.	three	1:22
trēs, tria, pl.adj.	three	1:22
tria	(*see* trēs)	
trīcēsimus, -a, -um, adj.	thirtieth	
trīgintā, adj.	thirty	
triplus, -a, -um, adj.	triple	
triumphus, -ī, m.	triumph, triumphal procession	1:26
Trōia, -ae, f.	Troy (a city-state in Asia Minor)	1:04
tū, tuī, pro.	you	1:19
tum, adv.	then	1:07
tunica, -ae, f.	tunic, long-sleeved garment	
turba, -ae, f.	crowd	2:13
turpis, turpe, adj.	unseemly, unsightly, ugly	2:18
turris, turris, f.	tower	2:12
tūtus, -a, -um, adj.	protected, safe	1:07
tuus, -a, -um, adj.	your, yours; your own	1:24/2:25
tyrannus, -ī, m.	tyrant, king	1:10
ubi, rel. adv. or conj.	where, when; inter. adv. where?	1:09/2:02
ūllus, -a, -um, adj.	any	1:21/2:18
ultimus, -a, -um, adj.	last; *ultimum* – the end	1:25
umbra, -ae, f.	shadow	2:06
umquam, adv.	ever, at any time	1:25/2:15
ūnā, adv.	together; together with; *ūnā cum* – together with	2:10
unda, -ae, f.	wave, water	2:22
unde, adv.	whence, from which place, from where	2:09
ūndecim, adj.	eleven	
ūndecimus, -a, -um, adj.	eleventh	
ūndecimus, -a, -um, numeric adj.	eleventh	
ūndēvīcēsimus, -a, -um, adj.	nineteenth	
ūndēvīgintī, adj.	nineteen	
undique, adv.	from/on all sides, from everywhere, everywhere	3:09
ūnifōrmis, -e, adj.	uniform	
ūniformiter, adv.	uniformly	
ūniversus, -a, -um, adj.	combined in one, whole, entire	2:27
ūnus, -a, -um, adj.	one	1:21
urbs, urbis, f.i.	city	1:14
urgeō, urgēre, ursī	to press, to push, to force, to drive	
ursus, -ī, m.	bear	2:06

ūsque, adv.	all the way, continuously; *ūsque ad* – unto, until, to the point of	2:22
ūsus, -ūs, m.	use, method	2:19
ut *or* utī, conj.	(with the ind.) as; when; (with the sub.) in order that, to	3:05
uter, utra, utrum, adj.	either, which (of two)	1:21/2:18
utī	(*see* ut)	
ūtilis, -e, adj.	useful	
ūtilitas, ūtilitātis, f.	good, usefulness, utility	2:09
utinam, adv.	would that!	
ūtor, ūtī, ūsus sum (+ abl.)	to use	2:26
utrimque (utrinque), adv.	from both sides, from each side	2:24
uxor, uxōris, f.	wife	1:10
vacca, -ae, f.	cow	
valeō, valēre, valuī, valitūrum	to be well; to be able; to be powerful	2:12
validus, -a, -um, adj.	well, strong, powerful, brave	1:08/2:22
vallēs, vallis, f.	valley	
vallum, -ī, n.	earthen wall, fortification	
vānitās, vānitātis, f.	emptiness, worthlessness	2:26
vānus, -a, -um, adj.	empty, void; useless	
vapor, vapōris, m.	steam, vapor, warmth	
vastō, -āre, -āvī, -ātum	to lay waste, to destroy	2:05
vectīgāl, vectīgālis, n	tax	2:23
vehemēns, vehementis, adj.	violent, impetuous	2:07
vehō, vehere, vexī, vectum	to carry, to convey	3:12
vel, conj.	or; *vel . . . vel* – either . . . or	2:15
vēlōcitās, vēlōcitātis, f.	velocity	
velut, adv.	as if, just as if	3:11
veluti	(*see* velut)	
vēndō, vēndere, vēndidī, vēnditum	to sell	1:23
venēnum, -ī, n.	poison	3:15
venia, -ae, f.	kindness, grace; forgiveness, pardon	2:15
veniō, venīre, vēnī, ventum	to come, to come back, to return	1:27
Venus, Veneris, f.	Venus (goddess of love)	
venustus, -a, -um, adj.	charming, delightful	3:13
verbum, -ī, n.	word; (in grammar) verb	1:18
vērē, adv.	truly	1:26
vereor, verērī, veritus sum	to fear, to be afraid	2:26/3:12
Vergilius, -ī, m.	Vergil (poet and author of the *Aeneid*)	
versus, -ūs, m.	line of poetry, verse	
vertō, vertere, vertī, versum	to turn	1:23/3:14
vērum, adv.	truthfully; (as a conj.) but	3:04
vērum, n.	true thing, truth	2:19

vērus, -a, -um, adj.	true	2:19
vester, vestra, vestrum, adj.	your (pl.)	2:25
vestīmentum, -ī, n.	garment; (pl.) clothes	
vestis, vestis, f.	clothing, garment	2:20
vetō, vetāre, vetuī, vetitum	to forbid, to prohibit	3:06
vetus, veteris, adj.	old, ancient	3:01
vīcēsimus, -a, -um, adj.	twentieth	
vīcēsimus, -a, -um; prīmus, -a, -um, adj.	twenty-first	
vīcīnus, -a, -um, adj.	neighboring, nearby; (as a noun) neighbor	1:18
victor, victōris, m.	victor, winner	
victōria, -ae, f.	victory	1:20
videō, vidēre, vīdī, vīsum	to see	1:08
vigil, vigilis, adj.	watchful, awake; (as a noun) watchman; (pl.) a fire brigade, firemen	1:24
vigilia, vigiliae, f.	a watching for the security of a place; sentinels, soldiers keeping watch	3:08
vīgintī ūnus, ūnus et vīgintī, adj.	twenty-one	
vīgintī, adj.	twenty	
vīgintī, indec. adj.	twenty	
vīlicus, -ī, m.	overseer of a villa	3:06
vīlis, vīle, adj.	cheap	1:23
villa, -ae, f.	farmhouse	1:13
vīnārius, -a, -um, adj.	of wine, for wine	3:05
vincō, vincere, vīcī, victum	to conquer	1:13
vīnum, -ī, n.	wine	
violēns, violentis, adj.	impetuous, vehement	
violentus, -a, -um, adj.	violent	
vir, virī, m.	man	1:06
virgō, virginis, f.	maiden	1:12
viridis, viride, adj.	green	
virīlis, -e, adj.	masculine	
virtūs, virtūtis, f.	manhood, courage; virtue	1:13
vīs, vīs, f.	force, power; (pl.) strength, troops, forces	2:18/3:01
vīsibilis, -e, adj.	visible	
vīsō, vīsere, vīsī, vīsum	to look at carefully, to contemplate	3:02
vīta, -ae, f.	life	3:07
vītālis, -e, adj.	vital, life-giving, alive	
vitium, vitiī, n.	vice	2:16
vītō, -āre, -āvī, -ātum	to avoid	3:08
vīvō, vīvere, vīxī, vīctum	to live	1:16
vīvus, -a, -um, adj.	living, alive	1:08
vix, adv.	scarcely	2:12
vocātīvus, -ī, m.	(in grammar) vocative case; *casus vocātīvus* – same meaning	

vocō, -āre, -āvī, -ātum	to call	1:03
volātus, -ūs, m.	flying	
Volcānus, -ī, m.	Vulcan (the fire god)	
volō, velle, voluī	to wish, to be willing, to want	1:21/2:10
volō, volāre, volāvī, volātum	to fly	
voltus, -ūs, m.	(*see* vultus)	
voluntās, voluntātis, f.	will, wish	1:29
voluptās, voluptātis, f.	pleasure	2:20
volvō, volvere, volvī, volūtum	to roll, to tumble	3:14
vōs, vestrī/vestrum, pro.	you (pl.)	
vōtum, -ī, n.	vow (lit., "a solemn promise to the gods")	2:04
vōx, vōcis, f.	sound, voice; (in grammar) voice	
vulgus, vulgī, n.	the crowd, the common people	2:10
vulnerātus, -a, -um, adj.	wounded, hurt	1:08
vulnerō, -āre, -āvī, -ātum	to wound	1:08
vultus, -ūs, m.	face, visage	1:28

Contributors

CHRISTOPHER R. SCHLECT

Christopher R. Schlect is a Fellow of History at New Saint Andrews College in Moscow, Idaho, and also teaches at Washington State University in Pullman, Washington. At both institutions he teaches introductory and advanced courses in classical, European, and US history. He also works in historical interpretation as a ranger for the National Park Service. He holds degrees in history from the University of Idaho (MA) and Washington State University (BA and PhD [ABD]). Schlect has earned numerous competitive fellowships in support of his ongoing research on American religion and the culture wars of the 1920s and '30s. He frequently lectures on topics related to classical education and church history. He is the author of *Critique of Modern Youth Ministry*, *The Christian Worldview and Apologetics*, and an official history of the Communion of Reformed Evangelical Churches. His articles have appeared in *Credenda/Agenda*, *Table Talk*, *Classis*, and the National Park Service's Getaway series. He has also contributed chapters to *Repairing the Ruins: The Classical and Christian Challenge to Modern Education* (Canon Press), the Omnibus series (Veritas Press), and the Latin Alive! series (Classical Academic Press). Schlect is a teaching elder at Trinity Reformed Church (CREC) in Moscow, Idaho. He and his wife, Brenda, have five children.

New Saint Andrews College: http://www.nsa.edu/

GRANT HORNER

Professor Grant Horner's academic specialty is the literature, theology, and philosophy of the Renaissance and Reformation, with primary concentration in Milton, Shakespeare, Erasmus, Luther, Calvin, and late sixteenth- and seventeenth-century intellectual and cultural history. His research and writing has focused on Christian humanism in the Reformation, particularly the complex relationship between developing Reformed thought and classical Graeco-Roman pagan mythology and philosophy. He has worked on the citation of classical Greek and Latin authorities by Renaissance writers, published on theology and the arts, and is actively researching and writing a full-length work on John Milton and John Calvin. His book *Meaning at the Movies* on film and theology (Crossway, 2010) was an Amazon bestseller and nominated for Book of the Year in Christianity and Culture by the Book Retailers Association.

Professor Horner has been with The Master's College since 1999, where he teaches courses on medieval and Renaissance literature, film studies, Shakespeare, Milton, John Calvin, drama, poetry and poetics, comedy, critical theory, Western art history, epic, classical Christian humanism, and classical Latin. Each year he teaches art history in Northern Italy for the AMBEX study-abroad program. He also serves as Chair of Humanities in the Rhetoric School at Trinity Classical Academy, the fastest growing classical school in the nation, where he designed the humanities curriculum.

The Master's College: http://www.masters.edu/academics/undergraduate/english/faculty.aspx

Professor Horner's Blog: http://profetcetera.tumblr.com/

ALDEN SMITH

Alden Smith is Professor of Classics at Baylor University. He studied as an undergraduate at Dickinson College and did his graduate work at Vermont (MA) and Penn (PhD), where he worked under Professor Joseph Farrell. Smith taught at Rutgers University, where he served as chair of classics for ten years. His main research area is Latin poetry, though he has also published on Pindar and on Greek epigraphy. He currently serves as associate dean in Baylor's Honors College.

Baylor University: http://www.baylor.edu/classics/

Selected Bibliography

Listed here is a select number of resources consulted during the writing of this book. This bibliography is by no means a complete record of all the works and sources consulted. Rather, it indicates the substance and range of reading upon which some of the concepts, information, and ideas presented in this text have been formed. It is our wish that it serve as a springboard for those who wish to further pursue the study and appreciation of the Latin language and those great masters who were instrumental in its evolution.

Burl, Aubrey. *Catullus: A Poet in the Rome of Julius Caesar*. New York: Carroll and Graf Publishers, 2004.

Califf, David J. *A Guide to Latin Meter and Verse Composition*. London: Anthem Press, 2002. Available at: <http://books.google.com/books?id=MTiwYDS4xPMC&printsec=frontcover&source=gbs_ge_summary_r&cad=0#v=onepage&q&f=false>.

Campbell, Gordon, and B.A. Wright, eds. *John Milton: The Complete Poems*. New York: E.P. Dutton & Company, 1980.

CELT: The Free Digital Humanities Resource for Irish history, literature and politics [online]. Available at: <http://celt.ucc.ie/index.html>.

Clough, Arthur Hugh, ed. *Plutarch's Lives: The Dryden Translation*. New York: The Modern Library, 2001.

Everitt, Anthony. *Cicero: The Life and Times of Rome's Greatest Politician*. New York: Random House Trade Paper Back, 2003.

Fairclough, H.R. *Vergil: Eclogues; Georgics; Aeneid, I–VI*. Cambridge, MA: Harvard University Press, MCMLXXVIII.

Gildersleeve, B.L., and G. Lodge. *Gildersleeve's Latin Grammar*. Wauconda, IL: Bolchazy-Carducci Publishers, Inc., 1997.

Glossa: A Latin Dictionary. Available at: <http://athirdway.com/glossa/>.

Greenough, J.B., G.L. Kittredge, A.A. Howard, Benji L. D'Ooge, Anne Mahoney, and J.H. Allen, eds. *Allen and Greenough's New Latin Grammar*. Essex, UK: Ginn & Company, 1916.

Harbottle, Thomas Benfield. *Dictionary of Quotations (Classical)*. London: S. Sonnenschein & Company, limited, 1906. Accessed July 25, 2012. Available at: <http://books.google.com/books?id=2rSZy0yVFm8C&printsec=frontcover&source=gbs_ge_summary_r&cad=0#v=onepage&q&f=false>.

Hooper, W.D., and H.B. Ash, trans. *Cato and Varro on Agriculture*. Cambridge, MA: Harvard University Press, 2006.

Johnson, Harold Whetstone. *The Private Lives of the Romans*. Honolulu, HI: University Press of the Pacific, 2002.

Kent, Roland G., trans. *Varro on the Latin Language.* Cambridge, MA: Harvard University Press, 2006.

The Latin Library. <http://www.thelatinlibrary.com>.

Lenormant, François and E. Chevallier. *A Manual of the Ancient History of the East: To the Commencement of the Median Wars, Volume 1.* Whitefish, MT: Kessinger Publishing Company, 2006.

Lewis, Charlton T., and Charles Short. *A Latin Dictionary: Founded on Andrews' Edition of Freund's Latin Dictionary.* Revised, enlarged, and in great part rewritten by Charlton T. Lewis and Charles Short. Oxford, Clarendon Press, 1879. Searchable format e-book. Available at: <http://perseus.uchicago.edu/Reference/lewisandshort.html#Source>.

"Magna Carta (Latin Original)." Accessed July 5, 2012. Available at: <http://www.magnacartaplus.org/magnacarta/latin.htm>.

Miller, Frank Justus, trans. *Ovid: Metamorphoses.* Cambridge, MA: Harvard University Press, 1994.

Moldenke, Charles Edward. *New York Obelisk, Cleopatra's Needle.* A.D.F. and Co., 1891. Available at: <http://books.google.ca/books?id=78I2AAAAMAAJ&printsec=frontcover&source=gbs_ge_summary_r&cad=0#v=onepage&q&f=false>.

Naville, Edouard. *Bubastis (1887–1889).* Kegan Paul, Trench, Trubner and Co., 1891. Available at: <http://books.google.ca/books?id=zHQTAAAAYAAJ&printsec=frontcover&dq=bubastis&hl=en&sa=X&ei=kTf2T4qNGJS-0QHht_CJBw&ved=0CDMQ6AEwAA#v=onepage&q=bubastis&f=false>.

Oxford Classical Dictionary. 3rd ed. New York: Oxford University Press, 1996.

Rawson, Elizabeth. *Cicero: A Portrait.* London: Bristol Classical Press, 2009.

Rose, H.J. *A Handbook of Latin Literature from the Earliest Times to the Death of St. Augustine.* Wauconda, IL: Bolchazy-Carducci Publishers, Inc., 1966.

Rutherford, Brett. "Preface: Raven and Dove." *In Last Flowers: The Romance and Poetry of Edgar Allen Poe and Sarah Helen Whitman.* Accessed July 25, 2012. Available at: <http://poetspress.org/poepref2.html>."Selected Works of Martin Luther." *Project Wittenberg.* Revised April 7, 2006. Available at: <http://www.iclnet.org/pub/resources/text/wittenberg/wittenberg-luther.html#sw-95>.

Tennyson, Alfred Lord. *The Works of Alfred, Lord Tennyson.* London: Macmillan, 1908.

Tennyson, Alfred Baron. *The Works of Tennyson.* London: MacMillan, 1913.

Thayer, Bill. *Pliny the Elder: The Natural History* [online]. Available at: <http://penelope.uchicago.edu/Thayer/E/Roman/Texts/Pliny_the_Elder/home.html>.

Ticknor, Caroline. *Poe's Helen.* New York: C. Scribner's Sons, 1916. Accessed July 25, 2012. Available at <http://books.google.com/books?id=vnBbAAAAMAAJ&printsec=frontcover&source=gbs_ge_summary_r&cad=0#v=onepage&q&f=false>.

Warmington, E.H. *Remains of Old Latin*, vol. 2. Cambridge, MA: Harvard University Press, 1936, rpt. 1967.

Wikipedia: The Free Encyclopedia. Available at: <http://www.wikipedia.org/>.

Appendix A:
Pronunciation Guide
- Roman Alphabet
- Phonics for Latin (pronunciation of consonants and vowels)
- Syllabication
- Accent

ROMAN ALPHABET

The earliest writings we possess in the Latin alphabet date from the sixth century BC. The Latin alphabet was adapted primarily from that of the Etruscans, a people who inhabited central Italy prior to the Romans, and consisted initially of only twenty letters:

A B C D E F G H I L M N O P Q R S T V X

The letters *k*, *y*, and *z* were later added from the Greek alphabet when Romans wanted to adapt Greek words to the Latin language. The letters *j*, *u*, and *w* were added at a much later stage, also for the purposes of adapting other languages to Latin. The letter *j* became the consonant form of *i*, *u* is the vowel form of *v*, and *w* was introduced as a "double-u" (or "double-v") to make a clear distinction between the sounds we know today as *v* and *w*. With these additions, the Latin alphabet, also called the Roman alphabet, has come to be the most widely used alphabetic writing system in the world.

PHONICS

In Latin, each consonant produces only one sound when on its own. Most are identical to our modern pronunciation, but there are a few variations that you should learn. Take a look at the following table:

CONSONANT	PHONETIC RULE	LATIN EXAMPLE
c	always hard as in **c**at, never soft as in **c**ent.	cantō cēna
g	always hard as in **g**oat, never soft as in **g**entle.	glōria genus
i (j)	as a consonant appearing before a vowel, pronounce as the *y* in **y**ellow.	iam Iuppiter
r	often rolled as in Spanish or Italian	rēctus

s	always like the *s* in sit, never like the *z* sound in please.	semper senātus
t	always like the *t* in table, never like the *sh* sound in nation.	teneō ratiō
v	sounds like the *w* in wine	vīnum victōria
x	sounds like the *ks* in extract, not the *gz* in exert.	nox rēx

In English, when two consonants appear together, their sound can change in a myriad of different ways. Take for instance these common pairing of *th*:

then   theatre   thyme

On most occasions that two consonants appear together in Latin, you will pronounce each one with its individual sound as prescribed above. There are a few consonant blends, but unlike English, each blend has one assigned sound that never varies.

CONSONANT BLEND	PHONETIC RULE	LATIN EXAMPLE
bs, bt	*b* sounds like *p*	urbs (urps) obtineō (op-tin-ey-oh)
gu, qu	sounds like **gw**, **qw** as in pen**gu**in and **qu**art (the *u* is considered a consonant here, not a vowel)	lingua quod equus
ch	each sound pronounced individually like **ch**orus, not like ba**ch**elor	charta Chaos
th	each sound pronounced individually like goa**th**erd, not like **th**en or **th**eatre.	thymum theātrum
ph	pronounced like *f* as in **ph**iloso**ph**y	philosophia Orpheus
double consonants	pronounced by taking approximately twice as long to say as a single consonant	ecce (ec-ce) puella (puel-la)

Vowels in Latin consist of the typical *a, e, i, o,* and *u*. They are either long or short by nature. Thus each vowel has two and only two sounds. Unlike English, vowels in Latin that are long by nature are usually clearly marked by macrons (from the Greek word *makros*, meaning "long"). However, as you progress in your study of Latin, you will read from texts that do not have macrons; this lack of macrons will be especially the rule in books printed in the United Kingdom. You will also notice that certain quotations in this book do not employ macrons.

SHORT	LATIN EXAMPLE	LONG	LATIN EXAMPLE
a as in alike	casa	*ā* as in father	stāre
e as in pet	memoria	*ē* as in they	cēna
i as in pit	inter	*ī* as in machine	īre
o as in pot	bonus	*ō* as in hose	errō
u as in put	Marcus	*ū* as in rude	lūdus

Diphthongs are two vowels blended together to create one sound. Latin has only six diphthongs.

Diphthong	Pronunciation	Latin Example
ae	sounds like the *ai* in **ai**sle	fēminae, aequus
au	sounds like the *ou* in **ou**t	laudō, auctor
ei	sounds like the *eigh* in w**eigh**	deinde
eu	pronounced *eh-oo*	heu
oe	sounds like the *oi* in c**oi**l	proelium
ui	pronounced *oo-ee* as in **twee**t	huic, cui

The final version of the alphabet in classical Latin is as follows:

Uppercase: A B C D E F G H I K L M N O P Q R S T U/V X Y Z

Lowercase: a b c d e f g h i k l m n o p q r s t u/v x z

The various sounds produced by the consonants and vowels in Latin total forty different phonetic sounds. Compare this to the seventy-two sounds produced by the English language, and you can begin to see why Latin could be considered the easier of the two languages to learn. However, there is still more to consider in learning how to pronounce words correctly.

Syllabication

The term "syllable" is used to refer to a unit of a word that consists of a single, uninterrupted sound formed by a vowel, diphthong, consonant, or by a consonant-vowel combination. **Syllabication** is the act of dividing a word in order to reveal its individual syllables. With English this can be tricky because there are often letters that remain silent. However, in Latin there are no completely silent letters, so any given Latin word will have as many syllables as it has vowels or diphthongs. The rules of syllabication indicate that words are to be divided as follows:

1. Between two like consonants:
   pu-el-la   ter-ra

2. Between the last of two or more different consonants:
   ar-ma   temp-tō
   (but phi-lo-so-phi-a because, remember, *ph* is considered a single consonant)

3. Between two vowels or a vowel and a diphthong (never divide a diphthong):
   Cha-os   proe-li-um

4. Before a single consonant:
   me-mo-ri-a   fē-mi-nae

Caveat Discipulus: As with most rules, there are sometimes exceptions to the syllabication rules just mentioned. The most common exception occurs with prefixes. A division will always occur between the prefix and the root word. The root word will always divide as if the prefix was never there. Consider the following example:

creō = cre-ō   prō-cre-ō

Notice how the division in the compound verb occurs between the prefix and the root word. Notice also that the *cr* is still not divided when the prefix is added.

Special Rules:

5. Before a stop + liquid combination, except if it is caused by the addition of a prefix to the word:
   pu-**bli**-ca (but **ad-lā**-tus according to the exception)

6. After the letter *x*. Though it is technically two consonants, it is indivisible in writing, so we divide after it:
   ex-i-ti-um   ex-e-ō

7. Before *s* + a stop, if the *s* is preceded by a consonant:
   mōn-stro   ad-scrip-tum

Each syllable has a characteristic called **quantity**. The quantity of a syllable is its length—how much time it takes to pronounce or say that syllable. A long syllable has twice the quantity or length of a short syllable. It is easy to tell the quantity of syllables in Latin and it will be important to know how to do so in order to properly accent words. Syllables are long when they have:

1. a long vowel (marked by a macron);

2. a diphthong; or

3. a short vowel followed by two consonants or a double consonant (*x* or *z*), except if there are two consonants that consist of a stop + a liquid (e.g., the second syllable of *a-la-cris* stays short before the *cr*).

Caveat Discipulus: The only exception for this two-consonant rule is the letter *h*. This letter is often reduced to an aspiration, barely audible.

Otherwise, syllables are short. The first two rules are said to make a syllable long by nature because the vowel sound is naturally long. The last rule is said to make a syllable long by position, because the length depends on the placement of the vowel within that word. Recognizing the length of a syllable becomes particularly important when reading poetry.

Caveat Discipulus: The quantity of the syllable does not change the length of the vowel. You should still pronounce short vowels according to the phonetic rules you have just learned. The quantity of the syllable will affect how you accent the words.

Accent

Accent is the vocal emphasis placed on a particular syllable of a word. In Latin, the accent can only fall on one of the last three syllables of a word. Each one of these syllables has a name. The last syllable is referred to as the **ultima**, meaning "last" in Latin. The next-to-last syllable is called the **penult** (from *paene ultima*, meaning "almost last"). The syllable third from the end is known as the **antepenult** (from *ante paene ultima*, which means "before the almost last"). Which one of these syllables carries the accent depends on the length of the syllables.

The rules for accent are as follows:

1. In words of two syllables, always accent the penult or first syllable: **aúc-tōr**.

2. In words of more than two syllables, accent the penult (next-to-last syllable) when it is long: **for-tú-na**.

3. Otherwise, accent the antepenult (third-to-last syllable): **fé-mi-na**.

4. The ultima will never carry the accent unless it is a one-syllable word: **nóx**.

Hint: Think in terms of the last syllable (the ultima) having a gravitational pull. If it is long, the "gravity" pulls the accent close to it. If it is short, then there is less gravity, as on the moon, and the accent floats away to the third position (antepenult). There is, however, an invisible force field on the other side of the antepenult, so the accent cannot float past that syllable.

Appendix B:
Reference Charts

Nouns

FIRST DECLENSION, FEMININE AND MASCULINE (*LA1*, Ch. 4; LA2, Ch. 2; LA3, Ch. 1)

Nota Bene: The great majority of first declension nouns are feminine. The few nouns that are masculine, such as those that denote jobs usually done by men in the ancient world, have the same endings as the feminine nouns.

Case	1st Decl. Feminine	Fēmina, Fēminae
Nom.	-a	fēmina
Gen.	-ae	fēminae
Dat.	-ae	fēminae
Acc.	-am	fēminam
Abl.	-ā	fēminā
Voc.	-a	fēmina
Nom.	-ae	fēminae
Gen.	-ārum	fēminārum
Dat.	-īs	fēminīs
Acc.	-ās	fēminās
Abl.	-īs	fēminīs
Voc.	-ae	fēminae

SECOND DECLENSION (*LA1*, Ch. 6; *LA2*, Ch. 2; *LA3*, Ch. 1)

Case	2nd Decl. Masculine	Servus, Servī	Ager, Agrī	2nd Decl. Neuter	Dōnum, Dōnī
Nom.	-us, -r	servus	ager	-um	dōnum
Gen.	-ī	servī	agrī	-ī	dōnī
Dat.	-ō	servō	agrō	-ō	dōnō
Acc.	-um	servum	agrum	-um	dōnum
Abl.	-ō	servō	agrō	-ō	dōnō
Voc.	-e, -r	serve	ager	-um	dōnum
Nom.	-ī	servī	agrī	-a	dōna
Gen.	-ōrum	servōrum	agrōrum	-ōrum	dōnōrum
Dat.	-īs	servīs	agrīs	-īs	dōn<līs
Acc.	-ōs	servōs	agrōs	-a	dōna
Abl.	-īs	servīs	agrīs	-īs	dōnīs
Voc.	-ī	servī	agrī	-a	dōna

THIRD DECLENSION (*LA1*, Ch. 10; *LA2*, Ch. 3; *LA3*, Ch. 1)

Case	3rd Decl. Masculine/Feminine	Regular Rēx, Rēgis	I-stem Urbs, Urbis	3rd Decl. Neuter	Regular Iter, Itineris	I-stem Mare, Maris
Nom.	*	rēx	urbs	*	iter	mare
Gen.	-is	rēgis	urbis	-is	itineris	maris
Dat.	-ī	rēgī	urbī	-ī	itinerī	marī
Acc.	-em	rēgem	urbem	*	iter	mare
Abl.	-e	rēge	urbe	-e (-ī)	itinere	marī
Voc.	*	rēx	urbs	*	iter	mare
Nom.	-ēs	rēgēs	urbēs	-a (-ia)	itinera	maria
Gen.	-um (-ium)	rēgum	urbium	-um (-ium)	itinerum	marium
Dat.	-ibus	rēgibus	urbibus	-ibus	itineribus	maribus
Acc.	-ēs	rēgēs	urbēs	-a (-ia)	itinera	maria
Abl.	-ibus	rēgibus	urbibus	-ibus	itineribus	maribus
Voc.	-ēs	rēgēs	urbēs	-a (-ia)	itinera	maria

Nota Bene: The third declension shows both regular and i-stem endings. Where the i-stem differs from the regular ending, it is enclosed in parentheses.

FOURTH DECLENSION (*LA1*, Ch. 28; *LA2*, Ch. 4; *LA3*, Ch. 1)*

Case	4th Decl. Masculine/Feminine	Frūctus, Frūctūs	4th Decl. Neuter	Genū, Genūs
Nom.	-us	frūctus	-ū	genū
Gen.	-ūs	frūctūs	-ūs	genūs
Dat.	-uī	frūctuī	-ū	genū
Acc.	-um	frūctum	-ū	genū
Abl.	-ū	frūctū	-ū	genū
Voc.	-us	frūctus	-ū	genū
Nom.	-ūs	frūctūs	-ua	genua
Gen.	-uum	frūctuum	-uum	genuum
Dat.	-ibus	frūctibus	-ibus	genibus
Acc.	-ūs	frūctūs	-ua	genua
Abl.	-ibus	frūctibus	-ibus	genibus
Voc.	-ūs	frūctūs	-ua	genua

*The locative case appears in the fourth declension only for the noun *domus*.

FIFTH DECLENSION (*LA1*, Ch. 29; *LA2*, Ch. 5; *LA3*, Ch. 1)

Case	5th Decl. Masculine/Feminine	Vowel Stem Diēs, Diēī	Consonant Stem Fidēs, Fideī
Nom.	-ēs	diēs	fidēs
Gen.	-ēī, -eī	diēī	fideī
Dat.	-ēī, -eī	diēī	fideī
Acc.	-em	diem	fidem
Abl.	-ē	diē	fidē
Voc.	-ēs	diēs	fidēs
Nom.	-ēs	diēs	fidēs
Gen.	-ērum	diērum	fidērum
Dat.	-ēbus	diēbus	fidēbus
Acc.	-ēs	diēs	fidēs
Abl.	-ēbus	diēbus	fidēbus
Voc.	-ēs	diēs	fidēs

LOCATIVE CASE FOR ALL DECLENSIONS (*LA2*, Ch. 5)

Reminder: The locative case indicates *place where* for a select group of nouns only: the names of cities, towns, small islands in the Mediterranean, and the nouns *domus*, *humus*, and *rūs*. (Remember, the locative in the first and second declension singular is the same as the genitive case; elsewhere it is the same as the ablative case.)

Declension	Singular	Plural
First	-ae	-īs
Second	-ī	-īs
Third	-ī or -e	-ibus
Fourth	*domī**	———
Fifth	-ē	———

Domus is the only fourth declension noun that appears in the locative case.

IRREGULAR NOUN VĪS, VĪS (*LA2*, Ch. 18; *LA3*, Ch. 1)

Case	Singular	Plural
Nom.	vīs	vīrēs
Gen.	vīs	vīrium
Dat.	vī	vīribus
Acc.	vim	vīrēs/vīrīs
Abl.	vī	vīribus
Voc.	vīs	vīrēs
Loc.	———	———

Adjectives

FIRST & SECOND DECLENSION, POSITIVE FORM (*LA2*, Ch. 6)

Case	Masculine	Feminine	Neuter
Nom.	bonus	bona	bonum
Gen.	bonī	bonae	bonī
Dat.	bonō	bonae	bonō
Acc.	bonum	bonam	bonum
Abl.	bonō	bonā	bonō
Nom.	bonī	bonae	bona
Gen.	bonōrum	bonārum	bonōrum
Dat.	bonīs	bonīs	bonīs
Acc.	bonōs	bonās	bona
Abl.	bonīs	bonīs	bonīs

THIRD DECLENSION, POSITIVE FORM (*LA1*, Ch. 15)

THREE TERMINATION: **celer, celeris, celere**

Case	Masculine	Feminine	Neuter
Nom.	celer	celeris	celere
Gen.	celeris	celeris	celeris
Dat.	celerī	celerī	celerī
Acc.	celerem	celerem	celere
Abl.	celerī	celerī	celerī
Nom.	celerēs	celerēs	celeria
Gen.	celerium	celerium	celerium
Dat.	celeribus	celeribus	celeribus
Acc.	celerēs	celerēs	celeria
Abl.	celeribus	celeribus	celeribus

TWO TERMINATION: **omnis, omne**

Case	Masculine/Feminine	Neuter
Nom.	omnis	omne
Gen.	omnis	omnis
Dat.	omnī	omnī
Acc.	omnem	omne
Abl.	omnī	omnī
Nom.	omnēs	omnia
Gen.	omnium	omnium
Dat.	omnibus	omnibus
Acc.	omnēs	omnia
Abl.	omnibus	omnibus

ONE TERMINATION: **ingēns, ingentis**

Case	Masculine/Feminine	Neuter
Nom.	ingēns	ingēns
Gen.	ingentis	ingentis
Dat.	ingentī	ingentī
Acc.	ingentem	ingēns
Abl.	ingentī	ingentī
Nom.	ingentēs	ingentia
Gen.	ingentium	ingentium
Dat.	ingentibus	ingentibus
Acc.	ingentēs	ingentia
Abl.	ingentibus	ingentibus

SPECIAL -ĪUS ADJECTIVES (*LA1*, Ch. 21; *LA2*, Ch. 18)

These adjectives are different from most others in that the genitive singular has *-ius* and the dative singular has *-i*. Compare the pronouns *ipse* and *ille* for other examples.

Case	Masculine	Feminine	Neuter
Nom.	ūllus	ūlla	ūllum
Gen.	**ūllīus**	**ūllīus**	**ūllīus**
Dat.	**ūllī**	**ūllī**	**ūllī**
Acc.	ūllum	ūllam	ūllum
Abl.	ūllō	ūllā	ūllō

Case	Masculine	Feminine	Neuter
Nom.	ūllī	ūllae	ūlla
Gen.	ūllōrum	ūllārum	ūllōrum
Dat.	ūllīs	ūllīs	ūllīs
Acc.	ūllōs	ūllās	ūlla
Abl.	ūllīs	ūllīs	ūllīs

COMPARATIVE FORMS (*LA2*, Ch. 6; *LA3*, Ch. 9)*

Case	Masculine/Feminine	Neuter
Nom.	laetior	laetius
Gen.	laetiōris	laetiōris
Dat.	laetiōrī	laetiōrī
Acc.	laetiōrem	laetius
Abl.	laetiōre	laetiōre

Case	Masculine/Feminine	Neuter
Nom.	laetiōrēs	laetiōra
Gen.	laetiōrum	laetiōrum
Dat.	laetiōribus	laetiōribus
Acc.	laetiōrēs	laetiōra
Abl.	laetiōribus	laetiōribus

*Notice that unlike other third declension adjectives, comparatives are *not* i-stem.

SUPERLATIVE FORMS (*LA2*, Ch. 6; *LA3*, Ch. 4)

Case	Masculine	Feminine	Neuter
Nom.	brevissimus	brevissima	brevissimum
Gen.	brevissimī	brevissimae	brevissimī
Dat.	brevissimō	brevissimae	brevissimō
Acc.	brevissimum	brevissimam	brevissimum
Abl.	brevissimō	brevissimā	brevissimō

Case	Masculine	Feminine	Neuter
Nom.	brevissimī	brevissimae	brevissima
Gen.	brevissimōrum	brevissimārum	brevissimōrum
Dat.	brevissimīs	brevissimīs	brevissimīs
Acc.	brevissimōs	brevissimās	brevissima
Abl.	brevissimīs	brevissimīs	brevissimīs

IRREGULAR COMPARATIVE AND SUPERLATIVE FORMS OF ADJECTIVES AND ADVERBS (*LA2*, Ch. 8)

Positive	Comparative	Superlative
bonus (good) bene (well)	melior (better) melius, potius	optimus (best) optimē
malus (bad) male	pēior (worse) pēius	pessimus (worst) pessimē
magnus (big) magnopere	māior (bigger) māius	maximus (biggest) maximē
parvus (small) parum	minor (smaller) minus	minimus (smallest) minimē
multus (many, much) multum	plūs,* plūris (gen.) (more)	plūrimus (most) plūrimē
superus (upper)	superior (higher) superius	summus or suprēmus (highest) summē or suprēmē

*The word *plūs* is not an adjective in the singular but is a neuter noun that takes a partitive genitive. It may, however, act as an adjective in the plural. In either case, it declines as the third declension: sing. n. *plūs*; plur. m/f. *plūrēs*; and neut. *plūra*, etc.

Numbers

(*LA1*, Ch. 22)

Numerals	Cardinal	Ordinal
I	ūnus, ūna, ūnum	prīmus, -a, -um
II	duo, duae, duo	secundus, -a, -um
III	trēs, tria	tertius, -a, -um
IV or IIII	quattuor	quārtus, -a, -um
V	quīnque	quīntus, -a, -um
VI	sex	sextus, -a, -um
VII	septem	septimus, -a, -um
VIII	octō	octāvus, -a, -um
IX	novem	nōnus, -a, -um
X	decem	decimus, -a, -um
XI	ūndecim	ūndecimus, -a, -um
XII	duodecim	duodecimus, -a, -um
XIII	tredecim	tertius decimus, -a, -um
XIV	quattuordecim	quārtus decimus, -a, -um
XV	quīndecim	quīntus decimus, -a, -um
XVI	sēdecim	sextus decimus, -a, -um
XVII	septendecim	septimus decimus, -a, -um
XVIII	duodēvīgintī	duodēvīcēsimus, -a, -um
XIX	ūndēvīgintī	ūndēvīcēsimus, -a, -um

XX	vīgintī	vīcēsimus, -a, -um
XXI	vīgintī ūnus, ūnus et vīgintī	vīcēsimus, -a, -um; prīmus, -a, -um
XXX	trīgintā	trīcēsimus, -a, -um
XXXX or XL	quadrāgintā	quadrāgēsimus, -a, -um
L	quīnquāgintā	quīnquāgēsimus, -a, -um
LX	sexāgintā	sexāgēsimus, -a, -um
LXX	septuāgintā	septuāgēsimus, -a, -um
LXXX	octōgintā	octōgēsimus, -a, -um
LXXXX or XC	nōnāgintā	nōnāgēsimus, -a, -um
C	centum	centēsimus, -a, -um
CI	centum ūnus, -a, -um	centēsimus, -a, -um; prīmus, -a, -um
CC	ducentī, -ae, -a	duocentēsimus, -a, -um
CCC	trecentī, -ae, -a	trecentēsimus, -a, -um
CCCC	quadringentī, -ae, -a	quadringentēsimus, -a, -um
D	quīngentī, -ae, -a	quīngentēsimus, -a, -um
DC	sescentī, -ae, -a	sescentēsimus, -a, -um
DCC	septingentī, -ae, -a	septingentēsimus, -a, -um
DCCC	octingentī, -ae, -a	octingentēsimus, -a, -um
DCCCC	nōngentī, -ae, -a	nōngentēsimus, -a, -um
M	mīlle	mīllēsimus, -a, -um
MM	duo mīlia	bis mīllēsimus, -a, -um

Cardinal numbers 4 through 100 do not decline. Numbers 200 and greater decline like first and second declension adjectives. The number *ūnus* declines as *ūllus* and the other special *-ius* adjectives. The numbers *duo* and *trēs* decline as follows:

DUO: TWO

Case	Masculine	Feminine	Neuter
Nom.	duo	duae	duo
Gen.	duōrum	duārum	duōrum
Dat.	duōbus	duābus	duōbus
Acc.	duōs	duās	duo
Abl.	duōbus	duābus	duōbus

TRĒS: THREE

Case	Masculine/Feminine	Neuter
Nom.	trēs	tria
Gen.	trium	trium
Dat.	tribus	tribus
Acc.	trēs	tria
Abl.	tribus	tribus

Pronouns

DEMONSTRATIVE PRONOUNS: ILLE, ILLA, ILLUD (THAT, THOSE) (*LA1*, Ch. 20)

Case	Masculine	Feminine	Neuter
Nom.	ille	illa	illud
Gen.	illīus	illīus	illīus
Dat.	illī	illī	illī
Acc.	illum	illam	illud
Abl.	illō	illā	illō

Case	Masculine	Feminine	Neuter
Nom.	illī	illae	illa
Gen.	illōrum	illārum	illōrum
Dat.	illīs	illīs	illīs
Acc.	illōs	illās	illa
Abl.	illīs	illīs	illīs

The word *iste* declines the same as *ille*.

DEMONSTRATIVE PRONOUNS: HIC, HAEC, HOC (THIS, THESE) (*LA1*, Ch. 20)

Case	Masculine	Feminine	Neuter
Nom.	hic	haec	hoc
Gen.	hūius	hūius	hūius
Dat.	huic	huic	huic
Acc.	hunc	hanc	hoc
Abl.	hōc	hāc	hōc

Case	Masculine	Feminine	Neuter
Nom.	hī	hae	haec
Gen.	hōrum	hārum	hōrum
Dat.	hīs	hīs	hīs
Acc.	hōs	hās	haec
Abl.	hīs	hīs	hīs

DEMONSTRATIVE PRONOUNS: IS, EA, ID (*LA1*, Ch. 19)

This may be a demonstrative pronoun meaning "that" or a personal pronoun meaning "he," "she," or "it."

Case	Masculine	Feminine	Neuter
Nom.	is	ea	id
Gen.	ēius	ēius	ēius
Dat.	eī	eī	eī
Acc.	eum	eam	id
Abl.	eō	eā	eō

Case	Masculine	Feminine	Neuter
Nom.	eī	eae	ea
Gen.	eōrum	eārum	eōrum
Dat.	eīs	eīs	eīs
Acc.	eōs	eās	ea
Abl.	eīs	eīs	eīs

DEMONSTRATIVE PRONOUN: ĪDEM, EADEM, IDEM (*LA2*, Ch. 24)

Case	Masculine	Feminine	Neuter
Nom.	īdem	eadem	idem
Gen.	ēiusdem	ēiusdem	ēiusdem
Dat.	eīdem	eīdem	eīdem
Acc.	eundem	eandem	idem
Abl.	eōdem	eādem	eōdem

Case	Masculine	Feminine	Neuter
Nom.	eīdem	eaedem	eadem
Gen.	eōrundem	eārundem	eōrundem
Dat.	eīsdem	eīsdem	eīsdem
Acc.	eōsdem	eāsdem	eadem
Abl.	eīsdem	eīsdem	eīsdem

INTENSIVE PRONOUN: IPSE, IPSA, IPSUM (*LA2*, Ch. 24)

Case	Masculine	Feminine	Neuter
Nom.	ipse	ipsa	ipsum
Gen.	ipsīus	ipsīus	ipsīus
Dat.	ipsī	ipsī	ipsī
Acc.	ipsum	ipsam	ipsum
Abl.	ipsō	ipsā	ipsō

Case	Masculine	Feminine	Neuter
Nom.	ipsī	ipsae	ipsa
Gen.	ipsōrum	ipsārum	ipsōrum
Dat.	ipsīs	ipsīs	ipsīs
Acc.	ipsōs	ipsās	ipsa
Abl.	ipsīs	ipsīs	ipsīs

INDEFINITE ADJECTIVE/PRONOUN: QUĪDAM, QUAEDAM, QUODDAM (*LA2*, Ch. 24)

Case	Masculine	Feminine	Neuter
Nom.	quīdam/quiddam	quaedam	quoddam/quiddam*
Gen.	cūiusdam	cūiusdam	cūiusdam
Dat.	cuidam	cuidam	cuidam
Acc.	quendam	quandam	quoddam/quiddam*
Abl.	quōdam	quādam	quōdam

Case	Masculine	Feminine	Neuter
Nom.	quīdam	quaedam	quaedam
Gen.	quōrundam	quārundam	quōrundam
Dat.	quibusdam	quibusdam	quibusdam
Acc.	quōsdam	quāsdam	quaedam
Abl.	quibusdam	quibusdam	quibusdam

*Remember that if used as a pronoun the neuter should be *quiddam* instead of *quīdam* or *quoddam*.

PERSONAL PRONOUNS: (*LA1*, Ch. 19)

Case	First Person	Second Person
Nom.	ego	tū
Gen.	meī	tuī
Dat.	mihi	tibi
Acc.	mē	tē
Abl.	mē	tē

Case	First Person	Second Person
Nom.	nōs	vōs
Gen.	nostrī, nostrum	vestrī, vestrum
Dat.	nōbīs	vōbīs
Acc.	nōs	vōs
Abl.	nōbīs	vōbīs

REFLEXIVE PRONOUNS: MYSELF, YOURSELF, HIMSELF, ETC. (*LA2*, Ch. 25)

Case	First Person	Second Person	Third Person
Gen.	meī	tuī	suī
Dat.	mihi	tibi	sibi
Acc.	mē	tē	sē*
Abl.	mē	tē	sē*

Case	First Person	Second Person	Third Person
Gen.	nostrī	vestrī	suī
Dat.	nōbīs	vōbīs	sibi
Acc.	nōs	vōs	sē*
Abl.	nōbīs	vōbīs	sē*

*Note: *Sēsē* sometimes appears instead of *sē* for emphasis, but the meaning remains the same.

RELATIVE PRONOUN: WHO, WHICH (*LA2*, Ch. 16)

Case	Masculine	Feminine	Neuter
Nom.	quī	quae	quod
Gen.	cūius	cūius	cūius
Dat.	cui	cui	cui
Acc.	quem	quam	quod
Abl.	quō	quā	quō

Case	Masculine	Feminine	Neuter
Nom.	quī	quae	quae
Gen.	quōrum	quārum	quōrum
Dat.	quibus	quibus	quibus
Acc.	quōs	quās	quae
Abl.	quibus	quibus	quibus

INTERROGATIVE PRONOUN: WHO, WHAT (*LA2*, Ch. 17)

Singular*

Case	Masculine/Feminine	Neuter
Nom.	quis	quid
Gen.	cūius	cūius
Dat.	cui	cui
Acc.	quem	quid
Abl.	quō	quō

*The plural forms are the same as those of the relative pronoun.

Verbs: Regular Verbs

First Conjugation: amō, amāre, amāvī, amātus

Second Conjugation: moneō, monēre, monuī, monitum

Third Conjugation: mittō, mittere, mīsī, missus

Third *-io* Conjugation: capiō, capere, cēpī, captus

Fourth Conjugation: audiō, audīre, audīvī, audītus

IMPERATIVE MOOD: PRESENT TENSE (*LA1*, Ch. 16, 21; *LA2*, Ch. 10)

1st Conj.	2nd Conj.	3rd Conj.	3rd *-io* Conj.	4th Conj.
Positive Imperative, Present Tense				
amā	monē	mitte	cape	audī
amāte	monēte	mittite	capite	audīte
Negative Imperative, Present Tense				
nolī amāre	nolī monēre	nolī mittere	nolī capere	nolī audīre
nolīte amāre	nolīte monēre	nolīte mittere	nolīte capere	nolīte audīre

IMPERATIVE MOOD: FUTURE TENSE (*LA3*, Ch. 7)

1st Conj.	2nd Conj.	3rd Conj.	3rd *-io* Conj.	4th Conj.
Positive Imperative, Future Tense, Second Person, Active Voice				
amātō	monētō	mittitō	capitō	audītō
amātōte	monētōte	mittitōte	capitōte	audītōte
Positive Imperative, Future Tense, Third Person, Active Voice				
amātō	monētō	mittitō	capitō	audītō
amantō	monentō	mittuntō	capiuntō	audiuntō

Nota Bene: For a negative future imperative, use the *nē* plus the positive future imperative; e. g., *nē amātō* (don't love).

INDICATIVE MOOD: ACTIVE VOICE

Present Tense: I love, I am loving, I do love (*LA1*, Ch. 2, 8, 11, 16, 27)

1st Conj.	2nd Conj.	3rd Conj.	3rd *-io* Conj.	4th Conj.
amō	moneō	mittō	capiō	audiō
amās	monēs	mittis	capis	audīs
amat	monet	mittit	capit	audit
amāmus	monēmus	mittimus	capimus	audīmus
amātis	monētis	mittitis	capitis	audītis
amant	monent	mittunt	capiunt	audiunt

SUBJUNCTIVE MOOD: ACTIVE VOICE

Present Tense: I would love, I may love (*LA3*, Ch. 4)

1st Conj.	2nd Conj.	3rd Conj.	3rd *-io* Conj.	4th Conj.
amem	moneam	mittam	capiam	audiam
amēs	moneās	mittās	capiās	audiās
amet	moneat	mittat	capiat	audiat
amēmus	moneāmus	mittāmus	capiāmus	audiāmus
amētis	moneātis	mittātis	capiātis	audiātis
ament	moneant	mittant	capiant	audiant

Indicative Mood: Active Voice

Imperfect Tense: I was holding (*LA1*, Ch. 3, 8, 13, 27; *LA3*, Ch. 2)

1st Conj.	2nd Conj.	3rd Conj.	3rd *-io* Conj.	4th Conj.
amābam	monēbam	mittēbam	capiēbam	audiēbam
amābās	monēbās	mittēbās	capiēbās	audiēbās
amābat	monēbat	mittēbat	capiēbat	audiēbat
amābāmus	monēbāmus	mittēbāmus	capiēbāmus	audiēbāmus
amābātis	monēbātis	mittēbātis	capiēbātis	audiēbātis
amābant	monēbant	mittēbant	capiēbant	audiēbant

Subjunctive Mood: Active Voice

Imperfect Tense: I would be holding, I might hold (*LA3*, Ch. 5)

1st Conj.	2nd Conj.	3rd Conj.	3rd *-io* Conj.	4th Conj.
amārem	monērem	mitterem	caperem	audīrem
amārēs	monērēs	mitterēs	caperēs	audīrēs
amāret	monēret	mitteret	caperet	audīret
amārēmus	monērēmus	mitterēmus	caperēmus	audīrēmus
amārētis	monērētis	mitterētis	caperētis	audīrētis
amārent	monērent	mitterent	caperent	audīrent

INDICATIVE MOOD: ACTIVE VOICE

Future Tense: I will love, I will be loving (*LA1*, Ch. 3, 8, 13, 27; *LA3*, Ch. 2)

1st Conj.	2nd Conj.	3rd Conj.	3rd -*io* Conj.	4th Conj.
amābō	monēbō	mittam	capiam	audiam
amābis	monēbis	mittēs	capiēs	audiēs
amābit	monēbit	mittet	capiet	audiet
amābimus	monēbimus	mittēmus	capiēmus	audiēmus
amābitis	monēbitis	mittētis	capiētis	audiētis
amābunt	monēbunt	mittent	capient	audient

Nota Bene: The future tense does not exist in the subjunctive mood.

INDICATIVE MOOD: ACTIVE VOICE

Perfect Tense: I loved, I have loved, I did love (*LA1*, Ch. 8, 27)

1st Conj.	2nd Conj.	3rd Conj.	3rd -*io* Conj.	4th Conj.
amāvī	monuī	mīsī	cēpī	audīvī
amāvistī	monuistī	mīsistī	cēpistī	audīvistī
amāvit	monuit	mīsit	cēpit	audīvit
amāvimus	monimus	mīsimus	cēpimus	audīvimus
amāvistis	monuistis	mīsistis	cēpistis	audīvistis
amāvērunt	monuērunt/monuēre	mīsērunt	cēpērunt	audīvērunt

SUBJUNCTIVE MOOD: ACTIVE VOICE

Perfect Tense: Translations will vary according to usage in context. (*LA3*, Ch. 6)

1st Conj.	2nd Conj.	3rd Conj.	3rd -*io* Conj.	4th Conj.
amāverim	monuerim	mīserim	ceperim	audīverim
amāverīs	monuerīs	mīserīs	cēperīs	audīverīs
amāverit	monuerit	mīserit	capit	audīverit
amāverīmus	monuerīmus	mīserīmus	cēperīmus	audīverīmus
amāverītis	monuerītis	mīserītis	cēperītis	audīverītis
amāverint	monuerint	mīserint	cēperint	audīverint

INDICATIVE MOOD: ACTIVE VOICE

Pluperfect Tense: I had loved (*LA1*, Ch. 27, *LA3*, Ch. 3)

1st Conj.	2nd Conj.	3rd Conj.	3rd -*io* Conj.	4th Conj.
amāveram	monueram	mīseram	cēperam	audīveram
amāverās	monuerās	mīserās	cēperās	audīverās
amāverat	monuerat	mīserat	cēperat	audīverat
amāverāmus	monuerāmus	mīserāmus	cēperāmus	audīverāmus
amāverātis	monuerātis	mīserātis	cēperātis	audīverātis
amāverant	monuerant	mīserant	cēperant	audīverant

SUBJUNCTIVE MOOD: ACTIVE VOICE

Pluperfect Tense: As with the perfect subjunctive, translations will vary according to usage in context. (*LA3*, Ch. 6)

1st Conj.	2nd Conj.	3rd Conj.	3rd -io Conj.	4th Conj.
amāvissem	monuissem	mīsissem	cēpissem	audīvissem
amāvissēs	monuissēs	mīsissēs	cēpissēs	audīvissēs
amāvisset	monuisset	mīsisset	cēpisset	audīvisset
amāvissēmus	monuissēmus	mīsissēmus	cēpissēmus	audīvissēmus
amāvissētis	monuissētis	mīsissētis	cēpissētis	audīvissētis
amāvissent	monuissent	mīsissent	cēpissent	audīvissent

INDICATIVE MOOD: ACTIVE VOICE

Future Perfect Tense: I will have loved (*LA1*, Ch. 27; *LA3*, Ch. 6)

1st Conj.	2nd Conj.	3rd Conj.	3rd -io Conj.	4th Conj.
amāverō	monuerō	mīserō	cēperō	audīverō
amāveris	monueris	mīseris	cēperis	audīveris
amāverit	monuerit	mīserit	cēperit	audīverit
amāverimus	monuerimus	mīserimus	cēperimus	audīverimus
amāveritis	monueritis	mīseritis	cēperitis	audīveritis
amāverint	monuerint	mīserint	cēperint	audīverint

Nota Bene: The future-perfect tense does not exist in the subjunctive mood.

INDICATIVE MOOD: PASSIVE VOICE

Present Tense: I am loved, I am being loved (*LA2*, Ch. 11; *LA3*, Ch. 2)

1st Conj.	2nd Conj.	3rd Conj.	3rd -io Conj.	4th Conj.
amor	moneor	mittor	capior	audior
amāris	monēris	mitteris	caperis	audīris/audīre
amātur	monētur	mittitur	capitur	audītur
amāmur	monēmur	mittimur	capimur	audīmur
amāminī	monēminī	mittiminī	capiminī	audīminī
amantur	monentur	mittuntur	capiuntur	audiuntur

SUBJUNCTIVE MOOD: PASSIVE VOICE

Present Tense: I would be held, I may be held (*LA3*, Ch. 4)

1st Conj.	2nd Conj.	3rd Conj.	3rd -io Conj.	4th Conj.
amer	monear	mittar	capiar	audiar
amēris	moneāris	mittāris	capiāris	audiāris
amētur	moneātur	mittātur	capiātur	audiātur
amēmur	moneāmur	mittāmur	capiāmur	audiāmur
amēminī	moneāminī	mittāminī	capiāminī	audiāminī
amentur	moneantur	mittantur	capiantur	audiantur

INDICATIVE MOOD: PASSIVE VOICE

Imperfect Tense: I was loved, I used to be loved (*LA2*, Ch. 12; *LA3*, Ch. 2)

1st Conj.	2nd Conj.	3rd Conj.	3rd *-io* Conj.	4th Conj.
amābar	monēbar	mittēbar	capiēbar	audiēbar
amābāris/amābāre	monēbāris	mittēbāris	capiēbāris	audiēbāris
amābātur	monēbātur	mittēbātur	capiēbātur	audiēbātur
amābāmur	monēbāmur	mittēbāmur	capiēbāmur	audiēbāmur
amābāminī	monēbāminī	mittēbāminī	capiēbāminī	audiēbāminī
amābantur	monēbantur	mittēbantur	capiēbantur	audiēbantur

SUBJUNCTIVE MOOD: PASSIVE VOICE

Imperfect Tense: I would be held, I might be held (*LA3*, Ch. 5)

1st Conj.	2nd Conj.	3rd Conj.	3rd *-io* Conj.	4th Conj.
amārer	monērer	mitterer	caperer	audīrer
amārēris	monērēris	mitterēris	caperēris	audīrēris
amārētur	monērētur	mitterētur	caperētur	audīrētur
amārēmur	monērēmur	mitterēmur	caperēmur	audīrēmur
amārēminī	monērēminī	mitterēminī	caperēminī	audīrēminī
amārentur	monēbantur	mitterentur	caperentur	audīrentur

INDICATIVE MOOD: PASSIVE VOICE

Future Tense: I will be loved (*LA2*, Ch. 12; *LA3*, Ch. 2)

1st Conj.	2nd Conj.	3rd Conj.	3rd *-io* Conj.	4th Conj.
amābor	monēbor	mittar	capiar	audiar
amāberis/amābere	monēberis	mittēris	capiēris	audiēris
amābitur	monēbitur	mittētur	capiētur	audiētur
amābimur	monēbimur	mittēmur	capiēmur	audiēmur
amābiminī	monēbiminī	mittēminī	capiēminī	audiēminī
amābuntur	monēbuntur	mittentur	capientur	audientur

Nota Bene: The future tense does not exist in the subjunctive mood.

INDICATIVE MOOD: PASSIVE VOICE

Perfect Tense: I was loved, I have been loved (*LA2*, Ch. 13; *LA3*, Ch. 3)

1st Conj.	2nd Conj.	3rd Conj.	3rd *-io* Conj.	4th Conj.
amātus, -a, -um sum	monitus, -a, -um sum	missus, -a, -um sum	captus, -a, -um sum	audītus, -a, -um sum
amātus, -a, -um es	monitus, -a, -um es	missus, -a, -um es	captus, -a, -um es	audītus, -a, -um es
amātus, -a, -um est	monitus, -a, -um est	missus, -a, -um est	captus, -a, -um est	audītus, -a, -um est
amātī, -ae, -a sumus	monitī, -ae, -a sumus	missī, -ae, -a sumus	captī, -ae, -a sumus	audītī, -ae, -a sumus
amātī, -ae, -a estis	monitī, -ae, -a estis	missī, -ae, -a estis	captī, -ae, -a estis	audītī, -ae, -a estis
amātī, -ae, -a sunt	monitī, -ae, -a sunt	missī, -ae, -a sunt	captī, -ae, -a sunt	audītī, -ae, -a sunt

SUBJUNCTIVE MOOD: PASSIVE VOICE

Perfect Tense: Translations will vary according to usage in context. (*LA3*, Ch. 6)

1st Conj.	2nd Conj.	3rd Conj.	3rd -*io* Conj.	4th Conj.
amātus, -a, -um sim	monitus, -a, -um sim	missus, -a, -um sim	captus, -a, -um sim	audītus, -a, -um sim
amātus, -a, -um sīs	monitus, -a, -um sīs	missus, -a, -um sīs	captus, -a, -um sīs	audītus, -a, -um sīs
amātus, -a, -um sit	monitus, -a, -um sit	missus, -a, -um sit	captus, -a, -um sit	audītus, -a, -um sit
amātī, -ae, -a sīmus	monitī, -ae, -a sīmus	missī, -ae, -a sīmus	captī, -ae, -a sīmus	audītī, -ae, -a sīmus
amātī, -ae, -a sītis	monitī, -ae, -a sītis	missī, -ae, -a sītis	captī, -ae, -a sītis	audītī, -ae, -a sītis
amātī, -ae, -a sint	monitī, -ae, -a sint	missī, -ae, -a sint	captī, -ae, -a sunt	audītī, -ae, -a sint

INDICATIVE MOOD: PASSIVE VOICE

Pluperfect Tense: I had been loved (*LA2*, Ch. 14; *LA3*, Ch. 3)

1st Conj.	2nd Conj.	3rd Conj.	3rd -*io* Conj.	4th Conj.
amātus, -a, -um eram	monitus, -a, -um eram	missus, -a, -um eram	captus, -a, -um eram	audītus, -a, -um eram
amātus, -a, -um erās	monitus, -a, -um erās	missus, -a, -um erās	captus, -a, -um erās	audītus, -a, -um erās
amātus, -a, -um erat	monitus, -a, -um erat	missus, -a, -um erat	captus, -a, -um erat	audītus, -a, -um erat
amātī, -ae, -a erāmus	monitī, -ae, -a erāmus	missī, -ae, -a erāmus	captī, -ae, -a erāmus	audītī, -ae, -a erāmus
amātī, -ae, -a erātis	monitī, -ae, -a erātis	missī, -ae, -a erātis	captī, -ae, -a erātis	audītī, -ae, -a erātis
amātī, -ae, -a erant	monitī, -ae, -a erant	missī, -ae, -a erant	captī, -ae, -a erant	audītī, -ae, -a erant

SUBJUNCTIVE MOOD: PASSIVE VOICE

Pluperfect Tense: Translations will vary according to usage in context. (*LA3*, Ch. 6)

1st Conj.	2nd Conj.	3rd Conj.	3rd -*io* Conj.	4th Conj.
amātus, -a, -um essem	monitus, -a, -um essem	missus, -a, -um essem	captus, -a, -um essem	audītus, -a, -um essem
amātus, -a, -um essēs	monitus, -a, -um essēs	missus, -a, -um essēs	captus, -a, -um essēs	audītus, -a, -um essēs
amātus, -a, -um esset	monitus, -a, -um esset	missus, -a, -um esset	captus, -a, -um esset	audītus, -a, -um esset
amātī, -ae, -a essēmus	monitī, -ae, -a essēmus	missī, -ae, -a essēmus	captī, -ae, -a essēmus	audītī, -ae, -a essēmus
amātī, -ae, -a essētis	monitī, -ae, -a essētis	missī, -ae, -a essētis	captī, -ae, -a essētis	audītī, -ae, -a essētis
amātī, -ae, -a essent	monitī, -ae, -a essent	missī, -ae, -a essent	captī, -ae, -a essent	audītī, -ae, -a essent

INDICATIVE MOOD: PASSIVE VOICE

Future Perfect: I will have been loved (*LA2*, Ch. 14; *LA3*, Ch. 3)

1st Conj.	2nd Conj.	3rd Conj.	3rd -*io* Conj.	4th Conj.
amātus, -a, -um erō	monitus, -a, -um erō	missus, -a, -um erō	captus, -a, -um erō	audītus, -a, -um erō
amātus, -a, -um eris	monitus, -a, -um eris	missus, -a, -um eris	captus, -a, -um eris	audītus, -a, -um eris
amātus, -a, -um erit	monitus, -a, -um erit	missus, -a, -um erit	captus, -a, -um erit	audītus, -a, -um erit
amātī, -ae, -a erimus	monitī, -ae, -a erimus	missī, -ae, -a erimus	captī, -ae, -a erimus	audītī, -ae, -a erimus
amātī, -ae, -a eritis	monitī, -ae, -a eritis	missī, -ae, -a eritis	captī, -ae, -a eritis	audītī, -ae, -a eritis
amātī, -ae, -a erunt	monitī, -ae, -a erunt	missī, -ae, -a erunt	captī, -ae, -a erunt	audītī, -ae, -a erunt

Nota Bene: The future perfect tense does not exist in the subjunctive mood.

INFINITIVES (*LA2*, CH. 11, 14, 23)

Tense	Active	Passive
Present: A: to ___ P: to be ___ed	amāre monēre mittere audīre esse	amārī monērī mittī audīrī ———
Perfect: A: to have ___ed P: to have been ___ed	amāvisse monuisse mīsisse audīvisse fuisse	amātus, -a, -um esse monitus, -a, -um esse missus, -a, -um esse audītus, -a, -um esse ———
Future: A: to be about to ___ P: to be about to be ___ed	amātūrus, -a, -um esse monitūrus, -a, -um esse missūrus, -a, -um esse audītūrus, -a, -um esse futūrus, -a, -um esse	amātum īrī monitum īrī missum īrī audītum īrī

Irregular Verbs and a Couple of Common Compounds

(*LA1*, Ch. 7, 18, 21; *LA3*, Ch. 9)

sum, esse, fuī, futūrum   ferō, ferre, tulī, lātum   nōlō, nōlle, nōluī   eō, īre, īvī/iī, itum

possum, potesse, potuī, futūrum   volō, velle, voluī   mālō, mālle, māluī

IMPERATIVE MOOD: PRESENT TENSE

Singular	es	fer	ī	nōlī
Plural	este	ferte	īte	nōlīte

IMPERATIVE MOOD: FUTURE TENSE

Singular	estō	fertō	ītō
Plural	estōte	fertōte	ītōte

INDICATIVE MOOD: FĪŌ (THE PASSIVE OF FACIŌ) – TO BE MADE, BECOME
(*LA3*, Ch. 9)

Present Tense	Imperfect Tense	Future Tense
fīō	fīēbam	fīam
fīs	fīēbās	fīēs
fit	fīēbat	fīet
(fīmus)*	fīēbāmus	fīēmus
(fītis)*	fīēbātis	fīētis
(fīunt)*	fīēbant	fīent

Appendix B: Reference Charts

*The forms in parentheses are rarely if ever used.

Nota Bene: The perfect system tenses are formed as for all other passive verbs (e.g., *factus sum*, *factus es*, etc.).

SUBJUNCTIVE MOOD: FĪŌ: WOULD BE MADE, WOULD BECOME, MAY BECOME (*LA3*, Ch. 9)

Present Tense	Imperfect Tense
fīam	fierem
fīās	fierēs
fīat	fieret
fīāmus	fierēmus
fīātis	fierētis
fīant	fierent

Nota Bene: The perfect-system tenses are as for all other passive verbs (e.g., *factus sim*, *factus sīs*, etc.).

The following verbs are illustrated in the present system tenses only, since all perfect system tenses are formed regularly as noted previously in the textbook and in this section on verbs.

PRESENT TENSE: INDICATIVE MOOD (*LA1*, Ch. 7. 18, 21; *LA2*, Ch. 10)

sum	possum	ferō	volō	nōlō	mālō	eō
es	potes	fers	vīs	nōn vīs	māvīs	īs
est	potest	fert	vult	nōn vult	māvult	it
sumus	possumus	ferimus	volumus	nōlumus	mālumus	īmus
estis	potestis	fertis	vultis	nōn vultis	māvultis	ītis
sunt	possunt	ferunt	volunt	nōlunt	mālunt	eunt

PRESENT TENSE: SUBJUNCTIVE MOOD (*LA3*, Ch. 4)

sim	possim	feram	velim	nōlim	mālim	eam
sīs	possīs	ferās	velīs	nōlīs	mālīs	eās
sit	possit	ferat	velit	nōlit	mālit	eat
sīmus	possīmus	ferāmus	velīmus	nōlīmus	mālīmus	eāmus
sītis	possītis	ferātis	velītis	nōlītis	mālītis	eātis
sint	possint	ferant	velint	nōlint	mālint	eant

IMPERFECT TENSE: INDICATIVE MOOD (*LA1*, Ch. 7, 18, 21; *LA2*, Ch. 10)

eram	poteram	ferēbam	volēbam	nōlēbam	mālēbam	ībam
erās	poterās	ferēbās	volēbās	nōlēbās	mālēbās	ībās
erat	poterat	ferēbat	volēbat	nōlēbat	mālēbat	ībat
erāmus	poterāmus	ferēbāmus	volēbāmus	nōlēbāmus	mālēbāmus	ībāmus

| erātis | poterātis | ferēbātis | volēbātis | nōlēbātis | mālēbātis | ībātis |
| erant | poterant | ferēbant | volēbant | nōlēbant | mālēbant | ībant |

IMPERFECT TENSE: SUBJUNCTIVE MOOD (*LA3*, Ch. 5)

essem	possem	ferrem	vellem	nōllem	māllem	īrem
essēs	possēs	ferrēs	vellēs	nōllēs	māllēs	īrēs
esset	posset	ferret	vellet	nōllet	māllet	īret
essēmus	possēmus	ferrēmus	vellēmus	nōllēmus	māllēmus	īrēmus
essētis	possētis	ferrētis	vellētis	nōllētis	māllētis	īrētis
essent	possent	ferrent	vellent	nōllent	māllent	īrent

FUTURE TENSE (*LA1*, Ch. 7, 18, 21; *LA2*, Ch. 10)

erō	poterō	feram	volam	nōlam	mālam	ībō
eris	poteris	ferēs	volēs	nōlēs	mālēs	ībis
erit	poterit	feret	volet	nōlet	mālet	ībit
erimus	poterimus	ferēmus	volēmus	nōlēmus	mālēmus	ībimus
eritis	poteritis	ferētis	volētis	nōlētis	mālētis	ībitis
erunt	poterunt	ferent	volent	nōlent	mālent	ībunt

Irregular verbs form their perfect tenses in the same way as the regular verbs.

Deponent Verbs

FIRST CONJUGATION: cōnor, cōnārī, cōnātus sum
SECOND CONJUGATION: fateor, fatērī, fassus sum
THIRD CONJUGATION: nāscor, nāscī, nātus sum
THIRD -*io* CONJUGATION: patior, patī, passus, sum
FOURTH CONJUGATION: mōlior, mōlīrī, mōlītus sum

IMPERATIVE MOOD

Positive Imperative (*LA3*, Ch. 3)

1st CONJ.	2nd CONJ.	3rd CONJ.	3rd -*io* CONJ.	4th CONJ.
cōnāre	fatēre	nāscere	patere	mōlīre
cōnāminī	fatēminī	nāscimini	patiminī	mōlīminī

INDICATIVE MOOD OF DEPONENT VERBS

Nota Bene: Deponent verbs are passive in form but active in meaning.

Present Tense: I try, I am trying, I do try (*LA2*, Ch. 11; *LA3*, Ch. 3)

1st CONJ.	2nd CONJ.	3rd CONJ.	3rd -*io* CONJ.	4th CONJ.
cōnor	fateor	nāscor	patior	mōlior
cōnāris	fatēris	nāsceris	pateris	mōlīris

cōnātur	fatētur	nāscitur	patitur	mōlītur
cōnāmur	fatēmur	nāscimur	patimur	mōlīmur
cōnāminī	fatēminī	nāsciminī	patiminī	mōlīminī
cōnantur	fatentur	nāscuntur	patiuntur	mōliuntur

SUBJUNCTIVE MOOD OF DEPONENT VERBS

Present Tense: I would, I might try (*LA3*, Ch. 4)

1st Conj.	2nd Conj.	3rd Conj.	3rd *-io* Conj.	4th Conj.
cōner	fatear	nāscar	patiar	mōliar
cōnēris	fateāris	nāscāris	patiāris	mōliāris
cōnētur	fateātur	nāscātur	patiātur	mōliātur
cōnēmur	fateāmur	nāscāmur	patiāmur	mōliāmur
cōnēminī	fateāminī	nāscāminī	patiāminī	mōliāminī
cōnentur	fateantur	nāscantur	patiantur	mōliantur

Nota Bene: The deponent verbs will continue to conjugate following the same patterns as for regular passive verbs.

Participles

PRESENT ACTIVE (*LA2*, Ch. 19; *LA3*, Ch. 2)

Case	Masculine/Feminine	Neuter
Nom.	agēns	agēns
Gen.	agentis	agentis
Dat.	agentī	agentī
Acc.	agentem	agēns
Abl.	agentī/agente	agentī/agente
Nom.	agentēs	agentia
Gen.	agentium	agentium
Dat.	agentibus	agentibus
Acc.	agentēs/agentīs	agentia
Abl.	agentibus	agentibus

FUTURE ACTIVE (*LA2*, Ch. 19)

Case	Masculine	Feminine	Neuter
Nom.	āctūrus	āctūra	āctūrum
Gen.	āctūrī	āctūrae	āctūrī
Dat.	āctūrō	āctūrae	āctūrō
Acc.	āctūrum	āctūram	āctūrum
Abl.	āctūrō	āctūrā	āctūrō

Nom.	āctūrī	āctūrae	āctūra
Gen.	āctūrōrum	āctūrārum	āctūrōrum
Dat.	āctūrīs	āctūrīs	āctūrīs
Acc.	āctūrōs	āctūrās	āctūra
Abl.	āctūrīs	āctūrīs	āctūrīs

PERFECT PASSIVE (*LA2*, Ch. 20; *LA3*, Ch. 3)

Case	Masculine	Feminine	Neuter
Nom.	āctus	ācta	āctum
Gen.	āctī	āctae	āctī
Dat.	āctō	āctae	āctō
Acc.	āctum	āctam	āctum
Abl.	āctō	āctā	āctō
Nom.	āctī	āctae	ācta
Gen.	āctōrum	āctārum	āctōrum
Dat.	āctīs	āctīs	āctīs
Acc.	āctōs	āctās	ācta
Abl.	āctīs	āctīs	āctīs

FUTURE PASSIVE (GERUNDIVE) (*LA2*, Ch. 21; *LA3*, Ch. 1)

Case	Masculine	Feminine	Neuter
Nom.	agendus	agenda	agendum
Gen.	agendī	agendae	agendī
Dat.	agendō	agendae	agendō
Acc.	agendum	agendam	agendum
Abl.	agendō	agendā	agendō
Nom.	agendī	agendae	agenda
Gen.	agendōrum	agendārum	agendōrum
Dat.	agendīs	agendīs	agendīs
Acc.	agendōs	agendās	agenda
Abl.	agendīs	agendīs	agendīs

Appendix C:
Abbreviations

1	first person
2	second person
3	third person
A	active
ab.	ablative (*see also* abl.)
abl.	ablative (*see also* ab.)
abl. abs.	ablative absolute
abl. acc.	ablative of accompaniment
abl. ag.	ablative of agent
abl. cause	ablative of cause
abl. com.	ablative of comparison
abl. ma.	ablative of manner
abl. me.	ablative of means
abl. place	ablative of place
abl. PfW	ablative of place from which
abl. pr.	ablative of price
abl. PW	ablative of place where
abl. res.	ablative of respect
abl. sep.	ablative of separation
abl. TW	ablative of time when/time within which
ac.	accusative (*see also* acc.)
acc.	accusative (*see also* ac.)
PtW	accusative of place to which
acc. sp.	accusative of space
acc. ti.	accusative of time
AcSI	accusative subject of the infinitive
adj. + dat.	adjective with the dative
adj.	attributive adjective
adv.	adverb
App.	appositive
c.	conjunction (*see also* conj.)/common (*see also* C)
C	common (= m *or* f)
CInf	complementary infinitive

conj.	conjunction	part. gen.	partitive genitive
CpAdj	comparative adjective	pers.	personal
CpAdv	comparative adverb	pf	perfect
CTF	contrary to fact	PfW	place from which
d/D	dative (*see also* dat.)/deponent	pl.	plural (parsing; *see also* p.)
dat.	dative	PNA	possessive noun adjective
dat. ag.	dative of agent	PPA	possessive pronoun adjective
dat. obj.	dative direct object	ppf	pluperfect
DA	direct address	part.	participle (labeling)
dem.	demonstrative	pos.	possessive
dep.	deponent	pr	present
dis. num.	distributive number	PrAc	predicate accusative
DO	direct object	PrAdj	predicate adjective
DP	dative of possession	PrCTF	present contrary to fact conditional
DPr	dative of purpose	PrN	predicate nominative
DR	dative of reference	pro.	pronoun
f.	feminine	PW	place where
F	future	refl.	reflexive
FLV	future less vivid conditional	refl. pro.	reflexive pronoun
FMV	future more vivid conditional	s.	singular (*see also* sing.)
fp	future perfect	sing.	singular (*see also* s.)
g.	genitive	S	subject (labeling) *or* singular (parsing)/subjunctive (parsing; *see also* sub.)
gen.	genitive		
gerd.	gerund	SbAdj	substantive adjective
gerv.	gerundive	sem. dep.	semi-deponent
hv	helping verb	SF	simple future
(hv)	helping verb in the English, but not in the Latin	Sinf.	subject of the infinitive
I	imperfect/indicative	SP	simple past
IAdv	interrogative adverb	SpAdj	superlative adjective
iden. pro.	identical pronoun	SpAdv	superlative adverb
imp.	imperative	SPast	simple past conditional
impf.	imperfect	SPr	subject pronoun
ind.	indicative	SPres	simple present conditional
indec.	indeclinable	sub.	subjunctive (*see also* S)
indef.	indefinite	SV	subject and verb (a verb containing the subject for the sentence)
inf.	infinitive (labeling)		
Inf	infinitive (parsing)	V	verb (labeling)
inten. pro.	intensive pronoun	V	vocative (parsing; *see also* voc.)
interj.	interjection	voc.	vocative (*see also* V)
inter. pro.	interrogative pronoun		
IO	indirect object		
irr.	irregular		
l	locative		
LV	linking verb		
m.	masculine		
n.	neuter *or* nominative		
nom.	nominative		
OP	object of the preposition		
p.	plural *or* passive (*see also* pl.)		
P	preposition (labeling)		
P	passive/participle (parsing)		
PaCTF	past contrary to fact conditional		
part. abl.	partitive ablative		

Appendix D: Noun Cases and Their Common Uses

The following is a list of the more common uses for each of the seven noun cases. This reference list also provides the location for the lessons in which these uses are described.

Case	Use	Book:Chapter
Nominative	Subject	1:4/2:2
	Predicate Nominative	1:4/2:2
Genitive	Possession	1:12/2:3
	Origin	1:12/2:3
	Material	1:12/2:3
	Partitive	1:12/2:3
	Cause/Purpose	2:16/3:1,7
	Quality/Description	3:12
	Objective	3:15
Dative	Indirect Object	1:6/2:3
	Reference	1:6/2:3
	Special Intransitive	1:17/2:3
	Use with Certain Adjectives	1:17/2:3
	Possession	1:17/2:3
	Predicate Dative (Dative of Purpose or Result)	2:3/3:1,7
	Agent	2:21
	Direction	3:14
	Compound Verbs	3:15
Accusative	Direct Object	1:5/2:2
	Place to Which (Motion Toward)	1:11/2:2
	Duration of Time	1:23/2:9
	Extent of Space	1:23/2:9

Case	Use	Book:Chapter
Accusative	Predicate Accusative	2:2
	Cause/Purpose	2:16,27/3:1,7
	Exclamatory	3:8
	Subject of Infinitive (Indirect Statement)	2:23/3:8
Ablative	Agent	2:13/3:2
	Means/Instrument	1:9/2:4/3:2
	Manner	1:9,11/2:4
	Separation	1:9,11/2:5
	Accompaniment	1:11/2:4
	Place Where	1:11/2:5
	Place from Which (Motion From)	1:11,28/2:5
	Price	1:23/2:9
	Time When	1:23/2:9
	Time Within Which	1:23/2:9
	Respect/Specification	2:8,27/3:9
	Cause	2:16
	Absolute	2:20/3:10
	Object of Deponent Verbs	2:26/3:3
	Comparison	2:6/3:9
	Degree of Difference	3:9
	Quality/Description	3:12
Locative	Place Where	2:5
Vocative	Direct Address	1:16/2:4

Appendix E:
Parsing, Declining & Conjugation Worksheets

Verb Parsing Worksheet

Nōmen: _____ Diēs: _____

Parse and translate the verbs provided in the chart below.

Verb	Person	#	Tense	Mood	Voice	Meaning
1.						
2.						
3.						
4.						
5.						
6.						
7.						
8.						
9.						
10.						
11.						
12.						
13.						
14.						
15.						
16.						
17.						
18.						
19.						
20.						
21.						
22.						
23.						
24.						
25.						
26.						
27.						
28.						
29.						
30.						

Declining Worksheet

Nōmen: _____ Diēs: _____

INSTRUCTIONS:
1. Choose six nouns from chapter(s) _____.
2. Find the stem of each noun.
3. Decline each noun.
4. On the line provided, translate the word in the box marked with an asterisk (*).

1. Stem: _____

Case	Singular	Plural
	*	

* _____

2. Stem: _____

Case	Singular	Plural
		*

* _____

3. Stem: _____

Case	Singular	Plural
	*	

* _____

4. Stem: _____

Case	Singular	Plural
		*

* _____

5. Stem: _____

Case	Singular	Plural
	*	

* _____

6. Stem: _____

Case	Singular	Plural
		*

* _____

Verb Conjugating Worksheet

Nōmen: _____ Diēs: _____

INSTRUCTIONS:
    1. Choose six verbs from chapter(s) _____.
    2. Find the stem of each verb.
    3. Conjugate the verb in the tense requested.
    4. Translate, in two different ways, the word in the box marked with an asterisk (*).

1. Tense: _____ Stem: _____

   *_____ | _____
    _____ | _____

   *_____
    _____

2. Tense: _____ Stem: _____

    _____ | *_____
    _____ | _____

   *_____
    _____

3. Tense: _____ Stem: _____

    _____ | _____
   *_____ | _____

   *_____
    _____

4. Tense: _____ Stem: _____

    _____ | _____
    _____ | *_____

   *_____
    _____

5. Tense: _____ Stem: _____

    _____ | _____
    _____ | _____
    *

* _____
  _____

6. Tense: _____ Stem: _____

    _____ | _____
    _____ | _____
                                                                             *

* _____
  _____

Notes

For grades 10-12

Rhetoric Alive! Book 1
by Alyssan Barnes, PhD

This course is a vital step for students before they leave high school.

Rhetoric Alive! Book 1: Principles of Persuasion, written by Alyssan Barnes, an experienced rhetoric teacher with a PhD in rhetoric, is a clear, compelling, and delightful text on rhetorical theory and practice.

The highly engaging *Rhetoric Alive!* explores the principles of winsome speech as developed in the foremost text on persuasion, Aristotle's *Rhetoric*. The 15 chapters of *Rhetoric Alive!* step through the essential components of persuasion—the three appeals, the three types of speech, and the five canons. Each chapter includes an exemplary classic text for analysis and discussion, spanning from Pericles's "Funeral Oration" to Martin Luther King, Jr.'s, "Letter from Birmingham Jail." Students also have plenty of opportunities to practice developing their own rhetorical skill through weekly workshops, imitation assignments, and oratory presentations.

Three appeals
Ethos (speaker's credibility)
Pathos (audience's emotion)
Logos (argument's reasoning)

Three types of speech
Deliberative (exhort or dissuade)
Ceremonial (praise or blame)
Judicial (accuse or defend)

Five canons (rules or standards)
Invention
Organization
Style
Memory
Delivery

What sets *Rhetoric Alive!* (*RA*) apart from other rhetoric texts?
- *RA* balances philosophical and practical application
- *RA* moves students from understanding into doing
- *RA* uses high school language, resulting in more comprehension
- *RA* includes discussion texts, workshops, and speeches
- *RA* brings Aristotle excerpts into contemporary moments
- *RA* has everything teachers and students need in one place
- *RA* is clearly laid out, comprehensive, and easy to use

Free Samples Online!

CONTINUE YOUR JOURNEY!

Latin Alive! Book 4
Latin Literature: From Cicero to Newton

This Latin reader features thirty-one annotated readings which include writings from early classical authors such as Cicero, ecclesiastical authors such as St. Patrick, medieval authors such as Aquinas, and neo-Latin authors such as Newton. This unique reader is an ideal capstone to the Latin Alive! series and will acquaint students with a broad range of Latin authors and writing styles. The readings are fully annotated, guiding students through any new and challenging grammatical constructions.

A team of three veteran Latin educators contributed to the book: Karen Moore, Gaylan Dubose, and Steven L. Jones.

For free sample chapters visit our store at:
www.ClassicalAcademicPress.com

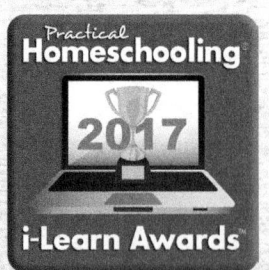

Live, Online Learning!

Live, online courses for grades 3–12 that are classical and restful, cultivating a deep engagement with learning.

SCHOLÉ ACADEMY
CLASSICAL ACADEMIC PRESS

ScholeAcademy.com